2—

THE SPEAKER'S TREASURY OF
Anecdotes

THE SPEAKER'S TREASURY
OF Anecdotes

Edited by MAXWELL DROKE

GROSSET & DUNLAP *Publishers*

NEW YORK, N. Y.

CONTENTS

CONTENTS—Continued

CONTENTS—Continued

CONTENTS—Continued

CONTENTS—Continued

WHEN TO TELL ANECDOTES

IT CAN be stated with reasonable assurance that there are no Federal or State statutes—and no municipal ordinances—which make it compulsory for any person to render, recite, or otherwise inflict anecdotes upon a public or quasi-public gathering. On the contrary, we sometimes are tempted to believe that in certain circumstances there should be a law *against* the practice!

If we may judge by the ungracious and awkward manner in which many individuals approach this business of story telling there seems to be a general impression that it is a civic duty which must be performed regardless of personal inclinations or aptitude. It is expected that a speaker shall lard his discourse with anecdotes; ergo, anecdotes must be dug up from some source and duly executed. To the speaker this practice may be as distasteful as paying taxes or taking out a license for the household canine. But tradition has laid a solemn obligation upon him, and he struggles manfully to do his duty.

The late Albert J. Beveridge (and what a tale-teller he was!) used often to tell of an able political speaker—a solemn, stately man whom the Maker had endowed with so many virtues that He apparently deemed it unnecessary to add even the traditional trace of humor. In this man's utterances there was that quality which impelled ACTION. On the platform he was a convincing, a deeply moving speaker, with an uncanny faculty for making up the other man's mind. But he would stand up and talk for an hour or more without indulging a single jest or sally. He told no stories. This worried his friends. They got to talking among themselves about this strange condition. And what was definitely worse, they talked with the speaker about it. Day upon day they dinned in his ears the counsel that he should "brighten his talk" with sundry jokes and jibes. With rare common-sense the solemn speaker responded that he was not the type. Well-wishers persisted that this glint of humor was essential. He demurred that he knew no jokes. Undaunted, his friends promised to supply them. They did. But unfortunately they did not likewise supply the tale-telling technique.

On the occasion of his next address our speaker, fortified with

1

his borrowed jokes, arose. For half an hour or more he talked in his usual earnest, humorless fashion, while his crestfallen friends sat dejected. He hadn't told a single story! The speaker paused. Over his countenance spread a look of evident distate. "Now," he said, in the manner of a mortician about to close the casket, "Now, I will tell some jokes." And he did! One after another, he grimly and gravely recited the examples of humor which his friends had gleaned from near and far. As each cruelly mangled corpse fell into a sepulcher of silence, he proceeded with the next. When he came to the last "—and the Second Scotchman replied," he heaved a sigh of relief, indulged in an expressive gesture indicating that he was heartily glad to wash his hands of the whole business, and returned to his argument where he had abruptly left off.

His friends, I believe, decided at that point to leave him alone. For which he was no doubt duly thankful.

I have set forth this incident in considerable detail with the hope that it may perhaps have a salutary effect upon others. Here, indeed, is a rare mortal—a man who could not tell funny stories; knew that he could not, and had no desire to do so. Such an individual is well deserving of a monument. Unfortunately, Chronicler Beveridge neglects to give us the name of this remarkable gentleman. I am fairly certain, however, that it is not Legion.

❖   ❖

So, I think that before delving into this question of when to trot out your anecdotes, you should carefully consider whether you really *want* to tell funny stories at all. Can you tell a story at least moderately well? Many excellent speakers cannot. On the other hand, there are persons who, on the whole, speak poorly, but who possess a certain knack of narration which enables them to enrich their talks with pert and pertinent anecdotes. So they get along very nicely and are sometimes even asked to fill return engagements!

There are few things more likely to give an audience collective pain than the spectacle of a speaker standing up there cracking dull and meatless jokes because he thinks it is *expected* of him.

Here is a pretty good rule to follow: Do you, in your everyday relations with your fellow humans, tell stories, relate bits of anecdote, dramatize your personal experiences? If you do, and if you have little difficulty in gathering an appreciative audience (aside from those who work for you and are impelled to laugh as a matter of policy) then it is more than likely that you are a pretty fair story-teller. In your public appearances you may safely venture to tell an extra-good story—in its proper time and place.

But if you are not a tale-teller in private life—if you have no inclinations or talents in that direction—why change character simply because you are talking to a hundred or a thousand persons, instead of one or two?

❖ ❖

Now, on this matter of timing . . .

The soundest counsel that can be given is this: tell your anecdotes when and where they are least expected. The speaker who gets up, clears his throat, and begins, "Your chairman's remarks reminds me of a story . . ." is off to an almost irreparably bad start. He is in the position of a pugilist who habitually telegraphs his punches. Fully half the charm of a good story lies in having it sprung unexpectedly upon you.

You will be well advised to spurn such outworn artifices as "That reminds me of a story," "It seems there were two Irishmen . . ." or "I heard a good one the other day."

Never announce to your audience that you are about to tell them a story, or label your impending anecdote as "funny." Let them discover the humor for themselves. They will appreciate it all the more. Humor is always emphasized by the element of surprise. Drift into your story as quietly and unostentatiously as you can. Be well under way with it before listeners realize that you *are* relating an anecdote. This takes some careful planning, and a good deal of skill, but it is well worth the effort.

It will help to give your story an authentic ring if you will tie it to some actual imaginary character out of your own experience. Instead of, "Well, the way I heard this joke, there was an old soak . . ." lead up to the point with more subtlety. Let's say you are discussing the virtue of dependability, and by contrast you seek to bring in this story of the old soak. Why not do it this way: "Some men are just naturally *born* dependable, I suppose, and others are—well, they're a good deal like Hob Jenkins, who used to do odd jobs around the little town where I was raised. Hob

was a regular old soak. . . ." From this point you can proceed with
the tale.

The advice I am now about to give is frankly revolutionary. It
is contrary to the common practice of at least three-fourths of our
public talkers—professionals and amateurs alike. It is simply this:
Do not launch your talk with a funny story!

This is a generality. Like most generalities it is subject to exception. I do not say that the practice of beginning a story with
your initial breath will result in invariable disaster. Maybe you
can get away with it. Many speakers do. But I do say that in most
situations—and for most speakers—it is not the best procedure.
And I will give you three reasons.

The first reason that I oppose the custom of starting right out
with a story is the fact that it *is* a custom. A lecturer may hold the
platform for an hour. Fifty-eight minutes of that period will be
given over to a serious discussion of some timely or scholarly
theme. But he feels that he will somehow be breaking with tradition if, in that initial two minutes he failed to give the customers what he believes to be an amusing anecdote. Well, I for
one would like to see him break that tradition, at least to the
extent of delaying his story until he has laid down a platform of
perfunctory preliminary remarks upon which to exhibit his gem.

The second reason in support of a delayed story is that comparatively few persons in an audience really *hear* the first fifty
words a speaker utters. Attention is likely to be distracted by
late-comers and early-goers. The general scuffing of feet and shift-
ting of *deriere* positions places the speaker at a decided disadvan-
tage. This is a good time to waste words; to pour out a considerable number of rather meaningless phrases, which no one will
mind in the least. It is a poor time to start a good story.

Finally, I like the idea of holding back your story for a season-
able time because you are thus permitted to build a pattern of
contrast. At the outset, you can be dull—decidedly and deliberately dull. You arise and thank the chairman for his kindly introduction. You refer, perhaps, to a previous appearance before this
particular group, or to an earlier visit in this fair city. You may
add a few sentences to whet civic pride, or pour on some laudatory
remarks concerning the worthy objectives of the aggregation you
are addressing. By this time most of what may technically be
termed listeners will have concluded that they are in for a session

of the same old tripe. Now, the time has come to spring your story! Watch them begin to prick up their ears. Note the look of pleased incredulity that spreads from countenance to countenance. Well, what do you know! We thought this was a dud. And look! The guy is going to be *good,* after all. A sigh of collective satisfaction emerges from the audience as they settle down earnestly to hear what you have to say.

This final point illustrates, I think, the primary mission of—and indeed the only valid reason for—the use of anecdotes in what is essentially a serious discourse. Humor should be employed carefully, discreetly, deliberately as a "change of pace." An average audience can absorb just about so much in the way of solid statistics and significant facts—and then it rebels. It cries out for a rest. A wise and experienced speaker will not push his auditors too far. He will employ frequent changes of pace, just as a thoughtful driver in the old horse-and-buggy days used to alternate trot, walk and canter. This "change of pace" may be attained in a variety of ways. You may inject a touch of pathos—an illustrative story to emphasize a particular point. You may turn to charts, graphs, or pictorial displays. And you may, of course, as we have pointed out, rely upon humor.

Not too much humor. That is an important warning. In a talk that is essentially serious humor should be a rare and sparing spice, never a major ingredient. Someone has shrewdly observed that laughing-stock pays no dividends. A clown may cause much merriment, but he is not likely to win many converts to a cause. This caution obviously does not apply in those instances when your primary purpose is to attain an atmosphere of gaiety. Then, and only then, can you afford the luxury of being as funny as you like.

At this point let us insert a few words on the importance of selectivity. Too many speakers appear to labor under the delusion that any sort of story will serve in any kind of situation. But the art of selecting your anecdotes is quite as important as the knowledge of when and how to relate them. We shall have more to say on this subject in subsequent sections. However, let us emphasize here and now that no story should ever be told without a plan and purpose. Have a *reason* for telling your amusing anecdote Make certain that it brings out a point—a point that is clearly pertinent to your discourse.

Whenever you hear a good story, ask yourself, "How can I *use* that?" Does it teach a lesson or point a moral? Does it denote the wisdom—or folly—of a certain course? This business of finding a *reason* for telling your story is not so difficult as you might imagine. If the story is really good the point of contact may be rather weak or far-fetched. The validity of your point isn't as important as is the fact that you have made a clear effort to tie in the story with the theme of your talk. An audience instinctively resents an anecdote that is obviously "dragged in by the heels," without rhyme or reason. It is an affront to the intelligence of your listeners. The implication is that you are trying to "buy" their interest with a cheap trick, and going about it rather clumsily. The reaction is likely to be a subconscious irritation as we try to puzzle out the speaker's motive. Sure, it's a good enough story, but *why* did he tell it? What has it got to do with the subject he is supposed to discuss? And when an audience becomes too critically analytical it bodes no good for the man on the platform.

Finally, I must confess to a personal fondness for the old vaudeville axiom: "Always leave them with a laugh." For the general speaker this hardly deserves the dignity of being termed a rule. There are a great many effective ways to conclude a talk. But certainly one of the best endings is a really good, appropriate anecdote.

A practical reason—not to be overlooked—is that by following this course you are sure to get a good, lusty round of applause!

HOW TO TELL ANECDOTES

"What kind of stories shall I tell?"

This is a question each individual must answer for himself, but perhaps a few pointers may not be amiss.

First and foremost, then: Never tell a story which does not strike you as extremely funny. Unless you enjoy a story—unless it strikes you as well worth telling—you will not get it across to your audience. Perhaps you heard another speaker tell the anecdote and reap a big laugh. To you it doesn't seem particularly pat, but you say, "Well, if that's what folks want, I'll give it to them." But, somehow, the story falls flat. Why? Because you didn't enjoy telling it. It didn't seem funny to you, and the audience, mirroring your mood, finds it humorless.

So again I say, tell the stories that appeal to you. Don't select anecdotes because they got a laugh for the other fellow.

Specialize on the kind of stories that you tell best. Unless you are perfectly at home with a dialect, you will probably do well to give it a wide berth. But the chances are that you will have at least a degree of familiarity with some one group—Hebrew, Irish, Scotch, Hillbilly, Negro, or whatever it may be. Enlarge and improve upon this knowledge. Grasp every opportunity for close study and observation of your chosen group.

Let's say your group is Irish. All right, then, make up your mind to be an authority on these people. Learn the lingo—the real McCoy, I mean, not the "Be jabers" jargon that is so often attributed to sons of Erin. Study the Irish. Familiarize yourself with their expressions, their habits, their reactions. Then, when you tell an Irish story it will be truly authentic. Your audience will be quick to sense and applaud these touches of realism.

In specializing on one of two or three dialects you are not so limited as you might at first conclude. Many good stories may be switched from one dialect to another without loss of point. Let us say that you run across a particularly good story in which a Negro character plays the principal role. You do not feel at home with the Negro drawl, but you have a certain facility in telling Hebrew stories. All right, then, analyze the anecdote. See if you cannot alter it, preserving the essence of the story, but making a

7

Hebrew your hero. You'll be surprised to see how often this can be done.

We cautioned you at the outset to tell only those stories that appeal to your sense of humor. To this we might add a supplementary warning: Never tell a story of which you do not approve, or one that makes you feel uncomfortable or undignified. The story may have been a "wow" when told by a less sensitive narrator; but it will fall flat for you, unless you give it your wholehearted endorsement.

Personally, although I have in my repertoire, for stag occasions, many sketches that are hilariously indecorous I do not tell dirty stories of the usual gutter or smoking-car variety. They simply strike me as rather stupid. They are too crude and obvious.

In selecting your material, I warn you to beware of repeating the funny story that you heard someone tell at a banquet or public gathering just the other day. Stories run in cycles, you know. There are very few basically new ones.

The danger of telling a story you have just heard is quite obvious. Other folks get around, too. A number of them may have been at the same meeting, and heard the story told much better than you are likely to tell it. Moreover, the woods are full of amateur speakers, waiting with ghoulish glee to pounce upon a good story the moment it shows its head above the white linen cloth of the banquet board. Because they have no adequate source of anecdotes, and little appreciation of the art of story telling, such speakers habitually repeat the last story which they recall hearing. If the story has real merit, you may be assured that it soon will be as torn and tattered as an army flag after a major engagement.

❖   ❖

Suppose we pause at this point to define an anecdote. Briefly, an anecdote is a short narrative of an entertaining character; a terse, pithy account of some happening, usually personal or biographical. This example we present merely by way of illustration:

"One day," relates a professor, "I gave a pupil a problem in algebra, and although it was comparatively easy, he couldn't do it. 'You ought to be ashamed of yourself,' I remarked. 'At your age George Washington was a surveyor!' The boy looked me straight in the eyes. 'Yes, sir, and at your age he was President of the United States!' was the prompt rejoinder."

Now, there's the anecdote as you might encounter it in a maga-zine or other publication. But it is by no means in the proper form for platform use. Because of the limitations of the written word, the stories which we find in print are burdened with all sorts of interpolations that retard action when the story is re-peated orally. One of the most common mistakes of the tyro is that of lifting a story bodily from a printed page and repeating it word for word.

How should this story be revised for platform use? Well, ideal-ly, it should be told by a professor as a personal experience. That is the most simple and direct form. If told by a third person it will lose some of its charm. There is an added advantage in tell-ing this story as a personal experience: an audience loves the speaker who "tells one on himself." But never, under any cir-cumstances, tell an anecdote in which you are the hero. In your stories, you must not outwit the other fellow, or get the best of the deal. No matter how innocently you may do this, you are promptly branded as a "smart guy" who is "stuck on himself." You will have a hard time warming up an audience after such a *faux pas*.

Well, let's say a professor is telling this story. He will probably begin informally. "The other day I gave one of my boys a prob-lem in algebra. It was comparatively simple, but he couldn't seem to get the answer. After he had struggled with it for half an hour, I said, 'Ralph, you ought to be ashamed of yourself! Why at your age George Washington was a surveyor!' "

You will see that the anecdote has been re-arranged so that the professor's comment to his pupil is not broken by the interpola-tion, "I remarked." On the printed page, this rather long quota-tion might be confusing, but when the words are spoken, this difficulty does not occur.

If the professor is a skillful story-teller, he will omit the words, "The boy looked me straight in the eyes." Altering his voice to impersonate that of the lad, he will jump directly from his own comment to the boy's response:

" 'Yes, sir, and at your age he was President of the United States!' "

Such interpolations as "he said," "she replied," and the like, invariably mark the inept story-teller. The writer, deprived of inflection and gesture, is compelled to clutter his script with detailed description. But the speaker should not permit these encumbrances. Instead of saying, "she exclaimed excitedly," put the excitement into your voice as you speak the words. Don't say, "At this point the Judge cleared his throat impressively and remarked . . ." Impersonate the Judge. Clear your throat impressively and begin at once to speak the words attributed to the Judge. The context of the story, with the proper change in the tone of your voice, will make the transition entirely clear.

And here's another little trick in transition that will often come in handy: It will help materially if you turn your head rather to one side while speaking the words attributed to one character. When it is time for another character to speak, turn your head in the opposite direction. The audience soon "catches on," begins to associate an Eastward glance with one character, Westward with another. This is a stunt long known and practiced by the ventriloquist.

But let's get back to our anecdote. Have you observed the most significant change which we made in re-drafting the story? It comes at the very end. The printed version, you recall, ran like this: " 'At your age he was President of the United States!' was the prompt rejoinder."

Those last four words are the trouble-makers. Personally, I dislike their use even in the printed form. In an anecdote for platform use, they become a catastrophe. These words represent an anti-climax. The response, "at your age he was President of the United States," is the point, or "explosion." Everything leads up to it. Nothing should be permitted to follow.

Every experienced public speaker will realize the soundness of this point. An anti-climax impedes the laughter or applause which the story has earned.

Right here we might well delve into the art of "waiting for the laugh." The matter of timing is one of the things which sets the professional well apart from the novice. Again and again, the tyro will "crowd his laughs"—that is, he will keep right on talking at a point where a laugh may logically be expected. This smothers the demonstration and if continued has a depressing effect on the audience.

Laughter breeds laughter. The speaker pauses significantly at a likely spot. A few alert individuals titter appreciatively; others join in the chorus. Presently, the more slow-witted members of the group "get the point" and, delighted with their ability to see what it's all about, they howl with glee. Thus is born a rousing ovation where, in less skillful hands, the demonstration might never have risen to audible proportions.

❖ ❖

Bear in mind that there is one technique for the written word, and quite a different one for the spoken word. Many a story that "reads all right" is hackneyed and stilted when spoken. How often have you heard someone tell a story in such a manner that you could almost trace it line for line from a printed page?

This story appears in a book of Toasts and Anecdotes. It is a pretty good example of the sort of thing I mean:

John Marshall, famous Chief Justice of the Supreme Court, once climbed upon a ladder in his library to get a law book from the topmost shelf. The eminent jurist was then very old and rather feeble. And when several books stuck he tugged and the whole row came down on his head; he was quite naturally bowled right over on the floor. Hearing the crash, his servant rushed to the library. He found his master sitting on the floor under the avalanche, laughing heartily and rubbing himself ruefully.

"Well, well," he chuckled. "I've been laying down the law for a good many years, but this is the first time I have ever been laid down by the law."

I cannot at the moment think of an occasion where this story would be apropos; but granted you did have a place for it, you certainly would not want to weary your audience with tedious and irrelevant preliminaries. The whole point lies in the epigramatic final paragraph. Then cut to the core with something after this fashion:

As Chief Justice John Marshall once remarked when a shelf of heavy law books came tumbling down upon his head, "I've been laying down the law for a good many years, but this is the first time I have ever been laid down by the law."

Doesn't that condensed version preserve the essence of the story? Here, it happens that what the Chief Justice said is the all-important point. To whom he said it, and the circumstances leading up to the classic remark are of no importance. Therefore, we relentlessly cut them out, preserving only enough background to carry the point of the anecdote.

In print, this condensed version looks rather sparse, I will admit. But picture yourself telling the story. On which version would you prefer to stake your chances?

This is not to imply that condensation is always practicable, or even advisable. On the contrary, quite often a story must be "padded" or drawn out in order to attain the maximum in suspense, contrast or surprise. In a story which is primarily a character sketch, it is essential to relate enough of the background to make the character credible to your listeners. You will learn from experience, and from natural instinct, when to strip the hampering verbiage, and when to "build up" your story.

❖ ❖

Avoid, in the telling of anecdotes, such banalities as " 'Oh, yes, indeed,' was the prompt rejoinder," or " 'Certainly, sir', was the surprising response." The old writing technique again, you see. These expressions and dozens more with which you are all too familiar, tend to give a story the bright spontaneity of a slightly moist fuse.

Most jokes are heavily burdened with phrases of this type. That is one reason why I rarely tell a joke. Practically all jokes read far better than they relate. They are too "quick" for platform use. There is no chance to employ the element of suspense, which is one of the most essential factors in successful story-telling. Jokes are best reserved for those occasions when there are two participants—one of them serves as the foil or "feeder." Even so, the comedian knows that one joke will not get him very far. He employs a volley of them, gradually "warming" his audience, until he comes at length to his master-piece which, he fondly hopes, will "wow" them.

So you will be wise, I think, to eschew the joke books, and select, in preference, anecdotes and character sketches. In choosing your repertoire, look carefully for the dramatic quality, or element of suspense, to which I referred in a preceding paragraph. Here is a story—one of the best from that master craftsman, Lou Holtz—that well illustrates my point:

A visiting Maharaja is being entertained elaborately at a banquet in an exclusive Washington club. All the distinguished dignitaries are gathered to do him honor. The Maharaja, unfortunately, speaks no English; his interpreter can do little better.

Presently, at a signal from the toastmaster, the distinguished visitor arises, jabbers a few sentences (Lou Holtz impersonates the character superbly) and abruptly resumes his seat. The interpreter then arises, bows profoundly, and in a sing-song Oriental voice explains, "The Maharajara he say America very great country; he say he like America very much." Again the Maharaja arises, jabbers a trifle longer; again the interpreter explains, "Maharaja he say American women very beautiful; he say he love American women very much."

An impressive pause, and the Maharaja is once more on his feet. This time he jabbers interminably, gesticulating with great enthusiasm. All eyes and ears are upon the interpreter. A Message of Vital Import is about to be delivered. Again the monotonous monotone: "Maharaja he say, please, where is the Gentlemen's Wash Room?"

I am fully aware that the story loses much of its charm in print. It is one of those gems that demand the vocal expression of a master to do it justice. But nevertheless you will be able to trace through this crude outline, the element of suspense to which mention has been made. See how the curiosity of the audience is built up, up, up—until the climax, or "explosion," which in this case is so outlandishly ridiculous that laughter comes as a natural consequence.

I invite your attention also to another feature of this story—namely, the application of the Rule of Three. You will find this element recurring again and again in stories that are constructed upon sound dramatic principles. It is not mere happenstance that the Maharaja's convulsive query occurs the third time he arises to his feet. No; it comes as the logical conclusion of our little dramatic plot. Had the Maharaja asked his question the first time, our story would be lacking in contrast; on the second occasion we still would have sacrificed much of the suspense that we were steadily building. But by the third appearance curiosity is at its peak. The time is ripe to strike. Nothing is to be gained and much may be lost by stringing the story out to four or five chapters, as many an amateur will be tempted to do.

Look for the Rule of Three in the stories that intrigue you. You will be surprised to see how frequently it figures. Every seasoned tale-teller applies the rule, although he may do so unconsciously. I urge you, consciously and carefully to re-draft your own pet stories, following this formula.

✧   ✧

It is worth noting, I think, that some of our most engaging speakers tell surprisingly few stories, depending almost wholly upon epigramatic sentences or sparkling references to brighten their talks. Will Rogers was a splendid modern example. Henry Ward Beecher, in his day, was a master of this somewhat difficult practice. This quotation is characteristic: "The churches of the land are sprinkled all over with bald-headed sinners, whose hair has been worn off by the friction of countless sermons that have been aimed at them, and have glanced off and hit the man in the pew behind."

What is commonly termed the "wise-crack"—usually a form of epigram or pun—has come into wider use in recent years. When they are good, they are very, very good, and when they are bad— they fall pretty flat. By "bad" I mean to imply that it probably is (a) so patently and artificially contrived, or so far-fetched that most of the humor is extracted, or (b) so vague, or so subtle that the audience fails to "get" it. We see many examples of both varieties.

If you employ the "wise-crack" make reasonably certain that you use no terms foreign to the ears of your auditors. Thus the assertion that "it takes jacks or better to open a Pullman window" will gain appreciation only from those versed in poker. And in these days of air-conditioning it is pretty well outdated.

Only recently I heard a speaker begin his discourse by saying, "I am here today to bring you facts, although I am well aware that nobody loves a fact man." There is a case where too much subtlety cheated a speaker of a deserved laugh. The remark was clever—too clever for a general audience. It failed to get across. The speaker should have "blue-printed" his jest. Possibly something like this: "Although, if I may be pardoned for paraphrasing an old familiar saying, I am well aware that nobody loves a fact man." Or, if he chose to be even more elementary: "Sometimes I am inclined to think that the old familiar saying 'Nobody loves a fat man' should be amended to read, 'Nobody loves a fact man.'"

❖   ❖

This subject of humor—what it is, and why—is far too complex to tackle exhaustively in the limited space at our command.* But, we will suggest a few fundamentals that possibly may prove enlightening.

What makes a story funny?

At the very head of the list I certainly should place incongruity. Go back over your list of stock stories. See how many of them depend for their humor upon incongruous situations—ridiculous, absurd, fantastic, perhaps. Distortion is one of the oldest, certainly the most primitive form of humor. It is my opinion that early examples of caveman art—showing composites of two or more animals—which scholars have believed may hold ceremonial significance, may be nothing more than Paul K. Paleolithic's clumsy efforts to siphon humor from the incongruous.

It is the basic humor of incongruity that leads us to laugh heartily at the sight of a silk hat cast rakishly upon an empty suit of armor. Individually, these articles possess a certain dignity, arouse a measure of awe. In combination they become sidesplitting. It is the same principle that leads small boys at Hallowe'en to hoist Deacon Albright's spring wagon atop the steeple of the First Baptist Church and tether Bossy to a leg of teacher's desk.

Yes, incongruity clearly heads our list. But a close second, and probably a cousin by marriage, is irreverence. By this I do not necessarily mean impiety, but more accurately a sort of gusty appreciation of the discomfiture of those in High Places. It is mildly amusing to observe a pedestrian slip upon a banana peel. But if that unfortunate individual chances to be a wearer of the cloth,

---

* Readers who wish to pursue a more comprehensive study of the subject are referred to a scholarly and engaging text, *Enjoyment of Laughter,* by Max Eastman (Simon & Schuster).

our enjoyment is greatly heightened. To go into all of the psychological ramifications of why this is so would take us too far afield. And the discussion would be pointless. You recognize the truth of the statement without argument.

Another type of story that is likely to go well is the unconscious humor of childhood. The unconscious *faux pas* of the adult may also be highly amusing. And we all like to laugh at fools. It may be cruel, but it gives us a feeling of superiority to guffaw at such absurdities as that of the hired man who was sent out to count the pigs and returned to report, "Well, I counted nine, but that other little son-of-a-gun ran around so much I couldn't count him."

Finally I should say that we will laugh at almost any story, granted it has a point at all, if the smart narrator has sold us the idea that it is funny. There's a whole lot more to this than most story-tellers realize.

In an earlier paragraph I pointed out as one of the essentials that you must believe in your story, and must enjoy telling it. That still goes. But the time is ripe for a word of caution:

Yes, you must enjoy telling your story—but not to the point of laughing uproariously at your own sallies. A certain sparkle in your eye, a quiet smile, an air of suppressed glee, will prove far more convincing than a boisterous display of self-satisfaction. Indeed, certain types of stories are greatly enhanced by what is termed in professional circles, "dead-pan" expression. The man who can say the most amusing lines while maintaining a perfectly grave countenance, is pretty sure to have his auditors doubled up with laughter.

And above all else, I urge you, never, NEVER encore a story. How often you have heard some one tell a story, get his applause (in which he joins heartily) then go back and, between fits of laughter, repeat the point some two or three times.

I know of no performance that is more boring to a group than this, and no trait that more surely marks the slovenly and unskilled mind.

I do not mean to infer that every person who enjoys story-telling is, *per se*, a good story-teller. We all know plenty of examples to the contrary. I am assured by those who have made a study of such matters that the jackass delights in his bonny brays. His enthusiasm is not shared by his auditors.

But it is a fact that the man who gets personal satisfaction from his performance has an excellent foundation upon which to build. He may need a bit of coaching, perhaps; but he has the right stuff in him and if he will frankly and resolutely face his shortcomings he CAN learn to tell a story as it SHOULD be told.

Let me illustrate that point with an example: In a middle-western city there dwells an influential banker who for more than sixty years confined his oral outbursts to board meetings and employee groups. No one had ever heard him tell a story, or suspected that he had the slightest inclination to do so. But after a lifetime of sitting silently at the Speaker's Table, on occasions great and small, he experienced an overwhelming desire to participate more actively in the goings-on. Yes, he wanted to be an after-dinner speaker. And he had the courage that so many in his position lack. For he began at once accepting invitations to "say a few words." And he started right out telling stories!

Simple candor forces me to admit that his exhibition was as inept as any I have ever heard. His anecdotes were terrible—picked at random without point or purpose. And he told them in a dry, cracking monotone, without the slightest emphasis or characterization.

But he got a big hand. To some, the spectacle of a staid banker turning himself into a verbal Joe Miller was highly hilarious. They laughed, not at the jokes, but at the ludicrous situation. Others felt that anything a Great Man said deserved approbation —and gave it without stint. Then, of course, there were the "policy" laughers. In every group there was sure to be a claque who owed the banker money. They could be counted on to make the rafters ring.

To our friend, the banker, these kudos were as heady wine. He enjoyed hugely his new prestige, and with uncommon acumen set to work to improve his performance. He sought the counsel of his bright young men, listened attentively to their criticisms, had them seek out new and better material. As a result, his speeches grew better and better. The last time I was privileged to hear the gentleman he spoke in a strange city to a group "that knew not Joseph." I will not say that he was precisely a Chatauqua attraction, but he acquitted himself most creditably.

And this is only one of dozens of cases out of my own observation, which tend to show conclusively that with enthusiasm and determination, any person who truly WANTS to do so, may make himself a good anecdotist.

❖ ❖

Like all professional story-tellers I am often asked where I get my material. And I am always at a loss to answer. We gather our stories from the warp and woof of daily life. Some we borrow; some we swipe; some are suggested by humorous incidents we encounter in our daily lives; and a good many are manufactured out of whole cloth. I have taken stories, as Kipling's character took his fun—wherever I have happened to find them; but rarely have I found it practicable to adopt an anecdote or character sketch without extensive alterations.

This art of taking stories and, through a few deft touches, making them distinctly and distinctively your own, is something that can be gained only by patient practice. Some men never acquire it. I know two business partners—both able speakers. One is a born story-teller; the other, although he tells a story acceptably, has never achieved brilliance. This latter gentleman, noting that his partner often pored over a tattered almanac, while preparing a speech, conceived the notion that if he could just get his hands on that precious book, he too could convulse an audience. So, when he had occasion to talk before a group of salesmen, he cajoled the book, but was depressed to find it filled with rather stupid stories. His associate had made them appear brilliant only through skillful window-dressing.

A favored practice of this anecdotist is to tie his story to some scene or circumstance of his boyhood or early youth, thus giving it an added ring of reality. Over a period of time, he has sketched from memory, or invented, a variety of characters that have become familiar to the firm's salesmen, to whom he talks regularly each fortnight. Thus, when he wants a point to stick in the memory of his men, he hammers it home with a story of "Butch" Gascomb, or old Cap Thane, the Civil War Vet.

Obviously, much care should be taken in the selection of the stories you are to tell. See that they coincide with the intelligence, experience and possibly the occupations of the audience. Equally important is the precaution of making certain that your material is in keeping with the spirit of the occasion. A small group met to pay tribute to a celebrated scholar is quite different from a sales convention of the Kolossal Kandy Ko. Generally speaking, at an evening meeting one may be allowed a little more latitude than at a luncheon or the business sessions of a convention. If ladies are present, the type of story is altered somewhat. Even though "dirty" stories are not indulged, the stag meeting brings out a certain robustious, all-good-fellows-together type of story that is more keenly appreciated by the male of the species.

Know in advance the precise point at which a story will be introduced, and the manner in which you will present it. Once your material is selected, and you have made the necessary transitions from the printed form, the next step is to learn your stories. This should be a needless admonition. Unfortunately, however, there are many who sadly neglect this important point. It may not be necessary—may, indeed, not be advisable—to memorize an anecdote word for word. But at least you should rehearse the tale again and gain, until you are very certain that you can relate it with the most telling effect. Few things are more disconcerting than listening to a speaker endeavoring to tell a story without adequate preparation.

❖   ❖

So now to sum up briefly: Tell anecdotes only if you like to do so; tell only those anecdotes that strike you as being really funny; select your stories thoughtfully for each occasion; master the story in every detail; know just how and where you are going to tell it; tell your story without a hackneyed introduction or preamble; build up the element of suspense as you go along without making the story involved or tedious.

Do these things faithfully, and it is tolerably certain that you will develop into a Grade A raconteur.

Here's the best of luck to you!

HERE ARE THE ANECDOTES

IN THE pages that follow we are presenting what your compiler believes to be the most *helpful* collection of anecdotes ever put together in a single source. Although the volume is large, we make no boast of size. It would have been a simple matter—indeed, a far *simpler* matter—to have included five times the number of stories actually selected. Setting up our standards and maintaining them with integrity and exactness has been the real time-consuming task.

Since this is above all a collection for the practicing speaker, the *usefulness* of a story has been our first, and in fact our only consideration. No bright bit is included for which we have not seen a valid purpose. This eliminates a great body of anecdotage (if we may coin the term) which while funny enough in its way, does not weigh enough when put to the test of practical platform use.

No collection of contemporary humor can ever be *complete*. For humor is not a static thing. Our fecund creators spawn new stories with every tick of the clock. But let us emphasize that this is not intended merely as a gathering of the newest bits of brightness. Many an old story stands boldly on these pages. By honorable service it has earned the right of inclusion. We hold that no story is decrepit so long as there are ears that have not heard it. And even a "chestnut" may be relished if given a new point and purpose. Old stories, like old songs, hold their cherished place in human hearts. "I like the old ones," says a very great speaker, "because an audience always kwows just where to laugh."

Since every anthology is bounded—and hounded—by human fallibility, it is obvious that we have made errors, both of omission and of commission. Doubtless we have screened from these pages certain old standbys in the mistaken belief that they are too threadbare to stand the strain of another telling. And in their stead we have set tales that may not seem to you as funny as we found them. In the main, however, it is our feeling, and certainly our hope, that we shall find agreement.

In conclusion, we remind you that these anecdotes come to you tested in the only crucible that really counts. Your compiler, his platform friends and associates, have used the stories in a variety of situations. They have seemed to be just about what the audience ordered.

Certainly we shall be first to admit that there remain outside our corral stories quite as good as any we have captured and brought to your service. But we are minded of the overseas soldier who wrote to his girl at home of a certain English lass named Nellie. He wrote frequently, and in glowing terms. Finally, the home-town gal grew weary. "What," she asked petulantly, "has this Nellie got that I lack?"

"Nothing," confessed the soldier blandly. "Nothing at all—but Nellie has it here!"

We have the stories here. It is our hope that you will help yourself!

SOME STORIES FOR THE
CHAIRMAN TO TELL

AT A meeting, not so long ago, I overheard a charming young matron ask the Chairman to define his duties. His response struck me as particularly appropriate, and I'd like to share it with you:

"My dear," he said, "the functions of a Chairman are very simple. He may be likened to the piece of parsley that is placed on top of an order of fish."

❖　❖

Let us assume that your meeting began rather tardily (as meetings so often do!) Now, with two or three speakers yet to be heard from, it is obvious that you will not conclude at the scheduled time. Yet, as the presiding officer, you don't want the remaining participants to feel uncomfortable, or under a sense of time pressure. As gracefully as you can, accept the blame for a late start—and tell this story to illustrate your point:

A suburbanite put on a last-minute spurt of speed to catch his train—but he missed it. A bystander remarked, "Well, if you had just run a little faster, you would have made it."

"No," the suburbanite replied with compelling candor, "it wasn't a case of running faster, but of starting sooner."

❖　❖

If you are a popular master of ceremonies, known to be in great demand, you may tell this as a personal experience. (The audience always loves the Chairman or speaker who "tells one on himself!") Or, if you are quite inexperienced as a presiding officer, you may say that you are not at all like the central character in this little farce—a popular toastmaster who found himself dining at home, for a change:

As soon as the family group was seated at the dining table, the toastmaster's wife arose and rapped for order. Smiling her sweetest smile, she began:

"Children, we have with us tonight a guest of whom you have all heard even if you do not know him personally. He is a man

22

who has a reputation for good cheer in every club in the city. This evening we are to have the honor and pleasure of being numbered among the admirers of his entertaining qualities. It is with great pleasure that I present to you—Your Father."

❖   ❖

Long-drawn-out introductions are usually a bore. You will make a hit if you tell this one—and then get on promptly with your specific mission:

A German mayor, in a small Wisconsin town, had been called upon to introduce Senator Spooner. His introduction provides a pattern which all of us might follow with pleasing results:

"Mine frents," said the mayor, "I haf been asked to introduce Senator Spooner, who is to make a speech. Vell, I haf did so, and he vill now do so."

❖   ❖

Another good approach to a brief introduction:

It has always seemed to me that the principal province of a presiding officer is to get out of a speaker's way as promptly as possible. The members of our craft should, I feel, take as their motto that excellent maxim: "Be Brief, Be Bright, Begone!"

❖   ❖

Here is an introductory story if you are presiding at a meeting of professional folk, where the rewards gleaned by members of the craft are likely to be spiritual and mental rather than monetary:

I have just learned of an editor (teacher, doctor, scientist, etc.) who started poor twenty years ago, and recently retired with a comfortable fortune of $50,000. This was acquired through industry, economy, conscientious effort, indomitable preserverance —and the death of an uncle who left him $49,990.

❖   ❖

Introducing a scholarly speaker, after a rather satisfying meal:

We have just enjoyed turkey stuffed with sage. It will now be our pleasure to give our attention to a sage stuffed with turkey.

❖   ❖

Introducing any speaker who is a recognized leader in his field:

A rather well-known Protestant bishop was making a journey

in a Pullman car. The porter eyed his guest carefully, and presently paused to inquire: "Anything I can do for you, Senator?" The bishop smiled kindly, and shook his head.

Later the porter returned: "Gov'ner," he suggested, "Would you-all lak a little bite o' somethin' from de dining car?" Again the bishop shook his head.

Finally, at the end of the journey, the porter asked: "Colonel, sah, kin I bresh yo' off?"

The bishop looked up. "Porter," he said, "I'm not a senator, a governor, or a colonel. I'm just a poor, common Methodist bishop."

"Yas, sah, Bishop," replied the darkey, "I knowed all de time yo' was one o' dem face ca'ds!"

Well, our speaker today is not only "one of the face cards," but an acknowledged king in his particular realm. . . .

❖   ❖

Frankly, I'm a little nervous on this occasion (admits the Chairman). In introducing our distinguished guest of the day, I feel that I must pick my words carefully. I don't want to be in the position of another presiding officer who had the great honor of introducing the shy and retiring Senator Hattie Caraway.

"Ladies and gentlemen," he thundered, "we are about to hear the most notorious woman in Arkansas."

❖   ❖

If you have the wit and audacity to get away with it, you can make quite a reputation for yourself by deliberately piling insults upon your associates along the banquet board. It's all in good fun, of course, and no one gets more of a kick out of it than those who are mercilessly ribbed by the master of ceremonies. It is only fair to say, however, that this sort of thing requires a specialized skill. A bungling amateur is likely to wind up making everyone mad. For safety's sake, your humorous digs should be so broad as to be readily recognized by victim and audience alike as burlesque. There should be no genuine animosity in what you say. Generally speaking, it is safest to twit your fellow speakers on their strong points, rather than their weaknesses. The reason for this is psychologically sound: The able lawyer knows that he is good. He has no inferiority complex where his profession is concerned. He will take any amount of kidding on a legal score. But he may be inordinately sensitive concerning his golf game. Hint that he isn't so hot on the green—and he may see red.

A very good technique is the collective insult. This embraces everybody at the table. Thus each man feels that you are really hitting at his neighbor. No one takes it personally, and everybody enjoys the jibe. Here is an instance:

My remarks this evening (said the toastmaster) will be brief. It isn't my mission to bore you, but to introduce others who will.

The great master of public insult is Clarence Buddington Kelland, the author. He achieved his reputation years ago as head of New York's famous Dutch Treat Club. Speakers writhed under Bud's caustic wit, but they were always eager to come back for more.

Once, when Kelland was presiding at a banquet, he arose, solemnly surveyed the assembled speakers, and said, very slowly and profoundly: "It isn't the intention that a toastmaster should be very entertaining. Indeed, he should strive to make his comments a trifle tedious, so that the remarks of the speakers will, by contrast, appear the more amusing." Then, after a long and eloquent pause, he continued. "Surveying the aggregation of talent before me this evening, I perceive that I shall have to rise to new heights of boredom."

It was Kelland who, introducing the ubiquitous Dr. Nicholas Murray Butler, of Columbia University, said:

"For years organizations have been besieging this retiring gentleman to address them—with remarkable success."

❖   ❖

Generally speaking, people do not relish too much of the apologetic attitude in their speakers. But the fellow who makes the introductions—well, he isn't supposed to be too good. And a little honest confession may serve to clear the atmosphere. If genuinely ill at ease, you might tell this one:

I feel a close kinship with the college sophomore who was reciting a memorized oration. He began bravely enough: "Washington is dead. Lincoln is dead." Then, forgetting the next lines, he hesitated, and finally concluded lamely—"and I—I'm beginning to feel pretty sick myself."

❖   ❖

You might use this one if it falls to your lot to introduce a speaker noted for his eloquence and vocabulary:

Many years ago, Jim Reed, then Speaker of the House of Representatives, went into a barber shop in Washington to be shaved. The barber, following the custom of his clan, began a program of urging additional services on the Speaker.

"Hair's pretty thin, sir?" he commented, fingering the few stray locks on an otherwise bald pate. "Been that way long, sir?"

"I was born that way," said Reed unemotionally. "Afterward, I enjoyed a brief period of hirsute efflorescence, but it did not endure."

The barber gasped—and said no more.

Later, someone remarked that the departing parton was Speaker of the House.

"Speaker!" exclaimed the tonsorial artist. "Say, don't I know it! That fellow really *is* a speaker!"

And tonight, ladies and gentlemen, we have with us another of whom we may speak in the same superlative terms. . . .

❖   ❖

Speakers are forever catching colds! It appears to be an occupational disease. If at least one of your stable of stars doesn't show up with something approaching a light attack of laryngitis, consider yourself uncommonly fortunate. If asked to apologize for a speaker's slight indisposition, you may do it with this story:

Our guest this evening has asked me to explain that he is a bit hoarse. I have assured him that the indisposition will not detract from our enjoyment of his message; in fact, it may serve to enhance certain eloquent passages. You recall the small boy who was seen wading ankle deep in a puddle of water. A well-meaning stranger paused to warn the lad that he was in danger of catching cold.

"That's jest what I'm after, mister," confided the small boy.

"I'm goin' to speak *Spartacus to the Gladiators* at school Friday, and I want to git my voice good and hoarse for it."

❖ ❖

Too often, an important speaker is unavoidably detained and makes his appearance only after the meeting has begun. You might introduce the tardy individual with this good story:

Well past the usual supper hour, a neighbor encountered Johnny playing marbles with some companions.

"You'd better hurry home, my boy," said the neighbor. "You'll be late for supper."

"Oh, no, I won't," replied Johnny, with an air of one who knows his stuff. "I won't be late 'cause I've got the meat!"

(The point, of course, being that the tardy one has the "meat" which he is now about to deliver.)

❖ ❖

To bring out by contrast that your speaker is a practical man who keeps his feet on the ground, tell this one of the army rookie who had just arrived at an army training camp:

The lad was curiously inspecting the live stock at too close range, when one of the mules kicked, knocking the boy cold. His buddies got him on the rebound, placed him on a stretcher and started for the infirmary. Regaining consciousness, the rookie felt the swaying motion of the stretcher, and cautiously lowering his hand over the side, found only space.

"Gosh," he moaned in horror, "I ain't hit ground yet!"

❖ ❖

Introducing a speaker who has labored long and earnestly to accomplish some worthwhile feat, you might relate this impressive anecdote:

When James A. Garfield was president of Hiram College, he was approached by the father of a prospective pupil.

"Can't you simplify the course?" he was asked. "My boy will never take all that in. He wants to get through by a shorter route."

"Certainly," answered Garfield. "I can arrange that. It all depends, of course, on what you want to make of him. When God wants an oak he takes a hundred years; but when He wants to make a squash, he requires only a couple of months."

✧   ✧

The Chairman of The Day

Here is a little essay on "The Chairman" which you may find of interest and value. It was written by ALFONSO JONES, *a Rotarian, of Dallas, Tex., and appeared originally in* The Rotarian.

The chairman of the day is a paradox. ("Paradox," springing from the Greek is not the singular of "Para-dice," which gallops from the African.) While sitting, he is not a chairman, but when he stands, he is. Neither is he a setter as he sits nor a stander-upper when he arises. He performs somewhat the duties of a piece of punk when we were kids; you will recall that the punk started the fireworks. But if the chairman of the day is too punk, we have no fireworks, and if he is too well lit, anything can, and does happen.

When the president turns the meeting over to the chairman, he does so with a sigh of relief; or just a sigh, period, depending on his faith in the chairman. Heaving a sigh, the president does not become a cipher; certainly naught.

A good program has its high points, its peaks, its mountain tops. Generally the chairman of the day is the valley, but he mustn't be a dip. He is like the platform of a railroad passenger car: of no further use when the train (of thoughts) gets started. If the chairman of the day talks too much, he is criticized for taking up too much time; if he doesn't talk enough, he is accused of not giving the speaker a good send-off; if the program goes over, the speaker gets the credit; if it is a flop, the chairman takes the blame.

The chairman of the day is chairman for not more than five minutes, but those five minutes can make or break a program; he should at least know the name of the speaker and the subject, but he shouldn't try to make the speech, even if he can do a better job than the scheduled performer. Regardless of how effective he is, the chairman of the day almost always receives sincere applause when he sits down; perhaps it is a vote of confidence. He will appreciate a kind word after the meeting adjourns; he has played an important part in the program. So here's to the chairman of the day; long may he rave.

THE SPEAKER AND CHAIRMAN

Where the speaker's discourse is preceded by a business meeting (and how often that happens!) this may prove a good opening story:

All this business of motions made and seconded brings to mind the case of an Easterner, making his first visit to a Kentucky community.

"Do you mean to say," the horrified Easterner asked a Kentucky colonel, "That this man you speak of was shot and killed by the chairman of the meeting just because he made a motion that was out of order?"

"Yes, suh," the colonel answered. "That's the way it was."

"What lawlessness!" exclaimed the Eastern man. "What wanton disregard for the sanctity of human life!"

"Well," said the colonel. "Just to keep the record straight, and the fair name of our community clear, I might state that the motion of the deceased was toward his hip pocket."

❖ ❖

The Chairman has lauded the speaker almost to a point of embarrassment—outlined the difficulties involved in securing his services, emphasized the good fortune of the group in having the opportunity to hear so renowned an authority. The speaker feels that he can't possibly live up to the booking, and must do something to ease the tension. Try this one.

My reaction to your chairman's extravagant introduction can perhaps best be summed up in the instance of an old colored man, homeless, friendless, penniless and sick, who slipped into a barn and crawled into the haymow to sleep. The farmer caught sight of him and came running with a shotgun in hand.

"I got you, doggone you," he yelled. "I got you."

The poor old Negro poked his head out of the hay. Scornfully he said, "An' a great git you got."

Your chairman's hyperbolic comment on my modest achievements (says the speaker) is reminiscent of the reaction of a country editor who had left his weekly publication in the care of a young assistant. Returning, he found that the burning of a livery stable

29

had been heralded in the largest, blackest type the shop afforded.

"Wh-wha-what do you think of it?" the assistant asked anxiously.

"Well," the editor pondered. "I reckon it's all right. But I—I was sorta saving that type for the second coming of Christ."

❖   ❖

The new editor of a southwestern town's little weekly was very young, shy, and nervous. His speech to the Chamber of Commerce had flopped miserably, for the presence of bearded men with .45 pistols hanging at their hips had not helped his presence of mind.

He stumbled to a halt, finally, and sat down. Immediately, a group of his armed listeners rose and walked ominously toward the speaker's table.

A grizzled old cattleman came over and placed a reassuring hand upon the youth's trembling shoulder.

"Now, you jes' sit still, son." he said. "They ain't gonna hurt you—they's comin' fo' the program chairman."

❖   ❖

Let it be clearly understood that, whatever happens, I am here at the invitation of your Chairman. You'll have to take it out on him. It's a case somewhat like that of a young man with a local reputation as a vocalist, who attended a dinner and was asked to sing. He had no music with him, and was hoarse as a frog, but consented to try. Midway through the first number he broke down.

"Never thee mind, lad," said an elderly Quaker. "Thee has done thy best. But the fellow as asked thee t' sing, ought to be shot."

❖   ❖

Most speakers are called upon from time to time to head committees. And, as reports are made, praise is accorded the chairman. The wise speaker will have a good story to subordinate his own efforts, throw the spotlight on associates. One way to do this is through ironic definition. Thus:

The presiding officer has referred in glowing terms to my executive ability, and while I am appreciative of his kindly remarks,

I can't help recalling the small boy who asked his father to define the term.

"Executive ability, my lad," said the wise parent, "is the art of getting credit for all the hard work that somebody else does."

(This is also an excellent story for the boss to tell at company meetings, where his praises are sung.)

❖ ❖

How fine it would be if all who serve on committees would take their work as seriously as the small girl who awoke one Monday morning with a cold and was told by her mother that she had better stay home from kindergarten.

"But, Mother, I *can't*," the child protested. "This is the day we start making our clay model of a cow, and I'm chairman of the udder committee."

❖ ❖

If you are asked to head an uncommonly large committee—or if such a committee is reporting at a meeting where you are to speak—this story may be used to good advantage.

"Is your town doing anything in the uplift way?"

"Oh, yes! We have a committee appointed to see all shows suspected of being immoral and report on them."

"Good!"

"Yes, a committee of one thousand."

"Indeed! Isn't that a-er-rather large committee?"

"Well, you see, we couldn't afford to create any hard feeling, and so we made it large enough to include about everybody."

❖ ❖

Said the chairman of a certain society at its annual meeting: "In most kindred associations, half the committee does all the work, whilst the other half does nothing. I am pleased to place on record that in the society over which I have the honor to preside it is just the reverse."

"MEET-THE-SITUATION" ANECDOTES

YOUR compiler believes that in his twenty-odd years of varied platform experience he has encountered practically every situation
that is likely to befall a public speaker. These situations have a
way of recurring again and again. And in a general sense, they are
common to us all.

The gathering of stories to meet situations is so obvious a step
that most veterans have collected and stored their private treas-
ures. Now, for the first time in any public tome, we undertake a
comprehensive grouping of "Meet-the-Situation" stories.

The stories we have selected are by no means the only ones
applicable to the given situations. You may find a story in another section of this book which strikes you as more acceptable
for a specific situation. Or, conversely, you may wish to use the
one of these suggested stories to illustrate a completely different
point. That is quite all right. We simply give you a *possible*
application. Your own ingenuity will find many more.

"Meet-the-Situation" anecdotes have been tested by able, experienced speakers in the manner indicated. They have met these
situations adequately. May you find this new department—and
new departure—of great practical value.

THE SPEAKER accepts a High Office

Let me assure you, in all seriousness, that I am deeply grateful
for the honor you have bestowed upon me, and that I appreciate
fully the responsibilities that this high office entails. You have
given me not an empty honor, but a full-time job, and I purpose
to put into it all that I have of energy and ability. My position in
this respect is quite different from that of the old darky who approached his employer and asked for a day off.

"Hit's on account ob de lodge," he explained, "We is gwine
hab a big 'nitiation meetin' wid a monstah unifawmed pee-rade
in de aftahnoon. Mighty big doin's, sah."

"Um-m," mused the boss. "You an officer in this lodge, Ras?"

"Yas, sah, yas, sah. I's de Mos' High Sublime Potentate ob de
ordah."

"Well, well," said the employer. "That's quite an honor. I couldn't very well keep the Head Man of the lodge away from such an important meeting. Go along, now, and have a big time."

"Thank you, sah," said the grateful servitor. "Thank you, sah. But, sah, I reckons I ought t' 'splain dat I ain't de head man, 'xackly. You see, sah, dey's six mo' in de lodge what holds offices above me."

THE SPEAKER accepts praise

Thank you, Mr. Chairman, thank you very much indeed for those sweet words. Now, I know how a buckwheat cake feels when molasses is poured on it!

THE SPEAKER accepts with pleasure

I want to set the record straight on one point. Perhaps from your Chairman's introductory remarks you may have gained an impression that the Program Committee faced quite a chore in dragging me here. The truth of the matter is that I am probably the most easily persuaded fellow you ever met. I am always ready to talk at the drop of a gavel.

I am somewhat like Henry Clay. He was once asked by a Southern lady if he would make a speech to a large gathering. "Madam" he replied, "I suffer when I don't!"

THE SPEAKER acknowledges a good introduction

Thank you for those kind words. You know, we all relish praise, even when we may be a bit dubious as to our deserts. It makes us feel important. A little girl I know came down to breakfast the other morning smiling happily. "Last night," she confided, "I had the nicest dream. I dreamed that everything I said was important."

❖ ❖

Thank you for that gracious and generous introduction. It certainly is a striking contrast to one I received last week. The speaker said he wouldn't waste much time in introducing me because he had a very important announcement to make. "Our next speaker," he concluded, "will be Dr. Blank, of Chicago, and I certainly hope it won't be as hard to sell tickets for him as it was for this meeting."

THE SPEAKER acknowledges applause

If you persist in telling funny stories you will sometimes get a trickle of laughter! It is well to be prepared. Here's an appropriate acknowledgment.

Thank you for that friendly demonstration. A friend, you know, is one who laughs at your funny stories, even if they aren't so good, and sympathizes with your misfortunes, even if they aren't so bad.

❖   ❖

I appreciate that applause—but don't worry, I'm not going to tell another story! You know, one of the most needed devices in this country is some sort of a gauge that would enable an audience to tell just how much applause would make a performer feel good without being mistaken for an invitation to give an encore.

❖   ❖

(Acknowledging the demonstration at conclusion of the Chairman's introduction.) Thanks for the applause. I'm always glad to get it this early in the program. You never can tell what might happen later. But then, of course, a speaker can never be sure whether the hand-clapping is a tribute to his sterling character, or to the chairman's masterful introduction. It's a good deal like the self-proclaimed football star who rushed to the observation platform when the train stopped at a small town.

He had no sooner made his way there than the train began pulling out. But ripplings of applause from a group of young ladies at the station was music to his ears.

"Too bad the train isn't staying longer," the great one said. "But it' nice of them to keep applauding me."

"Applauding you?" a disgusted team-mate exclaimed. "Why,

man, they're not applauding you. They're applauding the engineer."

❖   ❖

Thanks . . . but I really didn't think the story was *that* good! I appreciate the demonstration all the more because I have no ulterior motive. In that respect I'm rather different from the Governor of a mid-western state who recently paused in the crowded anteroom of his executive quarters to tell a stale and pointless story, and to observe carefully the resulting reaction.

Later, in the Governor's private office a friend remarked, "Gosh, that was an old chestnut you pulled out yonder."

"Sure, I know it," the chief executive agreed, "but I had to do it. I wanted to find out how many of those fellows were here to ask favors."

"And did you get the information?"

"Certainly," said the Governor. "They were the ones who laughed!"

❖   ❖

Thank you. . . thank you. I even observed some of the guests laughing on that one. You know, a story has to be pretty good to get a response from a guest. They don't have to laugh to get their money's worth. And that's my cue to tell you an amusing little experience:

A ladies' club in New Jersey invited a female book reviewer to speak at its meeting. She told the plot of a triple-A tear jerker, and the entire assembly broke into tears. All but one, that is—a lady who sat dry-eyed and unmoved thru the entire recital. After the lecture, the reviewer asked her why she hadn't cried. The lady's answer stopped her cold. "Oh," she explained, "I'm not a member."

THE SPEAKER acknowledges a scholarly title

I was gratified, to be sure, that your chairman elected to employ my honorary title of "Doctor." I don't get a great deal of use out of that title, and around home, I must admit, it isn't taken very seriously.

Shortly after my degree was conferred, some practical joker

called my home, pretending to seek my professional services in a dire emergency where medical skill was clearly indicated. The phone was answered by our maid of all work, and I chanced to overhear her part of the conversation. "Yas, sah, yas, sah," she said, "dis heah is Dr. ——'s residence. . . Oh, sah, I is afeared you-all has done made a mistake. He's a doctah all right, sah, but he ain't de kind ob a doctah what does anybody any good."

THE SPEAKER acknowledges a testimonial

I think I need not tell you that I shall always look back upon this meeting—and my good friends here—with the deepest affection. I cannot begin to tell you of my gratitude for all of the kind things that have been said here this evening. I feel that I am expressing myself almost as ineptly as did a speaker on another historic occasion:

A colonel was speaking at a dinner given in his honor before embarking for Africa.

"I thank you," he concluded, "for your kind wishes regarding my welfare, and I want you to know that when I am far away, surrounded by ugly, grinning savages, I shall always think of you."

THE SPEAKER addresses a rural audience

I hope I won't find myself today in the position of a speaker who had the bad luck to address a group such as this during a protracted dry spell. After the meeting, as the crowd was filing out, he happened to overhear an exchange between two farmers.

"That fellow was right good, wasn't he?" said the first.

"I suppose so," conceded the other, "but a half hour's rain would o' done us a heap more good."

❖   ❖

A gentleman farmer tells of a city lad who once worked for him. The lad was called one winter morning before dawn and told to harness the mule to the dearborn.

The lad was too lazy to light a lantern, and in the dark he didn't notice that one of the cows was in the stable with the mule.

The farmer, impatient at the long delay, shouted from the house:
"Billy! Billy! What are you doing?"

"I can't get the collar over the mule's head," yelled back the boy. "His ears are frozen."

❖   ❖

Down in southern Missouri, Mose White, a colored farm-hand, appeared at a neighbor's back door one morning and asked for the loan of a mule to do his employer's plowing.

"Why, Mose," said the neighbor, "your boss has a good mule. Why not use him?"

"Well, suh," replied Mose, "dat mule sit in de shade all day. Jes' won't work."

"What's the matter with him? Is he sick?"

"No, suh," was the answer. "Dat mule ain't sick. He jes' thinks he's a gentleman farmer."

THE SPEAKER addresses a Women's Club

Women relish a bit of good-natured bantering on their organized activities. A story, such as this one, gets you off to a good start:

In that trying period preceding the program, the visiting lecturer was being entertained by a local social leader of the fluttery type. Hard-pressed for conversational topics, she at length inquired, "And do you believe in clubs for women?"

"Oh, yes," said the lecturer. "Yes, indeed," and then pausing significantly, he added, "but of course only when kindness fails."

THE SPEAKER advises, "Go climb a tree!"

W. Rowland Allen, a department store personnel manager, says that years ago, when he was on a hunting trip in Maine, he became separated from his guide. He wandered about for several hours and became thoroughly panic-stricken. He saw in imagination a posse finding his body weeks later. Then he recalled his guide's earlier counsel:

"If you're lost, climb the tallest tree and look around. From up there, you may see something that will help you."

Allen climbed a tree; found to his chargrin that the impenatrable forest extended for only a quarter of a mile. His camp and his guide were less than a mile away.

THE SPEAKER answers questions

Question-and-Answer sessions are a bane to many speakers. No amount of preparation is any guarantee that you won't be tripped by a trick query! Experienced speakers know that the best course is to make no pretense of infallibility—and to have a few good stories handy! Tell 'em you don't want to be like the clerk in this narrative:

A learned professor, attending a convention at a well-known resort hotel, had occasion to consult a reference work. Approaching a desk clerk, he inquired, "Is there a copy of the *Encyclopedia Britannica* in the hotel?" he asked.

"No, sir," the clerk replied regretfully. And then, as an afterthought, "But what is it, sir, you wish to know?"

❖ ❖

If you are fortunate enough to share the question-answering session with one or more associates, tell the story of the small boy who boasted, "Me and my Pa together knows everything." Whenever he was asked a toughie he'd pass it off with the response, "Oh, that's one o' the things Pa knows." Tell the audience you shall avail yourself of a similar privilege and pass along the questions that are out of your special province.

❖ ❖

"If you don't know, ask" is a good rule to follow. But I do hope that some of the responses we are able to give at this session will prove more helpful than the reply received by a ministerial friend of mine. He had been called upon in an emergency to preach a funeral sermon. The dear departed was a complete stranger, and after the service was well under way the preacher realized to his horror that he had even neglected to inquire as to the sex of the corpse. The name supplied was one of those indefinite terms that might be applied to male or female. The meager notes were not enlightening.

In a cold sweat, the minister proceeded as diplomatically as possible, trying to avoid an incriminating declaration. But finally he came to a point where he simply had to know. So, while the choir sang, he beckoned to a nearby mourner, pointed to the casket, and whispered hoarsely, "Brother or Sister?"

The mourner answered, "Cousin!"

❖ ❖

I like simple, direct questions. But of course there is such a thing as being too embarrassingly direct. I recall the case of a principal telling his students of a forthcoming examination.

"I want you all to do your very best," he said, "If only for the honor of the dear old school. Questions are already in the hands of the printer. Now, is there anything further you'd like to know?" "Yes, sir," piped up one voice, "Who's the printer?"

THE SPEAKER apologizes . . .
for his presence at the festive board

This has been such an altogether delightful occasion that it seems a pity to inflict anything in the nature of a formal address upon you. Fortunately, we have dined exceedingly well. And I am comforted by the findings of a noted criminologist. I have his word for it that very few men commit acts of violence after a hearty meal. This fact alone, I am confident, accounts for the singular longevity of after-dinner speakers.

THE SPEAKER apologizes . . .
for inept performance

I am a good deal like a young Negro making his first political speech.

"Friends and fellow citizens," he stammered, "I 'clare to goodness, when I stand up to talk, my mind sets down."

❖ ❖

At this point I can sympathize with the four-year-old who was to take part in an Easter program.

"Are you frightened, Barbara?" she was asked.

"Oh, no," she said, "I'm not afraid, but my stomach is."

THE SPEAKER apologizes . . .

for inexperience

I suppose it is unnecessary to herald the fact that I am inexperienced at this sort of thing. I recall the fellow who, suddenly called on for a few remarks, stammered, "T-to tell the truth, I never did any public speaking except when I proposed to my wife on a party line."

❖　❖

A new maid had been employed for a special occasion. The mistress was a little dubious about her. "Now, Mary," she cautioned, "when you are in the dining room tonight I want you to be careful and not spill anything."

Mary looked at the mistress knowingly and smiled.

"You can count on me, ma'am. I don't talk much."

Well, I'm a good deal like Mary—I don't talk much. . . .

THE SPEAKER apologizes . . .

for lack of constructive content

It is a simple matter to criticize, to argue and to refute, but mapping a constructive course of action is quite a different matter. I don't want to be in the position of the old Negro preacher, much given to the use of big words and ponderous phrases. He was called on the carpet by a committee and told his preaching wasn't satisfactory.

"How come?" he asked. "Don't I argify and sputify?"

"Yes," conceded a committee member, "you does dat all right. You argify an' you sputify, but you don' show wherein."

❖　❖

I trust I shall not find myself in the position of the noted American journalist who, on a trip to China, was asked to address a Chinese audience. He was about half way through his talk when he noticed that a Chinese in a corner was writing on a blackboard. He became interested in watching this writer and observed that he set down less, and finally stopped altogether. Later, the journalist asked what the man had been doing.

"Why," explained the chairman, "he was interpreting your

speech for the benefit of those who do not understand English."

"But," said the speaker, "for the last twenty minutes he didn't put down a thing."

"Oh," said the chairman smoothly, "he was only writing the *ideas* on the blackboard."

❖   ❖

I have found it difficult to gather the specific data I desired and for that reason I have an apprehension that this talk may have less substance than I had hoped. I don't want to garnish a spare soup bone with fancy decorations and pass it off as a Chef's Special.

George Washington Carver, the great Negro scientist, once told of a man in his community who kept a horse so lean and hungry it could scarcely stand.

One day, when this fellow drove his horse to town, the animal was observed wearing a brand-new straw bonnet. "Well, Uncle Mose," someone observed, "your horse would be much better off with less millinery and more oats."

❖   ❖

Former United States Senator James E. Watson tells an amusing story about one of the first cases he ever tried. "My client was a rambunctious Irish woman and was almost irrepressible throughout the trial. I was the only lawyer on our side, while the opposition had employed two. The old lady kept insisting that we ought to have another on our side. I was not greatly disturbed about the outcome, but she kept insisting so vigorously that I finally turned to her and said, "Mary, why on earth do you want another lawyer?"

" 'Well,' she said, 'you see, on their side when wan is talkin' the other wan is a-thinkin', while on our side when yez are talkin' there's no wan a-thinkin'.' "

❖   ❖

I fear that I have said very little today that you will care to remember. But it is just possible that you may be able to draw a lesson even from this lack of constructive content.

Sidney Smith, the great English clergyman was once discussing the relative importance of two prominent men. "There is the same difference between their tongues," he observed, "as between the hour and the minute hand on a clock. The one goes twelve times as fast, the other signifies twelve times as much."

❖   ❖

If you have come here today hoping to be moved by a Momentous Message, I am afraid you're in for a disappointment. At the conclusion of my remarks you'll probably be somewhat in the mood of a woman I overheard in an art gallery not long ago. She had paused to examine a realistic portrait of a very dead fish. After considerable contemplation, she turned to her companion and remarked:

"Well, I must admit he doesn't say *a thing* to me!"

THE SPEAKER apologizes . . .
for lack of oratorical ability

I am not an orator—a fact that will become increasingly evident as we go along. I merely want to present to you a few facts, as clearly and as simply as I can. I have no wish to emulate the young Negro who claimed special oratorical talents. "But what," asked his companion, "is an orator?"

"You mean you don't know what is a orator? Lis'en an' I'll 'splain it to you. If you was to walk up to a ordinary nigger an' ask him how much is two an' two, he'd say 'fo'.' But if you was to ask one of us orators he'd say, 'When in de co'se of human events it becomes necessary to take de numeral of the second denomination and add it to de figger two, I says to you, an' I says it without fear of successful contradiction, dat de result invai'bly will be fo'.' Dat's a orator."

❖   ❖

H. I. Phillips, the humorist, has defined oratory as the art of making deep sounds from the chest seem like important messages from the brain.

❖   ❖

I certainly make no pretense of being an orator. And to tell you the truth, I'm a little suspicious of too-smooth talking. I am not sure the small boy was wide of the mark when he wrote, in answer to a quiz:

"Elocution is the way people are put to death in some parts of the United States."

❖   ❖

One reason I am not going to inflict oratory upon you, I must admit, is that I don't know the lingo. I'm a good deal like the litle girl who was rebuked for incessant chatter. "Well," she explained, "I don't know any big words, so I use lots and lots of little ones to make up."

THE SPEAKER apologizes . . .
for lack of originality

I fear that on this subject I have nothing startlingly new or original to present. My position it not unlike that of the little girl who returned from school to ask her mother if she knew that Christopher Columbus was an Italian.

"Oh, yes," said the mother. "And did you know" continued the little daughter, "that Queen Isabella furnished the money to buy his ships?" "Yes; I've heard the matter mentioned."

Kay mused for some time, then said reflectively: "Well, really, Mother, I don't see any use in my going to school if you already know the things I come home and tell you!"

THE SPEAKER apologizes . . .
for lack of preparation

I wish, for my appearance before this audience, I were as well prepared as an old fellow I once heard of—a resident of the Southern mountain country. This old fellow had to do his drinking on the sly. His wife had scruples against the use of intoxicants. So he kept a jug of moonshine in a hollow log out in the woods. Every once in awhile he'd slip away for a swig.

One evening, feeling low in the mind, he took several good, long swigs. Just as he was setting the jug down, he felt something brush against his foot. He looked down and there, almost touching him, was a six-foot diamond-back rattler, coiled, ready to strike.

The old man took another deep draught, then lowered the jug and addressed the snake:

"Strike, dern ye, strike! You'll never find me better prepared than I am right now!"

❖   ❖

To be quite frank about it, I have no planned approach for this talk of mine. In that respect, I'm a little like "Red" Grange the great Illinois football star. One day the coach called "Red" out of the line and cautioned him. " 'Red,' " he said, "you're leaning every time your signal is called. You're tipping off the other side as to just where you're going to carry the ball."

"Well," said "Red" apologetically, "I'm sorry about that, Coach. But I don't see just how I can be tipping them off. The truth is I don't know myself where I'm going with the ball!"

THE SPEAKER apologizes . . .
for lengthy discourse

I fear I have talked much too long. I don't want to be like the banquet speaker who had gone on for what seemed like days. Finally, one suffering auditor, leaving by a side door encountered another member of the audience who had preceded him.

"Has he finished yet?" the earlier deserter asked.

"Yes," was the reply. "He finished long ago; but he won't stop."

❖   ❖

Soon, I fear, you will be likening me to the long-winded lawyer who droned on and on until the judge finally gave vent to a suggestive yawn.

"I sincerely trust," said the lawyer, "that I am not trespassing on the time of the court."

"There is some difference," the judge observed, "between trespassing on time and encroaching on eternity."

❖   ❖

Sir Josiah Stamp, speaking some years ago at the Chicago Club, expressed a hope that he wasn't talking too long. "I wouldn't like to be in the position of the parson," he explained, "who in the midst of an interminable sermon broke off his discourse to chide: 'You know, I don't mind having you look at your watches to see what time it is, but it really annoys me when you put them to your ears to see if they are still running.' "

❖ ❖

This is a very old story—Irvin Cobb once said he got it from his grandfather. It concerns a minister who had a reputation for being long-winded. On this Sunday he was in especially good form. His topic was the Prophets of the Bible. For more than an hour he droned on.

"And, now," he said at length, "we have disposed of the Major Prophets. We next come to the Minor Prophets. What place, my friends, shall we assign the Minor Prophets?"

From the rear of the church arose a bored-looking stranger. He waved an explanatory arm toward the seat he had just vacated and spoke:

"Parson," he said, "don't worry. One o' them Minor Prophets can have my place. I'm goin' home."

❖ ❖

If I keep talking much longer I am likely to find myself in the position of a certain parrot of which I once heard. This parrot, left alone with a dog, kept teasing the animal, saying, "Bow-wow, bow-wow. There's a good dog. There's a good dog!"

Completely ignored, Polly got bolder, hopped down on the table, repeated its remarks. The dog took no notice until Polly hopped to the floor. It was immediately grabbed, eventually returned to its perch minus feathers.

"I know what's the matter with me," the parrot squawked, "I talk too much."

❖ ❖

At the outset, let me say quite frankly, that I am afraid this talk is a bit long. I tried to cut it down, but I couldn't decide where to amputate. I was rather like the old gentleman who had a walking-stick that was too long for him. He carried it anyway, because it had such a beautiful gold head. Friends suggested that he cut a piece off the stick. "Oh, no," he would gasp, "I-I couldn't cut off this beautiful head!"

"Not *that* end," his friends pointed out. "Cut off the *other* end."

"But, no," the gentleman protested. "You see, the other end fits!"

❖ ❖

The audience always applauds the speaker who tells "a good one" on himself. This is one that Captain Edw. J. Wynn, author of Bombers Across, *used to tell to groups of war workers. You can revamp it a bit, and tell it as a personal experience—the Captain won't mind. You might make the setting a sales meeting. It's the kind of story salesmen relish.*

My talks ran overtime with such chronic regularity that those in authority finally delegated a public relations man to accompany me. His duty was to stand in the back of the room, catch my eye, and signal for the conclusion by pointing to a clock, or to his wrist watch.

On one occasion, when I was more than commonly wound up, I completely forgot my mentor. It was rather dark in the back of the hall and I couldn't see clearly. But finally, when I chanced to look that way, there was the public relations man, standing up on a chair, frantically waving a calendar!

❖ ❖

Now, as I look at my watch, I am overwhelmed with a sense of guilt that must be comparable to that experienced by a minister of whom I once heard:

The minister of a local congregation approached the desk of the city editor. "I just dropped by," he said, "to thank you for the very generous report on my sermon in your morning edition, and—er—to register a mild protest."

"A protest? No serious mis-statement, I trust," said the editor.

"That's just the trouble," said the minister ruefully. "I'm afraid it may be too true. You referred to me as 'reverend,' but you spelled it 'neverend'!"

❖ ❖

I fear that I am too much like a certain talkative mother I heard about not long ago.

The child was out visiting with her mother. The stay was lengthy and the little girl became restless.

"Mother—" she interrupted.

"Mary," rebuked the mother, "it's rude to interrupt while I am speaking; you should wait until I finish."

"But," said the child, "you don't finish."

❖   ❖

I fear that at this point I am vulnerable to the same criticism as that made of one of our fighting men during the war. A young lady eagerly opened an envelope inscribed by her beloved, expecting the usual cargo of endearing phrases. Instead there was a note from the censor. It said: "Your boy friend still loves you, but he talks too much."

❖   ❖

On one occasion, a dull and long-winded member of Congress said to Henry Clay, "You, sir, speak for the present generation, but I speak for posterity." To which Clay responded, "And it seems that you are resolved to keep on speaking until your audience arrives."

❖   ❖

I don't want to be in the position of a speaker at a safety meeting who, after an hour or so of rambling, introduced what he believed to be some rather startling statistics:

"Do you know," said the speaker, "that while I have been speaking, one person has been killed, and several have been injured!" He paused to allow this arresting fact to sink in. And in the hushed silence a voice from the audience rang out:

"Then, don't you think it's time you stopped talking?"

Well, I *do* think it's time I stopped, so . . .

❖   ❖

I have talked for a very long time, and I appreciate your patience and your loyalty. It is reminiscent of another occasion when the speaker had talked for hours, with much arm waving and gesturing. When he finally concluded his discourse, he spoke to a friend who sat below him in the front row.

"How was it, Charlie? Did I get it across?"

"Yes, it was a fine speech. I enjoyed it."

"But didn't I see you yawning? You were yawning, weren't you?"

"That wasn't yawning. That was just a silent Indian war whoop."

❖   ❖

A housing expert took a trip up into the Scandanavian peninsula to make a talk on better housing to the Laplanders. He arrived at one of the small towns and set up his exhibit in the only available building. The hour for the lecture came, and while a huge crowd of the villagers had gathered outside the hall, none ventured inside. The lecturer stepped to the door and invited them to come in. There was a lot of mumbling and small talk, but the speaker could make out no definite reason for the delay. Finally he called aside a bright looking fellow and asked him what was the trouble.

"They want to have some understanding about the fee they are to receive for listening."

"Fee for listening?"

"Anyone can talk," he said, "but it is so hard to listen so long."

❖   ❖

Leon J. Bamberger, an executive of RKO Pictures made this comment at a recent convention session: "Really, I'm having such a good time spouting here that I'd just as leave go on all afternoon, but I hardly want to be embarrassed as I was on on another memorable Monday when talking at a convention. It seemed that I had hardly begun when I heard a fellow in the first row lean over and ask his friend, "Say, what follows Bamberger?" And the answer was: "Wednesday."

❖   ❖

Before long, I fear, you will be thinking me as difficult to stop as a certain motor car, of which I once heard. Before the dawn of the motor-car age, a passing motorist picked up a farmer who had never before seen an automobile. The farmer was duly impressed and delighted. To impress him still more, the motorist put his foot on the accelerator and for six or seven miles they tore along like the wind. Then something went wrong with the steering-gear and they ran into a tree. The farmer and motorist alighted unhurt on a bank of moss. The car was not damaged.

"That was fine," said the farmer, as he got up. "We sartinly went the pace. Tell me this, though—how do you stop her when there ain't no trees?"

❖ ❖

A stranger in an Indiana village thought he might improve the time by attending service in the local church. At the conclusion of a lengthy talk, the minister announced that he would like to meet the board. The stranger, in company with several other persons, proceeded to walk to the front of the church. The pastor, thinking there must be some misunderstanding, said to him: "I believe, sir, you are mistaken. This is just to be a meeting of the board."

"Well," replied the visitor, "I have listened to your talk for more than an hour and if anyone has been bored more than I have been, I should like to know who it is."

❖ ❖

A truly eloquent parson in the South had been preaching for an hour or so on the immortality of the soul.

"I looked at the mountains," he declaimed, "and could not help thinking: 'Beautiful as you are, you will be destroyed, while my soul will not.' I gazed upon the ocean and cried, 'Mighty as you are, you will eventually dry up, but not I!'"

❖ ❖

Mr. Brown was a senior in the theological seminary, and on one occasion had been sent to a country village to fill the appointment of the regular minister on Sunday morning. He had become well immersed in his sermon and was becoming more and more inspired with speech, when he realized that he had been talking for nearly an hour when only a half-hour had been allotted to the sermon. Seeing that he had gone far past the lunch hour, he made an apology and concluded his words.

The "sweet young thing," influenced more by his personality

than with his sermon, rushed up at the close and offered her words of consolation.

"Brother Brown," she breathed soulfully, "you needn't have apologized. You really didn't talk long—it just seemed long."

❖   ❖

I don't want to be in the position of the minister who was making an interminable call on a member of his congregation. Finally the member's small daughter was moved to inquire, "Mama, didn't the preacher bring his amen with him?"

❖   ❖

It is my firm conviction that most of us talk too much. At that, however, American audiences are probably more favored than they realize. Our British cousins are even more long-winded than we. Particularly in Parliament, they drone endlessly on. There is a very old story that the Duke of Devonshire once dreamt he was speaking in the House of Lords—and awoke to find that he was!

❖   ❖

You know, I used to take a certain amount of satisfaction that at least most of the members in my audiences managed to keep awake. But I am now a little shaky on that point since I heard of the case of a certain hypnotist. This hypnotist agreed to try his wares on a Negro messenger. His efforts were from a distance and somewhat desultory, which may account for what happened at the end of twenty-five minutes of conversation directed at the messenger.

Slowly the black boy lifted one eye-lid, looked at the hypnotist and said, "I'd have been sleeping by now if you hadn't been talking so much."

❖   ❖

I know that I have been talking for a long time—at least it probably *seems* a long time to some of you. Perhaps you are like the little boy whose mother had promised to be ready to take him to the movies "in about five minutes." He waited around for what seemed like an age and a couple of aeons. And then he timidly inquired, "Mother, are minutes any longer than they used to be?"

❖ ❖

I notice that my time is about up, and I don't want to keep you longer. I have always agreed with the fellow who observed that it is all right to have a train of thought, provided you also have a terminal.

❖ ❖

(The speaker looks musingly at his watch.) Have I really been talking as long as it *seems* to you?

You know, I think it might not be a bad notion if this organization would adopt a custom that I understand prevails in a certain South African tribe. As a practical means of limiting oratory, every public speaker is required to stand on one foot while addressing his hearers. As soon as his other foot touches the ground, his speech is brought to an abrupt close. . . Well, my other foot is coming down—right now. And, thanks for the use of the hall!

❖ ❖

James Whitcomb Riley, the Hoosier poet, and a fellow writer were discussing their platform experiences.

The other fellow confessed that his engagements had not been too successful. He asked Riley, who had several times been present on these occasions, to point out the trouble. "Why are you such a success?" he concluded, "while my talks fall flat?"

"Well," said Jim, "I'll tell you the big reason, as I see it: I talk until I get tired—you talk until the audience gets tired."

❖ ❖

The British judge, Sir Henry Hawkins, sat on his official bench listening, as a long-winded barrister, inordinately fond of the sound of his own voice, droned on and on.

Finally the judge picked up a pen, wrote a few words, signaled a bailiff to deliver the note to the pleading barrister. To his great discomfiture, that worthy gentleman read:

Patience Competition
Gold Medal—Sir Henry Hawkins
Honorable Mention—Job
The plea was quickly concluded.

❖ ❖

Here awhile back, I was practicing a talk that I intended to deliver to a sales group. I was going along at a great rate, and mentally patting myself on the back when my wife, who had been sitting quietly over in a corner, approached and handed me a printed instruction sheet that had come with a new-fangled fountain pen. I noticed she had underscored a couple of lines. So I put on my spectacles and read: *"When this pen runs too smoothly, it is a sign that it is nearly empty."*

I got the point. And I think that I had better act on it now. This is just about the place where I am going to bring my talk to an end.

THE SPEAKER apologizes . . .
for loss of memory

If you place too much dependence upon memory, one of these days it will fail you— and you will find yourself at a loss for words. If, on that tragic occasion, you can still recall a good story, you can get out of a bad fix. A safer course is to memorize ideas rather than precise words, and to supplement memory with adequate notes.

He had written a very fine speech, memorized it word for word. The opening sentence began: "One hundred years ago, the place where I now stand was a howling wilderness."

Came the night. The gentleman arose and bravely began, "One hundred years ago the place where I now stand was a howling wilderness. . ." To his dismay, he found that he had completely forgotten the remainder of his speech. His mind was a complete blank.

To give himself a bit of time, he said again the opening words, adding, "I repeat this for the sake of emphasis."

Still the speech did not come back to him. He stood a moment in silence. Then, for the third desperate time: "One hundred years ago tonight the place where I now stand was howling wilderness. . . . I wish to God it still was, and I was in the middle of it."

❖   ❖

You started out bravely enough, but now, half way through your speech you're stuck. What to do? The soundest counsel, of course, is NOT to get stuck. Usually you can avoid disaster by thorough preparation and adequate supporting notes. But this is no time for moralizing. Blind spots come to us all at times. You can't think what comes next? Then, don't let the lapse of memory trouble you unduly. Go on to the next point you can remember. Nine tenths of the people listening will never know!

If your difficulty seems too deep to get out of in that way, always remember you can get away with murder—almost literally— if you have a good story to ease the passage. And here IS a good one.

I had a point that I wanted to bring up in this connection, but for the life of me I can't think just what it was. Frankly, I'm stuck. I'm reminded of the two city lads who approached a barn in which there were a number of calves. The weather was hot and while switching their tails, whipping away flies, one animal's tail accidentally dropped through a knothole in the side of the barn.

One of the city lads, observing this phenomenon, remarked, "I've been trying to figure how that calf ever got through that hole."

The other one replied, "That doesn't worry me half as much as how he got through that far and now can't get the rest of the way."

❖   ❖

Well, I must confess to you that I have completely forgotten a point that I had wanted to make in this connection—but I do recall a very good story about another fellow in a similar predicament.

Examining lesson papers, the professor found one which, instead of being covered with historical names and dates, had a crude sketch of a cemetery, with a large tombstone on which was written:

"Sacred to the memory that always deserts me on an occasion like this."

THE SPEAKER apologizes . . .
for mentioning his Company and products

I certainly don't want to appear in the role of a press agent for our firm and its products, but an occasional direct reference is almost necessary in order to bring out a specific point.

In this connection I am in almost as tough a spot as was a certain Navy chaplain that Admiral Nimitz used to tell about. It seems that on a certain ship gunnery crews had developed so much interest and enthusiasm in their work that they talked of nothing else, even during the mess hours. The commanding officer, fearing his men would go stale, issued an order that there was to be no "shop talk" during meals. The men were struggling to obey, making a conscious effort to keep the conversation in general channels.

When the chaplain arose to give the prayer, a junior officer touched his sleeve, whispered, "Remember, now, padre, no 'shop talk' today!"

THE SPEAKER apologizes . . .
for nervousness

This happened to a judge, traveling to Charlottesville, where he was to deliver a speech at the University of Virginia. You might switch it around a bit, tell it as a personal experience:

The judge was pretty nervous. The last lap of the journey found him pacing up and down the aisle, going over his speech word for word. Finally, one of the other passengers spoke up: "Judge," he inquired, "do you expect to collect mileage for that speech."

❖   ❖

Naturally, as an inexperienced speaker I am somewhat nervous on an occasion such as this. However, I was a bit relieved when I read the other day something by Richard C. Borden: "Nervousness," he says "is the penalty you pay for being a race horse instead of a cow." That being the case, gentlemen, take a good look at *Man of War!*

❖   ❖

Yes, I'm a little nervous—and I am perfectly willing to admit it. In that respect I'm somewhat more frank than a speaker I heard about not so long ago.

A lady came into a room in a well-known hotel and saw a government official whom she recognized, pacing up and down. The lady asked what he was doing there.

"I am going to deliver a speech," he said.

"Do you usually find that you get very nervous before addressing a large audience?"

"Nervous? No, I never get nervous," he answered, smiling.

"In that case," demanded the lady, "what are you doing in the Ladies Room?"

THE SPEAKER apologizes . . .
for not bringing a Great Message

People often ask, as your Chairman did a few moments ago, concerning the nature of my talk. "What," they will inquire "is the Message you have for us?" Well, that sort of stumps me. I'm very much afraid I have no Great Message to deliver. What you get out of this talk will depend largely upon the way in which you view it. In that respect I'm somewhat like the small child who proudly presented to her mother an animal which she had modeled at kindergarten.

The mother had no wish to discourage creative talent. Yet she was frankly puzzled, and finally ventured to risk a tentative question:

"It is beautiful, dear—perfectly beautiful. And I am very proud of you. But I am not quite sure—is it a horse, or a dog?"

"Oh," beamed the small one, "you've got the very idea! If you like dogs, then it's a dog. But if you like horses, you can see a horse in it!"

THE SPEAKER apologizes . . .

for rambling discourse

Looking back on my discourse this evening I feel that while I may have covered a good deal of territory, I have not been as clear in emphasizing my points as I might have been. It brings to mind two tourists, on their way to Florida, who got lost on a country road in Georgia. Seeing an old colored mammy sitting on a porch, they called:

"Auntie, can you tell us where this road goes?"

The old woman took a pipe from her mouth, regarded the pilgrims deliberately, and replied:

"Well, honey, hit goes fust one place, an' den anothah."

❖   ❖

In trying to find my way through this maze of notes I feel somewhat like the Kentucky farmer who was giving directions to a pair of tourists. They had asked the way to Louisville.

"Well, let's see," the farmer reflected, "you go down this road a spell, maybe two, three mile, till you come to a little school house on the east fork. . . . No, I reckon that wouldn't be the best way, neither. . . . You drive in the barn-lot here, turn around and go back to the first cross-roads. . . . Um, well, come t' think of it, you can't go that way; bridge is out. . . . You might take that lane yonder and foller it till you come t' the pike—but then that would be right smart out o' your way. . . . Well, now, I'll tell y', folks, if I was goin' t' Louisville, I jest wouldn't start from here at all!"

❖   ❖

I don't want to get lost in my own circumlocutions, and wind up as the central figure in a narrative such as I heard not long ago.

A lank, disconsolate-looking farmer stood on the steps of the town hall during the progress of a political meeting.

"Do you know who's talking in there now?" demanded a stranger, briskly, pausing for a moment beside the farmer. "Or are you just going in?"

"No, sir; I've just come out," said the farmer, decidedly. "Congressman Smiffkins is talking in there."

"What about?" asked the stranger.

"Well," continued the countryman, passing a knotted hand across his forehead, "he didn't say."

❖　❖

A self-conscious and egotistical young clergyman was supplying the pulpit of a country church. After the service he asked one of the deacons, a grizzled, plain-spoken man, what he thought of his morning effort.

"Well," answered the old man slowly. "I'll tell ye in a kind of parable. I remember Tunk Weatherbee's first deer hunt, when he was green. He followed the deer's tracks all right, but he followed 'em all day in the wrong direction."

❖　❖

I hope that I have not too closely emulated a tiresome attorney in a western town, who in arguing a complicated case, had looked up authorities dating back to Julius Caesar and had consumed more than an hour and a half in the most intricate part of his plea when he was pained to observe what seemed to him inattention of the bench. It was as he had feared—His Honor was unable to appreciate the nice points of the argument.

"Begging Your Honor's pardon," said he, "but do you follow me?"

The judge shifted uneasily in his chair. "I have so far," he answered, "but I'll say frankly, Mr. Jones, that, if I thought I could find my way back, I'd quit right here."

THE SPEAKER apologizes . . .
for reading from manuscript

I hope, in this instance, your reaction will be more charitable than that of the old colored mammy who went to a church where the young minister always read his sermons. Someone asked how the minister was getting on.

"How he gettin' on?" she answered. **"Jest lak a crow in a cawn** field—two dabs an' a look-up!"

❖　❖

There is at least one thing to be said for the man who reads his discourse:

A wearer of the cloth in Scotland seeking a new pulpit was asked by a committee if he were a "paper minister."

"I read my discourse," replied the candidate.

"That's a'right then," said the spokesman. "When a man has a paper, we ken he'll end where the paper ends."

❖   ❖

I know it is discouraging for an audience to see a speaker get up and confront it with a bale of manuscript. But I have some statistics and other matters to present, and I want to be sure to get my facts straight. Unfortunately, I can't depend upon my tricky memory. My situation is not like that of Bill O'Dwyer.

While campaigning for District Attorney in New York O'Dwyer generally appeared on the platform with a piece of paper in his hand ostensibly covered with notes of the address he was about to make.

He'd look around the audience, say "Hello, Joe," to one listener, "Howya, Harry," to another. Then he'd smile and tell the audience:

"I didn't know I would have so many friends here tonight. I don't need notes to talk to you people," and he'd throw away the paper in his hand. "To you I can speak from here," he'd add, indicating his heart.

A reporter, curious because he had seen O'Dwyer do this in every Brooklyn neighborhood from Red Hook to Brownsville, one night mounted the platform and picked up the discarded paper.

It was an old laundry bill.

THE SPEAKER apologizes . . .

for reiteration

I am quite aware that I have dwelt repeatedly on certain points, but these are basic principles that cannot be too strongly emphasized. In this respect, I am rather like the old Negro parson, who outlined his preaching formula thus: "Fust I tells 'em what I is gwine t' tell 'em. Den I goes ahead an' tells 'em. Finally, I tells 'em what I has done tole 'em."

❖   ❖

It is true that I touched on this point earlier in my talk, but it is a basic consideration and, I think, worthy of special emphasis.

I don't want to be in the position of a professor who was chiding a pupil for a poor recitation.

"Why," said the prof, "I told you the answer to that question less than an hour ago."

"Well," replied the pupil, "I guess that's so; but you only said it once."

THE SPEAKER apologizes . . .
for repeating a stale talk

I observe that the Program Committee has given my talk a new title. That, I fear, is almost the only new thing about it. Those of you who have heard me before may as well get up and leave now.

My situation is rather like that of a well-known lecturer who, asked concerning fees replied candidly, "My charge is $500, if you pick the subject; $250 if you leave it to me. And in either case, you'll get the same talk."

Oh, to be sure, I do vary my talk a bit from time to time. Somebody asked my small daughter about my speeches the other day. "Well," she said, "they all sound pretty much the same, but I think he hollers in different places."

THE SPEAKER apologizes . . .
for tardy appearance; inability to fill
an earlier engagement

The popular speaker has many demands upon him. There will be occasions when conflicting engagements will make it impossible for him to arrive until shortly before he is to participate, or which will force his untimely departure. Or, again, he may have to decline several invitations to address a given group before an open date is found that is acceptable. It is well to have stories on hand to meet such situations.

I am truly sorry that I was unable to be with you for the earlier portion of this program. Unfortunately, another engagement made it impossible. It seems I never have time to be all the places and do all the things I'd like. It brings to mind the minister who was sympathizing with a recently bereaved widow.

"Your husband," he said, "was a man of many excellent qualities."

"Yes," sighed the widow, "I have heard him well spoken of. I wasn't much acquainted with him myself. You see, he belonged to seven lodges and three clubs."

THE SPEAKER apologizes . . .

for tedious talk

I am afraid this talk has been both too long, and too dry. It brings to mind the minister who was ill. His wife had been instructed to take the ministerial temperature. But through mistake the good woman used a barometer instead of a thermometer. When he asked, "Well, how does it read?" she answered: "Dry and windy."

❖   ❖

I am very much afraid that some of these facts and figures have proved a bit tedious to many of you. Perhaps I'm the fellow somebody had in mind when he observed:

"It took Sir William Ramsay sixteen years to discover helium; the Curies required thirty years to find radium, yet in five minutes you produce tedium."

❖   ❖

Perhaps I have let my own enthusiasm for this subject get the better of me. I hope, sincerely, that I have not put myself in the postion of an author whose work was being reviewed by a schoolboy: "This book," he wrote, "tells me more about penguins than I am interested in knowing."

❖   ❖

Let me say, in conclusion, that I realize this has hardly been what might be termed an inspiring or moving talk. By the very nature of things I have been obliged to quote numerous figures, and to bring in a good deal of rather dull statistical data. I could not have censured you had you elected to nod through portions of the discourse. But you have been most attentive, and I appreciate the compliment.

Now, I feel that you are entitled to some reward. I want to tell you about a certain minister of the gospel, and a certain practitioner of medicine, who are mighty good friends—such good friends, in fact that they enjoy bantering each other about their respective professions. The other day they met on the street, and in the course of their conversation the man of medicine informed the gentleman of the cloth that he was on his way to pay a professional call on elderly Mr. Blank, who had been in ill health for some time.

"How is Mr. Blank? Is he any worse?" inquired the clergyman.

"Ah," sighed the doctor, gravely. "He needs your help more than he does mine."

Taking the bait, hook, line, and sinker, the minister exclaimed: "Poor fellow! Is he as bad off as that?"

"Yes," said the doctor, without a smile, "I can't get him to take a much-needed nap in the daytime."

THE SPEAKER apologizes . . .
for unfamiliarity with the topic

If you talk very much in public you will sooner or later be asked to discuss a subject of which you have little or no knowledge. Whether you accept, or gracefully decline, here's a story that will stand you in good stead:

I must confess that my position in this matter is rather like that of Ephriam Whiffkins who, as a political reward, was appointed to the post of Smoke Inspector of a thriving Southern metropolis. In the course of time he was informed that he was expected to turn in a report. Having only the haziest notion of his duties, he wrestled with the problem for three days and nights, and finally came up with the following:

"This is to certify that I have inspected the smoke of the city of Boonville, for the month of October, and have found same to be of good quality."

❖   ❖

A long, lanky mountaineer applied for a job as lifeguard at a popular beach resort. He would have stood nearly seven feet in his socks—if he had worn socks, and on the whole, seemed like rather promising material. He was exposed to the usual questionnaire, and finally, as a matter of routine, inquiries were made as to the applicant's ability as a swimmer.

"Well," the mountaineer confessed, "I can't swim t' do no

good." And then, looking down at his long legs, he brightened visibly. "No; I cain't swim—but I can wade like blazes!"

(And so, if I can't progress swimmingly in the topic assigned to me, I will at least wade right into the subject.)

❖ ❖

My position (the speaker may say) is somewhat like that of the Scotch minister who was asked to pray for rain. His prayer was followed by such a downpour that crops were injured. One old farmer said to another: "This comes o' trustin' sich a request to a meenister who isna' acquaintit' wi' agriculture."

THE SPEAKER argues for a Minority

I know that my group probably is outnumbered on this issue, but nevertheless we want to register our point of view. President James B. Conant, of Harvard University, tells of an old fellow on his way to a Town Meeting.

"Don't you know, Ed," someone remarked, "there ain't no use goin' t' that meetin'? Doc Barnes and his crowd are in control."

"That's all right," the old fellow replied complacently, "I can worry 'em some!"

THE SPEAKER asks, "Can you hear me?"

The speaker who puts that query is asking for an obvious retort. He had best be prepared to follow it quickly with a story— such as this one:

The speaker was getting along pretty well with a talk that wouldn't hurt anybody when a little commotion in the rear of the room caused the people to turn their heads to see the cause of it. An old man, his hand back of his ear, evidently because he was hard of hearing, had left his seat and was walking toward the front. When he got down pretty far he stooped over and spoke to a man in a seat on the aisle and said quite audibly, "Say, Jim, is that fellow speaking or singing?"

"Can't you hear him at all?" Jim asked.

"Not a word," replied the old man.

Jim's reply gave some inkling as to how he liked the speech. "Well then, thank God, and sit down."

THE SPEAKER asks for order

Audiences, on the whole, are remarkably well behaved. But now and again the speaker may have occasion to ask for more concentrated attention. Scolding and nagging may serve only to aggravate the situation. A good story is far more effective.

Otis Skinner was playing a matinee once at which there was present a group of young women from a fashionable dramatic school. Throughout the performance they chatted and giggled without a stop. This was quite disconcerting to Mr. Skinner and the other actors, who found it well nigh impossible to get through their lines.

When the performance was over, the girls were taken backstage to meet the famous actor. They gushed over him, and one girl said:

"Oh, Mr. Skinner, we enjoyed the play so very much! You acted so magnificently! But there must be something wrong with the theater's acoustics. There were times when we could hardly hear you."

"That is strange," answered the actor. "I found not the least difficulty in hearing you."

THE SPEAKER asks, "Whither are we going?"

There's too much aimless drifting these days; too many of us like the elevator operator who stepped off at one of the floors and went over to speak to another girl. Returning, she looked off into space for a moment with puzzled expression, then turned to the occupants of the car and asked, "Was I going up or down?"

❖   ❖

Let us also try to maintain a sense of direction, remembering that it is important not only to keep going, but also to know where we are headed.

An ocean liner, westward bound, was overtaken by sudden disaster. All that was left on the surface of the sea were two Englishmen.

Not having met formally, they swam about for hours in stony silence. The sun began to sink; darkness crept over the waters. Finally, in desperation one swam toward the other.

"I say, old fellow," he shouted, embarrassed but determined, "I say, dash it all, which way is London?"

THE SPEAKER attends a Class Reunion

Two college presidents were discussing what they'd like to do when they retired. "I'd like to be superintendent of an orphans' home—no letters from parents," said one. The other suggested: "Why not be a penitentiary warden? The dog-gone alumni don't insist on coming back."

THE SPEAKER breaks a Long Silence

Mr. Chairman, I'd like to comment briefly on that motion before the house. It happens that I have some rather definite ideas on the subject. As you know, I've been a member of this group for some time, but I very rarely get up on my feet. My case is rather like that of a boy Bob Burns mentions—his Cousin Wilfred. This boy had reached the age of eleven without ever having uttered a word. One afternoon Wilfred sat on a fence, watching his father plow. A bull broke through a pasture and, attracted by the moving figure, made directly for it. It was then that Wilfred found words. "Hey, Pa!" he yelled. "Hey! Look out fer the bull!"

Later the old man expressed his gratitude. "Wilfred," he said "you done me a right smart favor that time. But how come you're speakin' all of a sudden? You ain't never said nothin' before."

"Well, Pa," explained Wilfred, "I just ain't never had nothin' t' say."

THE SPEAKER breaks Bad News

Every speaker has occasion, now and then, to present facts which he has reason to feel his audience will not relish. His integrity will not permit him to gloss over those facts, or to reach a conclusion they do not warrant. But at least he can divert censure from himself by reminding his hearers that he did not invent the condition he now presents; that he is merely the messenger bringing them the facts—in other words an "innercent man."

An old Negro in a remote area of a Southern state had long been on the county relief rolls. Yet he continued to have periodic increases in his family, much to the disgust of the young social worker assigned to his particular case.

Finally, on the arrival of the tenth child, the social theorist was completely exasperated. "Henry," she said, "if this happens just *one more time,* I want you to go out and hang yourself. You are a disgrace to the community. Now, remember, this must be *the last child!*"

But, in a matter of months, came another arrival. And the social worker faced a shamed and disconsolate specimen of humanity. "I 'members what you-all done said, Miss Alice," he declared miserably, without waiting for the challenging queries he knew were coming. "An' I done 'tended t' do what you said; 'deed I did. I get me a len'th o' rope an' I run it over de raf'tah. I maks me a noose in dat rope an' slips my haid thru. Den I gits me up on a cheer. Den jes' when I was 'bout t' step off, I thunk me a thunk. 'Wait a minute,' I says. 'Wait a *minute,* Henry. You-all jes' mout be fixin' t' hang a innercent man!'"

THE SPEAKER celebrates Ladies' Night

Oh, yes, if you have a genial manner and a bit of humor in your makeup, you will be asked to hold forth on those occasions when the luncheon club members invite the ladies to meet with them. And you had better have a stock of good stories bantering both sexes. As the feminine contingent will be composed chiefly of wives, the old threadbare theme of Married Life can be played to the limit. Here is a good starting story:

I hope you will not misunderstand anything I shall say this evening. I don't want to be put in the position of a male lecturer who recently addressed a woman's club. Among other things, he told the ladies that the best way to get along with their husbands was to mother them. "And now," he concluded, "who will promise to try it?"

A stocky, well-built female in the back of the room got to her feet at once. "Ah," beamed the lecturer, "I am glad to see at least one woman who will go home and try to be a mother to her husband."

"Mother!" rumbled the bulky one. "Did you say mother? I thought you said smother!"

❖ ❖

Someone has asked why there are so few women after-dinner speakers. Frankly, the only reason I can think of is that not many of 'em can wait that long to talk!

❖ ❖

We've done a lot of kidding tonight, but it all winds up to the fact that women are really one of the best sexes we have. Come what may, we wouldn't want to live without the ladies—and we sincerely hope they feel that way about us.

An old Southern Negress who had been visiting her Washington daughter was left at the Union Station awaiting her train. Having lived in a small community all her life, she was filled with wonder and amazement when two nuns came in and sat beside her. As curiosity got the better of her, she asked a porter: "Who's dose two ladies over dar, dress' in black?"

"Dey's nuns."

"Nuns? What's nuns?"

"Why nuns is very religious ladies dat lives by demselves whar dere ain't no men!"

"Laws, dey sho' does go into mighty deep mournin' about it!"

THE SPEAKER comments on Progress

Progress isn't a static thing—nor a condition that springs suddenly upon us. The trouble is that most of us are so close to our jobs we scarcely notice the revolutionary changes that are taking place. We are engrossed in some small detail and completely overlook the Main Show.

Recently a trade journal in the leather industry carried a feature story of a veteran who had spent half-a-century in the employ of one of the large processing houses.

"Well," commented a reporter, "in your time you must have seen some vast changes in this business."

"Yes," agreed the old man meditatively, "yes, I have. In the old days, I used to have to go down the cellar and carry the leather up three flights of stairs. But now," he brightened, "they bring it up to me."

THE SPEAKER comments on the weather

If you speak a good deal in public you will often find yourself in conflict with the Weather Man who has conspired to cut your audience down to a corporal's guard. But don't let it get you down. You can even use the weather as an opening topic!

Dr. Alexander Whyte of Edinburgh was famous for his pulpit prayers. He always found something to thank God for, even in bad times. One stormy morning a member of his congregation thought to himself, "The preacher will have nothing to thank God for on a wretched morning like this." But Whyte began his prayer, "We thank Thee, O God, that it is not always like this."

THE SPEAKER concludes a Long Program

The final speaker on a long program is certainly not in an enviable position. People are tired, restless, eager to get out into the fresh air. The speaker had better be good! Now, if ever, he'll need a story to get the audience with him.

On the closing night of the conference a Methodist brother prayed with considerable fervor:

"Oh, Lord, be with the first speaker and give him power to move this people. And be with the second speaker and inspire him with Thy spirit. And, Lord, have mercy on the last speaker!"

❖   ❖

Many distinguished speakers have appeared on a brilliant and varied program. The hour grows late—very late. And at long last you are announced—the final speaker of the occasion. What shall you talk about? Talk about a minute—and sit down!

Here's a little gem that may set the pace for your remarks:

A metropolitan symphony orchestra had given a special performance, enabling the inhabitants, for the first time, to attend a real big-time concert. The next day some of the audience, gathered around the general store, were expressing their opinions.

"Well, all I got to say," commented one old character, "is that was a long way to bring that bass drum only to bang it wunst."

✧ ✧

Too many speakers have talked for too long a time. You are the last man on the program. Maybe you'd better tell them this one—and cut your talk to the core:

I am reminded of the two skeletons imprisoned in a dark, musty closet. One said to the other, "What are we doing here, anyway?" "Darned if I know," said the second, "but if we had any guts we'd get the heck out of here!"

THE SPEAKER corrects an error in title

I feel that perhaps I should clear up a misunderstanding with respect to my title. Your chairman introduced me as the Sales Manager of the Consolidated Corporation. Officially, I am manager of the Sales Promotion department. Sometimes this matter of occupation can be rather important. I am minded of the Jewish recruit filling out his army papers. He listed himself as Herman Rabinowitz, C. P. A.

Being assigned to a camp where the accounts were in something of a mess, he was promptly given an office, a big pile of ledgers that needed attention, and a drill-free month in which to bring the books up to date.

At the end of the month, officers discovered that the books were in the same condition as before. They called on Private Rabinowitz, and asked why he hadn't done his work.

"Pleez," answered Herman, "I am not knowing how."

"Then why did you list yourself as a C P A?" barked the CO.

"Because that's my business," insisted Rabinowitz, "Cleaning, Pressing and Alterations."

THE SPEAKER counsels Concentration

No objective can be attained without concentration. That is one of the first and most important lessons we must learn. No matter how much ability you have, if you don't stick to a trail, you're bound to fail!

A southern sportsman once had the fastest, best-bred and keenest-nosed hound in that region. But the dog suffered from a temperamental defect that kept him from real success.

He would jump a buck and run him tirelessly for miles. When the buck was about at the point of exhaustion, the fickle hound's nostrils would catch a hint in the air where a fox had recently crossed the trail, and immediately would decide the fox ought to be a more attractive proposition. Later when he neared the fox and the chase became hot, his nose chanced to discover a rabbit—so he would start in pursuit with the inevitable result that by 4 o'clock the hound would be thirty miles from home with a chipmunk treed.

Some men, like that dog, lack a definite objective and the will to stick to it until they arrive.

THE SPEAKER counsels, "Don't let the prize blind your eyes!"

Sometimes we are so sure of reaching a specified goal that we neglect the prosaic steps that will take us there.

You remember the small boy whose father promised him a bicycle if he stood at the head of his class. However, the close of the term found the boy far from the honor post.

"What is the trouble, Henry?" the parent asked. "I am sure you have the ability. I can't understand why you didn't work harder. What have you been doing all this time?"

"Well," confessed Henry, "I—I've been learning to ride a bike!"

THE SPEAKER counsels, "Keep on the main road!"

Beware of bypaths! No matter how temptingly picturesque they may appear, they will waste your time and energy. If you ever hope to arrive at your goal, keep on the Main Road!

A Scandinavian, recently arrived in this country, bought himself a second-hand car and started for California.

In the fullness of time he arrived, and after the customary exchange of affectionate greetings the Pacific Coast relatives asked for a road report.

"Vell," said the Scandinavian judiciously, "that man Lincoln, he is great engineer; but that Frenchman De Tour—ach, he is no road-builder at all!"

THE SPEAKER counsels, "Keep your feet on the ground!"

One trouble, of course, is that some of us don't always know when our feet *are* on the ground. In that respect, we're a little like a certain colonel who was piloting a transport plane. The colonel had been given an "all-clear" signal to land, and as he swooped down over the runway, he looked up from the controls. "One of the best landings I ever made," he said proudly.

The engineer sergeant, standing behind his superior officer, cleared his throat nervously. "Sir," he said timidly, "you're still fifteen feet off the ground!"

THE SPEAKER counsels, "Make your handicap a help!"

We ran across a lad not long ago who is going to get along all right in this old world. Taunted by someone because of an inordinate number of freckles on his face, he replied good-naturedly:

"They ain't freckles. Y' see, I've been goin' swimmin' 'most every day, and them spots is just my iron constitution rustin' on me!"

✧ ✧

Seven-year-old Tommy is no mental giant—but stoutly refuses to harbor an inferiority complex. When someone asked recently how he was getting along at school, he replied, "I think I'm doing all right. I am the fastest one in the slow group."

THE SPEAKER counsels Persistence

What most of us need in our daily encounters is a good deal more of the Edison spirit. When told that his 2000th experiment to find a filament for his incandescent lamp had failed, the great inventor commented: "That means there are 2000 things we do not need to try again."

THE SPEAKER counsels, "Use your head to get ahead"

If the Lord hadn't intended you to use your head for something besides a walking ad for the latest dandruff cure, he would hardly have equipped you with the finest thinking apparatus in the animal kingdom. You are supposed to have *brains*. Use them!

A serviceman, stationed in the Philippines, greatly admired an elaborately embroidered handkerchief which his laundress had made of white parachute silk. He engaged her to make two for girl friends at home, giving detailed instructions as to the embroidering. Since the Filipino matron had only a sketchy knowledge of English, the cautious soldier carefully printed on a bit of paper the name to be embroidered on each handkerchief.

In due time the laundress returned with the commission neatly executed. The work was beautifully done. She had followed instructions in precise detail. And each handkerchief was delicately embroidered, "To Mary and Helen."

THE SPEAKER counts his friends

A signal honor has befallen you. Now, you are expected to stand up and make a modest acknowledgement. This is the time to remember your friends. Pay them generous tribute. Make clear that this thing couldn't have come to pass without their help. Your own stature will increase proportionately as you acknowledge your debt to others.

Frankly, I don't know who is responsible for this nomination. But I know that some of my good friends have been active. My position is rather like that of a prisoner who stood before the judge.

"Have you no legal counsel?" asked the surprised jurist.

"No, your Honor," said the confident defendant. "You see, I have some very good friends on the jury."

❖ ❖

I am glad to observe in the audience several friendly and familiar faces. It gives me a feeling comparable to that experienced by the small boy who was being enrolled in kindergarten.

The teacher, following the usual formula, brought out her records and began to ask questions of the mother:

"Does the boy have any older brothers?"

"No."

"Younger brothers?"

"No."

"Older sisters?"

"No."

"Younger sisters?"

"No."

At this point the lad, who had grown increasingly unhappy and self-conscious, put in a wistful word. "But," he said defensively, "I've got friends."

❖   ❖

I am glad to see so many of my old friends here tonight. This evidence of their loyalty is very touching. Friendship is a great thing, and I am always for my friends. In that respect, I'm a good deal like the old politician:

Down in Mississippi they had a law in one county against shooting squirrels for a certain time every year. Opinion was divided.

There was an old fellow running for sheriff and his managers were mighty scared he was going to say something about this law, and get in bad with one side or the other.

One night at a meeting a man got up and asked right out, "Where do you stand on the squirrel law?" The old fellow's managers shook their heads and made motions for him to dodge the issue, but he didn't pay any attention. "I'm glad you asked me that," he said. "I want to say something about it. I understand half my friends are in favor of the law, and half are against it. I want it definitely understood that I'm for my friends!"

THE SPEAKER credits others

In presenting this talk of mine, I must say very frankly that I am rather in the position of Charles Lamb, who explained how he wrote one of his entrancing essays:

"I milked twenty cows to get the milk; but the butter I churned is all my own."

❖   ❖

I feel that I have been given a great deal more credit than I deserve. If it hadn't been for the faithful service of many other persons in this endeavor, the results we have achieved would never have been possible. I don't want to be like the Scotchman who was complimented on his fine garden. "It must take a sight of work," the visitor observed, "keeping this plot so neat and trim."

"Ah," said the Scotchman, " 'tis nae work at a'. Maggie does it."

THE SPEAKER declines to talk

Every speaker is at times called upon to talk when he has nothing in particular to contribute, or when he is insufficiently prepared. In such cases it is best to exit gracefully. For this purpose keep a few clever "out-of-the-frying-pan" stories stored away in memory.

I find myself on this occasion somewhat in the position of the good Dr. Johnson. Being an indifferent speaker, and seeking to conceal the fact, the Doctor would arise, when called upon, clear his throat impressively, and remark, "So much has been said on this subject—and on the whole so well said—that there seems nothing further for me to add." After which he would bow gracefully (speaker bows) and resume his seat, somewhat in this manner (speaker proceeds to seat self, amidst laughter.)

The beauty of this story is that it gets you back into your seat, where you devoutly wish to be, without arousing a feeling that you have been a shirker, or shown discourtesy in failing to meet the Chairman's request.

❖ ❖

I once knew a fellow who had what he always claimed was "the best job in railroading." You know the guy who goes alongside the trains and taps the wheels with a hammer to see that everything's all right? Well, this friend of mine helped him listen.

I always envied my pal that job. And so, while I appreciate your invitation to participate, I think, if it's all the same to you, I'll just sit here quietly and help the rest of the folks listen.

❖ ❖

I appreciate deeply your courtesy in asking me to speak at this time. But, actually, I haven't anything to say—and I am going to say it in very few words. That has always impressed me as the best—and safest—course.

A stage driver of New Mexico, noted for taciturnity, took five passengers on a sightseeing tour over the mountains. Among these was a woman who began by exclaiming over the scenery, soon proceeded to cautioning the driver, fired a barrage of questions that showed more ignorance than curiosity. At journey's end a quiet man asked what the fare was. "Two-and-a-half," the old rawhide replied. Each passenger paid, the woman coming last. She handed over a five-dollar bill, which the driver put in his pocket.

"Where's my change?" she asked.

"Ain't any," was the response.

"But you charged the others only $2.50!"

The stage driver made a three-word reply: "They didn't talk."

❖   ❖

If I should undertake to express an opinion in this distinguished company, I fear that I'd be somewhat in the predicament of a young man who, in a similar position, began bravely enough:

"Someone has said that genius is ten percent inspiration and ninety percent expiration." And then he proceeded to expire!

❖   ❖

I appreciate very much your invitation to say a few words to this distinguished company. But I recall a saying that I once heard: There are two kinds of persons who speak in public—those who have something to say, and those who have to say something. Well, I haven't anything to say, and certainly don't feel that I have to say anything, so—

❖   ❖

I appreciate the invitation to talk, but believe I can do no better than repeat a brief form that Prof. William Lyon Phelps once developed. "I am a good linguist," he admitted. "I can speak three or four modern languages. Once I lived for a time near a deaf-and-dumb asylum, and learned to talk on my hands. But, unfortunately, I cannot talk on my feet."

Someone has very wisely observed that "an elocutionist may teach us how to speak, but none of them can teach us *when*."

THE SPEAKER decries Progress without Plan

To many of us, progress is merely motion. The main thing is to keep going—without any particular thought as to plan and purpose. We are too much like the camper who, having made his coffee, ran out of fuel. He lit a fringe of dry grass and held his frying pan over the moving blaze. The eggs cooked elegantly— but he found himself a mile and a half from his coffee!

THE SPEAKER defines Psychiatry

A psychologist you know, is a blind man in a pitch black basement looking for a black cat. A psychiatrist is that same man— on the same search—only the cat ain't there!

THE SPEAKER defines Psychology

Psychology, as near as I can figure out, appears to be the fine art of trading you something you don't want for something you'd like to have—and making you feel grateful in the bargain. Maybe some times these psychologists have sound reasons for their actions. But I have a hunch that now and then they just do it for practice. Like the case of a doctor I once heard about. The doctor's phone rang sharply. "Do you think I could have some pea soup?" a patient asked wistfully.

"No," said the doctor, firmly.

"Then," compromised the patient, "how about an oyster stew?"

"Yes, you may have oyster stew," agreed the doctor. Then turning to his secretary he said: "If the old fool had asked for oyster stew first, he could have had his pea soup."

THE SPEAKER denies "inside information"

Many a well-meaning Chairman has a diabolical genius for putting the speaker on a hot spot. He will present you confidently as a guy who has all the answers—an oracle who maintains a private pipe line to Secret Sources. This is considerably wide of the mark. You fear a let-down and wish to crawl off that spot as promptly as possible. Maybe you can do it with a story.

Once there was a certain bookmaker—my reference is to the racetracks and not the graphic arts—who became slightly "tetched in the head" and was confined to an institution for the mentally impaired.

He got along very well except that, in the course of time, he suffered a degree of nostalgia for the old haunts, and for his accustomed occupation. Being an ingenious fellow, he devised a plan for following his trade within the confines of the institution.

This bookie got himself a supply of small round pebbles, to pass as currency. These he dyed a bright red, to keep the boys from cheating on him, and passed them out to fellow inmates, together with elementary instruction in the art of gaming. Each morning he would accept bets on the races. Each evening, as the reports came in by radio, he would pay off. Since he made his own odds, it was a bookmaker's paradise. When the customers went broke, as they invariably did, the bookie would pass out more pebbles.

And so the game went merrily on until a certain morning a customer approached panting and puffing under the weight of a huge block of red sandstone, he had picked up somewhere on the premises.

"I want," he announced, "to bet this on the nose of *Goofus* in the fourth race."

The bookmaker regarded the huge lump dubiously, and slowly shook his head. "No," he decided, "I can't take that bet."

"Why?" asked the customer belligerently. "You're a bookie, ain't you?"

"Yeah; I'm a bookie, but I ain't no sap. If you want to bet that much, you must have inside information!"

(The speaker, picking up at this point, emphasizes that he has no "inside information" or secret sources.)

THE SPEAKER denies Prophetic Ability

Whenever I go any place to make a speech, people are always asking me about the future. They want to know whether business is going to be good, and what I think Congress is likely to do. The idea seems to be that anybody who comes from a distance ought to have the Real Dope. But I don't know. I don't pretend to know. When it comes to forecasting I'm about on a par with an Indian I once heard of. This Indian named Joe wowed a small Canadian community with his uncanny way of predicting changes in the weather. On a sunny day, along would slink Joe and say: "Bimeby rain come." And, sure enough, rain would usually come.

One day it was particularly miserable—rain, wind, cold. "Joe," inquired a hunter, "when will all this blow away? Bimeby nice day?"

The red man shrugged. "Dunno," he replied. "Radio he broke."

THE SPEAKER deplores Indecision

Making decisions is often a difficult—and always a necessary—function of life. The ability to decide is the first characteristic of a leader. You will make mistakes, of course. But the person who never makes a mistake will never make much of a mark in life. Speakers—especially in the industrial field—will have frequent occasion to use these stories bearing on indecision.

But be sure your decision is a real one—not merely a superficial solution. A drunk settled himself at a restaurant table and proceeded to wrestle with the bill of fare. Finally he said to the waiter:

"I'll have an omelette."

"What kinda omelette?" parried the waiter.

Another decision! The drunk settled down grimly to ponder this new and tougher problem. At long last, he cleared his throat impressively. The waiter, pencil poised, leaned closer to catch the impending command. "I will have," the drunk pronounced with utmost gravity, "an egg omelette."

❖ ❖

Indecision is our greatest curse. What we need—and need desperately—is more of the "Do-it-NOW" spirit. Do you know, psychologists have discovered that if you put a frog in a pail of hot water he will immediately jump out. But if you put him in cool water and then gradually heat it up the frog will permit himself to be cooked, apparently being unable to decide when the water is so hot as to be unbearable.

❖ ❖

If you hope to get out of the rut and into the race you must be willing to *decide things*—to seek and accept responsibility. It is the unwillingness to do this, more than any other one thing that keeps young men in the mire of mediocrity.

Too many of us are like a general utility man employed by a friend of mine to do a few odd jobs around the place.

The man was first put at digging postholes. The work was completed in half the expected time. The next task was sawing and piling wood. This chore, too, was accomplished in record time.

"Well," said the employer, "about the only other job I have at the moment is sorting some potatoes. You can put the biggest ones in this bin; the medium-sized ones here, and the little fellows over yonder. I figured it might take half a day, but at the rate you work, you'll probably be thru in an hour."

When nothing was heard from the new hand that day or the next, the business man set out to investigate. He found the workman seated on the floor, his head buried in his hands. "I can't take it!" he moaned. "It's getting me down!"

"But what on earth is the matter?" queried the employer.

"Well," admitted the hand, "it's just the strain of these everlasting decisions!"

THE SPEAKER deplores Lack of Progress

Too many of us in business are like the boy who fell out of bed. He said he went to sleep too near the place where he got in.

THE SPEAKER discusses Advance of Science

We err gravely in assuming that Science is a static thing. It is constantly on the march. We must keep pace or be left far behind. Here is an instance to illustrate the point:

A patient came to a field hospital with the complaint that he was unable to sleep at night. The doctor's advice was for the soldier to eat something before going to bed.

"But, Doctor," the patient reminded him, "two months ago you told me never to eat anything before going to bed."

The good doctor blinked, and then in full professional dignity replied, "My boy, that was two months ago. Science has made enormous strides since then."

THE SPEAKER discusses Changing Times

Times change. But we do not all change with them. Now and again, we are surprised, and perhaps a bit disconcerted to run across someone who is apparently oblivious to the march of minutes.

Our neighbor's child doesn't go for the urge most of the kids have to be a fighting airman. He's a little old-fashioned. He still dreams of being a pirate some day. He described to us his mental picture of himself boarding a merchant vessel by climbing over the side with a cutlass between his teeth.

"That's kind of out-of-date, isn't it?" we suggested. "That cutlass-in-the-teeth stuff went out long ago."

He thought for a moment. "Well," he said, "I wouldn't put it back in my mouth again after I'd killed somebody till I'd sterilized it in boiling water."

THE SPEAKER discusses "Conditions"

A husband, attempting to hang a picture, was standing precariously on a stool, placed atop a kitchen chair. Trying gingerly to balance himself, he gave the nail a few hesitating and uncertain taps with his hammer.

The wife, supervising operations, asked: "Why don't you give a brave blow or two, and settle it?"

"How can a man give a brave blow," asked the tottering one, "when he is standing on a foundation like this?"

Although we may sympathize with the author of this observation, the fact remains that most of the world's great achievements were made by men whose personal position was anything but secure, and in periods when "conditions" were much against them. While you wait for an ideal time to "give a brave blow" the world will pass you by.

❖   ❖

A hayseed Democrat was running for governor in Indiana during the depression that followed the panic of 1893. In one of his speeches he was be-laboring the Republicans on the tariff, taxes, and bad times when a fellow in the crowd shouted, "Old stuff! What we want to know is about this here panic."

Some members in the crowd tried to shut up the questioner, but the candidate told them to let him alone. "I'll answer his question," he said. "Times are going to get better, or they'll get worse, or they'll stay about the way they are."

THE SPEAKER discusses Faith and Works

The faith that really moves mountains believes in using dynamite and steam shovels.

THE SPEAKER discusses Grouches

The chronic grouch is the inspirational speaker's pet target. You can always take a few pokes at him with impunity. And since very few of us admit to that classification, we can always enjoy stories of the other fellow's ill temper and surliness. Add this to your collection.

Bert Truby, the feed merchant, could generally be counted on to find a quarrel or make one. Once he dropped in at the railway station to buy an 89-cent excursion ticket, belligerently tendering a twenty-dollar bill. Without a word of protest the station agent shoved the change across the counter.

Twice Bert counted the sizeable stack.

"What'sa matter," the agent finally asked, "ain't the change right?"

A third time Truby counted, slowly, coin by coin. Finally he spoke.

"Well," he said grudgingly, "it just is."

THE SPEAKER discusses higher Standards of Living

Some well-meaning souls hold to the idea that all we have to do to improve the living standards of the masses is to provide them with more money. That is an essential concomitant, to be sure. But the problem is not wholly economic. We must educate these people to appreciate their *need* for our commodities and services.

The dude and the hill-billy were both rear rank privates occupying adjoining bunks in the barracks. One day the dude inspected his toilet kit, glanced at his neighbor and demanded sharply. "Did you take my tooth paste?"

"No, I didn't take no tooth paste," came the answer. "I don't need no tooth paste. My teeth ain't loose."

❖   ❖

Someone has observed that the United States has the highest average living standards in the world, but you can't eat an average. If you average the millionaires and the poor together, the poor people are still hungry.

THE SPEAKER discusses "leaners" and "lifters"

There are two kinds of people in the world—those who carry their own weight, or a little more, and those who incline to "lean on the load" and be carried along by others. They might be called the "leaners" and the "lifters."

At first glance, you might conclude that the "leaners" have all of the best of it in life. They haven't, really. There's no true happiness for the "leaner" because he lacks personal security. He isn't making his way. Without that reassurance, his spirit is perpetually troubled.

Beware of the "rich uncle" philosophy—the lulling belief that somebody, some time is going to give you a push that will start your personal battery to functioning. The best helping hand you will ever have is right at the end of your own arm!

There is a very trite, but very true observation that the Lord helps those who help themselves. Don't be like the mountaineer who was hailed by a passing motorist with the cry that "Your house is a-fire!"

"I know it, mister," was the untroubled response.

"Then, why don't you DO something about it?"

"I am a doin' somethin'," the mountaineer asserted. **"I'm a prayin' fer rain!"**

THE SPEAKER discusses Man and the Job

A three-year-old child was once struggling in an effort to move a table. After several unsuccessful efforts, the mother finally said to the child, "Baby, you can't move that table, it's as big as you are."

"Yes, I can," answered the child, "I'm as big as it is."

THE SPEAKER discusses Obstacles

We talk a great deal about overcoming obstacles. That's all right in its way. Overcome them if you can, to be sure. But sometimes that isn't practicable. And, again, it just may not be worth the effort. However, there's always a way out.

A farmer had a stump in his field—too hard to uproot, too knotty to split, too wet and soggy to burn.

Somebody asked what he did about it. "Well," he replied, "if you'll keep the secret, I'll tell you: I just plowed around it!"

THE SPEAKER discusses Optimism

Optimism is a great thing—and we need more of it in this sorry old world. But this doesn't mean that we should blind ourselves to rational considerations. We need to temper optimism with a tincture of reason.

A prominent executive had asserted that he was very optimistic over the future of business.

"Then why," he was asked, "do you look so worried all the time?"

"Well, to tell you the truth," he confessed, "I'm worried about my optimism!"

THE SPEAKER discusses our Influence on Others

We are in a sense the product of our environment. And we do not begin to sense how profoundly our actions and reactions influence the lives of those about us. I heard of a striking instance which I'd like to share with you:

This is the strange saga of an expectant mother in the city of Chicago. An apartment-dwelling matron, she had a loathing for all forms of physical exercise.

"But," prodded the persistent physician-in-waiting, "you must have exercise. Force yourself to walk. Ten blocks a day. Every day."

So the matron walked. Dutifully. Five blocks up the street. Five blocks back. A dreary, monotonous trek, broken only by the twinkle of traffic signals.

And in the fullness of time, her child was born. A healthy, well-developed youngster. But attendants were surprised to observe: one eye was red, the other green.

THE SPEAKER discusses Perverse Human Nature

If you tell a man that there are 279,678,934,341 stars in the universe, he'll believe you. But if a sign says, "Fresh Paint," he has to make a personal investigation.

THE SPEAKER discusses Ruts

Most of us spend the greater part of our lives in ruts of one kind or another. Sometimes it becomes the speaker's mission to blast us out of them. Our actions and reactions are conditioned by what has happened—or failed to happen—in the past. Thus we become blinded to opportunities—and often to dangers as well, as this story testifies.

Down a steep, twisting grade came a ten-ton government truck, loaded to capacity with dynamite. It was on a TVA operation in Tennessee, some years ago. At the wheel sat a mountaineer youngster, a raw recruit from a neighboring settlement, taking a turn at "public works." As he guided his dangerous cargo over the treacherous path the boy puffed unconcernedly at a half-smoked cigarette.

From his temporary shack office a straw-boss looked up. At one quick glance he took in truck, dynamite and live cigarette. He sprang to his feet yelling and frantically waving his arms, as he raced in the direction of the truck.

"Throw away that cigarette, you xx!! xx! Throw it *away!*"

Slowly, methodically, the mountain boy applied the brakes, brought his craft to a groaning, screeching halt, and, finally, removing the cigarette from his lips, deposited it by the roadside.

When at last he could spare the breath, the boss expostulated. "You idiot! You lunatic! You lunkhead! Don't you know better than to smoke a cigarette when you're haulin' *dynamite?* Don't you know a spark is likely t' set off ten tons o' that stuff, and blow this whole countryside t' smithereens?"

The boy was frankly impressed, but bewildered. Slowly, he turned his puzzled blue eyes upon the excited speaker. A wrinkle of honest reflection was furrowed on his brow as he drawled, "Well, Mister, it ain't *been* a-doin' it!"

❖ ❖

At a certain crossroads in Canada, where the going is all but impossible in periods of heavy rain, this sign has been conspicuously posted: "Take care which rut you choose. You will be in it for the next twenty miles."

❖ ❖

Sometimes it's just about impossible to bring a new point of view to the fellow who's "sot in his ways." He *enjoys* his well-worn rut and doesn't want to be jolted out of it.

An insurance salesman was trying his level best to sell an accident policy to an unresponsive farmer who, perched twenty feet above him on a rickety scaffold, continued painting his barn.

Suddenly, the scaffold gave way, the prospect tumbled at the salesman's feet.

Quick to seize the opportunity, the insurance man whisked out his application form and pencil. "Now, you see how accidents happen. Are you ready to take that policy?" "Heck, no!" replied the farmer. "I didn't get hurt, did I?"

❖ ❖

Little Gladys, who had attended Sunday School with considerable regularity, surprised a fond parent the other Sabbath by announcing her intention of absenting herself.

"But why?" persisted her mother.

"Well, mother," said little Gladys, with resigned patience, "I have been going now ever since I was a child. And all they talk about is the Ten Commandments. I feel as though I am getting in a rut."

THE SPEAKER discusses "Technique"

Technique has been defined as the art of rendering the simplest passages with the utmost difficulty. It is something more than that; it is the art of "knowing the ropes"—all of the tricks and artifices of the trade or profession in which you are engaged. There are techniques in almost everything you undertake. You must master them, or go down in defeat.

A mid-western matron, coming by a Great Dane pup of impeccable pedigree, decided to send it to the dog training school at Harvard University.

When the pup was returned, the lady called family and friends to witness the results of perfect training. "Lie down!" she commanded. The dog blinked blankly. Neither coaxing nor threats would induce him to recline.

So the matron, who was journeying eastward to install a daughter in college, took the pup with her; deposited him indignantly at the threshold of the training school. She demonstrated the canine's contrariness by repeating the "Lie down" routine.

"Um-m," mused the Head Trainer. He spoke quietly to the pup, who at once fell over limply. Turning to the matron with just a trace of Harvard insouciance he exclaimed, "The command is 'Lay down!' "

THE SPEAKER discusses "the breaks"

I'll admit, sometimes it does seem that the fellow with the lightest load gets the most lifts.

When the elevator operators at New York's Radio City went on strike some time ago, the musicians on the Blue Network lugged their cumbersome instruments up and down stairs from one broadcast to another.

Finally, one of the musicians discovered that an emergency freight elevator was in operation and gratefully tugged his bull fiddle aboard.

"Well, hello, there," said the operator pleasantly. "Where have you been? The piccolo players have been riding all evening!"

THE SPEAKER discusses "Theory" vs. "Practice"

Often the best cure for "theory" is a very substantial dose of "practice." I recall the case of a young student of child behavior who frequently delivered a lecture called "Ten Commandments for Parents." He married and became a father. The title of the lecture was altered to "Ten Hints for Parents." Another child arrived. The lecture became "Some Suggestions for Parents." A third child was born. The lecturer—so the story goes—stopped lecturing.

✧   ✧

Maybe you can raise a baby strictly by the book, but a young couple I know is beginning to wonder. They started out with high hopes, but . . . One night the infant was wailing and the parents stood by its crib, peering through the index of their book and eyeing their little one with trepidation. Came a voice from the nursery door where their Irish cook stood in her nightgown: "If I was youse" she said, "I'd put down the book and pick up the baby."

✧ ✧

Perhaps the simplest way to distinguish between theory and practice is to say that theory is *thinking,* while practice is *doing.* Or, as the small boy put it when he was asked to define "agriculture." "Agriculture is something like farming, only farming is doing it."

THE SPEAKER discusses these Uncertain Times

A generation ago, we used to feel that we lived in a stable world—a livery stable world, if you want to put it that way. But now, well, the man who bets on a sure thing had best hold out the rent money. I heard about such a case not so long ago.

Three times the enthusiastic patron had made his way to the ticket window to place heavy wagers on Bluebells in the fourth race.

On the fourth pilgrimage, an observer tapped the bettor on the shoulder: "Brother," he said, "it's none o' my business, I reckon, but if I was you, I wouldn't be puttin' all that money on Bluebells; he ain't goin' to win no race."

"Yeah?" said the other, "How'd you figure that?"

"Well, if you must know," responded the counselor "I own Bluebells, an' I jes' know he ain't goin' t' win."

"Um-m," was the meditative response. "Well, all I can say is that it's going to be a mighty slow race; I own the other four horses."

THE SPEAKER discusses Vanity

We are all vain creatures. And we may as well admit it quite candidly. If we did not have our little vanities—honors and accomplishments which we cherish fondly—life would become pretty intolerable at times.

The late Stephen Leacock, Canadian humorist and philosopher, used to tell an amusing experience on himself:

(NOTE: *The speaker boasting an honorary degree might alter this story a bit and relate it as a personal experience.*)

When I first got my Ph.D. degree I was inordinately proud of it; used to sign myself, "Dr. Leacock" in season and out. On a trip to the Orient I put myself down that way on the passenger list of the liner.

I was just getting my things straightened out when a steward knocked at my cabin door and asked, "Are you Dr. Leacock?" "Yes," I answered. "The captain's compliments, Dr., and will you please come and have a look at the second stewardess' leg?"

I was off like a shot, realizing the obligations of a medical man. But I had no luck. Another fellow got there ahead of me. He was a Doctor of Divinity.

THE SPEAKER draws to a close

Bringing your talk to a successful conclusion is often something of a problem. A good rule is to "leave them with a laugh." You might tell this story and say to your audience that, like the immigrant boy, you, too, are "closing up."

I now think of the young Irishman who recently came to this country. He and his brother were passing a grocery store.

"What's the green things on that stand?" he asked.

"Persimmons," replied the merchant; "fine when ripe but those are green. I'll give you a few; put them in your pocket. Take them home and let them ripen."

But the immigrant boy couldn't wait. When a block or two away from the store slyly he took a persimmon out of his pocket and bit into it. A moment afterwards he touched his brother on the arm.

"Tim," he said with some difficulty, "is there anythin' I ought to say to you?"

"Why, I dunno," said Tim, "why do you ask that?"

"Because," said the immigrant boy with a wry face, "if there is, it's got to be quick, because I am—I'm closing up."

❖   ❖

I believe that I have now covered the principal points that I had in mind to discuss with you. I have always tried to keep in mind the response made by a college president when a visiting speaker asked how long he should talk.

"There is no time limit," said the president. "Your message will determine when you are through."

❖   ❖

I hope that I have been able to bring you something of interest and value, but now, as I come to my conclusion, I am frankly a little dubious. I feel somewhat like the professor in a well-known medical college who was delivering his final lecture to the graduating class.

"Gentlemen," he confessed, "I have been lecturing to you for the past four years. I am afraid that half of what I told you is wrong. The trouble is, I don't know *which* half!"

THE SPEAKER dwells on the Flight of Time

Your Chairman has just told me that three years have passed since I last met with this group. So clear, and so pleasant are my recollections of that visit that it seems hardly possible so many seasons have passed. It does seem that time gallops by in these later years. I am reminded of the farm lad who went down to enlist in the Navy. When they asked his birth date he shuffled awkwardly and confessed that he didn't know. "Maw never told me," he added.

He brightened. "But I'm thirty-two years old," he added. "Maw told me once how old I was, and I added a year every plowing."

"When did you add the year," asked the recruiting officer, "at spring or fall plowing?"

The candidate scratched his head.

"Why dern it all," he said, "that explains it. I thought I was getting old too fast."

THE SPEAKER encounters a Confusion of Names

Occasionally, at the speaker's table, you will run into a situation where two individuals bear the same, or a very similar surname. It may be a little confusing, and if you chance to get them mixed, pass it off with this story:

Cohen and Goldman, partners in ten-percentage, were discouraged with the world and with business. One morning Cohen announced he was going to change his name. "From now on, I'm McCarthy." That night Goldman thought it over. Why should he have the Jewish name in the firm? He would change his, too. "I also," he announced, "am going to call myself McCarthy!" They instructed the telephone girl to sing-song "McCarthy and McCarthy." All moved smoothly until a voice demanded to speak to Mr. McCarthy. "Which McCarthy do you want?" she asked. "Cohen or Goldman?"

THE SPEAKER endorses an Improvement Program

I was very much interested in listening to the report of your Committee on Civic Betterment. These are great projects you have afoot, and I am all for them. I need hardly caution you, however, that there are practical limits. Don't let your enthusiasm carry you too far. A program of this kind is a little like planning a garden in the early Spring. Really, a man should never lay out a bigger plot than his wife can take care of comfortably.

And don't let your enthusiasm for Improvement carry you to extremes. I am reminded of a lady trustee of a home for delinquent girls. One day she approached the director with something on her mind. "I have been thinking," she said, "that the time has come when we really ought to try to get a better class of girls in this institution." She wanted a committee to start working on it right away!

THE SPEAKER enjoys the Banquet

I want to say that I have thoroughly enjoyed myself—up to now. In fact, I was just thinking what a contrast this affair has been to one I heard of, not so long ago. That other banquet had dragged pretty sadly. The food was terrible, the service inadequate, the speakers unpardonably dull. Finally, the chairman introduced the final speaker with the announcement that he would "now give us some of his biggest and best after-dinner stories."

"Well," said the unfortunate speaker, "to begin with my biggest story, let me first tell you how much I have enjoyed this meeting."

❖   ❖

I suppose the best proof that I am not much of a speaker (aside, that is, from listening to me make a speech) is the fact that I eat too much at these affairs. I look up and down the table and watch others nibble while I gnaw.

Now, it is a well-known fact that the good speakers at public banquets eat practically nothing. And it once occurred to me, during the food conservation period, that if we could just find some way of getting more people to make more speeches, the resulting economy in food would be something terrific!

THE SPEAKER expresses gratitude for a large turnout

It is always heartening to a speaker to face a large audience such as this fine gathering. My especial regard is extended to those persons I see standing in the rear of the hall. I appreciate their valor, but may question their judgment. Certainly, I wouldn't care to stand in order to hear myself talk! However, come to think of it, I'll be standing, too—I hope!

Mark Twain, I recall, once told a little personal-experience story to illustrate that point.

In the course of one of his lecture trips Mark Twain arrived at a small town. Before dinner he went to a barber shop to be shaved.

"You are a stranger?" asked the barber.

"Yes," Mark Twain replied. "This is the first time I've been here."

"You chose a good time to come," the barber continued. "Mark Twain is going to read and lecture tonight. You'll go, I suppose?"

"Oh, I guess so."

"Have you bought your ticket?"

"Not yet."

"But everything is sold out. You'll have to stand."

"How very annoying!" Mark Twain said, with a sigh. "I never saw such luck! I always have to stand when that fellow lectures."

THE SPEAKER faces the Facts

We must appreciate that in this situation there are some facts that cannot be evaded. They are as immutable as the laws of mathematics. We can't be like the little girl who was having trouble with fractions. The teacher tried earnestly to make the matter clear, employing about every artifice in her repertoire. Finally, in desperation, she asked: "Don't you understand *at all*, Ethel?"

"Oh, I understand all right," said the child, "I just don't happen to agree with you."

THE SPEAKER fills a long-promised engagement

If you will promise to guard my secret, I'll tell you why I am here this evening. It is simply because your Program Chairman exacted the promise from me last January. You see, I am one of those fellows who, if he is asked to do something four months hence, will always readily agree. That seems practically a lifetime away. You can hardly plead a pressing engagement for that particular evening. And so, before you realize what has happened, you're hooked!

THE SPEAKER fills a return engagement

I am delighted not only to be with you again, but to note a substantially increased attendance on this return engagement. Apparently, you are either a particularly hardy breed hereabouts, or else word of my initial performance has not been widely spread.

At any rate, I am glad to see you—all of you. I shall not be in the position of the college president who at the beginning of a new school year expressed his gratification over the large number of freshmen enrolled, and then announced the Bible lesson for the day—a portion of the third Psalm, which goes: "Lord, how they are increased that trouble me!"

❖   ❖

You will, I am sure, be glad to know that I have reformed since my last engagement. My talk today, if not funnier, will, at least, be shorter. I have learned my lesson. People used to listen to me with open mouths—which I was simple enough to regard as a good omen, until I noticed on closer inspection, that their eyes were simultaneously closed.

THE SPEAKER gets down to Brass Tacks

Now, what I have given you thus far has been chiefly a theoretical discussion of the subject. I know that you are waiting impatiently for a more practical application. That is a perfectly natural reaction.

A distinguished churchman had been speaking for upwards of an hour on the subject of the Immaculate Conception. He had developed the theme with theological subtlety, learning and brilliance. Afterward, when he asked for questions, there was a long silence, broken by a somewhat hesitant voice: "Can you tell us, please, what are the advantages?"

THE SPEAKER gives Advice

Candidly, I dislike the role of oracle. And if, in this talk I seem at times a bit on the didactic side, please bear in mind that I am only relating my own experience and observation. You are free to accept or discard, as your judgment dictates.

I don't want to put you in the position of the Indian who was converting a log into a canoe. A man came along and said, "Chief, I think she's too wide for her length." So the Indian narrowed her down. Another said, "Chief, the stern's too full." So he cut down the stern. A third said, "The bow's too sheer, Chief." So he fixed up the bow. . . . When he launched the canoe it capsized. He hauled it back on the beach, found another log and began again. Once more a stranger offered advice, but this time he answered. "That's everyman's boat over there," pointing to the monstrosity that wouldn't float. Resuming his work, he mumbled, "This will be Indian's boat."

❖   ❖

I realize that giving advice is usually a thankless business, and I assure you I shall not venture far in that direction. I have always kept in mind the unconsciously profound summation written by a small schoolgirl:

"Socrates," she wrote, "was a Greek philosopher who went about giving people good advice. They poisoned him."

THE SPEAKER greets a large audience

This gratifyingly large attendance reminds me, by contrast, of an experience I had some years ago. Finding myself unable to meet a certain lecture date, I telegraphed the chairman to make the necessary refunds. In due course came the response: "We have given the audience back his money, and he has gone home perfectly satisfied."

✦   ✦

It is a continuing marvel to me that men will pay money to hear a public talker, when they can get more eloquent talk at home—without putting out a penny!

It was three o'clock in the morning when a minion of the law encountered an inebriated gentleman staggering uncertainly down the street.

"Hey, you!" called the officer. "Where y' headed at this hour of the mornin'?"

"Offisher," replied the drunk, with visions of his waiting wife, "I'm now on my way to a lec'shure!"

THE SPEAKER in a mercenary mood

Clarence Darrow, at a women's club in the West, had been delivering a lecture on ancient history, in the course of which he had touched upon the arts, customs, and achievements of the ancient Phoenicians. "Oh," said the portly and laudatory chairlady, when Mr. Darrow had run down, "how can we thank Mr. Darrow for the fascinating lecture he has given us tonight."

Darrow returned to the lectern and added the following postscriptum: "I entirely forgot to tell you that it was the Phoenicians who first invented money."

THE SPEAKER introduces a newcomer

You may have occasion to introduce, at some public gathering, a newcomer of unusual distinction. You can tell this story, then, outlining the newcomer's accomplishments, emphasize the point that he has been delivered to us "full-growed."

Army paratroopers were practicing their jumps in a backwoods region. A parachutist started to come down on a field, near which lived an old mountaineer and fifteen children. One of the youngsters saw the parachute floating down with a man attached to it, and he ran into the house yelling: "Bring your shotgun, Pappy —the darn stork is bringin' 'em fullgrown now!"

THE SPEAKER injects an extraneous note

Quite often the speaker has some special announcement, or extraneous note to present to an audience. Here is a good way to to get it in:

Before we come to a formal discussion of our topic, there is one observation I should like to make. Or, as a lecturer of my acquaintance unfortunately phrased it the other day: "Ladies and gentlemen, before I begin my address, I have something I want to say to you."

THE SPEAKER is "Glad to be here"

When I say I'm *glad* to be here, I really mean it. I'm not one of those shy, taciturn fellows who has to be coaxed to talk. My great problem—as I am frequently reminded in the home circle —is failure to keep my big mouth shut.

I'm somewhat like the very small boy who was crying papers on a street corner. A kindly passerby asked the lad if he was making much money. "Oh, I don't make nothin' " said the boy. "I git my papers from Butch over yonder fer five cents each, and sell 'em for a nickel."

"Then, why, my little man, do you sell papers?"

"Oh," said the lad blandly, "just t' git a chance t' holler!"

THE SPEAKER is "hard to get"

Due to a combination of circumstances, you have been obliged to cancel one or two engagements to appear before this particular group. You and the program committee have had some difficulty in getting together on a satisfactory date. But at long last you have arrived! The Chairman, in his introductory remarks has dwelt upon these circumstances; built you up as a big, busy executive. It's a little embarrassing. You'd like to do something to convey the idea that you don't take yourself that seriously. Tell them the "horse-trader" story.

Some years ago a friend of mine was buying a horse from a local trader. After the deal was concluded, the vendor appeared a bit hesitant. Finally, he blurted out: "Mister, they's a couple o' things about that there animal I sorta think you ought t' know."

"Okay," said my friend. "A deal's a deal, but if there are any special points you want to bring up, I'll be much obliged for the information."

"Well, for one thing," said the trader, "that there hoss is mighty flighty. Turn 'im loose in a pasture and it'll take a whole company o' infantrymen t' round 'im up."

"Oh, that's all right," the buyer said in a relieved tone. "I'm going to keep the horse in a stable, anyway. What—er, what was the *other* thing?"

The trader leaned over, cupped his hand and whispered: "After ye ketch 'im, he ain't wuth a damn!"

THE SPEAKER is misunderstood

If you talk in public, soon or late, you will be misunderstood. Some innocent remark will hold hidden implications, and will be met with gales of unexpected laughter. Yes, you'll feel pretty foolish. But the only course you can follow is to join in the general merriment—and perhaps come back with a story of some other classic misinterpretation.

The Duchess of Marlborough, so the story goes, had been presented with a pair of those remarkable birds that have brought despair to countless crossword-puzzle addicts—our old friend the emu.

The birds were housed in Blenheim castle, and there were well-bred expressions of hope that they would get along congenially and multiply. At long last, to the Duchess, visiting in Paris, came this telegram from a well-meaning retainer:

"Emu has laid an egg. In absence of Your Grace, have put a goose to sit on it."

THE SPEAKER is paid a dubious compliment

Not infrequently, a well-meaning Chairman will phrase a compliment in such a clumsy or thoughtless way as to convey a possible meaning quite the reverse of the original intent. In such cases, the audience is quick to see the point and howl with glee. And the speaker is placed in quite a quandry. His best move, probably, is to laugh it off with an account of another similar experience.

While Lord Halifax was British ambassador to the United States he made a speaking trip to Iowa. After one talk he was approached by a farmer who told him that he had made a great contribution to American understanding of the British.

"Before we heard you," the ruralist continued, "we used to be scared of the British. We thought they could outsmart us. Hearing you, we ain't afraid any more."

THE SPEAKER is pressed for time

It happens more often than it should. The Program Committee has scheduled too many speakers—or the organization has too much business to transact. In either case, your time has been whittled down to a minimum. What to do? Better tell a brief story—and make the best of a bad situation.

Two young vaudeville actors from New York went over to London to set the English capital on fire. They gave a dress rehearsal of their clever act before one of the big booking agents, who listened to it solemnly from the pit one foggy morning.

When they had finished he said, "Very good, boys; but it runs twenty-five minutes, and that's pretty long. However, if you'll cut it down to eight minutes we may bill you."

"Eight minutes!" cried one of the team, glaring down at him. "Why, man, we *bow* eight minutes!"

❖ ❖

Your time has been whittled to a fraction of the original allotment. You dislike to be in the position of directly rebuking the Chair. But you are not pleased and would like to convey your displeasure in a subtle—but not too subtle—way. A suggestion:

Arise deliberately and, without comment or elaboration, make this statement of fact. The folks out front will get the point!

At a meeting of the Presbyterian General Assembly sometime ago, the moderator announced: "The next number will be an address by Rev. James McCosh, Chancellor of Princeton University. Subject: 'The Immortality of the Soul.' Time allotted: Fifteen minutes."

❖ ❖

Whe practically all of your time eaten up by other features on the program, you might acknowledge the Chairman's introduction, look at your watch, and pointedly remark:

"I am reminded of the little girl who put a nickel up on the counter for a candy bar.

" 'But we have no nickel bars,' said the clerk.

" 'May I please have a soda pop?'

" 'But they are seven cents.'

Puzzled, the girl made a final attempt by ordering a popsicle. When told they were also seven cents she reached the sidewalk before the clerk could remind her of the nickel on the counter.

" 'That's all right,' she said, 'I can't buy anything with it anyway.' "

❖ ❖

Too many speakers have seen their time encroached upon by extraneous matters that somehow find their way into the poorly-managed program. Maybe one of these days an exasperated speaker who finds that he has left a net of fourteen minutes to deliver a forty minute message will have the nerve to tell this story to a program chairman who has been "a bit liberal wid my time." Anyway, we sincerely hope so!

An old Negro who had been sentenced to five years in the state penitentiary was asked by the judge if he had anything to say.

"Naw, sah," said the old man hesitantly, "Ah reckon not, sah, 'ceptin' maybe t' say dat youall sho' is a bit lib'ral wid my time."

THE SPEAKER kids his audience

There is nothing an audience relishes more than a collective ribbing. Strickland Gillilan has, for many years, had a sure-fire opening that he employs on festive banquets and other gay gatherings. Arising with the air of a cheer-spreading evangelist, he beams benevolently upon the group: "I am happy to be here this evening and look into your faces" *(a long, sweeping, quizzical look)* "and God knows there are some faces here that need looking into!"

Fritz Kreisler, the violinist, tells one which you can tell on him.

"I was walking with a friend one day when we chanced to pass a large fish market. There was a fine catch of codfish, neatly arranged in rows. Somehow, those wide open mouths and eyes staring fascinated me. Then I remembered.

"Clutching my friend in frantic haste, I exclaimed: 'Heavens! That reminds me—I should be playing at a concert!'"

THE SPEAKER lauds Coming Attractions

I am especially glad to learn that—— and—— are to be with you at future meetings. Both of these gentlemen are outstanding speakers and you have a real treat in store. I congratulate you. To attract lecturers of such renown, your budget must be at a rather high level. You know, that reminds me of a little incident I think you might enjoy.

A prominent churchman had been invited to address a community group. A collection was taken and after the session the speaker was offered a substantial part of the "take."

"No, thank you," he demurred, "I'd rather not accept compensation." Then, as an afterthought, he asked, "What do you usually do with this money you collect?"

"Oh," said the chairman, "it goes into a special fund."

"And what is the purpose of the fund?" persisted the churchman.

"Why," the chairman explained, "that's so we'll have money to get better speakers next year!"

THE SPEAKER lauds an Unconquerable Spirit

It is an accepted axiom that the man who won't admit defeat simply can't be beat. There are many illustrations to attest this truth.

Hoagy Carmichael, Hoosier composer of *Stardust,* tells of Uncle

Jed Sproul, down in Spencer County, Indiana. He was the best shot with a gun in those parts.

One day he was guiding a party through the White River valley and finally Jed said, "Now, we ought to see some quail in just a minute—I'll take a pot shot at the lead bird and the rest of you follow suit." The quail flushed and Jed took his time at aiming at the lead bird and finally he let go. But the bird kept flying, to the amazement of all concerned. Uncle Jed looked around sort of sheepish like for a moment and then he wheeled around, looked up in the sky and shouted:

"Fly on, you gosh-durned fool with your heart shot out!"

THE SPEAKER "lays an egg"

Well—I didn't expect too much of that one. And I'm grateful for the delayed ripple of laughter. I hope it wasn't inspired by a situation similar to the one that confronted a professor friend of mine.

This professor told what he fondly thought was a funny story to his class of bobby-soxers—and laughed loudly, as he often does at his own jokes. He was the only one who *did* laugh. The bobby-soxers sat mute and motionless. And as the silence was getting rather painful, a little girl in the front row whispered hoarsely, "For heaven's sake, kids, laugh or he'll tell it again!"

THE SPEAKER opens his discourse

Naturally, I want to get off to a good start. You know, a good beginning oftentimes means a great deal. To emphasize the point, there is the case of the young man who, desiring to marry, secured a favorable hearing from his sweetheart's irascible father by opening the interview with these words: "Sir, I know a way whereby you can save a lot of money!"

❖ ❖

"And now, in conclusion . . ."

I begin my speech with those words, because I have observed that this is the phrase everybody looks for and welcomes in a speech—and I want to make you folks happy right from the start.

THE SPEAKER pays tribute to a "grand old man"

I sincerely believe one of the greatest tributes that can be paid to our distinguished guest of the evening is that no one ever thinks of his age. He has always been too busy to bother with birthdays.

With no thought of irreverence, I would like to share with you what seems to me an especially appropriate paragraph I picked up some time ago, attributed to Mary McLeod:

"Years should be regarded as an asset. Come to think about it, God must be very old. But has anyone ever suggested that the years must have robbed Him of His ability to hold the stars in their courses, and that it is about time He was retiring and making way for someone younger?"

❖ ❖

THE SPEAKER pleads for *Action*

No speaker can have too many "action" stories in his repertoire. Human nature being what it is, there's always occasion to punch, poke and prod people into the spirit where they will say, "Come on, let's do it NOW!"

The story is told of a young preacher, who, somewhat embarrassed, was to preach before the examining board preparatory to his admission into the ministry. He began, "I want to speak from these words about Paul, when his enemies said, 'These men are come here to turn the world up-side-down.' My sermon is divided into three parts: first, the world was up-side-down and Paul had come to set it right-side-up. Second, the world is wrong-side-up today, and needs to be set right-side-up. And third, we are the ones to do it!"

❖ ❖

Mr. Chairman, we have passed this matter on from one meeting to the next. It seems to me the time has come to do something definite about it. Caution is a fine thing, but it can be carried to an extreme. It's a little like the hotel page with a telegram to deliver.

Through the hotel lobby and corridors, the mezzanine, the barber shop and the men's retiring room, a page had patiently wended his way, repeating at intervals, "Telegram for Mr. Niedspondiavanci!"

On the second round a timid, hesitant little man approached: "You are heving," he said dubiously, "a talegrim for Mr. Niedspondiavanci?"

"Yeah," said the page.

"Um-m," pondered the guest. "Vat initial, please?"

❖   ❖

There is always a psychological time to strike. And in my opinion that time is NOW. I am reminded of the two pugilists who had been making quite a sorry spectacle of themselves. For several rounds they had done nothing but circle each other, with no punches being thrown. A forbidding silence mounted in the arena. Then—

"Hit him now, ya bum," a spectator called, "you got the wind wit ya!" Well, I think we have got the wind with us. The time has come to hit!

❖   ❖

It strikes me that this group has already wasted a great deal of precious time. Can't we come to a definite decision? I am reminded of the small boy on his first day at kindergarten. "Now, David," the teacher said kindly, "would you like to model an animal? The clay is all ready for you."

"Naw," said David scornfully. "I don't want to play with mud. When do we get down to business?"

❖   ❖

Some persons seem to have no conception of the value of *time*. Oh, yes, they agree that such and such a thing should be done, but they hesitate to take simple, direct steps to accomplish a desired result quickly.

Aart van den Hoek, Rockefeller Center's crack gardener, had just completed his most spectacular undertaking—planting the first of several fifty foot elm trees along Fifth Avenue, in front of the Center. The giant tree—weight, eight tons—had finally been put in place, with the aid of fifteen men. As Mr. van den Hoek patted the last clod of earth in place, a little old lady—a fascinated but puzzled spectator—looked up at the gardener and asked: "Tell me, sir, wouldn't it be much simpler to plant a seed?"

✧ ✧

Too many of us are like the hired girl who had been sent to the brook for a pail of water. Instead of "fetching" she stood gazing at the stream, apparently lost in thought.

"What's she waiting for?" someone asked.

"I dunno," hazarded the head of the household, "maybe she hasn't seen a pailful yet that she likes."

THE SPEAKER pleads for Clarity

Never take anything for granted. Some of the things which seem to us perfectly obvious may prove pretty obscure to the other fellow. Remember he lacks your specialized knowledge and experience.

A traveler, pausing at a crossroads, remarked to a farmer that the arrow on a sign had been reversed. It read "Bangor" but pointed toward Monroe.

"Yes," agreed the farmer, "that sign ought to be over on this side of the road, but when we tried to set it we struck a stone ledge, so we put it in over there."

"But—but," expostulated the amazed traveler, "that makes the directions the wrong way!"

"Sure, sure," agreed the farmer complacently, "but anybody knows enough t' git t' Bangor!"

THE SPEAKER pleads for simple, effective language

Speaking of efficiency in expression, I am reminded of the old Southern darky who had been condemned on rather flimsy evidence for murder, and sentenced to death. There had been hints that the Governor was dissatisfied with the verdict and intended to exercise his powers in the interests of clemency. Mose had been waiting patiently for something to happen. Finally, he decided to jog the official memory. So he moistened his stubby pencil and wrote:

"Dear Massa Govner: They is fixin to hang me on Friday and here it is Tuesday."

❖ ❖

Let me take just a moment to repeat that last point in simpler terms. I think it is important, and you know it's so easy to be misunderstood. Some years ago a woman clerk in the Department of Agriculture at Washington noticed a farmer lad wandering aimlessly about the lobby. "Perhaps," she suggested helpfully, "you'd like to see the forty-foot mural on the floor above. It's really quite interesting."

Half an hour later came an irate call from the Bureau of Animal Husbandry: "Who the heck," a voice inquired, "sent a guy up here looking for a forty-foot mule?"

❖ ❖

A good many of our high-flown phrases bring to mind a sign that once appeared in the window of a dingy tailoring establishment in Birmingham's Darktown. In that window were a pair of the bluest blue trousers ever beheld, enlivened with a stripe of incredible width and ostentation. Beside the startling exhibition was this sign, crude but expressive:

"These pants were uncalled for."

❖ ❖

About Muncie, Indiana's lower Mulberry street cluster the city's Negro and foreign population. At a strategic point in that district an enterprising black, some years ago, established an eating house. From time to time he would hoist above his establishment a huge American flag, large enough completely to envelop the shack.

Though the restaurant enjoyed a fair regular patronage, executives in a neighboring plant observed that trade was uncommonly brisk whenever the Stars and Stripes chanced to fly. They were curious to know why this display of patriotism should be so closely linked with profits. A little investigation revealed a sign, tied to the flagpole. Roughly lettered in pencil, on the bottom of a shoe-box, were these welcome words:

"Chicken served when flag is out."

❖   ❖

Someone has defined "technique" as the art of rendering the simplest passages with the utmost difficulty. Many a person has attained a reputation for profundity merely because he uses words no one else can comprehend. But if you wish really to REACH people—to touch their hearts and perchance their pocketbooks, you must use words and phrases that have meat and meaning for them. Souls aren't saved through synthesis.

"Doctor," a wife asked a renowned medical man, "can you tell me why it is that some people are born dumb?"

"Why—" replied the medical man. "It is due either to some congenital inhibition of the faculty of articulation, or to some anatomical deficiency in the organs of vocalization."

"There, now," she remarked, triumphantly, glancing at her husband, "see what it is to have an education? I've asked Henry more than a hundred times why it was, and all he could say was, 'because they're naturally born that way.'"

❖   ❖

They tell an amusing story of a man who received as a gift a volume on Einstein's theory of Relativity. "I found," he said in a somewhat puzzled confession, "that I could identify all of the words, but when I started to read the book, I could not understand any of the sentences."

❖   ❖

A noted clergyman was asked by a colleague why the loud, vehement preaching of his earlier days had given way to a more quiet persuasive manner of speech. The man laughed. "When I was young," he said, "I thought it was the thunder that killed people, but when I grew up I discovered it was lightning. So I determined that in the future I would thunder less and lighten more."

❖   ❖

Down in the hog country of Arkansas, they don't believe in wasting words.

Aunt Charlotte, who had been put on the witness stand to tell what she knew of the sudden end of a large porker under a loco- motive, considerably annoyed the questioning lawyer by the meagerness of her responses. Finally, in some desperation, he said: "Madam, what I'd like for you to do is to tell the court in as much detail as possible, exactly what happened."

"Wall," said Aunt Charlotte, after some deliberation, "hit jest tooted and tuck 'im."

❖ ❖

When we use big words to disguise simple facts, there's always the danger that we may be found out—with disastrous results.

Moriarity went to call on his friend, the Doctor. "It's me wife," he explained, "that's sendin' me here. She's concerned with the state o' me health."

"Hm-m," said the Doctor meditatively. After an hour's exami- nation and a series of searching questions, the medico gave his verdict: "All that's the matter with you, Moriarity, is that you've been drinking too much."

"Well, that may be," admitted Moriarity, "but I can't be goin' back and tellin' that t' me wife."

"Oh," said the Doctor, "just tell her you're suffering from syncopation."

"Shure," said the pleased patient, "you be writin' that on a bit of paper and I'll give it to her." Which he did.

And the trusting but inquisitive Mrs. Moriarity, spelling out the strange word, letter by letter, in the dictionary, read the defi- nition: "Irregular movement from bar to bar."

❖ ❖

Cy, the sage of a little Mohawk Valley community, is an unre- lenting enemy of ostentation in any form. During an argument in the corner store, one of the participants made the mistake of using fancy language in Cy's presence.

Cy interrupted. "What was that last word?"

"I said it was a defalcation; any man who does what Joe Doakes is doing is committing a defalcation—"

Cy pointed an accusing finger at the speaker. "That," he bellowed scornfully, "is an out-of-town word!"

❖ ❖

The career gentlemen of our State Department are renowned for their tendency to indulge in high-flown and often unintelligible language. George Dixon, the Washington correspondent, tells of one of these elegant exponents of the art of circumlocution who was talking with Rep. Luther A. Johnson, of Texas, and chanced to remark that he had been having trouble with his liver.

"Your liver?" echoed Johnson, pretending to be aghast, "You mean your pate de foie gras, don't you?"

❖ ❖

Bernard Iddings Bell, the well-known minister, tells of performing a marriage ceremony for a Scandinavian couple.

All went as usual until Dr. Bell asked the question: "Nels, do you take this woman to be your wedded wife . . . ?"

The big chap grinned broadly and gave an unconventional but convincing response:

"Father, vat the hell you t'ink I come here for?"

Dr. Bell proceeded with the ceremony.

❖ ❖

What we need are more persons who do not say, "Regardless of their pigmentation or coloration under normal illumination, felines of all species, it has been learned authoritatively, have been found to be cinereous when the earth becomes enveloped in tenebrosity" when they mean "All cats are gray at night."

THE SPEAKER pleads for Tolerance

Too many of us are like the fellow who readily agreed that there are two sides to every question—"My side," he would say, "and the *wrong* side." We need to comprehend that there is often much to be said for *both* sides—depending upon the point of view.

George V. Denny, Jr., founder and moderator of the *Town Meeting of the Air* has a little ball that he likes to display when the question of tolerance comes up for discussion. Grasping the ball tightly in his hand, he asks, "What color is it?" The person questioned takes a quick look and answers: "Black."

Denny then shakes his head. "The part I see is white." He gives the ball a twirl. The other half *is* white.

"We could never agree on the color of this ball," he points out "unless you knew my point of view, and unless I realized you were looking at it from another point of view. Many of our disagreements could be settled if people would only look at *both sides* of the ball."

❖ ❖

Charles V was determined to compel all his subjects to adopt his way of thinking about religion. Thousands died rather than conform. Weary of a long reign, Charles abdicated in 1556, and retired to a monastery, where he amused himself by trying to make a dozen clocks run absolutely together.

When he failed, he exclaimed: "How foolish I have been to think that I could make all men believe alike about religion when I cannot even make two clocks run together."

THE SPEAKER points to the Danger of a Middle Course

A good many years ago, in the early days of the automobile, a Southern Negro was sent to deliver a mule a few miles away. It was night and the owner of the mule cautioned, "Now, Sam, if you see a light coming down the road, you get the mule off to one side until it goes by."

The next day, after diligent search and inquiry, Sam was located in a hospital, undergoing heavy repairs. "Sam," inquired the owner of the mule, "why didn't you do as I said, and drive off to one side until that light went by?"

"Ah, aimed t' do dat, boss," replied Sam, "but they was two lights, so Ah took aim fo' de middle!"

THE SPEAKER points to the Limits of Logic

Logic is great—we're all agreed on that. But it goes down better if you mix it with a little common sense. Which is something an applicant failed to do in a recent civil service examination. One of the questions asked was the following:

"If a man buys an article for $12.25 and sells it for $9.75, does he gain or lose by the transaction?"

One of our modern young sweet things, with good looks unmarred by brains, after studying for a while, gave the following answer:

"He gains on the cents but loses on the dollars."

❖   ❖

Logic is good, and we ought to be governed by it—up to a reasonable point. But there's such a thing as carrying a point too far.

Two colored golfers went out for a round of eighteen holes. One was a skilled golfer, but the other was a duffer. To equalize matters, the better golfer gave his friend a stroke a hole.

The duffer played better than usual, and his one-stroke handicap helped him to tie or beat his buddy on the first few holes. Then they came to a short hole, which the good golfer played so well that his ball rolled into the cup. A hole in one!

"Man, just try to beat that!" he said.

The other just stood there, frowning and scratching his head. Suddenly his face lighted up. "I wins dis hole," he announced.

"Boy, are you crazy?"

"I wins," maintained the other.

"How?"

"I claims my stroke. That gives me a hole in nothin'!"

THE SPEAKER praises a small group

Wherever a group, limited in numbers, has chalked up a record out of proportion to its size, this story can be worked in to fit the situation.

Drought struck the country-side and the parson of the church prayed for rain. Rain came in such torrents that a flood followed.

A rescue party in a boat spied a devout church member sitting on the roof of his house watching the current swirl by.

"Your prayers were sure answered," shouted one.

"Yes," said the careful stranded one, "I figger it ain't bad for a little church like ours."

THE SPEAKER presents a gift

I had prepared an eloquent speech for this august occasion, but somehow, in the spirit of gay informality and good fellowship, it seems quite out of place. Let me, instead, tell you about a certain captain of a fire department who was about to retire. The men banded together and bought their beloved leader an elegant embossed silver horn, and planned to present it to him at a meeting in the town hall. The fireman who was chosen to make the presentation practiced his speech for days beforehand. The chief, who had been informed of what was to happen, also practiced his speech of acceptance. They rehearsed together and were "letter perfect" when they mounted the platform in the town hall. The throng which confronted them had, however, a disastrous effect. Holding the horn at arm's length, the fireman stalked across the platform and with a ghastly expression on his face, said:

"Well, Bill, here's your horn!"

The chief rose slowly to his feet and gasped: "Heck! Is that it?"

(At conclusion of story speaker may proceed with his own simple build-up and presentation of gift, taking care, of course, to keep the entire ceremony quite informal and in the spirit of the gathering.)

THE SPEAKER presents a New Viewpoint

I realize that some of the things I have said today may strike you as a bit radical—that my point of view differs from that of other authorities to whom you may have listened. However, in the end we are all seeking the same objective, and in the end we may come to it by differing paths.

There were three travelers who, when they came to a certain crossroads, fell to disputing.

Said the first: "We must go to the left." "Oh, no," said the second, "I am sure we turn to the right." "You are both wrong," laughed the third, "I know it's the road straight ahead!"

After much disagreement they parted, each in a different way. And that evening, quite to their surprise, they met at the same inn.

THE SPEAKER projects "The Voice of The People"

Even in Russia, I am told there is a growing determination on the part of the people to have a voice in their own government.

An emissary from Moscow was persuading village peasants to install a radio loud-speaker. "With this invention," he said, "you can hear for yourselves what Stalin and Kalinin are saying in Moscow."

"Very good, Comrade talker," interjected an old, bearded peasant. "But will this new contraption talk backward? Will they, in Moscow, be able to hear what we are saying in the villages?"

THE SPEAKER promises Brevity

I note that your closing time is 1:30 and I certainly shall not keep you beyond that limit. I have never forgotten a story that Generalissimo Chiang Kai-shek used to tell concerning an old Chinese sage who conducted classes in public speaking many centuries ago.

A young man who was a sort of a chatterbox came to the sage, sent by his parents to learn oratory. In their first interview, the young man talked so much that the old teacher became annoyed. So when the time came to discuss terms of tuition, he asked double his usual price.

"Why charge me double?" asked the young man indignantly. The sage smiled blandly. "Because," he said, "I shall have to teach you two completely different things: the one to hold your tongue, the second, how to speak when the occasion arrives."

❖   ❖

An English manufacturer of motor car tires was the speaker at a businessmen's luncheon. In response to a toast, he said: "I have no desire or intention to inflict upon you a long speech for it is well known in our trade that the longer the spoke, the bigger the tire."

❖   ❖

I have observed, in a long and varied career, that while short speeches are not always the best, the best speeches always seem short.

❖ ❖

I remember Irvin Cobb's classic remark: "No speech can be entirely bad if it is short enough."

❖ ❖

Sometimes I become very much afraid that we all talk too much. This conviction was impressed upon me anew when I read some time ago that twenty minute speeches before the United Nations assembly usually require less than five minutes in their translated form. And an interpreter, listening to half an hour of Chinese testimony, merely shrugged his shoulders and explained: "He says, 'No'."

❖ ❖

I am going to try to be brief, and to keep directly to the point. I am reminded of the railway maintenance-of-way man who had been counseled to cut out long-winded reports. So the next time —relating damage done by a sudden cloudburst—he wrote: "Dear Sir: Where the railroad was, the river is."

❖ ❖

I haven't a great deal to say, and I assure you that I shall not be a great while in saying it. I have always been rather taken with Bruce Barton's suggestion that talk should be taxed, and that these taxes should be graded like income taxes are graded—the larger the income the higher the tax. It has been suggested that the first five minutes be exempt, the next five bear a tax of two percent, fifteen minutes ten percent, twenty minutes twenty-five percent, all over thirty minutes sixty percent, and all after-dinner speakers and all members of Congress be required to pay double tax.

❖ ❖

I don't want to bore you with a long-drawn-out exposition and I think on this occasion, I shall follow a plan which I believe was originated by one of the Supreme Court justices.

When asked to comment, the justice gets up, lights a cigarette, then, without puffing it, holds it in his hand until it burns his fingers. That is a signal that he has talked long enough! So he sits down.

❖   ❖

In my opinion, audiences are altogether too patient with long-winded speakers. I can recall only one instance where a group did anything constructive to reduce the volume of oratory to proper proportions. It was during the war. Fed up with lengthy speeches at launching ceremonies, workmen kicked the blocks away and let a ship slide in the middle of a peroration. I have always felt they did just the right thing.

❖   ❖

One thing, at least, I can promise: I shall not hold you long. Brevity, I believe, is one of the essential qualities of good public talk.

I was interested in the formula followed by a program committee in St. Paul, not so long ago. Each speaker was limited to the length of time he could—or would—hold a twenty-five pound cake of ice in his bare hands.

❖   ❖

It is my purpose to shape this discourse upon a Spartan pattern. The Spartans, you will recall, were celebrated for their laconic style. They loathed nothing more than talkativeness.

Once a neighboring island in the Aegean Sea was struck by a famine and the population sent an envoy to Sparta to ask for help. He made a long speech describing the distress of the islanders but the Spartans sent him back empty-handed and told him: "We have forgotten the beginning of your speech and we understood nothing at the finish."

The famine-stricken population sent another envoy to Sparta urging him to be as concise as possible in his request. He took a lot of empty flour bags with him and opening one for the Assembly of Sparta, he said: "It is empty. Please fill it." Which the Spartans immediately did and they filled the other bags as well, but before he left, the chairman of the assembly told him: "You need not have pointed out to us that your bags were empty. We would have seen it, anyway. It was not necessary to ask us to fill them. We would have done so, anyway. Remember, if you come another time do not talk so much."

❖ ❖

It is my purpose to take a moral from a little story I heard not long ago.

A minister who lived in the suburbs during his discourse said, "In each blade of grass there is a sermon."

Late the following afternoon a broker, a member of his flock, discovered the good man pushing a lawn mower about his garden and paused to remark:

"Well, parson, I am glad to observe you engaged in cutting your sermons short."

❖ ❖

This talk may not be good—but at least it won't be long. I recall too distinctly the experience of a luncheon club speaker who, just before he was to be introduced, leaned over and asked the chairman, "How long do you want me to talk?"

"You can talk as long as you want to," said the chairman graciously, "but we usually leave here at 1:30."

❖ ❖

I quite agree with the observation that the average public speaker is not only loquacious, but he also talks too much.

❖ ❖

Let me say here and now that I'm not going to inflict a *long* address upon you. I've always been guided by a precept that was given to me by a veteran speaker many years ago: "If you don't strike oil in two minutes," he advised, "stop boring."

❖ ❖

My problem is to present this matter briefly, yet in sufficient detail to give you a clear picture. I hardly think you would want me to go to the extreme adopted by my friend Mike.

Mike, the foreman of a logging camp employing a hundred men and a couple of women cooks, was inclined to be extremely verbose in his reports to the management. Finally, after several broad hints, an executive issued positive orders.

"Mike," he said, "I haven't time to read page after page of minute details. Boil it down. Give me the picture in percentages; that's all that really matters."

So, in his next report, Mike wrote: "Last month, one percent of the men married fifty percent of the women."

THE SPEAKER quotes

When and how to give credit in your public remarks is sometimes quite a problem. The insertion of too many "verbal quotation marks" may tend to disrupt the continuity of your talk. The matter is best settled by individual judgment and conscience. Here is a clever little twist you can sometimes use in quoting an indefinite source:

"Let me respond to your chairman's generous tribute with a few appropriated words . . ."

In this talk I shall borrow liberally from the opinions expressed by authorities in the field. So, if you observe me making some unusual gestures—well, perhaps I'd better tell you about the educator who was visiting a Negro church in a small Georgia community. This educator was impressed by a very distinctive gesture which the pastor employed. At intervals during the course of the sermon this leader of the flock would extend his arms in front of him; raise and lower them with a slow rhythmic motion.

Later, the white visitor asked his Negro brother to explain the significance of the unusual movement. "Well," said the parson, "de congregation knows 'bout dat. I done 'splained it to 'em. Y' see, sah, dem is de quotation mahks!"

THE SPEAKER reminds us of our Obligations

There is an old and true saying that "Salvation is free"—and so it is, within limits. But we must pay for having it piped in to us. And, after all, we must not be unmindful of our obligations.

Faithfully each year, for a full decade, Mrs. O'Flaharity had journeyed to the cathedral for the christening of the latest addition to the family. And on each occasion she had given the new baby five names.

On the eleventh occurrence the good father laboriously entering all of the names in the register, looked up from his labors:

"Mrs. O'Flaharity," he beamed, "it is the joy and the privilege of the Church to welcome these little charges into the fold, but the next time—the next time, you really must bring your own ink!"

THE SPEAKER reminds us, "You can't have everything!"

With the third drink, the little man with the wan look began to talk. "I married the woman of my dreams," he confided to his neighbor of the bended elbow. "She is as beautiful to me as the day I met her. Her hands are always white and soft. Her hair is never untidy. Her appearance is always immaculate."

"So," said the neighbor, "your marriage is a happy one?"

"Yes," said the little man, with just a trace of wistfulness in his voice. "Yes, but do you know, I sometimes get pretty tired of eating in restaurants."

THE SPEAKER responds to an Unexpected Call

As your reputation for public talking increases, you will be more and more called upon to speak—often without opportunity for careful preparation. You do not always need to speak, in the formal sense. But you had best be prepared, at least, to get up and tell a story.

A bashful young man had just been married to a somewhat masterful and entirely self-possessed young woman. A wedding supper followed the ceremony. The couple sat at the head of the table receiving congratulations. Several guests offered toasts. Finally, the supposedly happy bridegroom was asked to say a few words.

He demurred, but the guests became increasingly insistent. At last, the bride took a hand.

"George," she said, "you must say something to them—you really must. I insist upon it."

So the young man, beginning a long life of accepting commands, got reluctantly to his feet. He placed a wavering hand on the shoulder of his bride, coughed nervously, and began:

"This thing has been thrust on me!"

THE SPEAKER returns to Old Haunts

Getting back to the old home town is always a pleasure. And, fortunately, I am not in the position of a couple of fellows I heard about recently.

"Do you know," one said to the other, in an exchange of confidences such as train journeys foster, "I just got out of prison this morning. It's going to be tough, facing old friends."

"I can sympathize with you," said the other, "I'm just getting back from the state legislature!"

❖   ❖

I recall (the speaker may say, returning to his home town after the lapse of many years) the case of another pilgrim.

A middle-aged childless couple moved from an Indiana community to an Eastern city. After a space of years, the wife returned for a visit and called on the local dentist for some needed repairs.

"Evalina," said the practitioner, cautiously exploring dental cavities. "Evalina, we've been hearin'—that is—well, to come right out with it, there's right smart talk that Jim has had goat glands grafted on him. Is—is they anythin' to it?"

Evalina replied that it was quite true. "And maybe you haven't heard," she added coyly, "we have a son now—a fine boy nearly seven years old. He's waiting for me out in your reception room."

The dentist extended congratulations, and expressed a wish to see the lad. So Evalina called him in.

"Well, well!" exclaimed the tooth tinkerer. "What a fine, healthy boy! And how are things with you, son?"

Smiling confidently the sturdy youngster looked up and spoke: "Not ba-a-a-d!"

THE SPEAKER returns from a vacation

You have just returned from a vacation, and have been asked to take part in a program. Everyone says how fine you look—even the Chairman, in his introduction makes sly reference to your pleasure pilgrimage. Okay, then, that's your cue to give them this delightful little yarn:

Moe Silverstein was a devoted family man, as well as something of a braggart. Mama Silverstein lived in the lap of luxury. The most expensive and showy raiment was piled on her. And Moe rarely overlooked an opportunity to impress the price-tags on his circle of acquaintances.

When Mama died suddenly, the neighbors called to pay their last respects.

"How wonderful she looks!" clucked Rachel Goldfarb sympathetically.

"And vy shouldn't she be looking wonderful?" demanded Moe, "Ain't it she is just spending the whole winter in Miami?"

THE SPEAKER says, "Check and double-check"

Appearances ARE deceitful. And even when you have the evidence you'd best examine it closely. It pays to use your own powers of deduction. Here's an instance:

When a midwestern reporter turned in a story about a farmer's loss of 2,025 pigs by theft, an alert copyreader thought the figure pretty high; phoned the farmer to check on it.

"Did you lose 2,025 pigs?" he asked.

The distraught farmer answered, "Yeth."

So the smart newsman thanked him; changed the copy to make the loss two sows and 25 pigs.

THE SPEAKER says, "If the foe is tough, you must get rough!"

Once there was a preacher who didn't want to offend any of his somewhat touchy parishioners. Yet he felt that it was incumbent upon him to preach a sermon on Sin. So he went at it one Sunday, and wound up something like this:

"Brethren, I say unto you repent of your sins (in a measure). Ask for forgiveness (more or less) or you will be damned (to some extent.)"

I guess maybe the sermon satisfied all who heard it—but there is no record of any conversions.

THE SPEAKER says, "It's all a matter of opinion"

An artist who wanted a home among the Taconic Hills of Vermont was talking the matter over with a farmer who allowed that he had a good house for sale. "I must have a good view," said the artist. "Is there a good view?"

"Well," drawled the farmer, "from the front porch yuh kin see Ed Snow's barn, but beyond that there ain't nothin' but a bunch of mountains."

✧ ✧

A Negro child had been told by his mother that the lion was the strongest animal in the world. "A lion can whup anythin'," the boy's mother assured him, "—a horse, a man, even a elephant, I 'spec—anythin'."

One day the boy brought home a colored print showing a young man, with his bare hands, tearing the jaws of a lion. "Mammy," he said, dubiously, "how come this picture, if a lion is so strong, lak you say?"

"Honey chile'," the mother replied without hesitation, "Ah reckon no lion done painted dat picture."

THE SPEAKER says, "Remember your objective!"

An employer told a group of boys the owl story, and hired the boy who gave the right answer:

The farmer went into the barn to shoot an owl. The gunfire set the hay ablaze. The barn went up in flames, the cattle were burned, the farmer's wife lost her life trying to rescue her husband, the farmer himself almost lost his life.

The boys who, on hearing the story, would talk about the cattle or the barn or the farmer's wife, did not get the job. It went to little Willie who never forgot the objective and who asked, "Did the farmer hit the owl?"

THE SPEAKER says, "Stand up for your convictions!"

What you believe is of course, important. But even more important is the willingness to stand up and defend that belief with everything that's in you. Beware of taking a neutral stand on any issue in which you really ought to have firm convictions. Believe in something! And don't hesitate to back that belief.

Remember what happened to the borderland citizen, back in civil war days, who resolved to remain neutral. He wanted to play safe so he dressed himself in Confederate trousers and a Union jacket. The result was that the Confederates shot him in the chest and the Union soldiers shot him in the seat of the pants!

❖   ❖

We all love the person who has strong convictions. But of course there's a difference between sincere conviction and plain bull-headedness. In a country church there was a hot quarrel over the question of whether to buy a new organ. Somebody asked one of the elders what he thought about the matter.

"I have not yet made up my mind," he said ponderously, "but when I do, I shall be very bitter!"

❖   ❖

Yes, stand up for your convictions. But choose them with care. There are two sides to everything—including a sheet of flypaper. But it makes a lot of difference to the fly which side he's on!

THE SPEAKER says, "We all make mistakes!"

What we need is more patience and understanding. Remember, the fellow who never makes a mistake never makes much of anything else. Temper your temper when something goes wrong. Consider the other fellow's *intentions*. They ought to outweigh a lot of other considerations. And, you know, there's always the chance that he was using horse sense!

That reminds me of a ranchman living alone in deep Wyoming —a fellow who claims to have the smartest horse in the world.

"Here awhile back," he recalls, "I slipped and broke a laig. And do you know what that horse done?"

"Well, he drug me t' my bunk, and then run five miles to fetch a doctor. But I got t' admit tho," the rancher added grudgingly, "he did slip a mite. He fetched back a horse doctor!"

THE SPEAKER says, "We must take the medicine!"

All too often, we tear up the prescription—and then blame the doctor for our slow recovery. I heard of a case like that just the other day.

A not-too-intellectual employer called in one of his trusted workers. "Isidor," he said, "you're a happy man? What's the secret?"

"Well," said Isidor tentatively, "I don't know. I haven't thought much about it. I—well, I like to read."

"That's it," said the employer. "You read. Reading's good."

The next morning the employer again called Isidor to his office. "Boy," he groaned, "did you give me a bum steer! So you read, eh? Well, I went home and read last night. Friends wanted me to go out, but no! I was going to read. I read one hour. I read two hours. After all, how long can you read? By that time it was too late to make a date. So what do I do? I go to a speakeasy alone and swill the worst liquor I've ever tasted in my life. Now look at me!" he concluded bitterly. "And that's what you call happiness, is it?"

THE SPEAKER scourges an opponent

When you must follow an opposition speaker usually the best tactic is to take a course directly opposite to the one he has followed. This avoids invidious comparison, and your points stand out all the more by contrast. Let us say the preceding speaker has been deadly serious. Then, perhaps the good-natured kidding approach is indicated. Has he leaned heavily on sentiment? Very good, then spurn the sentimental, and strike in deadly earnest with all you have. The following story illustrates our point.

Mr. Kleverleigh, the attorney for the defendant, had made a masterly plea. When he concluded nearly everybody was in tears. The jury, made up of hardheaded, weather-beaten old country-men on whose ears oratory and sentiment fell like snowflakes into a warm chimney, was unmoved. The other attorney took its measure at a glance.

"Gentlemen," he said coolly, "let it be understood to begin with that I am not boring for water."

❖   ❖

I am not questioning the ability, the integrity, nor the good intentions of my opponent. All these qualities have been abundantly demonstrated in the past. But he appears to have what amounts to a genius for backing the wrong horse at the right time. His performance in this respect brings to mind the two farmers who ran racing stables and were keen rivals. They each entered a horse in a local steeplechase, and one of them, thinking he would get the better of his friend, engaged a crack jockey. The two horses were leading at the last fence, which proved to be too stiff for them. They fell, unseating their riders, but the expert jockey quickly remounted and won the race. On returning triumphant to the paddock he found the farmer who had engaged him fuming with rage.

"What's up?" asked the jockey. "I won, didn't I?"

"Yes," roared the farmer, "you won all right, you idiot, but you were on the wrong horse!"

THE SPEAKER seeks to explain

Chairmen who know a speaker intimately are forever trying to "tie something on him," in their introductory remarks. And of course the speaker, not to be outdone, wants to come back at the guy. Here's a good story to pave the way for your own special explanation:

"Now, this little matter your Chairman mentioned awhile ago: I can explain the whole thing—and I'd like to. But, you'll have to give me a little time, and space.

I'm somewhat like a meek little guy named Isaac Goldfarb who somehow got himself involved in an argument with an opponent who believed in action rather than altercation. The result, for Ike, was a battered hat, a broken nose and two purple eyes.

When the police arrived tardily, the assailant had escaped, but Ike was promptly dragged to the police station.

Next morning, when the magistrate had gone over the evidence and ruled that Ike was not to blame, he said to him:

"Why didn't you explain the matter to the officers, and save yourself all this trouble?"

"Exblain?" blurted the injured innocent, gesticulating wildly. "How could I exblain? They handcuffed me before I could say a vord?"

THE SPEAKER serves as a substitute

If you are replacing a star performer, your position is hardly an enviable one. It becomes doubly important, therefore, to min-

*imize the disappointment of your audience by giving them an
early laugh. Try this one:*

I can appreciate your disappointment in not being able to hear
Mr. —— on this occasion. And I can assure you that I share that
disappointment with you. I feel somewhat as I imagine Cornelia
Otis Skinner must have felt when Madam Chairman arose for the
usual introduction and, with engaging frankness said: "Since we
cannot afford Admiral Byrd, we are having Cornelia Otis Skinner."

❖   ❖

*"Filling in" for another speaker is never a very tempting role.
The audience is likely to be a bit "let down." In such a situation,
try to build yourself up with a good story, at the outset. With a
few introductory remarks, this one should serve very well.*

The little country parish near a famous ocean resort was having
"supplies," as they call visiting ministers. On one Saturday they
learned that the expected preacher could not come. They were
sore beset, but they heard of the sojourn of a very distinguished
doctor of divinity at the hotel, by the sea. With some misgivings
they appointed the stoutest member of their committee to invite
the noted preacher to occupy the pulpit. He received the committee-man with graciousness, and to the latter's surprise and joy,
accepted. The committee-man, wishing to round out the happy
transaction, remarked, "You know, Doctor, we would have been
satisfied with a poorer preacher if we could have got one."

❖   ❖

I can appreciate the disappointment of this audience in not
being able to hear the distinguished gentleman who was originally
billed for this occasion. But I must add that I am deeply grateful
to your chairman for his generous introduction. In this respect,
I certainly fared much better than did Dr. Burris Jenkins, the
eminent Kansas City divine, on a somewhat similar occasion. The
chairman, in that instance, arose and detailed the disappointments of the committee in their endeavors to secure a number of
notable speakers, concluding with the statement that Dr. Jenkins
was present to serve as a stop-gap.

Dr. Jenkins, acknowledging the introduction, remarked that he
felt like a bundle of rags stuffed in a crevice to replace a broken

window-pane. Later, a well-meaning old lady in the audience did her best to console the somewhat discomfited speaker. "Oh, Dr. Jenkins," she insisted, "you're not old rags; you're a pane!"

THE SPEAKER shares the spotlight

There are so many distinguished persons present on this occasion that I feel as I imagine George Jessel must have felt on another program years ago. A fraternal organization had asked George to play a benefit, and since it was in his home territory of Brooklyn, George agreed.

A few days later someone phoned and suggested that the actor might also be able to line up Eddie Cantor. George said he would try, and was finally able to report Cantor's acceptance.

"Ah, that's fine," beamed the officer in charge of arrangements. "Now, just one thing more: If you can also get Bing Crosby, you won't have to come!"

THE SPEAKER sidesteps an issue

Perhaps some of you will conclude that I'm a good deal like an Arkansas politician who had been dodging issues through an hour's oration. Finally, someone in the audience whispered to his neighbor, "You know, if that feller two-steps as well as he side-steps, I'll bet he's pop'lar at the Little Rock dances."

I don't want to appear to evade an issue, but . . . *(Proceed with an explanation of why no clearly defined answer can be given at this time.)*

THE SPEAKER silences a heckler

Hecklers fall into two classifications—and we've often wished they might fall into something a good deal worse than that! These are the truly obnoxious, drunk or otherwise, and the hazers who simply seek, in a goodnatured way to discomfit the man who is on his feet.

Obnoxious hecklers, if they persist, should be dealt with by someone in authority. The other type can best be handled by a good-natured exchange of badinage. Whatever you do, try not to

*lose your temper, for it is the prime purpose of the heckler to
"get your goat."*

Try to get your tormenters off the track with a story.

Look, fellows (you might say) let's stop right now and decide
among ourselves who's going to make this speech. I had sort of
got the notion that I had been nominated, but maybe I was mistaken. Reminds me in a way of the sheriff who drove down to the
station with an insane man handcuffed to his wrist—a fellow he
was supposed to take to a nearby institution. It was not exactly
clear which should board the train first, and some difficulty was
experienced in getting up the steps. The porter offered his services and seemed to make the mix-up worse, so he backed off and
remarked:

"Jes' which one of yo'-all ge'mens is de nut, anyway? Ah specks
Ah could be mo' he'p if Ah find dat out fus'."

THE SPEAKER stumbles over a name

*If you falter or fumble on a name (and you will!) it is well to
have a few selected "name" stories in your repertoire. They relieve tension and help you to get back on the main track.*

"So," sobbed Nadya Oblomovivitch, "my beloved Ivan per-
ished in battle. Do you say he spoke my name as he lay dying?"

"Well," said the returned soldier truthfully, "he said anyway
part of it."

✧   ✧

*Sometime you may even make the grave error of miscalling the
name of the city in which you are speaking. McNair, while mayor
of Pittsburgh, once made this mistake—and got out of it neatly.*

"I am glad to be in your fine city of Johnstown—"

"GREENSBURG!" called some one in the audience.

"I know, I know," said McNair, recovering quickly. "I just
wanted to see if you were awake. Now, I hope you'll stay awake
until I've finished."

THE SPEAKER sympathizes with listeners

My six-year-old son and I had been attending church services.
He had behaved quite well through a long and somewhat tedious
sermon, and I was rather proud of him.

"Daddy," he inquired on the way home, "what does a preacher do on the days that aren't Sunday?"

"Oh," I replied, "a preacher has lots of duties. There's a good deal of church business to take care of. He has to visit all of the people who are sick or in trouble. Then, he has to prepare his sermon for the next Sunday. And, of course," I concluded, "he has to rest up some, too. Talking in public is hard work, you know."

My son pondered this last point thoughtfully. "Well," he observed after a pause, "listening isn't easy, either!"

THE SPEAKER talks about Prejudices

There is no such thing as an unprejudiced person. The individual who claims complete freedom from prejudice is either an outrageous liar, or woefully weak on self-analysis.

Somehow, I have always had a sort of admiration for the forthright old lady who met a neighbor at a political rally. "Why," said the surprised neighbor, "I always thought you were a staunch Republican. What are you doing at this Democratic meeting?"

"Well," sniffed the old lady, "I came with a perfectly open and unbiased mind to listen to what I am convinced is pure rubbish."

❖ ❖

A college class was asked to give its reactions to a group of words. Did each name, in turn, suggest something pleasant, unpleasant or indifferent? Did it arouse a feeling of fear, hatred, distrust?

This is the list, as submitted: Scotchman, Nazi, Swede, Pole, Methodist, Negro, Walloonian, New Dealer, Jew, Italian, Presbyterian, Ku Klux Klan, Catholic, CIO, Frenchman, Pirenian, Moslem, Protestant, Russian.

Many names were checked on the unfavorable side. Prominent on the list of unfavorables were Walloonians and Pirenians.

Strangely enough there are no people called Walloonians or Pirenians. They were inventions of the professor.

THE SPEAKER talks about Trouble

Everybody has troubles—and likes to talk about them. But who wants to listen to the other fellow's? We can't avoid troubles, the speaker may point out, but at least we needn't go out of our way to borrow an additional load—as did the central character in this amusing tale.

The local express agent in a Southern community had bad news for Judea Hollis, a neighboring Negro planter.

"Jude," he said regretfully, "them strawberries you shipped to market t'other day—they got in at a bad time; mighty bad time. Commission man couldn't use 'em. Fact is, you not only ain't a-goin' t' git any money on them berries, but you owe me 89 cents for the carryin' charges."

Judea, with visions of being locked up for the duration of the jail, tremblingly confessed that he had no money.

The express agent reflected. "You got fryin' chickens, ain't y', Jude?"

"Yas, sah, Cap'n. Pow'ful fine fries."

"Well, I'll tell y', Jude. Next time you come t' town fetch me one o' them fries, and I'll fergit the 89 cents."

Three days later the Negro planter returned carrying *two* squawking cockerels. "Nex' Chuesday, Cap'n," he explained, "I aims t' ship me 'nother crate o' them berries."

❖　❖

Trouble is the one thing you can always find in abundance, if you really set out to look for it—and too many people, these days, are doing that very thing.

A young matron thought she was getting used to the eccentricities of day help, but was frankly nonplussed when the new girl continued to work with her hat on.

Finally, a bit timorously, she ventured a query: "Mona, why do you wear your hat in the house? I prefer that you take it off when you come to work in the morning—and leave it off until you go home."

"'Taint hurtin' nothin'," replied the maid belligerently. "And I want it on, 'cause effen anybody insults me, I'll be ready to leave right off."

THE SPEAKER talks of "motes and beams"

Before we go about finding fault, let us make very sure that the difficulty is not with our own vision.

A little girl had not dusted the furniture to the satisfaction of her grandmother. She was required to repeat the task a second, and then a third time. Finally, when there was still no word of approval, she looked up and said: "Grandmother, that dust is not on the furniture; it is on your glasses!"

❖ ❖

Before you flare up at anyone's faults, take time to count ten—ten of your own!

THE SPEAKER talks of our Obligations

Too many of us have been taking a ride through life and trying to dodge the demand, "Fares, please?" A little boy, riding with his parents on a train, had his first experience on an observation car. Enamored of his experience he came running into the Pullman and cried, "Daddy, come out and ride on the obligation car!"

THE SPEAKER talks of Peace on Earth

A writer in the *New York Times* once observed that Man is a wonderful fellow, learning as he does from the other created animals.

He studies the hawk and the vulture and flies through the air with the greatest of ease. He learns from the crab with its shell and the skunk with its tear-gas. He considers the ways of the squirrel and becomes a hoarder; the ways of the snake in the grass and goes in for espionage. He observes the caterpillar and the hippopotamus, the shark and the crocodile, the mole and the hedgehog, and makes himself terrible on land and sea and underneath both. . . . About the only creature left in nature for him to learn something useful from is the dove.

THE SPEAKER talks of Teamwork

Every speaker should have at his command good stories to illustrate the importance of co-operative action—all working together for the common goal. Here is one of the best:
An old Negro, on a Southern plantation, was an expert with the

whip and delighted to show his prowess. One afternoon he had given a demonstration by striking the blossom from a dandelion, and, later, hitting a fly in mid-air. Finally, a guest pointed to a hornets' nest, but the old darky resolutely shook his head.

"A blossom is a blossom," he observed sagely, "an' a fly is a fly, but a hornets' nest—man, that's an organization!"

THE SPEAKER talks straight from the shoulder

Tact and diplomacy are essential tools in the kit of all who perform in public. But there comes a time when only plain talk—strong and straight—will serve. In such a situation the speaker may wish to preface his remarks with the story presented below, building his subsequent remarks on the "I don't keer who hyars me" theme.

An old negro woman had lived with a certain family in the South for many years. One day her mistress had occasion to reprimand her quite sharply for something that had gone wrong. The negress said nothing, at the time, but a little later her voice could be heard in shrill vituperation of everything and everybody, with a rattling accompaniment of pans and kettles. So loud became the clamor and so vindictive the exclamations that Mrs. C. went hurriedly down to the kitchen.

"Why, Liza," she began, in amazement, "who on earth are you talking to?"

"I ain't talkin' to nobody," the old Negress replied, "but I don't keer who in dis house hyars me!"

THE SPEAKER talks to fill time

The one thing no Program Chairman can tolerate is a vacuum. If a certain speaker is tardy in arriving—or if there is some hitch in the program—you may be, and indeed often will be asked to "extend your remarks." This is just another way of asking you to stand up there and keep your jaw moving until the crisis has passed. For such an emergency you'll need a collection of stories. This one seems especially indicated.

The pulpit was being occupied by a distinguished visiting clergyman and the ambitious young lady organist decided to leave no stone unturned to impress the great man with the power of her playing. The stubborn old sexton who pumped the air for the instrument had been rather lax in his performances, so she decided to write him a note and demand sufficient air.

The note was handed to the old man just before the beginning of the service and he, quite mistakenly, proceeded to hand it down unopened to the visiting clergyman. The great man opened the communication and read:

"Kindly blow away this morning 'till I give you the signal to stop."

THE SPEAKER tells an Old One

I rather imagine some of you have heard *that* one. Well, anyhow, it was new to me. I guess maybe I just don't get around much. I'm somewhat like the little girl who came home from school with a sensational adventure tale to tell.

"Mother," she said breathlessly, "we learned all about Columbus today. He set out from Spain with three little ships, the *Nina,* the *Pinta* and—and—"

"The *Santa Maria,*" prompted her mother.

"Yes, that's right. And the Queen that pawned her jewels and gave him the money to buy the ships was—was—"

"Isabella," said mother.

"Yes," admitted the child, with a sudden suspicion, "but, Mother, have you *heard* this story before?"

THE SPEAKER urges, "Give while you live!"

A rich man said to his minister: "Why is it everybody is always criticizing me for being miserly, when everyone knows that I have made provision to leave everything I possess to charity when I die?"

"Well," said the minister, "let me tell you about the pig and the cow. The pig was lamenting to the cow one day about how unpopular he was. 'People are always talking about your gentleness and your kind eyes,' said the pig. 'Sure, you give milk and cream, but I give even more. I give bacon and ham—I give bristles and they even pickle my feet! Still nobody likes me. I'm just a pig. Why is this?'

"The cow thought a minute, and then said: 'Well maybe it's because I give while I'm still living.' "

THE SPEAKER urges Great Expectations

It isn't merely a catch-phrase, but a well-established truism that we get from life just about what we *expect* to garner. Too often our attitude is that of the Pullman porter who reported to an associate on the results of an excursion: "Well, I didn't get as much in tips as I expected, but then I hardly expected that I would."

Keep your expectations high! The next time you are in a slump recall John Wesley's analysis:

A young Wesley convert had been sent up to North England to preach. After a year, he returned to Wesley, searching for the reason his preaching did not make more converts. Wesley asked him:

"You don't expect to have converts at every meeting, do you?"

"Oh, no," said the young preacher, "not at *every* meeting."

"Then," concluded John Wesley, "*that's* the reason you aren't having more of them!"

THE SPEAKER urges, "Make the most of your time"

Time is about the only commodity that is equitably divided in this uneven world. We each have twenty-four hours a day to spend, and while many of those minutes may be mortgaged, no one can completely cheat us of our inheritance. The problem is to use that time to assure a maximum yield of happiness and satisfaction.

But of course there are practical limits. I would hardly counsel you to go as far as did old man Brown, who made every moment pay on his big farm. One fine haying day he fell into the cistern and his wife, hearing the splash, came running. Poking her head over the rim she yelled, "That you, Arthur?"

"Yup," came the answer. "I just fell in."

"Just hold your hosses!" said his wife. "I'll ring the dinner bell and get the hired men from the field to pull you out."

"What time be it, Mary?" came the gruff voice of her husband.

"Just 11:30."

"No, Mary, don't ring the bell yet. Water's cool and not so bad. I'll just swim around till dinner time."

THE SPEAKER uses statistics

I believe in statistics. I'm going to quote quite a few before I come to the end of this talk. Yes, statistics have their proper place —and we should try to keep them in that place.

A preacher in Georgia had the custom of telling the Lord all the news in his prayers. On one occasion he began a petition for help against the corruption in his town with this statement: "Thou great Jehovah, crime is on the increase. It is becoming more prevalent daily. I can prove it to You by statistics."

THE SPEAKER visits a school

If you are ever called upon to address a group of school children —and want to make a sure hit with them—tell them this "hound dog" story:

I once visited a school where the mascot was a beloved hound dog. I was somewhat surprised to hear the mascot referred to as "Principal."

"Why do you call your mascot by that name?" I asked.

"Well, sir," a student explained, "he just weaves in and out of the rooms all day."

Several years later I returned to the same school and found the same hound dog. But now he was referred to as "Superintendent." I asked about the change of name.

"Oh," said a student, "he's pretty old now; doesn't get around much any more. We call him 'Superintendent' because he just sits in one spot and howls all the time!"

THE SPEAKER warns, "Don't leave it to luck!"

I gravely doubt that a buckeye ever brought a buck to anyone! As for hoarding a rabbit's foot as a talisman against disaster: Well, okay, if you feel that way about it. But, remember, the rabbit had *four* of 'em, and they didn't keep him out of trouble!

THE SPEAKER warns, "Don't outsmart yourself!"

Sales stratagems are great stuff. But they can't take the place of sound, common-sense precautions.

A house-to-house salesman ran the bell of a cheap-looking apartment. As the door opened he tossed in a carefully prepared mudball which disintegrated and made a mess on the front room rug. "Now, don't get excited, lady," he said calmly. "I am demonstrating the Super Duper electric vacuum cleaner. If this little wonder doesn't remove every trace of dirt on your rug, I'll eat the whole mudball!"

The indignant housewife left for the kitchen, returning in a few moments bearing a tray containing a bottle of ketchup, a jar of mustard, salt, pepper—and a rolling pin. She deposited the condiments with elaborate care, then picked up the rolling pin and hefted it expertly.

"But, madam," exclaimed the startled salesman, "I don't understand."

"Start eating!" commanded the housewife. "We ain't got no electricity!"

THE SPEAKER warns of the perils of laying down on the job

If you want a horrible example of what may happen to the guy who lies down on the job, listen to this:

"Yonder," said the Town Oracle, "in the sheltering branches of that oak tree lies the laziest man in this community."

"Oh, now," said the stranger charitably, "you may be too harsh in your judgment. After all it's a hot day. What's the harm of catching a little nap?"

"Nap, heck!" snapped the Oracle. "Do you know how that lazy loafer got up into that tree? Well I'll tell you. Thutty year ago, he laid his'se'f down on an acorn!"

ANECDOTES FOR ALL OCCASIONS

BE IT ever so funny, no anecdote is of any real value to a speaker unless and until he can find a way to use it. The experienced platform artist insists that his stories must fit neatly into an appointed groove. He seeks to avoid that "dragged-in-by-the-heels" appearance. The story must have both point and purpose.

It is to aid in the selection of appropriate stories—stories that make specific points—that we have arranged the bulk of our selections under subject headings. It is understood, of course, that these groupings are arbitrary and that in no sense do they represent the limits of a given story. To illustrate by example: Stories involving the ubiquitous drunk are, with a few exceptions, grouped under the heading: "DRINK—Drinking," yet any single story in that classification may very well serve to illustrate several additional points. To list the entire catalog of possibilities is obviously impracticable since the only limits are set by the searcher's own ingenuity.

In looking for an anecdote to make a specific point, it is our suggestion that you run through the alphabetically arranged subject headings, pausing to scan the stories under those heads which seem rewarding. In this way you will practically always find the story you seek, with an investment of only a few moments.

In addition, we recommend occasional browsing, without fixed plan or purpose. This will bring to light many usable stories which might otherwise be overlooked. And at occasional intervals you may find it worth your while, as a memory-refreshing measure, to read the anecdotes in this entire section quite methodically. In this connection, we may suggest a time-saving technique: Read the final or "point" lines of each story *first*. Thus you can determine quickly whether the anecdote is a familiar one. Do not, however, discard a good story simply because you have heard it before. Every platform veteran knows that he is likely to get his loudest laughs from his oldest gags.

ABSENT-MINDEDNESS

Then there was the absent-minded professor who sent his wife to the bank and kissed his money good-by.

And second thought, he wasn't absent-minded.

ABSENT-MINDED PROFESSOR

You have all read jokes about the absent-minded professor. Well, I'm married to one, says a lady of our acquaintance, and its no joke, though the experience does provide amusing interludes.

Among other things, my husband has difficulty in remembering the color of his current toothbrush and which towels and washcloths have been assigned to him. After several futile reminders that the blue linens were for his particular use, I had an inspiration: "Let's make up a jingle," I suggested, " 'Baby blue, that's for you.' Remember that and all will be well."

A couple of mornings later I was obliged to bring up the matter again. "Charles," I chided, "I'm afraid you've forgotten our little jingle."

"Certainly not," he replied stiffly. "Recited it just this morning, 'Baby blue, that's for you.' So I left them for you and used the yellow ones."

ABUNDANCE

Two Negro soldiers were on a transport going overseas. Standing on the deck they gazed out across the vast expanse of water. "That's the mos' water I've eber seen in all my life," said one. "Did yo' eber see so much water?"

Said his companion: "Yo' ain't see nothin' yet. That's jus' the top ob it."

"ACCIDENTALLY ON PURPOSE"

Dinah Shore tells this one: While we were in France entertaining the GI's, I was dining one night at mess with some officers. We were having steak and it was very tough.

Noticing my struggles, the colonel apologized. "I know it's tough," he said, "but my orderly chased that cow ten miles before she would step on a mine!"

ACCIDENT—Prevention

An automobile accident resulted in the death of the driver and the injury of two passengers.

The coroner summoned several witnesses, among them a farmer living near the scene of the accident. There was voluminous testimony regarding the high speed at which the car traveled. Witnesses said, too, that the road was in bad need of repair. The coroner finally reached the farmer who lived near the scene.

"What would you say about this accident, Mr. Swiggert?" the coroner asked.

"Well, if I was writin' that young man's epitaph," the witness drawled, "I'd say he died tryin' to get sixty miles out of a ten mile road."

ACCOMPLISHMENT—Questioned

An old grouch had a son in Cornell. At the end of the first year the son came home in high feather. He stood second in his class. "Second," said the old man. "Second! Why didn't you stand first? What do you think I'm sending you to Cornell for?"

The young man returned for his second year, determined to win first place. At the end of the year he went home and announced his standing to his father. The father looked at him a few minutes in silence, then shrugged his shoulders, and said:

"At the head of the class, eh? Well, Cornell can't be much of a university after all!"

ACCURACY

"That crater is 70,004 years old," he explained.

"How do you get the exact age?" asked the newcomer. "I can understand the 70,000, but how do you calculate the four?"

"Well, I've been here in the islands for four years, and that crater was 70,000 years old when I arrived."

❖   ❖

A surveyor, working around an Army post on the edge of a western town, became acquainted with the soldier who fired the cannon for retreat each evening. The surveyor questioned the soldier: "Do you fire this cannon at the same time each evening?"

"Yes," the soldier replied. "At 6:00 o'clock on the dot, and I time it carefully with this watch. I check it every day by the jeweler's clock, about two blocks from here."

Several days later, the surveyor . . . entered the jeweler's shop and began talking to him. "That's a mighty fine clock you have there," he said, indicating the prominent time-piece in the window.

"It keeps perfect time," answered the jeweler. "In fact, that clock hasn't varied a second for two years."

"That's really a wonderful record."

"Yes, and we have a perfect check on it too. Every evening at exactly 6:00 o'clock, they fire a cannon over at the Fort and this clock is always right on the dot."

✧ ✧

Roscoe, the Rookie, scored a bulls-eye on his first attempt at rifle practice, but the other nine shots didn't even leave a mark on the target.

"How do you account for these misses?" barked the sergeant. "That first one must have been beginner's luck."

"Sorry, sergeant," apologized Roscoe. "I thought I had to get all the bullets through the same hole!"

ACHIEVEMENT—In Moderation

The eight year old niece of a well-known suffrage worker has the optimism of the family to which she belongs. When asked if she had passed her examination in arithmetic, she answered cheerfully, "No, I did not, but I was the highest of those who failed."

ACTION

In the long run, it is useless to shout louder than you act.

✧ ✧

Arthur and Mary were ensconced on a suitably placed seat in a park. For a time there was a silence, and then Arthur sighed: "I wish I were an octopus." "Whatever for?" asked Mary. "Because I should then have eight arms to hold you with," returned her companion. Again there was a lengthy silence broken at last by Mary. "Why don't you use the two you have?"

✧ ✧

At the monthly meeting of the Brookside Garden Club, Molalla, Oregon, members were asked to report on "What I should be doing at home this afternoon instead of attending the club."

When the gathering ended, the ladies voted to skip their next scheduled meeting.

ACUMEN

The Englishman wanted to know the Yankee's secret for getting ahead in business.

"I'll tell you," said the Yankee. "You should eat more fish. Fish is brain food. Give me five dollars and I'll get you some of the fish my wife gets me. Eat it and then see how you get on."

The Englishman forked over the five. The fish was duly delivered. Next day the two met and the Yankee asked whether any improvement had been noted.

"Well, no," said the Englishman regretfully. "But tell me, old chap, isn't five dollars quite a lot for a small piece of fish?"

"There, now!" beamed the Yankee. "Already your brain is beginning to work!"

ADULT—Responsibility

A boy of eight years had been given a beautiful globe in the hope that it would increase his interest in geography. The little fellow became so interested in it the first evening that, when that time came for retiring, he took it to his room and set it on the table by the head of his bed. Some time later, in the belief that the youngster was asleep, his father tiptoed in, picked up the globe, and was carrying it out to the light. As he did so, the lad roused up and said, "Hey, Dad, what are you doing with my world?"

ADVERSITY

Trouble teaches us two things: who our friends really are, and who have been waiting to catch us bent over at the right angle.

❖　❖

Every day the world turns over on someone who has just been sitting on top of it.

ADVERTISING

Two million Americans never saw an elephant. That's why the circus will come back next year.

That's why the same old elephant walks serenely confident that among every bored group of people who say, "That's just an elephant," some eager voice will shout, "Oh! that's an elephant!"

And so when you talk your business you are not talking to a grandstand, but rather to a parade that is constantly moving with new faces—new buyers—coming into the picture every day.

❖ ❖

The sales manager of a very reputable firm held up an order book. "This," he said, "is the thing that put business on the books of our company year after year." And then turning to the advertising manager, he asked, "Can you show me a single order that advertising ever put on my order book?"

"I think I can answer your question," replied the advertising executive, "if you will first answer one of mine. Will you show me a single load of hay that the sun ever put in a barn?"

ADVICE

Max Gordon, the theatrical producer, is noted for his efforts to get free advice. No matter whom he meets—he had a question to ask. At a recent party he was introduced to a "Dr. Smith."

"It's a funny thing, Doc," Gordon observed. "Some people say I have a flutter in my heart, and others say I haven't. If you could just listen for a moment . . ."

"Hey," interrupted a guest, "Dr. Smith isn't a physician—he's a professor of Economics!"

"Is that so?" exclaimed Gordon, completely unperturbed. "Well, then, tell me, Doc, do you think American Car & Foundry is a good buy?"

❖ ❖

The one vice all of us shun is advice. But once a man advertised that for $1 he would send a bit of sound practical advice that would be applicable to any time of life, to any business or to any activity. A reader who sent in his dollar received a card on which was printed: "Never give a boy a quarter to watch your shadow while you climb a tree to look into the middle of next week. It doesn't pay."

AGE—Feminine

The seven ages of woman—the infant, the little girl, the miss, the young woman, the young woman, the young woman, the young woman.

AGE—YOUTH

An aged woman was compelled to testify as a witness in a lawsuit.

Asked to tell her age, she appealed to the judge. "Do I have to tell that?"

"Why, yes, madam," replied the judge. "It's a proper question, and at your time of life you surely need not be sensitive about your age."

"Well," she answered reluctantly, "I'm 97."

"Now, madam," interposed the judge, "that admission didn't hurt much, did it?"

"Oh, yes, it did, judge," was the embarrassed reply. "You see, everybody thinks I'm 100."

❖ ❖

Once when Clarence Darrow was a fledgling lawyer beginning his career, he was opposed in court by a veteran attorney who, during the course of the trial repeatedly and insultingly referred to Darrow as "that beardless youth."

At length Darrow rejoined: "My opponent seems to condemn me for not having a beard. Let me reply with a story. The King of Spain once dispatched a youthful nobleman to a court of a neighboring king, who received the visitor with the outraged complaint: 'Does the King of Spain lack men, that he sends me a beardless boy?' To which the ambassador rejoined, 'Sir, if my

King had supposed you imputed wisdom to a beard he would have sent you a goat.' " Darrow won the case.

✧ ✧

Discussing his tennis technique Jack Goodman tells of a stout, amiable bald man who panted, "My brain immediately barks out a command to my body. 'Run forward speedily!' it says. 'Start right away! Lob the ball gracefully over their heads, and then walk slowly back to receive your partner's congratulations.' "

"And then what happens?" he was asked.

"And then," replied the bald man, "my body says: 'Who, me?' "

✧ ✧

The five-year-old who has succeeded in taking a simple toy apart and putting the pieces back together again, declares with boyish enthusiasm, "Daddy, I know how to do everything!"

"If you want the real low-down on just any old thing, ask me!" confidently advises the jaunty youth of twenty.

"If it's in my line, maybe I can tell you. I know my business from A to Z," says the man of thirty-five.

"The field of human knowledge is so vast that even a specialist can hardly have more than a speaking acquaintance with the more important facts of his subject," admits the man of fifty.

"I have lived a good many years," confesses the man of seventy, "but I haven't learned much. What I know is very little; what I am ignorant of is immense."

✧ ✧

The old say: "I remember when . . ." The young say, "What's the news?"

✧ ✧

"Look at me," spieled the patent-medicine quack, "I am 300 years old, and hale and hearty—all from taking this miraculous potion."

"Is he really that old?" asked a somewhat skeptical lady to the faker's youthful assistant.

"Lady, you'll have to ask somebody else," said the lad with a fine display of candor, "I've only worked for him 100 years."

❖ ❖

Asked why he was going to marry a glamor girl from the city instead of some woman his own age, Grandpappy opined: "I'd a heap ruther smell perfume than liniment!"

❖ ❖

The old lady had passed her ninetieth birthday, but her face was serene and unlined as that of a child. Life's troubles had left no mark on her and the new minister was admiring and curious.

"What," he asked "has been the chief source of your strength and sustenance all these years?"

The old lady raised her head. A sweet smile was on her lips, her eyes glowed with fond memories as she answered simply:

"Victuals."

❖ ❖

Claude Rains, well-known actor, is amused by a story told of that illustrious jurist, the late Justice Oliver Wendell Holmes. Out strolling with an associate one afternoon, the nonagenarian and his companion passed an intriguing young damsel. Wistfully the Justice turned for a lingering glance. "Ah," he said, "Ah, to be seventy again!"

ALIBI

The culprit, arrested for speeding stood before the judge, who asked the man if he had an alibi for his action.

"Yes, Your Honor. My wife's church was having a rummage sale, and I was hurrying home to save my other pair of pants."

❖ ❖

A certain not-too-trustworthy Negro contractor in the deep South was making some repairs on a church for a colored congregation.

A deacon dropped by to inspect the work. All went well until

the deacon chanced to see a plumb line fastened to a corner of
the roof. His eye followed the line on its downward course, and
he turned to the contractor in some perplexity.

"Look heah," he questioned, "dat buildin' 'pears to' be leanin'.
Jes' take a look at dat plumb line!"

"Oh, no, sah, Deacon," protested the contractor. "No, sah, dat
buildin' okay. Hit jes' an old plumb line what ain't reliable."

❖   ❖

He had arrived home late, and was being told all about it by
his wife. At last he lost his temper, too, and said a few things back.

"I don't care," he said. "I mean exactly what I say. I'm a man
who calls a spade a spade."

His wife snorted. "Maybe, James," she said icily, "you do call
a spade a spade, but you don't call a club a club—you call that
working late at the office."

❖   ❖

Pfc Harold Gordon, orderly room clerk, asked the first sergeant
for permission to take a short break to attend to a very important
but mysterious personal matter. He returned in a quarter of an
hour with red smudges around his mouth. When the top kick
pointed this out Gordon thought for a moment and said, "My
Good Conduct Ribbon must have run."

❖   ❖

A certain worker in a war plant was almost invariably tardy in
the morning. His foreman finally took him to task. "Jim," he
asked, "how is it that you are always late? You live right next to
the plant. Tom, over there, who has to travel quite a distance is
always on time."

"Well," said Jim reflectively, "if Tom's a bit late in the morning
he can always hurry, but if I'm late, I'm here."

❖   ❖

Two rabid Californians, during a heavy rainstorm in Los Angeles, watched the downpour with embarrassed expressions. Fi-

nally, after a deep silence, one said to the other: "Boy, some terrible weather certainly blows in from Nevada, doesn't it?"

❖   ❖

Friend of ours, who has had the same Negro cook for twenty years, is given to bragging on the culinary skill of her treasure. But recently, at company dinner, the biscuits were a flat failure.

The embarrassed hostess apologized profusely. Later, she took the cook to task.

"Well, ma'am," Mandy replied, "I sho' is regretful, but 'pears lak it couldn't be he'ped. Dem biscuits squated t' rise, but dey got cooked in de squat."

ALLERGY

The speaker was much annoyed by a man in his audience who coughed and sneezed and blew his nose almost constantly. Finally, the speaker could stand it no longer. As politely as he could he suggested to the brother who was having so much discomfort that a visit to the open air might be good for his cold.

"I haven't any cold," came the answer. "I'm just allergic to applesauce."

ALL OUT

"Marse" Henry Watterson, owner and publisher of the Louisville Courier-Journal in the old days, was the despair of his accounting department. When he needed a bit of spending money the old gentleman had a habit of going downstairs to the business office, opening the cash drawer and taking what he wanted.

Finally a young bookkeeper, after spending hours trying to balance the records, exacted a promise from the penitent "Marse" Henry. "All right young fellow" he said, "the next time I take out money, I'll put in a slip."

True to his word, Mr. Watterson, on his next foraging expedition, duly filled out and deposited a memo. It said eloquently: "Took it all!"

ALTITUDE

On week-end leave, a soldier attended a movie house in the city near camp. He was taken in tow by an usher who led him skyward on ramp after ramp to the floor level of the top balcony, where he stopped and pointed upward into the grayness. "You'll find a seat up there somewhere. This is as far up as I go. Above this level, my nose bleeds."

AMBITION

The itching sensation that some people mistake for ambition is is merely inflammation of the wishbone.

❖   ❖

A Negro sharecropper had raised a fair crop of cotton. He took it to town and turned it over to a merchant on his account. When the settlement was made he had $40 to his credit. The merchant counted out four $10 bills.

As the old man started to put the money in a worn tobacco sack, the merchant said, "Mose, that's no way to carry money; let me wrap it up for you."

The darkey handed over four $10 bills, which the merchant wrapped in a neat little package and returned. That evening, after supper, the old man drew his chair up to the fireplace and turned to his precious package. Upon unwrapping the money, he could find only three bills. For a long time he sat, miserably reflecting, then he philosophically opined: "They's trick in all trades, but I reckon I'd ruther be a good 'money-wropper' than mos' anything."

AMERICANA

Donald Nelson once told this story of a new school in China. An instructor called one of the children and asked: "Can you describe an American?"

"An American," the child answered, "is a man who has two legs and four wheels."

❖ ❖

Camping on an especially muddy locale, several of our soldiers in Italy appropriated a stack of straw from a nearby farmyard to serve as flooring for their tents.

Later a gesticulating Italian farmer appeared and demanded payment. Unable to make themselves understood, one of the soldiers took a scrap of paper from his pocket and very carefully wrote something on it. This satisfied the complainant for the moment, but the next day he was back looking for il capitano.

The paper had been inscribed, "Good for 100 rides on the merry-go-round at Coney Island."

❖ ❖

An Englishman and an American were presented to the ruler of one of the small Eastern countries. On looking over the Englishman's passport, the dusky monarch said:

"I see, sir, that you are a British subject."

"I am, sir."

"And you, sir, are a subject of the United States?"

"Subject, hell!" the American shouted. "I own part of the United States!"

ANCESTRY

A bigot was trying to brush off Max Mefofsky and exploded: "One of my ancestors signed the Declaration of Independence!"

"Oh, nertz," yelled Max. "One of my ancestors signed the Ten Commandments!"

❖ ❖

A Mayflower descendant once asked an acquaintance: "Were your ancestors Pilgrims?"

"No," was the acidulous reply, "my forebears came over when the immigration laws were more stringent."

ANGER

Men are like steel. When they lose their temper they are worthless.

ANTICIPATION

A comely colored girl had just been baptized in the river. As she came to the surface she cried, "Bless de Lawd, I'se saved! Las' night I was in de ahms of Satan, but tonight I'm in de ahms of de Lawd!"

"Sistuh," came a baritone voice from the shore. "How is yo' fixed up for tomorrow ebening?"

ANTIQUITY

A tourist with a mania for collecting, passed through a small village one day. He stopped to watch a very old man chopping wood with a very old ax.

"That's an old ax you have there," he remarked.

"Yes," said the old man, "it once belonged to George Washington."

"Indeed, I should hardly have thought it as old as that."

"Well," the old man said, "it ain't exactly. It's had three new handles and two new heads since then."

APPEARANCES—Deceptive

Although straws usually tell which way the wind blows, occasionally even the proverbial straw proves misleading.

Previous to entering the railroad yard, an able-bodied loafer picked up a small, glittering object from the sidewalk and, without examining it very closely, pinned it to his coat. Three minutes later he collided with a slowly moving freight train, was hurled against a post, and picked up insensible.

The train dispatcher, notified by telephone, called up Patrick Doyle, the yardmaster's assistant, and said:

"You'd better search his pockets, Doyle. Find out who he is, notify his friends, and report to me."

A few moments later the report came.

"There's not a line of writing on him," said Patrick, "but we've identified him by the badge on his coat. He's a Lady Maccabee."

APPETITE

Someone asked a little boy to define the word "appetite." His answer was prompt: "When you're eating. you're 'appy. When you get through, you're tight, that's appetite!"

APPRECIATION

Emily Kimbrough (author of *How Dear To My Heart*) had just made an ingratiating speech at a Philadelphia Book & Author luncheon. A waiter brought her a note from her nine year old daughter.

"Appreciated in my own home at last," murmured Mrs. Kimbrough happily, as she unfolded the note. It read: "You were pretty good, Mummy. Can I go to the dentist now?"

APPRECIATION—Self

It is interesting to note that when God made man he didn't arrange any of the joints of his bones so he could pat himself on the back.

APPROPRIATE

Robert St. John, the author, was standing in the lobby of the NBC studios, in Chicago's Merchandise Mart, where his luxuriant beard attracted considerable attention.

A woman visitor asked a page the identity of the owner of that hirsute splendor.

"That's St. John," she was told.

"Um-m," mused the visitor, turning again to the beard. "Here for the Baptist Convention, I presume."

APTITUDE TESTS

The general had been without a secretary for weeks. The Establishments Branch notified him that their psychologist was going to examine several candidates and perhaps he'd like to come down and watch.

The psychologist called in the first girl and said sharply, "What's two and two?" The girl replied promptly, "Four." The second girl thought for a moment, suspecting a catch, said, "Twenty-two." The third applicant answered, "Four, but it could be twenty-two."

After they had gone, the psychologist turned to the general. "Those tests were very revealing. The first girl has a conventional mind. To her, two and two is always four. The second girl has imagination. She realized it might be twenty-two. The third girl is a combination of both. She's practical and at the same time has imagination. Clearly she will make the best secretary. Now, which would you like?"

The general said without hesitation, "I'll have the one with blond hair."

ARBITRATION

He was a man of peace, and when he came upon two youths fighting in a back street he pushed through the crowd and persuaded the comrades to desist.

"Let me beg you, my good fellows," he said, "to settle your dispute by arbitration. Each of you choose half-a-dozen friends to arbitrate."

Having seen the twelve arbitrators selected to the satisfaction of both sides, the man of peace went on his way. Half an hour later he returned, and was horrified to find the whole street fighting.

"Good gracious, what's the matter now?" he asked.

"Sure, sorr," was the reply, "the arbitrators are at work."

ARGUMENT

A certain man was the most constant arguer in the community. Whatever anyone said he disagreed with it. But one day . . . one of the loungers at the crossroads store in the course of a meandering conversation, remarked, "I've heard tell that Cy Smith over at Boomtown was one of nineteen sons."

The words were no sooner said than the arguer laughed and

sneered: "That's whar ye heard wrong, then," he said. "Twa'n't Cy Smith at all. 'Twas a brother o' his'n."

❖ ❖

One of the justices of the Supreme Court tells of a young lawyer in the West who was trying his first case before Justice Harlan. The youthful attorney had evidently conned his argument until he knew it by heart. Before he had consumed ten minutes in his oratorical effort the justice had decided the case in his favor and told him so. Despite this, the young lawyer would not cease. It seemed that he had attained such a momentum that he could not stop.

Finally Justice Harlan leaned forward and, in the politest of tones, said:

"Mr. Smith, despite your arguments, the court has concluded to decide this case in your favor."

❖ ❖

"The less a thing can be proved the madder people get when they argue about it."

❖ ❖

Many an argument is sound—just sound.

ARMY—Discipline

The colonel was lecturing a class of incipient officers. "A 40-ft. flagpole has fallen down," he said. "You have a sergeant and a squad of ten men. How do you erect the flagpole again?"

The candidates offered suggestions involving a block-and-tackle, derrick, and so on.

"You're all wrong," replied the seasoned officer. "You'd say, 'Sergeant, get that flagpole up.' "

A SLOW ONE

This is what might be termed a "slow burner." It brings a laugh if you give the "customers" time to get it:

There was an old-fashioned pawn shop with a pile of cheap suitcases in front of it. The suitcases were packed pyramid-style, with a big one at the base, a little one on top. An impecunious wanderer paused to view the display. His eye strayed to a sign on the top case: "This size for 50 cents." Thrusting his hand into an empty pocket, he said feelingly, "And so do I!"

ATHEISM

The Portuguese tell with glee the story of the man who, at the period when Alfonso Costa announced that henceforth there was to be no more religion and the people were no longer to believe in God or go to church, stood in a public square announcing his pleasure in this edict with the following words: "I am more than glad that I no longer need go to church. I no longer believe in God; I am an atheist and from now on I intend always to be an atheist, please God."

❖   ❖

The atheist is a man who has no invisible means of support.

❖   ❖

The infidel assured the Quaker he would believe in God if he ever saw him, but not otherwise.

"Does thee believe in Spain?" inquired the Quaker.

"Sure," replied the unbeliever, "but, although I have not seen that country myself, I know several people who have."

"Did thee ever see thy own brains, or anybody that ever did see them?" the Quaker asked.

"No," said the other, "but that's different."

"Does thee believe thee has any?" asked the defender of the faith.

❖   ❖

Voltaire, the French atheist, lost no opportunity to scoff at religion. On one occasion, dining with the King of Prussia, he concluded, "I would sell my place in heaven for a Prussian dollar."

"Monsieur de Voltaire," observed a stout burgomaster, who was present, "in Prussia we never buy costly goods without feeling sure of the owner's right to them. If you can prove your right to a place in heaven, I will buy it for $10,000."

For once the quick-witted atheist had no reply.

ATOMIC AGE

The scientists don't seem to be sure whether splitting the atom was a wise crack.

❖   ❖

It is the year 1965. The atomic bomb has come actively into our world and laid it waste. Man has vanished from the face of the earth. And with him have gone the creatures great and small. Throughout the universe there is no stirring sign of life. No sign save one.

From a deep, dark cavern in a remote corner of the continent of Africa, two small animals emerge to stare in blinking awe at the wreck and ruin. Scratching his head reflectively, the boy monkey turns presently to his mate. "Well," he says in a tone of deep resignation, "let's start over again!"

❖   ❖

On a beautiful starlit night, Einstein was strolling the Princeton Promenade. He looked up at the sky and said, with a weary sigh: "Anyway, THAT the atom cannot destroy!"

❖   ❖

Idealists maintain that all nations should share the atomic bomb. Pessimists maintain that they will.

❖   ❖

The Nashville Tennessean presents this allegory which parodies rather uncomfortably the attitude of some of our statesmen in relation to the atomic bomb:

"We can imagine that the caveman who discovered fire called in his family and said:

"'We have a secret that none other shares. It gives us great power and protection. We must sit on it because if our neighbors were to find it out they would be as powerful as we are. They haven't the brains to figure out how to strike one stone on another to get a spark; moreover, they haven't as many stones as we have to strike together. It would be folly to pass this knowledge around.'"

AVARICE

Mark this earnest declaration of an English statesman, speaking in Parliament: "Sir, put these men on an uninhabited island and they would not have been there an hour before they would have their hands in the pockets of the naked savages!"

AVERAGE MAN

The average man, as his neighbors see him:

If he is poor, he is a bad manager. If he is prosperous, everyone wants to do him a favor.

If he is in politics, it's for pork. If he is not in politics, one can't place him, and he is no good for his country.

If he gives not to charity, then he's a stingy dog. If he does give, it's for show.

If he is active in religion, he's a hypocrite. If he evinces no interest in matters spiritual, he's a hardened sinner.

If he shows affection, he's a soft sentimentalist. If he seems to care for no one, he's cold-blooded.

If he dies young, there was a great future ahead of him. If he attains old age, he has missed his calling.

AVIATION

Aunt Melissa's definition of a paratrooper:

"He's a soldier what climbs down trees he never clumb up!"

AWKWARDNESS

They were dancing. The music was heavenly. The swish of her silken skirts was divine. The fragrance of the roses upon her dress was intoxicating.

"Ah," she smiled sweetly, with an arch look up into his face, "you remind me of one of Whitman's poems."

A sudden dizziness seemed to seize him. It was as if he were floating in a dream. When he had sufficiently gained his breath he spoke:

"Which one?"

"Oh, any one," she replied. "The feet are mixed in all of them."

BANQUETS

A student for the ministry wrote the following after an experience with a certain church. "Behold! . . . The club clubbeth together and they eat. The businessmen take counsel and they eat. And even when the missionary society meeteth together they eat. But this latter is in good cause, because they 'eat in remembrance' of the poor heathen who hath not to eat. Behold! Hath man's brains gone to his stomach and doth he no longer regard intellectual dainties that thou canst no longer call an assembly or get together even a 'bakers' dozen' except thou hold up the baker's dainties as a bait? Be it true, that the day cometh that to get a crowd at prayer meeting the preacher must hold up a biscuit? Even as one calleth unto the child and saith, 'Come hither, sweet little one, and I will give thee a stick of candy,' so must thou say to his grown-up papa and mama. 'Assemble ye together and we will serve refreshments.' And lo, they come like sheep into a pen. Selah."

✧　✧

Banquets have killed more people than bullets. The latter punch holes into you from the outside; banquets punch holes on your inside, right through the lining of the stomach. Death by bullet is speedier, less painful.

✧　✧

The great American institution, the banquet, is an affair where a speaker first eats a lot of food he doesn't want and then proceeds to talk about something he doesn't understand to a lot of people who don't want to hear him.

✧　✧

"One of the tragedies of life," said Channing Pollock, at a banquet in honor of a famous theatrical man, "is the fact that no one ever gives us a dinner until we don't need it."

BAPTISM

In an eastern city a pastor of a colored Baptist church consulted a plumber and steamfitter about the cost of putting in a baptistry. The estimate was soon furnished and the figure was regarded as satisfactory.

"But," said the plumber, "this covers only the tank and the water supply. Of course, you will want some sort of an arrangement to heat the water."

But the colored pastor had a truly economic idea in mind, and his own ideas of religion also, for he promptly dissented.

"You see," said he to the plumber, "I don't 'low to baptize nobody in that there baptistry what hain't got religion enough to keep him warm."

❖   ❖

Although late March, the day of the Baptism at Miller's dam was cold and the preacher had to break the ice for the ceremony.

"Is the water cold, John?" asked a deacon of one of the new members stepping ashore after his immersion.

"No, not a bit cold," replied John.

"Better put him under again, parson," advised the deacon. "He hasn't quit lying yet."

❖   ❖

A Negro spinster of uncertain years decided at long last to join the church—the Baptist Church.

As the deacons plunged her into the river the first time she gasped "I believe." The second time, she chattered, "I believe." A third time, gulping for air, she sputtered, "I believe." One of the elders interposed: "You believe what, sister?" She eyed him savagely: "I believe you stinkers are trying to drown me."

BEAUTY—Appreciation

A botanist in Scotland was scrutinizing a common heather bell under his microscope. An old shepherd, curious to know what was going on, was shown the beauty of the simple flower. He raised his head after a moment. "Mon, I wish ye had never shown it to me. I have trodden on so many of those beautiful things."

BEHAVIOR

The youthful mountaineer had just been brought into court and sentenced for breach of the peace. Testimony showed that he had done some feuding, featured by his adept handling of a knife.

After the trial, his grizzled old father stood with a group of cronies on the courthouse lawn. "I swear," he said, "I don't know whar that boy gits all his meanness. Now, you take me—I never stuck a knife deep in nobody."

BIBLE

At a meeting of the Council of books for our men in the armed forces, someone suggested printing a service edition of The Ten Commandments (a collection of short stories, each based on a Scriptural precept).

"It is much too long," objected one director.

"In that case," suggested Philip Van Doren Stern brightly, "we might select five and call it a 'Treasury of The World's Best Commandments.'"

❖ ❖

A minister taught an old man in his parish to read, from the Bible. He proved a proficient scholar. After the teaching had come to an end, the minister was not able to call at the cottage for some time and when he did, he found only the wife at home. "How's John?" he said.

"Fine," said the wife.

"How does he get on with his reading?"

"Nicely, sir."

"I suppose he can read his Bible easily now?"

"Bible, sir, bless you. He is out of the Bible and into the news-paper, long ago."

❖ ❖

Little Timothy had bought Grandma a Bible for Christmas and wanted to write a suitable inscription on the fly-leaf. He racked his brain until suddenly he remembered that his father had a book with an inscription of which he was very proud. So Tim decided to copy it.

You can imagine Grandma's surprise on Christmas morning when she opened her gift, a Bible, and found neatly inscribed the following phrase: "To Grandma, with the compliments of the Author."

✧ ✧

Someone has suggested that if all the neglected Bibles were dusted simultaneously, we would have a record dust storm and the sun would go into eclipse for a whole week!

✧ ✧

Roger Babson likes to weave religious paragraphs into his talks. At one meeting of business men he quoted the Ten Commandments verbatim.

After the dinner one of the guests rushed up to the head table to tell him how helpful that quotation would be if it were only printed and distributed. "Wherever did you get it?" asked the eager and appreciative listener. "Do you know if it is copyrighted?"

BIBLE—Attacks

Voltaire boasted his work would make the Bible extinct in 100 years. Recently his 92 volumes sold for $2.

BIBLE—History

A young minister who had been taking what his congregation deemed undue liberties in the "modernizing" of Scriptural text, was waited upon by a committee representing the conservative element in the church. He was told quite plainly that the group would approve of no streamlined Scripture. "What we want," said the spokesman, "is to hear the Bible read just as it was originally written, with nothing added to or taken away."

"Very well," agreed the minister, "I shall be glad to comply."

The following Sabbath he read a passage from the Old Testament in Hebrew, followed by a chapter from the New Testament in the original Greek!

BIBLE—Interpretation

Dr. Ralph Sockman in a recent radio sermon gave a new interpretation of the familiar words of Jesus: "Joy shall be in heaven over one sinner that repenteth more than over ninety and nine just persons who need no repentance." "I don't think Jesus meant," explained Dr. Sockman, "that a repentant sinner is worth ninety-nine good men. No! I might interpret the passage this way—that there is more fun in catching a live trout than in caring for a lot of frozen fish."

❖ ❖

A colored sexton was asked how he liked the new Georgia pastor.

"I spects I don't like him very much."

"And why not? I hear he is a brilliant scholar."

"Maybe. He sho is smart in some ways and then, agin, not smart. He's de greates' man I ebber know'd to take de Bible apart; but he don't know how to put it togedder agin."

BIBLE—Lore

In a western town a man who had come into possession of a considerable fortune decided to erect a large office building. During his discussion of the plans with an architect, the latter said:

"As to the floors, now. You would want them in mosaic patterns, I presume?"

"I don't know about that," replied the other dubiously. "I ain't got any prejudice against Moses as a man, and he certainly knew a good deal about law; but when it comes to having floors, it kind o' seems to me I'd rather have 'em unsectarian like. Don't it strike you that way?"

❖ ❖

The itinerant minister serving a small rural community failed to arrive at the time for beginning the usual service. One of the waiting congregation, a local farmer, rich in grace but meager of education, was eventually persuaded to officiate as a substitute. The lesson was the chapter from the book of Daniel which contains the oft-recurring passage: "At what time ye shall hear the sound of the cornet, flute, harp, sackbut, psaltery and dulcimer, and all kinds of music."

Three times the farmer, with evident trepidation, waded through the comprehensive catalogue of ancient Babylonian instruments. When, however, he again came to "At what time ye shall hear," he paused for a moment, wiped the perspiration from his brow, and then continued: "It's the same old band again, friends. Ah needn't read 'em out."

❖   ❖

Two men were arguing furiously over something and one of them said: "Listen, Bill. You don't agree with anything or anybody. I'll bet you don't even endorse the Ten Commandments." The other one replied casually: "Well, you make one small change in them and I'll go right along with them." "What small change do you want made?" And the pessimist said: "Just strike out that word 'not' all the way through."

❖   ❖

Paul au Chaillu, the one-time African explorer, performed a good Samaritan act one night—assisting along the street an intoxicated stranger. The man told him where his home was, and after considerable difficulty Chaillu got him to his door. The bibulous one was grateful, and wanted to know his helper's name. As the explorer did not particularly care to give his name in full, he merely replied that it was Paul.

"So it'sh—hic—Paul, ish it?" hiccuped the man, and then after some moments of apparent thought, inquired solicitously:

"Shay, ole' man, did y' ever git any—hic—ansher to those lo-ong lettersh y' wrote to th' Ephesians?"

❖   ❖

Two girlhood friends were exchanging confidences over their afternoon tea.

"I saw you in church, dear, yesterday," murmured the younger one.

"Oh, you were there? I didn't see you," gurgled the other.

"Yes. And I was so glad to see that you finally induced your husband to accompany you to divine worship."

"Yes, Frank came along with me. He'd much rather go to the theater, but the theaters are not showing anything on Sundays now. But he disgraced me."

"Really? In church? How, pray?"

"The minister read four chapters from 'The Acts of the Apostles,' and my husband insisted on going out after every act."

❖ ❖

A group of first graders was asked by their teacher to draw an imaginary picture of anything they wished. One paper turned in contained a picture of a fine big car. An old man, with long whiskers flying in the breeze, was driving, and two people, a man and a woman, were seated in the back seat. The little six-year-old, after being asked to explain, said: "Why that is God. He is driving Adam and Eve out of the Garden of Eden."

❖ ❖

Upon their return from Europe a movie producer and his frau were telling a writer about the painting of Adam and Eve and the Serpent in the Louvre. "You see," gushed Mrs. M P, "we found it especially interesting because we knew the anecdote!"

❖ ❖

A few months ago the agent for the Bible Society in Mukden, China, received this letter from a Chinese gentleman living in a distant Manchurian city. He wrote, "My son is going to the big city to college. He will be studying English there. Has the Bible been translated into English? If so, I would like to give him a copy in that language."

❖ ❖

It was part of the services for the congregation to repeat the Twenty-Third Psalm in concert, and one lady with a loud voice was about twelve words ahead. A stranger at the services asked about her.

"Who was that lady who was already by the still waters while the rest of us were lying down in green pastures?"

❖ ❖

A ten-year-old, under the guidance of his grandmother, is becoming something of a Bible student. The other evening he floored the assembly at dinner with the question, "Which virgin was Christ's mother—The Virgin Mary or the King James virgin?"

BIG STUFF

Back in the old days when every producer was a character, there was one who resolved to film the life story of Napoleon, in a truly spectacular way. Everything was to be on a grand scale.

Presently, the casting director began interviewing actors to play the title role. He sorted out the most promising and sent them in, one by one, to the producer.

After he had talked to the whole lot, the producer, disappointed and somewhat hot under the collar, summoned the casting director.

"I am not un'nerstanding it," said the exasperated big shot. "Here we are meking big plans—a colossal picture already—and you are sanding me positively the shortest ectors in Hollywood!"

BIG WORDS

The superintendent recently called upon a visitor to "say a few words" to the Sunday school, the members of which were mostly children of tender age.

The speaker, well known for his verbose and circumlocutory manner of speech, began his address as follows:

"This morning, children, I offer you an epitome of the life of St. Paul. Some of you may be too young to grasp the meaning of the word 'epitome.' It is in its signification synonymous with synopsis."

✧   ✧

Two colored men were discussing the eloquence of a certain member of the faculty of an educational institution for negroes.

"That Professor Biggs sure do like to use high-soundin' words, don't he?" asked one of them.

"Maybe dat's jest an affection on his part," said the other darky. "Some folks do like to put on airs in talkin'."

"No, I don't figure it out dat way," said the other. "I kinder thinks he uses them big words because he's afraid dat if people knew what he was talkin' about they'd know he didn't know what he was talkin' about."

BLAME—Shifted

A Jewish businessman was persuaded to use a dictaphone on a trial basis, and if he liked it, he could buy it. The next day the dictaphone representative called at his office and asked him how the machine was.

"Vell, I'll tell you," said the customer, "it ain't so bed, bott it tuks mit a awful hexent."

BLAME—Shifting

Man is inclined, when in the wrong, to lay the blame on some one else. He is like the small boy who was standing on his cat's tail. The mother, hearing the terrible outburst, called from an adjoining room: "Tommie, stop pulling that cat's tail!"

"I'm not pulling the cat's tail; I'm standing on it. He's the one that's doing the pulling."

BLUNDER

Two men left a banquet together; they had dined exceptionally well.

"When you get home," said one, "if you don't want to disturb your family, undress at the foot of the stairs, fold your clothes neatly and creep up to your room."

The next day they met at lunch.

"How did you get on?" asked the adviser.

"Rotten," replied the other. "I took off all my clothes at the foot of the stairs, as you told me, and folded them up neatly. I didn't make a sound. But when I reached the top of the stairs—it was the 'L' station."

BORROWING—LENDING

A man refused to lend a rope because he was going to tie up a heap of sand with it. "But you can't tie sand with a rope!" exclaimed his neighbor. "Yes," he replied, "you can do anything with a rope, when you don't care to lend it."

BRAGGING

A couple was ushered into the court-room as their case was called. The wife was a strong, healthy, broad-shouldered Irish woman; her husband a meek and obviously submissive little man.

The judge looked sharply at the meek male and spoke:

"You are accused of beating your wife. What have you to say?"

"Guilty, sir," said the little man unhesitatingly.

"Seven dollars or seven days," was the magistrate's prompt decision.

Later, a court official, commenting on the case, asked the magistrate if he hadn't been a bit severe in punishing the poor little fellow.

"Well," was the response, "I had to give him something for bragging!"

BRAINS

A Rochester merchant questioned the bill submitted by the Mayo Brothers for an operation on his wife. "I want an itemized account of this bill," he wrote. "I'm required to do that in my business and I expect it in yours."

"You may be able to itemize calico," Dr. Will wrote back, "but you can't itemize brains."

The bill was paid promptly.

❖   ❖

"I have a remarkable office boy," said a business executive in a group recently discussing labor shortages. "This lad," he continued, "has an unusual brain. It starts working the moment he gets up in the morning and doesn't stop until he gets to my office."

BREAKING-THE-NEWS

Two Irishmen (yes the same two) were using dynamite in a stone quarry. After the resulting explosion, only one remained. It became his duty to convey the news to the widow.

(No, don't leave yet. Maybe this is a new version.)

"Mrs. Flanagan," he began, "is it today the man will be calling for a payment on your husband's life insurance?"

"It is that," agreed Mrs. Flanagan.

"Then," said the bearer of tidings, " 'tis yourself that can be snapping your fingers at him."

BUREAUCRACY

An officer, home from strenuous service overseas, was assigned to a desk job in the Pentagon building. Each day for a week he shifted location of his desk—finally wound up in the men's wash room.

"Must be shell-shocked," associates opined.

But the officer explained grimly, "It's the only place around here where people seem to know what they're doing."

✧　✧

A manufacturing concern during the war period applied for priority on 100 ft. machinery belt. In due time came a letter from the agency asking how much of the firm's production was for war purposes. The firm filled out the questionnaire, stated that about 75% of its work was war production. Back came the requested priority—for a 75 ft. belt!

✧　✧

Here is one man's formula for success in Bureaucracy: "Shoot the bull, pass the buck, and make seven copies of everything."

✧　✧

An army officer was sent to a remote inland army post. Among his inheritance from the previous post commanders, he discovered a room full of musty files consisting of post cards and orders dating well back into the days of the Indian wars. Needing filing space, he wrote Washington asking permission to destroy the obsolete correspondence. After a number of weeks he received this reply: "You may destroy the files of 1868 to 1900, but you are to make a copy of everything before you do so."

BUSINESS

No wonder the tired business man gets that way. Eight hours a day he plays ball, shoots the works, greases the skids, knocks 'em dead, pushes his line, pulls in his horns, holds his own, hangs on, digs down, coughs up, follows through, hits hard, goes overboard and cashes in.

❖   ❖

If you have tears to shed—save them for the man in business. These days, his path is a hard and harried one.

The other evening, John came home from work and slumped dejectedly in a chair. "Well," he said with an air of resignation, "the worst has happened, dear."

"Why whatever is the matter?"

"The boss called me in just before quitting time and gave me the business."

BUSINESS IS BUSINESS

Goldberg hated Rosenbloom and plotted to kill him. But as he stuck his gun in Rosenbloom's face and was about to fire, Rosenbloom asked, "How much you esking for the gun?"

"And how," said Goldberg disgustedly, "am I going to kill a man ven he is talking business?"

❖   ❖

Milton Goldberg, owner and operator of the Goldberg Cleaning and Pressing Service, left his little shop with a suit under his arm. Halfway down the block he met his friend Baumgartner.

"Hallo, Goldberg," his friend saluted, and paused to inquire, "Where are you going?"

Goldberg jerked a thumb toward the clothes under his arm. "I'm taking my suit down to Horowitz to hev it pressed," he explained.

Baumgartner stepped back for a moment and looked at his friend with amazement, "I don't understand," he said. "You, Goldberg, run a pressing business, and yet you take your suit to Horowitz, your competitor, to have it pressed?"

"Ebsolootly!" replied Goldberg, "and why not? Dot feller's prices are so much more rizzonable!"

CAUTION

The bank teller was inexperienced, but resolved not to be lacking in caution. In a brisk manner he challenged practically everyone who presented paper to be converted into cash.

At the end of the line, an old patron of the bank, amused by the passing parade, decided to try an experiment. When his turn came, in response to the usual query, "Have you any identification?" he fumbled in his pocket, produced a snapshot and handed it to the teller. The young man eyed the print judiciously, then gave the patron a careful scrutiny. "Okay," he said at length, "you look like your picture. I guess it's all right to cash the check."

✧   ✧

Cordell Hull's caution, almost legendary, is best illustrated by an anecdote from his Tennessee days:

A fellow townsman bet that he could make Judge Hull give him a direct answer to a question: He asked the time of day; Hull pulled out his own timepiece but replied: "What does your watch say?"

CERTAINTY—UNCERTAINTY

"A certain young man sent me flowers," Mary confided to her girl friend.

"Never say 'certain young man'," cautioned her more experienced companion. "No man is certain until you've got him."

CHARACTER

The applicant for the job of office boy presented his credentials in a manner that bespoke his entire confidence that the position would be his. The sour-looking old gentleman at the head of the establishment read the paper carefully and then surveyed the boy searchingly.

"It is certainly a very nice thing for you to have these recommendations from the minister of your church and your Sunday school teacher," said he, "and I must admit that you look honest.

All the same, I'd like to have a few words from someone who knows you on week days."

CHARITY

A Negro child had asked for a quarter to take to school. "A quatah's a lot of money," commented the mother. "What's it fo'?"

"Teacher say hit t' he'p po' folks."

"Humph! What you think we is if we ain' po' folks? You go tell that teacher Ah say taken you offen de givin' list and put you on de gittin' list!"

❖   ❖

A woman of my acquaintance enjoys doing charity work. It not only is a satisfaction to her to help others, but it is a positive pleasure if she can go about it in the proper way. Last week when a party was given for charity this woman entered into it wholeheartedly. When she thought of the distress of others she began making preparations to attend the party and do her bit. She didn't have suitable clothes to wear, so she bought a new dress for herself and then bought hat, shoes, gloves and a handbag to match the dress. With the sufferings of others in mind she spent more than $40 getting herself ready for the party, and when she got there she contributed 50 cents to help the deserving poor.

❖   ❖

An observant rabbi noted that members of his congregation had a custom of touching fingers to lips, then touching the Torah with finger tips.

"Kiss the Torah," he advised, "not with fingers, but with your mouth. On the other hand, when it comes to charity, be more free with your hands, and less with your mouth."

CHARITY—Contributions

At a benefit performance the hall was crowded and the performers were generously applauded. But the offering amounted to less than $4. "Well," said the promoter, addressing the group,

"this offering, as you understand, is for the benefit of the poor—
and they all seem to be here."

CHAUVINISM

The ladies' church society was having one of its banquets. In
line with custom, the president, a sweet old soul, sat next to the
minister.

First on the program was a solo, "The Evening Star," from
Tannhauser, sung in German.

At its conclusion, madame president confidentially whispered
to the minister:

"I'd like those songs just as well if they sang them in English
like the apostles did."

CHILD—Behavior

"Now, children" said the bright young teacher, after a nature
lesson, "I have told you how the little new birdies learn to fly. So
suppose we have a 'flying lesson' of our own. I'll play the piano,
and you imitate the little birds learning to fly."

At a signal chord, the children began waving their arms ener-
getically—all except little Johnny.

"Come, come, Johnny" coaxed the b y t, "don't you want to imitate a newly-hatched little bird?"

"Aw" said Johnny, "I ain't hatched. I'm a bad egg."

CHILD CARE

Soon after her fourth child was born, a young mother received
a play-pen as a gift. "Thank you for the pen," she wrote. "It is a
Godsend. I sit in it every afternoon and read and the children
can't get near me."

✧   ✧

A mother of thirteen children was asked, "How in the world
do you have time to care for thirteen children?"

"Well," she replied, "when I had only one child it took all my
time; what more can thirteen do?"

CHILD DISCIPLINE

"There's one advantage in usin' love instead of a stick to control younguns. Your control don't stop when you get arthritis."

✧ ✧

"Go on away, Mother," said a small boy who had been naughty. "I want to talk to God."
"Is it something you can't tell me, dear?"
"No-o-o, but you'll just scold and scold, and God will forgive me and forget about it."

CHILDREN—Maturity

"Mother," asked a little girl out of a sudden silence, "when will I be old enough to wear the kind of shoes that kill you?"

CHILD TRAINING

If a child annoys you, quiet him by brushing his hair. . . . If this doesn't work, use the other side of brush on the other end of the child.

✧ ✧

Arthur Murray tells of a woman at an amusement park who gave her small son a dollar and, before turning him loose to his own devices, asked what he intended to do with it.
The lad announced his budget of saltwater taffy, ice cream cones, hot dogs, cotton candy and popcorn.
"Anything else?" asked the mother sarcastically.
The well-trained young man, recalling sundry dietary lessons, gulped a couple of times and added, "Yes, mama; a green vegetable!"

CHISELING

A great feast was to be held in a medieval village. To insure its success a huge cask was built into which each participant agreed to pour a bottle of wine.
"If I fill my bottle with water," soliloquized one, "and empty

the water into the barrel with others, surely it won't be noticed."

The big day arrived. All the villagers assembled. The great cask was tapped. Lo, only water flowed forth.

Each of the villagers had also reasoned, "My bit won't be missed."

CHIVALRY

He (at the movies)—Can you see all right?
She—Yes.
He—Is there a draught on you?
She—No.
He—Is your seat comfortable?
She—Yes.
He—Will you change places with me?

CHRISTIANITY

A wise person truly said, "It ought to be as impossible to forget there is a Christian in the house as it is to forget that there is a ten-year-old boy in it."

CHRISTIAN LIVING

"Can I lead a good Christian life in New York City on fifteen dollars a week?" a young man once asked Dr. S. Parkes Cadman. "My boy," was the reply, "that's all you can do."

CHRISTIANS AND JEWS

While he was in the Holy Land, Bart Crum looked around at some of the Christian shrines, noted with dismay the disrepair into which they had fallen, and remarked to Agronsky, publisher of the Palestine Post: "Frankly, I'm ashamed of the Christians here."

Agronsky replied patiently: "Now, Mr. Crum, you shouldn't generalize like that. Some are good, some are bad. You might find this hard to believe, but really—some of my best friends are Christians." Agronsky looked surprised when the San Francisco attorney burst into uncontrollable laughter.

CHRISTMAS—Gratitude

It was the day after Christmas in a Catholic church in San Francisco. The father was in the church looking over the representation of the stable in Bethlehem, when he noticed to his surprise that the infant Jesus was missing. Then he looked outside the church and saw a little boy with a red wagon, and in the red wagon was the little infant Jesus.

He walked up to the boy and said, "What have you got in your wagon?"

"I have the little Lord Jesus," replied the boy.

"Where did you get him?" inquired the kindly priest.

"I got him from the church," was the reply.

"And why did you do this?"

"Well, father, a week before Christmas I prayed to the little Lord Jesus and I told him if he would bring me a red wagon for Christmas I would give him a ride round the block."

CHURCH—Attendance

A bishop was being patronized by a millionaire.

"I never go to church, bishop," the millionaire said. "Perhaps you've noticed that?"

"Yes, I have noticed it," said the bishop gravely.

"Well, the reason I don't go to church is that there are so many hypocrites there."

"Oh, don't let that keep you away," said the bishop, smiling. "There's always room for one more, you know."

✧   ✧

Mrs. Callahan and Mrs. Donohue had quarreled bitterly. Meeting on a Sabbath morning, Mrs. Donohue seemed inclined to continue the spat. Mrs. Callahan, with heroic effort controlled her temper. After a moment she spoke:

"Mrs. Donohue, I've just been to church and I'm in a state of grace. But, plaze Hivin, the next time I meet yez I won't be—and thin I'll tell yez what I think of yez!"

✧   ✧

A young man of very limited means, after the marriage ceremony, presented to the minister twenty-seven large copper cents, all spread out on the palm of his right hand. "This is all I've got, parson," he said. Seeing a disappointed look in the minister's face, he added, "If we have any children, we will send them to your Sunday school."

❖ ❖

It was Sunday morning. Old Zeke sat on a log at the river bank, his fishpole and can of bait beside him, casting anxious glances at the sky. Rain seemed imminent. Just then the preacher passed by on his way to church.

"Well, Brother Zeke," he inquired, "is you goin' to church, or is you goin' fishin'?"

Zeke gave one more lingering look at the clouding sky.

"I dunno—yet," he confided. "I'm a-wrestlin' with my conscience."

❖ ❖

A minister told a poor washer-woman how glad he was to see her in her place in the church every Sunday, and so attentive to his sermons.

"Yes," she replied, "it is such a rest after a hard week's work, to come to church and just sit down and not think about anything."

❖ ❖

With the advent of a new minister, farmer Bates, always regular in his church attendance, had conspicuously absented himself from services. When a neighbor inquired the reason, the old fellow explained:

"Well, you recollect, I sold butter, milk and cheese to parson Brown. He patronized me, and so, in a manner o' speakin', I patronized him. But now this here young new feller, he's set up keepin' a cow. So I says to m'self, 'Well, if that's your game, we'll have a bit of home-grown religion, too!' "

❖ ❖

On a recent November day huge crowds drove distances up to 100 miles or more to sit for two hours in a cold, drizzling rain to watch two football teams. In the crowds were hundreds of women who will begin to shiver any time the house gets below 75 degrees; thousands of people who will not go two or three blocks to church if there is the least sprinkle.

✧ ✧

On a board in front of a little Protestant church in Dublin is printed the following: "If absence makes the heart grow fonder, then this church must have many friends."

✧ ✧

Why do people take their children to the circus but send them to Sunday School?

✧ ✧

A woman, after the sermon, thanked the minister for his discourse. "I found it so helpful."

The minister replied: "I hope it will not prove so helpful as the last sermon you heard me preach."

"Why, what do you mean?" she asked.

"Well," the minister said, "That sermon lasted you three months!"

✧ ✧

Daniel Webster was once asked why he went Sunday after Sunday to hear a poor country minister and neglected the more brilliant preachers of Washington. He replied, "In Washington they preach to Daniel Webster, the statesman, but this country parson has been preaching to Daniel Webster, the sinner, and it has been helping him."

✧ ✧

The Rev. E. Paul Conine, young Presbyterian pastor at Chittenango, N. Y., has found that work in the dairy barns keeps many men away from Sunday church services. So he addressed this letter to members:

"We have never lived or worked on a farm. We know very little about farming, and less about farm animals. However, we are learning to dislike cows. They cut down church attendance. Cows have developed this undesirable trait only within the last twenty or thirty years, for previous to that they allowed their owners to attend church regularly.

"We don't know what we can say to the cows, for we don't know cows well enough, but we feel that there must be something that will induce the cows of 1941 to let their owners come to church, even as their bovine ancestors allowed their owners to do thirty years ago. We think it very unfair of the cattle to demand so much more than God himself gets."

❖ ❖

Any golfer can be devout on a rainy Sunday.

❖ ❖

Hoffman, the famous German chemist, visited Glasgow, arriving in town late Saturday night. The following morning he went to call on Sir William Thompson, afterward Lord Kelvin. The doorbell was answered by a maid, of whom Hoffman asked if Sir William were at home. "Sir, he most certainly is not." "Could you tell me where I might find him?" "You will find him in church, sir," was the reply, "where you ought to be."

❖ ❖

A Maine newspaper once observed that if the Angel Gabriel had showed up Sunday evening he would have found the congregation scattered far and wide. Too hot in summer to go to church and too cold in winter and so only a short time in spring and fall that we can sit still and listen to a sermon. Many churches now hold no services during August. Wonder when Satan takes a vacation.

❖ ❖

Clarence Darrow, relentless critic of the churches, was listening to a discussion of some of the programs and devices which the churches were using to entice people to attend services on Sunday evenings. Darrow commented scathingly, "Why don't they try religion sometimes?"

❖ ❖

Each time I pass a church.
I stop to make a visit,
So that when I'm carried in
Our Lord won't say, "Who is it?"

CH—CH doesn't mean a thing to you unless U R in it.

✧ ✧

> Some go to church to take a walk,
> Some go to church to laugh and talk,
> Some go there to meet a friend,
> Some go there their time to spend,
> Some go there to doze and nod,
> The wise go there to worship God.

✧ ✧

Mother was trying to persuade her eight-year-old son to accompany her to church.

"You go to the movies once a week and you enjoy two or three hours' entertainment," said the mother, "and you go down to Billy's house to play or over to Harry's house and you have a nice time. Now, don't you think it is only right that once a week you should go with me to God's house for just an hour?"

The eight-year-old thought it over for a few minutes. Then said, "Well, gee, Mom! What would you think, if you were invited somewhere and everytime you went, the fellow was never there?"

✧ ✧

"Mother goes to the Baptist Church," said a little girl to the new neighbor.

"And isn't your father of the same denomination, dear?"

"I don't know zackly what daddy is. He don't go to church with mother. Uncle Robert said daddy must be a Seven Day Absentist."

✧ ✧

Someone has offered the non-church-goer the following little letter to think about:

"I never go to the movies nowadays because my parents made me go too often when I was a boy. Also, no one at the movies ever spoke to me, and every time I go someone asks me for money. The manager never calls on me, and people who attend are not all they should be."

❖   ❖

Introducing his Easter sermon to a church filled to overflowing, a popular San Francisco preacher remarked slyly:

"Now that I have you all before me I want to take this opportunity to wish each and every one a Merry Christmas as I won't see many of you here again until then."

❖   ❖

It is said that the great preacher Rowland Hill was so troubled by latecomers to his services that one Sunday morning he prayed, "O Lord, bless those mightily who are in their places; give grace to those who are on their way; and have mercy on those who are getting ready to come, and will never arrive."

❖   ❖

Margaret, age five, had been interested in an explanation of how her mother's social obligations could be simplified by the skilled use of calling cards.

The next day she attended church for the first time, and was tired out before the lengthy service ended. At bedtime she talked over with her mother her first visit to the Lord's house.

"Mother," she asked, "does the Lord expect us to call at his house every Sunday?"

"Yes, Margaret, every Sunday," was the reply.

"Well, mother," inquired this budding casuist, "some Sundays mightn't we just leave cards?"

❖   ❖

Henry Ward Beecher was buying a horse. The owner described the animal:

"This horse is perfectly sound," he said. "He can go any gait. He will stand without hitching and work any place you put him— on the off side or near side—buggy, plow or wagon. He is perfectly gentle, though full of spirit; goes when you want him, or stops when you say 'Whoa.' He has no bad traits; will neither bite nor kick; comes when you call him, and does not run off when he sees anything strange."

Beecher looked admiringly at the animal and said wistfully, "Ah, I wish that horse were an attendant of my church!"

✧ ✧

This bishop made quite an impression. "Only think, children!" he stated impressively, "in Africa there are 10,000,000 square miles of territory without a single Sunday school where little boys and girls can spend their Sundays. Now, what should we all try and save up our money and do?"

The class of children was, indeed, impressed. "Go to Africa," they cried in unison.

✧ ✧

Why, asks Dr. Daniel A. Poling, are there seventy million unchurched men and women in this country? If competition with amusement enterprises is the answer, then churchmen should be red in the face. My father used to say, "Fill the people and the people will fill the pews."

CHURCH—Construction

A fortune awaits the person who will design a church without any front pews.

CHURCH—Contributions

"Breddern an' sistahs," the visiting colored preacher announced, "I'se got a five dollah sermon, an' a two dollah sermon, an' a one dollah sermon. De deacons will now pass de plate so I will know which o' dem sermons dis congregation wants to heah."

✧ ✧

Bessie had just received a bright new dime and was starting out to invest in an ice cream soda.

"Why don't you give your money to the missionaries?" asked the minister, who was calling at the house.

"I thought about that," said Bessie, "but I think I will buy the ice cream soda, and let the druggist give the money to the missionaries."

❖   ❖

The minister said: "We are now going to pass the hat. Give if you possibly can; and if you can't don't pull any excuse that will get you into trouble."

A stranger sitting in the rear realized as the hat came toward him that he did not have a cent with him; so when the usher reached him he whispered to him, "I never give to missions."

The collector whispered back, "Then reach in and take some out of the hat; the collection is for the heathen."

❖   ❖

Dad criticized the sermon. Mother thought the organist made a lot of mistakes. Sister didn't like the choir's singing. But they all shut up when little Billy chipped in with the remark: "I think it was a darn good show for a nickel."

❖   ❖

One of the local ministers was walking along Main street, wrapped in thought—plus his overcoat, of course—when he was hailed by a friend.

"Why so meditative?" asked the friend.

"Oh," said the minister, "I was just thinking."

"About what?"

"Well," said the minister, "about the fact that if the churches had received as much money last year as will be listed as contributions on income tax reports, they would have nothing to worry about."

❖   ❖

Donald selected the aisle seat, and when the contribution plate was passed, deposited in it the combined offerings of his family. The vestryman, not realizing this, moved as though to pass the plate to others in the pew, when he was arrested by a highly pitched distinctly audible stage whisper announcing:

"I paid for five."

❖   ❖

The Reverend Moses White was holding services in a small country church, and at the conclusion lent his hat to a member to pass around for contributions. The brother canvassed the congregation thoroughly, but the hat was returned empty to its owner.

Reverend White looked into it, turned it upside down, and shook it several times, but not a copper was forthcoming. He sniffed audibly.

"Breddern," he said, "Ah sho' is glad dat Ah got mah hat back ergin."

❖   ❖

He marched into the store early Sunday morning, approached the druggist and asked, "Give me change for a dime, please."

"Sure," was the obliging response, "and I hope you enjoy the sermon."

❖   ❖

Junior was given two pennies, one for Sunday School, the other for candy. Walking along the street, he stumbled, the coins rolled away and one went down the sewer. Looking at it ruefully, he observed, "Well, Lord, there goes your penny!"

❖   ❖

The young pastor, preaching in the absence of the regular clergyman, was somewhat astounded to observe an aged deacon remove a half dollar from the collection plate and slip it into his pocket. After the services, he felt impelled to take the deacon to task for his action.

"Oh," smiled the elderly official, "you mean that lead half dollar? Why, man, I've been leading with that counterfeit coin for fifteen years!"

❖   ❖

"When I look at this congregation," said the preacher, "I ask myself, 'Where are the poor?' And then, when I look at the collection, I say to myself, 'Where are the rich?'"

❖   ❖

It was on the old camp-ground. "Pass de hat," suggested Bruddah Wheatly. But the parson raised his hand. "No, sah," he shouted, "dere'll be no hat about it. Pass a tin box wid a chain to it. De las' time a hat was passed around hyah, it nevah came back, and Ah had to go home bareheaded."

❖ ❖

Bulletin in Scotch church: "Those in the habit of putting buttons instead of coins in the collection plate will please put in their own buttons and not buttons from the cushions on the pews."

❖ ❖

Ernest Thompson-Seton, the naturalist, was discussing some of his experiences with a clergyman. "I found after a few tests," he said, "that I could attract squirrels, howsoever wild, by singing to them. Whenever I sang they would come out of their holes, sit and listen with apparent enjoyment. I remember one day, however, when I tried 'Old Hundred' on them. Would you believe it, the instant they heard that hymn they scampered off, nor could I induce them to return that day. I can't understand why."

The clergyman reflected and then suggested, "Probably they were afraid that you would next proceed to take up a collection."

❖ ❖

> Once there was a Christian
> He had a pious look.
> His consecration was complete
> Except his pocketbook.
> He'd put a nickel on the plate
> And then, with might and main,
> He'd sing: "When we asunder part
> It gives us inward pain."

❖ ❖

Father Jos Regan, a missionary in South China, concluded a recent sermon with a strong plea to support the parish.

Immediately after the service, his washer-woman, San Sao, advanced to the sanctuary and placed $2 on the altar rail. Others, magnetized, followed suit. The collection totaled $10.30.

The next day the priest sought San Sao to thank her for the liberal contribution.

"Contrib?" said the old woman, puzzled. "I just bring what I find in your pocket when I wash last week."

❖　❖

In one of the nursery schools, made necessary by the increasing number of working mothers, the tiny tot who brings an extra nickel is permitted to trade it for ice cream.

One little lady, aged three, who had come to associate the shiny coin with a delectable dessert, was found in tears when her mother called for her after Sunday School. "They tooked my nickel," she sobbed, "and they didn't give me an i-i-ice cream!"

❖　❖

A Negro preacher announced from the pulpit that a brother had neglected to lock the door of his chicken house the night before, with the result that most of his fowls were missing.

"I has my s'picions who stole dem chickens," said the parson, "an' I also b'lieves dat sech a low-down pusson ain' noways likely t' put money in de collection plate dat will now be passed."

The result was a record-breaking collection. The pastor viewed it with approval and continued: "Now, bredr'n, I don' want yo' dinners spoilt by wonderin' where dat brothah lives dat don' lock his chickens up. Dat brothah jes don' exist. He is jes' a parable fo' pu'poses ob finances."

❖　❖

Remember the story of the Scotsman who by accident dropped a sovereign into the plate instead of a shilling? After church was over he tried to get it back.

"Na, na, money that be paid to the Lord is na returnable," announced the elder who had passed the plate.

"Well," said the man, after reflection, "I'll get a sovereign's worth o' credit in heaven."

"That you weel not," announced the elder. "You'll get the shilling's worth you meant to drap in. The balance be just velvet for the Lord."

❖　❖

A minister was puzzled. He found that several I O U's were dropped in the offering plate. He thought it was being done by a practical joker, but some weeks later he found in the plate an envelope containing bills equal to the I O U's. They ranged from $5 to $15 and were apparently based on whatever the donor happened to think the sermon worth.

Then came a Sunday when the sermon was not up to par. After the service the usual envelope was in one of the plates. But the slip of paper read: "U O Me $5."

✧ ✧

Billy Sunday once said: "Sometimes, before sending out my ushers, I urge people to give according to their means. When the report comes from the treasurer, I am tempted to believe they gave according to their meanness."

✧ ✧

A veteran church deacon announced to an associate the other day that he had developed a device that was bound to make him rich. "Every church" he said confidently, "is sure to want this patented collection-plate of mine."

"What's the special feature?"

"Well, you see, it works like this: Coins fall through slots of different sizes. Dollars, half-dollars and quarters fall on velvet; dimes, nickels and pennies drop on a Chinese bell!"

✧ ✧

It is not a matter of how much of our money we give to the Lord, but how much of His money we keep for ourselves.

✧ ✧

A group of white men in a southern community owned a rather valuable piece of property in a Negro section, which could not be sold because of a popular belief that the place was haunted. They offered a reward of fifty dollars to any Negro who would stay all night there. The offer stood for some time with no takers, but finally the news came to the ears of old Uncle Mort, and Uncle Mort immediately applied to the person who had signed the offer.

To shorten the tale a little, Uncle Mort successfully endured the trials of the Yancy house and collected the fifty dollars.

"What was it like in there, uncle?" the white folks asked him.

"Well," was the reply, "Ah opens up de do' t' dat ole house and Ah goes in. Fust Ah buil's me a big fiah in dat fiahplace, en Ah say, 'Ain' no ghos' comin' down dat chimbly.' Den Ah locks de do' an Ah say, 'Dey ain' no ghos' comin' in no locked do'.' Den Ah farsten de windeh en Ah say, 'Dey ain' no ghos' comin' in dat windeh.' En Ah look aroun' en dah stan's th'ee ghos's—one in front ob de fiah, one in front ob de do', en one in front ob de windeh! Den Ah takes mah Bible en Ah reads a chapteh. Ah looks aroun', en dah stan's dem same ghos's. Ah sings me a hymn chune outden de book, en dem ghos's still stan's dah. Ah gits down on mah knees en Ah rassles wid de Lawd in prah. En dem ghos's still stan's dah. Den Ah say, 'Ah guess Ah'll take up uh kerlection.' Ah gits ma ole hat en stahts handin' it aroun' en be-hole, all dem ghos's is gone!"

❖ ❖

"Am dere anybody in de congregation what wishes prayer fer dere failins'?" asked the colored minister.

"Yassah," responded Brother Jones. "Ah's a spen'-thrif', an' Ah throws mah money 'round reckless like."

'Ve'y well. We will join in a prayer fo' Brothah Jones—jes' aftah de collection plate hab been passed."

❖ ❖

"Look whut de good Lawd is done for you all," exhorted the negro preacher. "You ought to give a tenth of all you gits."

"Amen," shouted a perspiring brother catching the spirit of the occasion, "but a tenth ain't enough. Ah say le's raise it to a twentieth."

CHURCH—Hospitality

A man failed to remove his hat when he entered a church, and was presently sighted by a horrified deacon, who quietly drew the man's attention to his apparent forgetfulness.

The man explained that he had been worshiping in that church for three years, without anyone speaking to him, and he thought the hat might do the trick.

CHURCH—Improvement

Some churches remind us of the Irishman's wife. She was in the hospital for months. Every day the husband visited her, and asked the nurse at the desk how she was getting along. Each time he got the same answer: "Showing quite a bit of improvement." Finally the patient died, and some one asked the sad husband the cause of her death. "She couldn't," he said, "stand all that improvement!"

CHURCH—Jealousy

In a small rural community the four leading churches are close together only in a geographical sense. Petty jealousy and bickering prevail. About the only thing these congregations have in common is the problem of dwindling attendance. A member of one of these churches was asked recently how his group was getting along. He had to confess that they weren't making much progress. "But, thank goodness," he added, "the others aren't doing anything either!"

CHURCH—Politics

A Negro deacon was tried before court for some minor crime.
"How does it come," asked the judge, "that you are a Deacon, and also a criminal?"
"Well, sah, jedge, yo honor," the Deacon replied, "hit was lak dis: de rough element in ouah church rose up an' demanded representation!"

CIVIC PRIDE

Every speaker at the dinner had boosted the town, which was inland some 800 miles from the coast. The speakers all said that had the city been on the coast it would have been the world's first city. The visiting speaker was called on next.
"Gentlemen, I am impressed with your city as much as you are and believe that I can suggest a way in which you can get your wish."

All leaned forward. The speaker continued: "This is what you should do: obtain a large pipe, run it from the center of your city into the ocean, and if you can suck as hard as you can blow, the ocean will soon be in your city."

CIVILIZATION

In another hundred years civilization will have reached all peoples except those that have no resources worth stealing.

❖ ❖

During the early days of the war, a little group of people was shipwrecked on a desert island in the middle of the Pacific. After many weary months a passing ship saw their plight and sent a boat ashore. But the boat did not land at once; one of the sailors threw a bundle of newspapers on the beach, shouting that they were from the captain, and saying:

"After you've read them, he wants to know whether you want to be rescued."

COINCIDENCE

"I have always been intrigued," says Bobby Jones, the renowned golfer, "by the veteran caddies at St. Andrews, Scotland. They are in a group to themselves in experience, dignity, wisdom. One, in particular, a veteran perhaps 70 years old, was carrying the clubs of an unpleasant duffer who played very poor golf and who blamed everything on the caddy."

"Throughout the ordeal the old caddy maintained a dignified silence. But finally when the duffer, addressing the other members of his foursome, remarked: 'I believe on this round I've drawn the worst caddy in the world,' the veteran quietly interposed: 'Oh, no, sir. That would be too great a coincidence.'"

COMMUNISM (see also SOCIALISM)

A candidate for the Communist Party was undergoing an oral examination.

"Comrade," he asked, "what would you do if you were left two million dollars?"

"I would give one million to the Party and keep the other million for myself."

"Very good. And if you had two houses?"

"I would keep one and give the other to the Party."

"Excellent. Now, what would you do if you had two pair of trousers."

There was a long pause. Finally the candidate blurted, "I don't know. You see, I have two pair of trousers!"

❖ ❖

His single listener merely stood there and said nothing. The Communist leaned forward.

"Comrade," he cried, "you seem to be a man of intelligence. Do you agree with everything I have said?"

The other man nodded.

The Communist seemed startled.

"What's that?" he asked. "Did you signify that you agree with everything I say?"

"Absolutely," returned the listener.

The Communist stepped down from his soap box and began to pack up his things.

"Bah!" he mumbled. "What's the sense of talking to you!"

COMPETITION

God and two men make a universe. He might have a hard time making it if His two men were my competitor and I.

❖ ❖

Moe and Izzy, broom merchants, are discussing business. "I don't see how you do it" complained Moe. "All the time you undersell me, and I'm telling you confidentially I steal the straw and I steal the handles—yet you're selling for less money. I don't see how you do it."

"Oh," said Izzy, "I'm stealing brooms ready made!"

COMPETITION—Meeting

It was a rough sea and a number of pallid individuals were leaning over the rail of the ocean liner.

A man, walking the deck, stopped to sympathize with one individual who was experiencing a particularly violent attack.

"Stomach a bit weak, eh?" he inquired solicitously.

"Weak, nothin'," gasped the sufferer, "if you'll notice, I'm throwin' as far as any of 'em!"

COMPLAINT

Into the office of Frank Sturm, Chicago, area rent control administrator, walked a worried man. "Who's my landlord?" he asked a clerk. "He's the man you pay your rent to," he was told. "I don't pay no rent." The man explained that nine years ago he had moved into a vacant house. "Well, then if that's the case, what is your complaint?" "My roof leaks," replied the man, "and if it isn't fixed pretty soon, I'm goin' to move out."

COMPROMISE

The middle way is frequently taken by those who do not know where they are going, and so find comfort in having company on both sides.

❖ ❖

Alexander Stephens, v-pres. of the Confederacy, who had a wizened body, was challenged by a big chap to fight a duel. On the field the big chap complained, "I am a full-sized target for that shrimp to fire at, while he offers me hardly any mark at all. It ain't fair."

"All right," said Stephens, "we will chalk out my size on your body and agree not to count any shots outside that." The challenger laughed. The duel was off.

CONCEIT

Conceit is the only disease known to man that makes everyone sick except the one who has it!

❖ ❖

The bigger the man's head gets the easier it is to fill his shoes.

❖ ❖

If you get too certain that you're a comer, you may be a goner.

CONCENTRATION

A man once came to Kid McCoy and offered him a high price for boxing lessons. "Very well," said the ring artist. The man put up his "dukes" ready for the start. "Who is that coming through the door?" asked McCoy. The man turned his head and McCoy handed him a wallop on the jaw. "That is the first lesson," announced the teacher. "Learn to concentrate. Don't take your mind off what you are doing or your eyes off the fellow you are boxing. . . . Ten dollars, please."

CONDITIONS

" 'Dis mornin'," said the Negro preacher, "I is goin' to preach to you-all on de subjec' ob *status quo*." He paused for an impressive moment. "*Status quo* is de name ob dis heah mess what we all is in."

CONDUCT

So live that after the minister has ended his remarks, those present will not think they have attended the wrong funeral.

❖ ❖

An Irishman was seeing his son off on the steamer to a new land where the lad was to seek his fortune. "Now Michael, my boy," he said, as they parted, "remember the three bones and ye'll always get along all right."

A stranger standing nearby overheard the remark and asked what three bones he referred to.

"Sure, now," said the Irishman, "and wouldn't it be the wishbone, the jawbone and the backbone? It's the wishbone that keeps you going after things, and it's the jawbone that helps you find out how to go after them if you're not too proud to ask a question when there's something you don't know; and it's the backbone keeps you at it till you get there."

❖ ❖

One day a devout Scotsman, member of Holy Trinity, Boston, announced to the famous Phillips Brooks that he planned to visit the Holy Land, climb to the very top of Mount Sinai.

"When I get there, mon, I weel read the Ten Commandments aloud."

"Sandy, I can tell you something better."

"Better, dominee?" gasped the astounded Scotsman.

"Indeed, Sandy, and simple and—real thrifty."

"Thrifty?" Sandy caught at this. "And what be that?"

"Just stay right here at home, Sandy, and keep them."

❖   ❖

A curb-cruising wolf pulled his car up beside a cute bobby-soxer and asked, "Going my way, baby?"

Said the bobby-soxer: "No! I get a harp at the end of mine."

CONFIDENCE

"Now that you are through college, what are you going to do?" the young man was asked.

"I shall study medicine and become a great surgeon," was the reply.

"But the medical profession is pretty well crowded already, isn't it?"

"I can't help that," was the confident reply. "I shall study medicine and those who are already in the profession will just have to take their chances. That's all."

CONFIDENCE—Excess

We heard the other day of a man who paid a psychologist $50 to cure him of an inferiority complex—and later was fined $25 and costs for talking back to a traffic cop.

CONFUSION

There are some amusing stories that are difficult to classify. This one, for example: An Arizona man hanged himself to the bedpost with his suspenders. The coroner's jury brought in a verdict: "The deceased came to his death by coming home full and mistaking self for pants."

❖   ❖

A dear old New England spinster, the embodiment of the timid and shrinking, passed away at Carlsbad, where she had gone for her health. Her nearest kinsman, a nephew, ordered her body sent back to be buried—as was her last wish—in the quiet little country church-yard. His surprise can be imagined when opening the casket, he beheld, instead of the placid features of his aunt Mary, the majestic body of an English General in full regimentals, whom he remembered had chanced to die at the same time and place as his aunt.

At once he cabled to the General's heirs explaining the situation and requesting instructions.

They came back as follows: "Give the General quiet funeral. Aunt Mary interred today with full military honors, six brass bands, saluting guns."

❖ ❖

An old Negro had just paid the last installment on his little homestead. The real estate man congratulated him. "Now, Uncle Joe," he said, "I'll make you a deed to the place."

"Thank ye, sah," said the old man, "but iffen hits jes' de same t' you-all, I'd ruther you'd gim-me a mortgage to de place."

"But you don't understand, Uncle Joe," said the kindly realtor. "A deed is what you really want."

"Well," said the old man hesitantly, "all I knows is dat I owned me a farm one time befo'. I had de deed an' de bank had de mortgage. An' first I knowed, the bank done got de farm."

CONSCIENCE

Conscience is a walkie-talkie set by which God speaks to us.

❖ ❖

Quite often when a man thinks his mind is getting broader it is only his conscience stretching.

❖ ❖

When Mrs. Stewart Edw. White—who is half Spanish, half Scotch, visited Scotland, a fine old gentleman of that land said to her:

"Weel, weel, my dear, so ye hae Scottish bluid in ye! That gives ye a Scottish conscience. It won't keep ye from sinning; it just keeps ye from enjoyin' it!"

❖   ❖

The Devil's best-selling lotion is a balm he has invented to be smeared on people's conscience—this concoction being called, "If I don't, somebody else will."

CONSERVATION

A government man was recently investigating the condition of the small farmers in the hill section of one of our eastern states. He found one farmer who was willing to talk, and he pumped him for information. "You can't raise anything on these stony hills, can you?" the man from Washington ventured.

"Raise anything!" exclaimed the native, with indignation. "Of course, we can. We raise plenty. We raise barley. We raise a sight of barley back here. I don't know what us farmers would do if we didn't raise barley."

"What do you usually get for barley?"

"Oh, we don't sell it. We don't sell a grain of it," the farmer answered.

"Then I suppose you feed it to your stock," the investigator suggested.

"No, siree!" returned the farmer. "You don't catch us wasting barley that away."

"Well, what do you do with it then?" pursued the rather puzzled agent.

"Why, doggonit, we save every grain of it for seed. That's what we do with it."

❖   ❖

A middle-aged Negro, employed for 20 years at a southern plant, began to develop an increasing aptitude for avoiding work. Every time the foreman looked for George, he'd find him behind the rain barrel, sitting in the sun. Finally, taking the veteran to task, the foreman asked why he didn't stop loafing and buckle down to work.

"Boss," replied the Negro, "Ah hears tell good men am mighty scarce dese days, so Ah says to mahself, 'George, yo' bettah take good care o' yo'se'f.' "

CONSERVATISM

The conservative residents of Maine seldom give direct answers. They don't like to commit themselves on any proposition.

"Who lives on that farm?" a visitor asked an old chap to whom he was giving a lift.

"Willie Richardson," he replied. Then, as if startled by his own definiteness, he added, "Leastwise I think his name's Willie. He's always been called that since he was a little boy."

❖ ❖

A conservative is one who does not think that anything should be done for the first time.

CONTENTMENT

A Quaker put up a sign on a vacant piece of ground next to his house: "I will give this lot to anyone who is really satisfied."

A wealthy farmer, as he rode by, read it. Stopping, he said, "Since my Quaker friend is going to give that piece away, I may as well have it as anyone else. I am rich. I have all I need, so I am able to qualify." He went up to the door and explained why he had come.

"And is thee really satisfied?" asked the Quaker.

"I have all I need and am well satisfied."

"Friend," said the other, "if thee is satisfied, what does thee want with my lot?"

CONVERSATION

Vera Vague, actress and radio star, tells this one. The other day her thirteen-year-old daughter came to her seriously.

"Mother," she asked, "how do you talk to boys?"

"Why, what do you mean?" replied Vera.

"Well, when my boy friend comes over I say, 'Hello, Butch,' and he says, 'Hiya Stinky. What's cookin'?' and then I don't know what to say next."

CONVERSION

A Salvation Army band was grimly playing its solemn airs on a street corner. When a sizable crowd had gathered the leader stopped the hymns and called on each member of the band to give a short testimonial. One by one they told how they had been saved, until finally the solemn-faced woman with the drum was beckoned to the front.

"Well," she began, "before I was saved I used to smoke one cigarette right after another. Then I was converted. And now I don't smoke no more.

"I used to drink, too, at least a pint a day. I've been saved and now I don't drink at all.

"Time was when I used to sin. I warn't no good at all. But I was saved. And now I don't sin no more. In fact, I don't do one damned thing 'cept beat this old drum!"

❖   ❖

An oysterman in Boston got converted at a meeting, and took for his text, "Thou knowest I am an oysterman." He said: "Isn't it wonderful that Christ revealed himself as an oysterman? He found us in the mud. He cracked our hard shells open, and found what we were meant for." After the meeting one of the men who was not quite so moved told him that the text really was. "Thou knowest I am an austere man." "I don't care what it is," was the reply, "I got eight converts from it."

CONVICTION

Convictions are what an employee has after he knows what the boss thinks.

CO-OPERATION

Perhaps we shall not realize for years to come the extent to which American industrial genius contributed to the winning of the war.

Early in the struggle, Wm. S. Knudsen, head of OPM, telephoned K. T. Keller, head of the Chrysler Corporation.

"K. T.," he asked, "will you make tanks?"

"Yes, Bill," was the quiet response. "Where can I see one?"

❖ ❖

A salesman died, went to Heaven, and was assigned by St. Peter to the Sales Division. There he found all former salesmen separated into two groups—the failures in one hall and the successes in another.

Around meal time he entered the Hall of Those Who Failed and was surprised to find the occupants thin and hungry-looking.

When the Angels began to serve dinner, large platters of delicious foods were placed upon the table, but before anyone was seated another Angel came along and attached a long iron spoon to each salesman's arm. This spoon was strapped around the wrists and biceps, making it impossible to bend the arm. As a result they could only look at the food.

Walking over to the Hall of Those Who Succeeded he was surprised to find these gentlemen looking fat, well-fed and healthy. Dinner was already on the table and an Angel had just finished strapping the long iron spoons to the arms of the diners. To his astonishment he found that each man in this room dipped his spoon into the food and fed the man seated next to him!

❖ ❖

A man who went into a bird store to buy a canary spotted a bright-looking bird that was singing merrily. "I'll take that one!" he said.

"Fine," agreed the clerk, "but you'll have to take the one in the cage below, too."

The customer protested: "I don't want that old, battered, broken-down bird. I just want the singing one—the one in the cage above."

"Look," he said, "you can't take the one above without the other one."

"And why not?" asked the exasperated customer.

"Because," said the merchant, with a note of finality, "the one below is the arranger."

❖ ❖

Said the bullet, "I do the work." Said the powder, "You would be useless without me." Said the cap to the powder, "You would be useless without me." Said the trigger to the cap, "You would be useless without me." Said the gun to the trigger, "You would be useless without me." Said the man who held the gun, "Hush! I need you all."

COST

A young chap, whose sweetie had just made him the happiest man alive, went into a jewelry store to buy the engagement ring. He picked up a sparkling diamond and asked its price.

"That one is $100," replied the jeweler gently.

The young man looked startled, then whistled. He pointed to another ring, "And this one?"

"That, sir," said the jeweler still more gently, "is two whistles."

COST-OF-LIVING

Kitty was going over the grocery bills. "Lookit" she said, "Guess what. I ordered fifteen cents worth of mild cheese last week, and here it is on the bill, written down just the way I ordered it: 'fifteen cents worth of mild cheese—twenty cents.' "

❖   ❖

No matter how high the cost of living may soar, there's some consolation in the fact that it is still cheaper to live than to die.

A live man pays 25 cents for a shave; a dead man $5 to $10.

A woolen overcoat costs $35 to $50; a wooden one $250 plus.

A taxi trip to the theatre and back costs $2; a hearse ride to the cemetery costs $10 to $25.

The good wife will lecture you about your bad points for nix; the preacher expects $15 or more to lecture about your fine points.

❖   ❖

It's almost as difficult to live within an income today as it was to live without one in the early '30s.

COUNSEL

And there is an aged Methodist who prayed: "Oh, Lord, use me as Thou wilt—if only in an advisory capacity."

COUNSEL—Confounded

A hard-working Irish wife came to her priest with the tale of her husband's unfaithfulness, his constant drinking and terribly late hours. The Father was kindly and suggested that he talk to Pat and tell him that his way was folly, but that she should be patient until the Father had an opportunity to do this.

One morning, sometime later, the Father sat down on a street car beside Pat, who seemed to be buried in the morning paper. He looked up, greeted the priest, and then continued reading. The Father waited, and finally Pat again looked up.

"Father, what causes lumbago?" Here was his chance, the Father thought.

"Well, my son, it is sinful living. Unfaithfulness to those who love you, liquor, late hours, and overindulgence are the causes of that suffering. Why do you ask?"

"Well, Father, it says here that the Pope has it."

COURAGE

Many a man who is proud of his right to say what he pleases wishes he had the courage to do so.

❖   ❖

A dear old lady was about to have an operation for the removal of one of her eyes. Just as the surgeon was ready to administer the anesthetic, she stopped him and said: "I have a favor to ask of you, doctor." She looked up and smiled. "When you select a glass eye for me, be sure that it has a twinkle in it."

❖   ❖

During the Marshall Islands operations in the spring of '42 five Jap dive-bombers swooped out of the clouds on Adm. Halsey's flagship. "I hit the deck," he recalls, "fustest and hardest. My staff trampled up and down my prostrate form."

Next day Halsey's eye fell on a first-class petty officer stationed at a near-by direction finder. "Rate that man a chief," he barked. "He had the guts to stand there and laugh at me when I was so scared yesterday!"

COURTESY—Lack

A charming Virginia woman said recently, "I believe my husband would die for me, but he never thinks to pass me the salt."

COURTSHIP

A man picks a wife about the same way an apple picks a farmer.

CREATION

One of Gutzon Borglum's great works is the head of Lincoln, in the capitol at Washington. He cut it from a block of marble which had long been in his studio. It is said that into that studio every morning came an old Negro woman to dust. She had become accustomed to seeing that marble block standing there, and for days had not noticed it. One morning she came in and saw to her astonishment and terror the unmistakable lineaments of Lincoln appearing in the stone. She ran to the sculptor's secretary and said, "Am dat Abraham Lincoln?" "Why, yes," answered the secretary. "Well," said the old woman, "how in de world did Massa Borglum know that Abraham Lincoln was in dat block of stone?"

CREDITS—COLLECTIONS

In the deep days of the depression, a traveler reported this sign, posted by a small Negro tradesman in rural Alabama:
"No more Credick til I gits my Outs in."

❖ ❖

Bustling into his tailor's, Jones handed him a pair of pants. "Here's that last pair of trousers you made for me," he said. "I want them reseated. You know, I sit a lot."

The tailor looked at him dejectedly. "I had hoped," he replied mournfully, "that you brought the bill to be receipted. You know I've stood a lot."

❖ ❖

Once cured, the out-of-town patient carefully avoided the chiropractor; ignored statements and collection letters.

The chiropractor hit upon an ingenious idea. He wrote:

"If I do not receive your check covering this statement within the next ten days, I shall donate the account to the Woman's Circle of the leading church in your town."

The account was promptly paid.

❖ ❖

In Portuguese East Africa the authorities have a neat way of collecting taxes but we have grave doubts that it would work in our social system.

If a native doesn't pay, they put his wives into jail until he comes and redeems them.

❖ ❖

This is from the Fibber McGee radio program. We find Fibber dickering with a neighborhood tailor on the reconstruction of an old suit.

"The price is being feefteen dollars—wid a slight addetional charge for cash," the tailor explained.

"Hey, hold on there!" Fibber exploded. "For cash I should get a discount, not an extra charge!"

"And why should I be giving a deescount for cash, I am esking? If you pay cash, I am having no bills to mek out, I am going by the peectures show to pass the time and who is paying for that—me?"

❖ ❖

"The wool for this suit I am wearing," observed Smith, "was grown in Australia. The cloth was woven in Mass. The thread came from England. The suit was made in Chicago and I bought it in San Francisco."

"So what?" commented his companion. "I don't see anything so remarkable in that."

"But isn't it wonderful," continued Smith, "that so many people can make a living out of something I haven't paid for?"

❖ ❖

An old Southern Negro was asked by the proprietor of a store how he happened to need credit when he had such a good cotton crop.

"De ducks got 'bout all dat cotton, suh," was the mournful reply.
"What do you mean—the ducks got it?"

"Well, you see," explained the old man, "I sent that cotton up
to Memphis, and dey deducks the freight and dey deducks the
storage and dey deducks the commission and dey deducks the
taxes. Yes, suh, de ducks got 'bout all dat cotton—and dat's why I
needs credit."

❖   ❖

A tourist visiting a country fair stopped by a merry-go-round.
Presently he noticed a miserable looking little man seated on one
of the wooden horses. But what struck him as strange was that
every time the machine stopped, the little man made no attempt
to get off the horse. At length, curiosity overcame the tourist,
and when next the man on the horse stopped opposite him he said:
"Pardon me, sir, but do you enjoy going round and round like
this?"

The unhappy one grimaced. "Not a bit," he replied.

"Then why do you do it?" asked the tourist.

"The man who owns this affair owes me five dollars, and this is
the only way I can get it out of him."

❖   ❖

In one of those little towns in Maine, where Summer residents
are the principal source of revenue, almost everyone trades at the
the lone grocery store. Bills commonly run for the season and
patrons pay the charge with a single check.

One city man, long after his return to town, was surprised to get
a bill from the grocer. He looked up his cancelled check, to make
sure he'd met his obligation, and upon his next visit to the community, dropped in to explain the matter.

"Oh, that's all right," said the tradesman's son. "You see, it gets
mighty lonesome up here sometimes in the dead o' winter, so Pa
goes over the books and sends out bills to all our Summer customers. You'd be surprised, too," he concluded, "how many of
'em pays up again!"

CREED—AND DEED

"Get your sins washed away," the Negro Baptist minister
pleaded.

"I already have," said a member of the congregation, "over at the Methodist church."

"Ah," replied the Baptist clergyman, "you ain't been washed, you jest been dry cleaned."

❖ ❖

Jerome Davis, educator, sociologist, and author of *Capitalism and its Culture,* is most amused by a story of his boyhood.

"My father," he says, "was a Congregational Missionary in Japan. When he was home on furlough, he was visiting my uncle who was an Episcopalian and was entertaining the local rector for dinner. My sister had been teasing to go to the Episcopal Church on Sunday, but my father thought, since we were only going to be in the city one Sunday, we should go to the Congregational Church.

"In the middle of the dinner, with the Episcopal rector sitting near by, my sister broke out with:

" 'Oh, daddy, if you'll only take us to the Episcopal Church we'll promise not to believe one word the minister says.' "

❖ ❖

Jones had been nominated as candidate for senatorship. To be a senator had always been his greatest ambition and now finally he seemed to be in sight of his goal. One day he traveled to a small community in the district to make a speech. Realizing that a candidate's religious denomination was exceedingly important to these villagers, he attempted to find out to what church his audience belong without having to ask anyone.

He started speaking:

"My great-grandfather belonged to the Episcopalian Church (stony silence); my great-grandmother was a member of the Presbyterian Church (continued silence); my grandfather was a Methodist (still silence), but my grandmother belonged to the Independent Church (cold silence). However, I had a great aunt who was a Baptist (loud cheers)—and (triumphantly) I have always followed my great aunt in this respect."

❖ ❖

An anecdote is related of a Hebrew who went into a restaurant to get his dinner. The devil of temptation whispered in his ear,

"Bacon." He knew if there was anything that made Jehovah real white mad, it was to see anybody eating bacon, but he thought, "Maybe He is too busy watching sparrows and counting hairs to notice me," and so he took a slice.

The weather was delightful when he went into the restaurant, but when he came out the sky was overcast, the lightning leaped from cloud to cloud, the earth trembled, and it was dark. He went back into the restaurant, trembling with fear, and leaning over the counter, said to the clerk, "My God, did you iver hear such a fuss about a little piece of bacon!"

✦　　✦

A Baptist preacher was strolling along the sea walk during a convention of his church members in Charleston. As he walked, the preacher chanced upon an old colored man fishing from the pilings along the pier. For quite a while the preacher watched the negro sit patiently waiting for a bite. At last, with a grunt, the darky pulled in a fish that appeared to be a cross between a toad and a bullhead.

Knowing little about fishing, the minister asked, "And what kind of a fish is that, George?"

"Dey calls it a Baptist fish," croaked the old man.

"A Baptist fish?" inquired the minister skeptically.

"Sho'," answered the old darky, as he threw the fish into the ocean, "dey calls em dat 'cause dey spoil so fast after dey's taken out of de watah."

✦　　✦

An Episcopal clergyman who was passing his vacation in a remote country district met an old farmer who declared that he was a "Piscopal."

"To what parish do you belong?" asked the clergyman.

"Don't know nawthin' 'bout enny parish," was the answer.

"Who confirmed you, then?" was the next question.

"Nobody," answered the farmer.

"Then how are you an Episcopalian?" asked the clergyman.

"Well," was the reply, "you see it's this way: Last winter I went to church, an' it was called 'Piscopal,' and 'heered them say that they left undone the things what they'd oughter done and they'd done some things what they oughtenter done, and I says to myself, says I, 'That's my fix exac'ly,' and ever since then I've been a 'Piscopalian.' "

❖ ❖

Graham McNamee's favorite story concerns a priest and a minister.

The two reverend gentlemen were the best of friends, notwithstanding their religious differences. One evening they were chatting together at a party to which both had been invited, and in the course of the conversation had come to extolling their friendship and its strength in withstanding their many long arguments on religious points.

"But," said the priest, "it is only as it should be. After all, we both teach the same lessons, and both preach the same gospel—you in your way, and I in His."

❖ ❖

A minister was discussing with an illiterate member of his flock, in an orthodox church located in Georgia, religious topics of various interest. The member said that even the best were none too good in this vale of sin and tribulation. "You believe, then," interposed the preacher, "in the doctrine of total depravity?"

"Yes, I do," responded the member, "that is,—er—er where it's lived up to."

❖ ❖

Little Margaret, who was reared in a liberal religious atmosphere, visited relatives whose creed was definitely the opposite.

"In Aunt Marie's church," she announced, "the sermons are much louder and much longer and full of strange words. I didn't like them, but of course I didn't show it. When the minister said things I knew were not so, I just crossed my fingers."

❖ ❖

An Irishman and a Jew were discussing the relative merits of the great men of their respective races, and, naturally, got into a heated argument. Finally the Irishman said:

"I tell ye, Isaac, fer ivery great Jew ye can name, ye can pull out one of me whiskers, and fer ivery great son of Erin, I'll pull out one of yours. Are ye on?"

Isaac agreed. Pat reached over, got hold of a whisker, and said "Robert Emmett" as he pulled.

"Moses," said Isaac, and pulled one of Pat's.

"Dan O'Connell," said Pat, and took another.

"Abraham," Isaac retaliated, with a vicious yank.

"Patrick Henry, rest his soul," cried Pat.

"The twelve apostles!" yelled Isaac, pulling out a handful of whiskers.

Pat let out a howl of rage and pain. He seized the Jew's full beard with both hands and roared: "The Ancient Order of Hibernians."

❖   ❖

At a family dinner table, when a young person expressed appreciation for the moral leadership of an outstanding minister, an elderly aunt, steeped in religious prejudice, took exception. "The trouble with that minister," she said, "is that his sermons are just as good for Catholics and Jews as for Presbyterians."

❖   ❖

Way down in the South, a traveling man found himself stranded for the night and in his rambles around town noticed there were two Baptist churches. He asked a colored man why there should be two churches of the same denomination.

"Well, boss, Ah'll tell you," said the informant. "They just can't agree. One of the churches believes dat Pharoah's daughter found Moses in de bull-rushes. De odah church claims dat's what she sez!"

❖   ❖

When the late Dr. S. Parkes Cadman was holding his question-and-answer session on the radio, someone asked, "Dr. Cadman, do you believe the time will ever come when all Jews, Catholics and Protestants will worship one religion in the same church?" This was a pretty big question for the doctor because he was talking to millions of Jews, Catholics and Protestants, but he replied, "Yes, I do; but I don't mind saying that I would hate to be the first arch-bishop of the church!"

❖ ❖

Al Smith and a party of friends, both Catholic and Protestant went into the Canadian wilds for a camping trip. All week long they fished and loafed and ate. On Saturday night while they were talking around the camp fire, one of the men suggested that to-morrow was Sunday, and that there was a little church down in the village where they ought to go down to mass. The Catholic mem-bers agreed and told Pat that he should wake them up in the morn-ing. The Protestants smiled and remarked how nice it was going to be to sleep as late as they wished.

In the morning, Pat awoke and amidst great protest got the men ready. The water was too cold for shaving, the fires had gone out, and they had a miserable time finding their good clothes. They finally got themselves together and started down the trail, closing the door of the cabin on the sleeping friends.

Longingly one of the church goers looked back and whispered to Al Smith: "Wouldn't it be a shame if we should find out that those boys are right after all?"

❖ ❖

A Kansas editor thought to poke fun at Dr. C. Oscar Johnson because of the statement that appeared somewhere that there were 2,500 people at a service in his St. Louis Church. Said this editor: "Every one knows that your church seats only 1,800 people." Dr. Johnson refused to be drawn into a controversy, simply retorting: "You do not know what narrow Baptists we have in Missouri."

❖ ❖

Our Army and Navy chaplains venturing into remote Pacific outposts were often surprised to find among the natives a fair per-centage professing the Christian faith—disciples of missionaries who visited the territory in some distant prewar period.

It was not uncommon for our chaplains, when circumstances per-mitted, to meet with these converts in a spirit of fellowship. Since a single group might embrace a variety of denominations one chaplain followed a custom of asking those present to identify themselves. After the Methodists, Baptists, Presbyterians, etc., had been sorted out, one very large and very black native stepped forward. "Me," he said with superb dignity, "Norwegian Lutheran."

❖ ❖

Lawrence Lariar, cartoon editor of Liberty, reports an overheard conversation between his seven-year-old daughter and the child of a neighbor.

"What church do you go to?" asked the other youngster.

"I don't go to church," said Lariar's daughter. "I go to a temple. I'm a Jewess."

"A Jewess?" questioned her companion. "What's that?"

"Well," said the seven-year-old patiently, "you know, there are Protestants, Catholics and Jews, but they're just different ways of voting for God!"

❖ ❖

An Irish Catholic was taken dangerously ill with smallpox. He insisted that in his illness he must have absolution. Turning to his wife, he said, "Bridget, I know I am going to die. Send for a Jewish rabbi at once."

"No, Patrick dear," replied Bridget, "you're not going to die. You're going to be well again. But of course if you want absolution, you shall have it. You want our own dear priest though, Patrick,—not a Jewish rabbi."

"No, Bridget, not the priest. I want a Jewish rabbi. Do you think I want our priest to get the smallpox!"

❖ ❖

An old colored farmer was asked by an evangelist what denomination he belonged to. He did not reply directly, but said: "Bress ye, sah, dah's t'ree roads leading from hyah ter town—de long road, de sho' road, and de swamp road—but when Ah goes ter town wid er load er grain dey don't say ter me, 'Uncle Calhoun, which road did you come by?' but, 'Cal, is yo' wheat good?' "

❖ ❖

On a train, some years ago, a high church dignitary was approached by a slightly inebriated young chap who invited him to join a card game. The bishop quite naturally refused. And something in his manner may have been a tip-off, for his chance acquaintance asked:

"Shay, are you a preacher?"

"I am a Southern Methodist bishop."

"Southern Methodist? Gosh! Always thought that was a football team!"

CRIME—Punishment

An old man who had served on many juries was asked what most influenced his decisions—lawyers, witnesses, or the judge.

"Well," the old man said, "I'm an ordinary man with a reasonin' mind. I don't let nothing none o' them fellers says influence me. No, sir! I jest take a good squint at the prisoner, an' I says t' myself, 'If he didn't do nothin' why is he here?' Then I bring 'em all in guilty."

CRITICISM

The United States Army of Occupation is making a valiant effort to instill in the German people some elements of democracy and self reliance. The experiment is not proving too successful. The tradition of subservience is too strong to be thrown off lightly.

Some months ago one of our public relations officers, in a periodic meeting with German newsmen, sought to make clear to them that they are now privileged to criticize the military government, so long as the criticism isn't malicious.

"Very good," responded a spokesman for the group. "Now, what is it you wish us to criticize?"

DECEPTION

We are reminded, by current propaganda stories, of the two rival Greek merchants who always tried to deceive each other about their commercial trips. One day Hadshikyriakos met his competitor Papazoglu on the Athens-Salonika train. Papazoglu, it seems, had told Hadshikyriakos he was going to Salonika.

"Papazoglu, why did you lie to me?" complained the second merchant. "You told me you were going to Salonika, and you really are going to Salonika!"

DECEPTION—Danger of

It is in our efforts to deceive others that we so often come to grief. Like the nearsighted girl. Determined that her lover should not learn of her defect, she planned an elaborate strategy.

One day, when her lover was due to call, she placed a pin in a tree about 50 feet from a bench where she was certain they would sit.

Later, she remarked quite casually, "Oh, look at the pin in that tree over there!"

The boy was incredulous. Such eyesight, he persisted was phenomenal. "Then come with me," the girl invited, "and I'll prove it's a pin."

She grabbed him by the hand, and they started for the tree. But on the way, she stumbled over a cow and broke her leg.

DECISION

Joe McCarthy had a dream that he had gone to heaven. Up there behind the Pearly Gates he saw the greatest baseball players of all time and just couldn't resist the temptation to form a team. Then the question arose of arranging a schedule.

He was trying to puzzle that out when the phone rang. It was the devil. "I have a team that can beat yours," Satan told him.

"Impossible," answered McCarthy. "I've got all the great ball players that ever lived. How could you expect to beat me?"

Replied the devil, "I've got all the umpires."

❖   ❖

A woman being interviewed on the secret of her successful marriage, insisted, "My husband is The Boss. I believe in letting the man make all important decisions."

"Who made the decision that he was to be The Boss?" she was asked. "Why," was the reply, "naturally, I did."

DEFEAT

Defeat is not bitter if you do not swallow it.

DEFINITION

Overheard in conversation between two biology students emerging from laboratory period: "Aw, everybody knows a skeleton is just a pile of bones with the people scraped off."

DELINQUENCY—Juvenile

Most homes nowadays seem to be on three shifts. Father is on the night shift; mother is on the day shift, and the children shift for themselves.

DELUSION

A student who had been loafing for most of the semester, approached a professor. "Do you think," he asked anxiously, "that if I 'bone up' for the next two weeks I can pass the exam?"

"Sir," replied the prof, "you make me think of a thermometer in a cold room. You can make it register higher by holding your hand over it, but you won't be warming the room."

DEMOCRACY

In a democracy, when people aren't sure what they want, they vote for something different from what they have.

DETAIL

The editor of a country weekly employed a correspondent who frequently forgot essential details in the stories he filed. Ye Ed sharply warned him to get names in his dispatches. Several days later the correspondent filed this: "Due to possibility of there being rabies spread in this town, our police force has rounded up four dogs. Their names are Towser, Rover, Fido and Prince."

DIET

"Doctor," growled the man who had been put on a diet, "why do you always order a fellow to cut out the things he likes?"

"Because," snapped the doctor, "he never eats or drinks the things he doesn't like, so it stands to reason it must be the things he does like that are disagreeing with him."

❖ ❖

Methuselah ate what he found on his plate, and never, as people do now, did he note the amount of the caloric count—he ate it because it was chow. He wasn't disturbed, as at dinner he sat, destroying a roast or a pie, to think it was lacking in glandular fat, or a couple of vitamins shy. He cheerfully chewed every species of food, untroubled by worries or fears lest his health should be hurt by some fancy dessert—and he lived over nine hundred years!

DIPLOMACY

In the days when the West was younger and a shade more robust than it now is, a young Harvard graduate inherited a cattle ranch and went out to operate it. He was an easy-going lad, with a natural horror of rough tactics. Presently, he encountered the inevitable cattle rustler, in the person of a neighboring rancher. His suspicions fully verified, the Harvard man sat down to indite a letter to the offending rustler.

"I shall appreciate it" he wrote, "if you will refrain from leaving your hot branding irons about, where my cattle can lie down on them."

❖ ❖

A good many of us in our attitude toward the evils of this world are rather like the dying Irishman.

"Well, Pat," said a friend at the bedside, "have ye made peace with God and denounced the divil?"

"Shure," said Pat, "I've made peace with God—but I'm in no position to antagonize anybody!"

❖ ❖

The Christ of the Andes statue, standing on the Chile-Argentine boundary line symbolizes a pledge made by the two countries. As long as the statue stands, it was agreed, there shall be peace and good-will between Argentina and Chile.

But, ironically enough, the statue itself was the cause of what almost resulted in open conflict. When the work was completed, someone pointed out that the Savior's back was toward Chile. Chileans felt they had been slighted. But while indignation was at its height, a Chilean newspaper man saved the day. In an editorial he explained: "The Argentineans need more watching over than the Chileans." This satisfied the people. They laughed good-naturedly—and went back to their daily tasks.

❖   ❖

When Voltaire visited England in the year 1727, feeling ran high against the French, and the great author felt this dislike keenly. Once he was accosted by an angry crowd of people as he went for a walk. "Kill him! Hang the Frenchman!" cried threatening voices around him. Voltaire stood on the curbstone and cried out: "Englishmen! You want to kill me because I am a Frenchman! Am I not already punished enough in not being an Englishman?"

The crowd applauded this speech and escorted him home in safety.

❖   ❖

A number of years ago, an excited gentleman came up to a Representative from New Jersey. "Mr. Eaton" he said, "are you for or against prohibition?"

The Representative straightened up and thundered impressively, "I am, sir!"

"Well," said the voter, "I thought you were." And he went away perfectly satisfied.

DISASTER

A gentle old lady's consuming desire was to own a large hat smothered in violets. Penny by penny she saved until she had the price demanded—twenty dollars.

Her first opportunity to wear her dream was at a funeral. The church was banked with flowers, and yet our gentle old lady removed her hat, feeling somehow that it was a bit too gay for so solemn an occasion. She placed it on a window sill and wept herself into a coma.

Presently the coffin was borne forth, piled high with flowers.

The old lady watched fascinated. On the very top of the heaped flowers was her hat. She is now saving her pennies again.

DISCIPLINE

A candidate for public office stopped at a farmer's house for the night. He talked with the farmer, got his promise of support then turned his attention to a long, lanky boy who had come to show him his room. "Young man," he said, "you look old enough to vote. What's your age?"

"Well," said the lad, "I was 21 last April, but I didn't bow my head when Pa ast the blessin', so he sot me back two year, an' now I cain't vote."

❖   ❖

Wilbur, an only child, had just entered kindergarten. Fascinated by everything that occurred there, he talked of nothing else. After father got home in the evening Wilbur followed him everywhere, telling him what had happened, who the children were, what they played, what the teacher said. Finally the parent could control himself no longer. "Young man," he said, "go over there and sit down and shut up."

Abashed, Wilbur obeyed, but not without a final thrust. "At school," he said in a small voice, "we say 'Please be seated.' "

DISCONTENT

Mrs. Higgins was an incurable grumbler. She grumbled at everything and everyone. But at last the vicar thought he had found something about which she could make no complaint; the old lady's crop of potatoes was certainly the finest for miles round. "Ah, for once you must be well pleased," he said, with a beaming smile, as he met her in the village street. "Everyone's saying how splendid your potatoes are this year." The old lady glowered at him as she answered: "They're not so poor. But where's the bad ones for the pigs?"

DISCOURAGEMENT

The spirit of despair laid its withering hand on Martin Luther, and he almost lost his grit to grapple with life. While he was in this frame of mind, Mrs. Luther appeared before him dressed in deep mourning. When Luther looked up and saw her strange attire, he inquired the reason for her behavior, she replied, "God is dead and I am mourning His decease." "Nonsense," shouted Luther. "From the way you were acting," said she, "I thought God must be dead and that you were running the universe for Him."

DISTRUST

Two Alabama farmers were wrangling in front of the village post office. A traveling salesman asked the cause. "Oh," explained the postmaster, "they swapped mules here awhile back, and now each is accusing the other of skinning him."

"Well," suggested the salesman, "why don't they trade back?"

"Why," said the postmaster, "they're afeared they'll git skinned again!"

DIVORCE (see also MARRIAGE, MARRIED LIFE)

The divorce problem exists simply because there are too many married couples and two few husbands and wives.

❖ ❖

Some of our modern customs cause complications. On registration day at a junior high school in one of our western cities, a girl came to the teacher with this problem: "What shall I put where it says 'Father's name?' Do you want the man my mother's divorced from, or the one she's married to now, or the man she's going to marry after she gets her divorce next week?"

❖ ❖

"The increasing divorce rate is rapidly making America the land of the free," a visiting Englishman acidly observed.

"Yes," admitted his American companion, "but remember the marriage rate is increasing too. That shows America is still the home of the brave."

❖ ❖

A young housekeeper, who lives in a small Kentucky town, had occasion to reprimand her cook for neglecting her duties.

"Well, Miss Lucille, Ah'se been worrited," was the reply. "Ah'se studyin' a most important question. Tell de trufe, Ah doan know which t' get—a winter coat or a divohce."

DOCTOR BILLS

"How much does it cost," a doctor was asked, "to say 'hello' to you?"

"There's no charge for that," said the doctor thoughtfully. "That's thrown in free."

"Well, hello."

"Hello to you," said the doctor.

"And good-by."

"Oh, you should have asked me about that," said the doctor. "Good-by costs $2."

DOMESTICITY—Lack

No woman's hand had ever touched the domain of the rough settlers' cabin, and the grime reigned triumphant. The conversation drifted from politics to cooking.

The two settlers sat smoking and talking about the cooking they had been doing. One suggested that they get a cook-book and try to improve.

"No," said the other. "I bought one of them things oncet, but I never could do nuthin' with it."

"What's the hitch?" inquired the other.

"Well, everyone of those recipes began in the same way. 'Take a clean dish—' and I never got no farther."

DRINK

The shoemaker, a Temperance man, was passing an inn one night when the landlord emerged struggling with a hefty customer.

"Give me a hand to get Bill home," he urged.

"Not I," chuckled the shoemaker. "You do as I do when I've done a really good job—just stick him up in the window as an advertisement!"

DRINK—DRINKING

The appraiser had been sent to a home to take inventory of its contents. The first entry was:

"One bottle old Scotch whisky—partially full."

The next item:

"One revolving Turkish rug."

❖ ❖

"They call this stuff moonshine!" the mountain traveler exclaimed after his first swallow. "Gosh! It ought to be rechristened. It tastes like bottled sunstroke!"

❖ ❖

A definition of intoxication: To feel sophisticated, and not be able to pronounce it.

❖ ❖

Soon after four in the morning the husband returned home in the usual state of intoxication. He was lucky in getting the key to fit the lock at the tenth try, but as he literally climbed the stairs an unfortunate side slip aroused attention. When he reached the bedroom his wife, whose tongue was fond of exercise, gave a prolonged exhibition of shrewish oratory. In conclusion she lamented the fate that had tied her to a man who came home at four in the morning.

"My dear," expostulated the husband, "itsh only one o'clock. Just now I heard it shtrike one several times mosht distinctly."

❖ ❖

She puts vitamins in her gin so she can build up while she's tearing herself down.

❖ ❖

A man went to a fancy dress party. Another said to him, "Pardon me, but you're 'Titus Andronicus,' are you not?"

"What, me?" said the man in the toga angrily. "I haven't even found out where the bar is yet."

❖ ❖

The late Justice Charles P. Thompson of Massachusetts while practicing law, once defended a client named Michael Dougherty, accused of the illegal sale of liquor. The sole evidence against the man was a single pint bottle of whiskey, which had been found in his alleged kitchen barroom.

After the prosecution had made a thumping good presentation of its case, the defense attorney arose and said, "Michael Dougherty, take the stand."

Mike, with big red nose, unshaven face, bleary eyes, and a general appearance of dilapidation and dejection, came forward.

"Michael Dougherty," said Thompson, "look upon the jury. Jury, look upon Michael Dougherty."

After the jury had taken a good, long look at the prisoner, his attorney said, "Gentlemen of the jury, do you mean to say to this court and to me that you honestly and truly believe that Michael Dougherty, if he had a pint of whisky, would sell it?"

Mike was quickly acquitted.

❖   ❖

Said the glass of beer to the bottle of gin: I'm not much of a mathematician, but I can and do Add to a man's nervous troubles, Subtract cash from his pocketbook, Multiply his aches and pains, Divide his property with bootleggers, so that fractions only remain for him.

Moreover, I take interest from his work, and Discount his chances for health and success.

❖   ❖

"Beverage alcohol," said a doctor who knew whereof he spoke, "gives you a red nose, a black eye, a white liver, a yellow streak, a green brain, a dark brown breath and a blue outlook."

❖   ❖

The trouble with people who drink like fishes is that they don't drink what fishes drink!

❖   ❖

In his youth, before he became a god, Bacchus discovered a plant which he wished might grow in his own country. Uprooting it, he placed it in the bone of a bird to protect the roots. The roots grew too big for the bird bone and as he was then passing through

Africa he picked up a lion's bone and placed the plant in it. But soon even the lion's bone could not hold it. Seeing a large bone of a jackass Bacchus pushed the lion's bone into it.

In his own country he planted the vine and bones in the ground. From the plant grew a vineyard, and from the grapes he made a wine. But strangely, when his friends drank some of the wine they sang like birds. When they drank more they were brave and mighty as lions. But when they drank too much they behaved in the manner of jackasses.

❖ ❖

In standard liquid measure, two pints make one cavort.

❖ ❖

"While summering in Maine," says N. C. Wyeth, the illustrator, "I offered an old shipwright a drink. He refused, adding that he had not touched a drink in thirty years.

"I asked what had happened to make him take the pledge.

" 'Wal,' he said reflectively, 'I was asked to make a coffin for a member of the community who had just passed away. They brought me a jug o' applejack and a bottle o' whisky and I started to work. I kept at the job straight through the night. By dawn the applejack and whisky was gone. I stepped back to take a good look at that coffin—an' right then I swore never t' touch another drop.'

"Naturally I asked what had been the matter with the coffin.

" 'Nothin',' said the old Yankee dryly, 'except I'd put a keel on it!' "

❖ ❖

Where there's a swill there's a sway.

❖ ❖

Two members of the old fraternity who hadn't seen each other in many moons paused to exchange the mystic grip and a bit of gossip.

"How's old Bill these days?"

"Oh, he's much improved since his operation."

"Operation? Didn't know he'd had one."

"Oh yeah; they removed a brass rail that had been pressing against his foot for years."

❖   ❖

It may be contrary to the laws of nature, but wild oats and old rye produce the same kind of crop.

❖   ❖

An inebriate dreaded the tongue lashing from his wife that invariably accompanied his return home in the early hours. So, after a night of tippling, he returned home, went to the kitchen, tied a rope about his waist, and tied skillets, pots and pans to the rope so they dragged behind him as he walked. Then he took off his shoes and stole softly upstairs.

"She'll never hear me in this infernal din," he whispered to himself as he crept toward the bedroom.

❖   ❖

Papa Hog wandered down to the brewery and found a big puddle of sour beer that had been poured out. When he staggered home, Mama Hog met him and quickly shunted him around the barn, out of sight of the baby pigs. With a furious grunt she exclaimed:

"You shameless thing! What do you mean by making such a human being of yourself before the children?"

❖   ❖

The minister found Mike on the sidewalk, drunk. He picked him up. He told Mike that it wasn't possible to drink up all the brewery could make. Mike looked at the brewery, all lighted up, and said, "Anyway, I got them working nights."

DRUDGERY

A farmer's wife had lost all semblance of sanity and it was necessary to remove her from her home by means of a strait-jacket and ambulance, and confine her to a nearby institution for the insane. Her husband, a day or so later, in trying to explain her sudden loss of sanity, said he just couldn't understand it. "Why, nobody ever bothered her. She hasn't been out of the kitchen in nearly twenty years!"

EARLY RISING

A maiden lady from the city was spending her vacation on a midwestern farm. Arising at what seemed to her the unprecedentedly early hour of seven, she found that the farmer had breakfasted and was well along with the chores.

"Ah," said the sentimental urbanite, inhaling briskly, "how glorious to be up at the dawning of a new day. And look! The larks are on the wing!"

The agriculturist looked up to observe a dozen sparrows flitting by. "Yeah," he said dryly, not bothering to correct the ornithological error, "I reckon they must be knockin' off fer lunch."

ECONOMICS

Once upon a time, so the story goes, there was a canny and powerful king who ruled a great and prosperous country. There came a time, however, when things were not going so well and there was hunger throughout the land. The good king called in the experts in his kingdom and told them to prepare a brief and complete text on economics so he could use it to do something for his people. In due course they made their report. It consisted of five words: "There is no free lunch."

ECONOMY

A small boy was seen by his father going upstairs three steps at a time.

"What you taking such big strides for, Isaac?" he asked.

"To save wearing out the carpet, pa."

"Good boy, Isaac," the father said approvingly. "But don't split your trousers."

❖   ❖

The Scot stepped into a telegraph office and picked up one of the blanks.

"How much," he asked, "is a telegram to California?"

"Five cents a word for ten words," informed the clerk. "There will be no charge for the signature.

The Scot looked musingly at the clerk.

"There will be no charge for the signature?" he repeated questioningly.

"That's right," declared the clerk.

"The Scot rubbed his forehead and finally suggested:

"Suppose you just send my signature then."

The clerk grinned. "All right," he said, "I'll do that for you. What's your name?"

"Well," said the Scot, "I may not look it, but I'm an Indian and my name is I-Won't-Be-Home-Till-Friday!"

ECONOMY—Simplified

Charlie Stow, press agent for the Adam Forepaugh circus, used to delight in telling this experience with a midwestern weekly. Stow dropped in on the editor and asked the cost of a full page ad for a single insertion.

"One hundred dollars," was the response.

"That's a lot of money," mused Stow. "How much for a half page?"

"One hundred dollars."

"That's an odd rate schedule," observed the press agent, "a new one on me. How do you figure it?"

"Well, sir," said the editor candidly and cannily, "your show is due here on July 12, and on the 13th I've got a note due for one hundred dollars."

He got the ad!

EDUCATION

This is a good time for the colleges to try to work their way through some of the students.

❖   ❖

A wise man once defined education as that which remains when we have forgotten all that we have been taught.

❖   ❖

Does education pay? Does it pay to sharpen the tools before working with them?

❖   ❖

"In my early youth," says Homer Croy, magazine writer, "I got a small 'vest-pocket' dictionary, determined to master every word in it. I came to the word 'coxcomb.' The definition was a 'fop,' but I had never heard the word fop. I looked it up.

"The dictionary said: 'Fop: a coxcomb.'

"It pretty well discouraged me from getting an education."

❖   ❖

Theodore Roosevelt was talking with the then president of the General Education Board, and during the conversation mentioned that he was going to endorse industrial and agricultural training for the Negro, but no more.

"And where will you train teachers for these subjects?" asked the educator.

"Yes, of course," said the Rough-rider President, "there must be normal schools. But I stop there."

"Where shall we train the teachers for the normal schools?" was the next question.

"Ah, I see," replied Roosevelt. "Once you start in education, you cannot stop!"

❖   ❖

Someone has observed that the trouble with the school system today is: the teachers are afraid of the principals, the principals are afraid of the superintendent, he is afraid of the school committee, they are afraid of the parents, the parents are afraid of the children, and the children are afraid of nobody.

❖   ❖

A college education was roaming around in search of a job. "Take of your coat," said a practical idea. So the college education took off his coat.

"Now, take off your waistcoat," said the P.I.

The college education did so.

"Now," said the P. I., "remove your collar and tie, your shirt, your——"

"But," interrupted the C. E., "there'll soon be nothing left of me."

"I know it," replied the P. I., "then you can begin."

❖   ❖

A group of professional men had gathered in the lobby of a hotel and proceeded to make themselves known to one another.

"My name is Fortesque," said one, extending his hand. "I'm a painter—work in water colors chiefly."

"Indeed," remarked another. "I'm a sculptor. I work in stone."

Then the quiet little fellow who had been inclined to keep apart stepped up, a dry smile on his face.

"Glad to make the acquaintance of you gentlemen," he remarked, "for I have a common interest with you. I work in ivory. I'm a college professor."

❖ ❖

The small Jewish boy brought home very poor marks from school. His alibi was that anti-Semitism was so strong he didn't have a chance. His parents finally decided that nothing should prevent the boy from getting the most from his schooling. At all costs, he must be converted to Christianity and thus escape the fate of his tribe.

The next report card was anticipated with great enthusiasm. The parents were much chagrined to note no improvement. Looking innocently into his father's face, little Abie explained:

"Well, you know, our kind can't learn as fast as those blamed little Jewish kids."

❖ ❖

A stranger to the city drove to Salem to inquire about a prospective building on the campus. Mistaking the State Hospital for the Insane for the university, he asked a man idling near the entrance if this were Willamette University. The man, a patient, replied that it was not, that it was the asylum.

"Oh, well," said the stranger, wishing to be affable, "I suppose after all there isn't much difference between them."

"But there is, and you're mistaken again," flashed the sane insane man. "In this place you've got to show improvement before you can get out."

❖ ❖

St. Peter, guard at the Pearly Gate, was suffering from a streak of boredom. They just hadn't been getting the right kind of people in Heaven for the past few years, and he was getting discouraged. A knock on the gate, and the famous keeper perked up his ears with hope.

"Who's there?" he called.

A suave, cultured voice responded, "It is I."

With a groan of despair, St. Peter growled, "Get to hell out of here. We have all the Harvard men and school teachers we can stand now."

❖   ❖

The postman was shoving the letters and the magazines into the farmer's mail box when the farmer's son came scooting out of the drive in his roadster, and breezed off to town. The postman called to the farmer in the yard, "Your son is a college graduate, isn't he?"

"Yes," drawled the farmer, "he is, but I'll have to give the college its just dues. He didn't have no sense to begin with."

❖   ❖

There is quite an old anecdote that seems particularly appropriate to this season when a new school year is just beginning:

"And how do you like going to school, Roger?" a kindly lady inquired of a very small lad.

"Oh, I like the going all right," the boy replied, "and I like coming back, too. It's having to stay after I get there that bothers me."

❖   ❖

A high school girl, seated next to a famous astronomer at a dinner party, struck up a conversation, asking, "What do you do in life?"

He replied, "I study astronomy."

"Dear me," said the young miss, "I finished astronomy last year."

EDUCATION—Limited

A hill woman came to a small mountain school to "pick up a little l'arnin'." Her desire was modest; she wanted only to learn to write her name. Having accomplished this feat in a single term, she thanked the teacher and took her departure.

But when school "took up" again in the fall, this woman was among the first arrivals. Once more she explained that she was interested only in learning to write her name.

"But you learned that last year," the teacher pointed out.

"Shore," agreed the pupil amiably, "but since then I've gone and got married."

EDUCATION—Progressive

"What's the fuss in the school yard?" asked a passer-by.

"The doctor's been around examining us," replied the boy, "and one of the deficient kids is knocking the stuffin' out of a perfect kid."

✧   ✧

Young Oswald has just been enrolled at a "progressive" school. His grandmother, who did not quite "take" to the newer knowledge was asked how the boy was getting along and what he had learned.

"Oh, he's progressing nicely," she replied. "He has learned that he will have to be vaccinated, that his eyes aren't mates, that his teeth need repairing, and that his method of breathing is entirely obsolete."

EDUCATION—Religious

If religious instruction is to mean something, there must be more than a mere verbal repetition of Scriptures.

We are reminded of the little girl whose Teddy Bear had shoe-button eyes that slewed about in a peculiar fashion. She named it "Gladly" after "a cross-eyed bear" she had heard mentioned in Sunday school. Investigation proved she had reference to the hymn, "Gladly, the Cross I'd Bear."

EFFICIENCY

In the early days of the campaign, General MacArthur summoned an engineer and asked: "How long will it take to throw a bridge across this stream?"

"Three days," was the reply.

"Good," snapped MacArthur. "Have your draftsmen make drawings right away."

Three days later, the general sent for the engineer and asked how the bridge was coming.

"It's all ready," was the answer. "You can send your men across now, if you don't have to wait for them pictures. They ain't done yet!"

✧   ✧

A Dutchman was recently expatiating on the folly of giving women the vote. . . . He declared that in Holland there was greater efficiency among the female sex where they did not possess that doubtful privilege. He pointed to the fact that the Dutch woman sits with one foot on the spinning wheel or churn and with the other she rocks the cradle containing twins; with her hands she knits socks for her husband, while on her knee rests a book from which she is improving her mind by study. And all the while she sits on a cheese, pressing it for market.

✧   ✧

The management of a certain factory has been much annoyed lately by the tardiness of the employees in responding to the noon whistle to start work again. The men like to loiter outdoors, talk, pitch horseshoes and play pass ball, during the noon hour after lunch, and few of them were at their machines when the whistle blew. The management posted a sign beside a suggestion box, calling attention to the matter, and offering five dollars for the best answer to this question: "What should we do to insure that every man will be inside the factory when the one o'clock whistle blows?"

Many suggestions were offered, ranging from a system of demerits and fines to an actual lockout of persistently tardy workmen. One of these schemes received the five dollar award, but a duplicate award was unanimously voted to the nimblewitted Irish sweeper who turned in the following answer to a perplexing problem: "Let the last man in blow the whistle."

✧   ✧

A minister of Scotch descent, rather noted for his close calculations, also operated a small farm in Vermont.

One day he observed his hired man sitting idly by the plow, as the horses took a needed rest. This rather shocked the good man's sense of economy. After all, he was paying the man twenty-five cents an hour. So he said, gently but reproachfully, "John, wouldn't it be a good plan for you to have a pair of shears and be trimming these bushes while the horses are resting?"

"That it would," replied John agreeably. "And might I suggest, your reverence, that you take a peck of potatoes into the pulpit and peel 'em during the anthem."

EFFICIENCY—Army

A cadet was running the obstacle course, but fell on the last hurdle and lay on the ground. The O-in-C saw him prone and rushed up: "What's the matter, why don't you finish the course?"

"I'm sorry, Sir, but I've broken my leg."

"Well," responded the officer, "don't waste time lying there—do pushups."

EFFICIENCY EXPERT

The efficiency expert will tell you that if a farmer's boy can pick six quarts of cherries in an hour, and a girl five quarts, the two of them together will pick eleven quarts. But any farmer knows that the two of them together won't pick any.

❖   ❖

Once upon a time two efficiency experts were out on a lake, fishing from a rowboat. The boat leaked so badly that it was in danger of sinking. Both worked at bailing out the water until they wearily agreed that such labor was unseemly and inefficient. One proposed that they punch a hole in the bottom of the boat and let the water run out by itself, which they did. But by some singular perversity, the water didn't run out—it ran in. Whereupon, the second expert had a happy inspiration. He advised that another hole be punched in the bottom of the boat, near the first hole, so that water could run out as fast as it ran in. Both were rescued, with their ingenious ideas somewhat damp but otherwise intact, and both are now busily engaged devising ways and means to keep the good ship Business afloat.

EFFORT

One day a vacationist at a remote New England farm was walking toward the village. He met a farmer mowing grass. "How long will it take me to get to town?" asked the visitor. The scythe stopped, a level glance came up, "How fast are you going to walk?"

EFFORT—Conserved

Old Paw was in his rocking chair on the front porch, rocking due east and west. Beside him was Sonny Boy, an innocent of forty, rocking north and south. Presently Paw said, "Son, why wear yo'self out that-a-way? Rock with the grain and save your strength."

EFFORT—Limited

The Northwest Indians when drying their winter's supply of salmon, hang the fish on trees thirty-three feet above the ground. An old buck was asked why the Indians always hung their fish thirty-three feet above the ground. He answered, "Flies no get him."

The Indians discovered that flies do not rise of themselves to more than thirty-two feet from the ground, so they fooled the flies by hanging the fish just one foot above the fly-line.

By exerting themselves just a little more, the flies could make the grade and get the fish. But they have always stopped trying at thirty-two feet and probably always will.

EFFORT—Minimized

An eastern pilgrim, motoring through rural Kentucky, paused at a particularly dilapidated farm to inquire directions.

"What are you raising?" he asked the farmer. "What's your main crop?"

"Hawgs," was the laconic response.

"Hogs?" repeated the pilgrim. "Do they pay better than corn or tobacco?"

"Wal, no," admitted the farmer. "No, I cain't say 's they do. But," and he brightened perceptibly, "hawgs don't need no hoein'."

EFFORT—Unrewarded

One of the tales left untold by Col. Starling, the late White House guard, is the one about the time he approached one of the natives of a small Vermont town where Calvin Coolidge was spending his vacation, and inquired: "Is there much good hunting around here?". . . The native glanced around him for a minute and then said: "Well, sure, there's plenty of huntin', but damned little findin'."

EFFORT WASTED

Two stuttering blacksmiths had just finished heating a piece of pig iron and one placed it upon the anvil with a pair of tongs.

"G-g-g-g-go on, h-h-h-h-hit it" he stuttered to his helper.

"Wh-wh-wh-where sh-sh-sh-shall I h-h-hit it?" asked the other.

"Ah, h-h-heck, now we'll have to he-h-e-he-heat it all over again!"

EGOTISM

An actor was strolling down Broadway one afternoon, when he stopped before a scale and decided to weigh himself.

He inserted a penny in the machine, and a hand showed his weight, and then a character card dropped out of a slot. It read: "You are extremely egotistical and if you don't change soon, you will never get anywhere."

Of course the actor felt there must be some mistake, so he inserted another penny, and promptly another little card came out. It read, "You are extremely egotistical and if you don't change soon, you will never get anywhere."

This made the actor very angry. With a snort, he pushed another penny into the scale, and immediately a third card came out. It staggered him. It read, "Maybe you think I'm kidding!"

❖ ❖

Jack Lait tells of a Hollywood producer preparing for a radio interview with a woman commentator. As usual, the big-shot took over, began dictating a script to one of his own writers. The interviewer, it developed, was to say:

". . . is one of the great producers of all time. Hollywood bows before him. He combines amazing genius for true art and popular appeal . . ."

At this point the producer paused, turned to his writer and asked, "Do you think that sounds too strong?"

The writer opined that it was maybe a little on the bombastic side.

"Well, then," said the producer, "after she says that, you have me say, 'Lady, you embarrass me!' "

ENCORE—Denied

One day Billy Rose was approached by a man who requested a job in his new show.

"What can you do?" asked Rose.

"I can dive head first from a 500-foot ladder into a barrel of sawdust," said the man.

"I'd like to see you do that," announced the showman.

The stunt was performed by the man much to the amazement of Rose.

"You are hired," exclaimed Rose excitedly. "I'll pay you $250 a week!"

"Oh, no," said the man.

"Then, I'll pay you $500 a week!"

"Oh, no," said the man.

"Then, I'll pay you $1,000 a week—but that's my top figure!"

"Oh, no," said the man.

"Why not?" asked Rose.

"You see," replied the man, "that was the first time I ever did that trick—and I don't like it!"

ENDURANCE

Returning to the capital during the war period after a whirlwind tour which would have knocked out most other men, President Roosevelt was asked how he managed to accomplish so much without getting weary. The President was silent for a few moments and then answered: "You're looking at a man who spent two years trying to learn how to wiggle his big toe again."

ENEMIES

Speak well of your enemies; remember you made them.

ENERGY—Wasted

The Mississippi, sailing from the port of New Orleans, had the largest steam whistle of any ship on the Mississippi river. As a matter of fact, it consumed so much steam in blowing the whistle when it neared the port that it did not have sufficient steam to dock. So it is with a great many people in their daily work—they consume so much steam telling about what they are going to do, or have done, that they do not have sufficient energy left to accomplish anything.

ENTERPRISE

One evening a Jew was received into a hospital for minor injuries, and was placed in a ward. Next morning, he prepared for his prayers by adjusting the tfilin to his arm. The Irishman who was in the bed next to his, watching the Jew intently, finally turned to the occupant of the bed next to his and said: "You certainly got to hand it to these Jews. He came in last night and this morning he's already taking his own blood pressure."

❖   ❖

In front of a grocery store, a well-known art connoisseur noticed a dirty little kitten lapping milk from a saucer that he realized was a rare piece of pottery. He dashed into the store and bought the kitten for $5. "For that sum," he told the proprietor, "I'm sure you won't mind throwing in the saucer. The kitten looks so happy eating from it."

"Nothing doing," said the proprietor. "That's my lucky saucer. From that saucer so far this week I've sold thirty-two cats."

❖   ❖

A storekeeper had for some time displayed in his window a card inscribed, "Fishing Tickle."

A customer drew the proprietor's attention to the spelling. "Hasn't anyone told you of it before?" asked the patron.

"Oh, yes," said the dealer placidly, "many have mentioned it, but whenever they drop in to tell me, they always buy something."

❖   ❖

Recently an admirer jestingly asked heavyweight champ Joe

Louis who he thought would ever beat him. Louis replied seriously:

"The fellow who comes along who can box better'n I can and who can hit harder."

"What are you going to do when he comes along?" was the next question.

"Try to sign him up," replied Joe, "so I can manage him."

❖   ❖

The sensational and spectacular have their place, but often the man who can see opportunity on the sidelines reaps the greater benefits.

W. Buchanan-Taylor, the English journalist, tells of a barber who, as a stunt, agreed to enter a den of lions and shave the lion-tamer.

The lions growled, but the barber went ahead with his work. But when he came out of the cage he was considerably chagrined to learn that a competing barber, with a shop in the same street, had been going through the crowd distributing his own advertising cards.

❖   ❖

"Almost every man can find work if he uses his brains," insists Henry Ginsberg, who tells of a piano-tuner he met in the far west.

"Surely piano-tuning can't be very lucrative way out here," I said to him. "I shouldn't imagine pianos are very plentiful in this region."

"No, they're not," admitted the piano-tuner, "but I make a pretty fair income by tightening up barbed-wire fences."

❖   ❖

Have you heard the story of the toothless Alaskan trapper who, finding a bear in one of his traps, made himself a very satisfactory set of dentures from the animal's molars, and then sat down contentedly to chew succulent bear steak, *with the bear's own teeth!*

❖   ❖

Those who have tried to drive through Georgia backroads of red clay will like this one:

The motorist had paid a farmer $3 to pull him back on the road, and inquired if many other persons were stuck.

"Oh, yes," said the farmer. "Sometimes we pull out as many as ten or twelve a day."

"Do you pull them out at night, too?" asked the tourist.

"Nope; we haul water for the roads at night."

ENTERPRISE—Lack

A Georgia cracker sitting, ragged and barefoot, on the steps of his tumbledown shack, was accosted by a stranger who stopped for a drink of water. Wishing to be agreeable, the stranger said, "How is your cotton coming on?"

"Ain't got none," replied the cracker.

"Didn't you plant any?" asked the stranger.

"Nope," said the cracker. " 'Fraid of boll weevils."

"Well," said the stranger, "how is your corn?"

"Didn't plant none. 'Fraid there wa'n't going to be no rain."

The stranger, confused but persevering, added: "Well, how are your potatoes?"

"Ain't got none. Scairt o' potato bugs."

"Really, what did you plant?" asked the astonished visitor.

"Nothin'," answered the cracker. "I jes' played safe."

ERROR

To err is human, but when the eraser wears out before the pencil, look out.

ESTEEM—Self

Uncle Zeke, patriarch of a small Mississippi village, was asked why he enjoyed talking to himself.

"Firstly," said the old darky, "Ah laks to talk to a smart man; and secondly, Ah laks to hear a smart man talk."

ETHICS

A minister, a doctor and a lawyer, adrift on a raft, sighted a distant island. There were signs of human habitation, but no persons in view.

Since the drift was away from the island, the lawyer volunteered to swim ashore and bring help. Just as he was about to dive into the sea, the minister urged a word of parting prayer, and a brief religious service was held.

Eagerly the two remaining voyagers watched their companion. Presently they were horrified to see a huge shark making directly for the lawyer. At the last moment, however, the shark ducked and the swimmer was saved. Later, another shark came into view and he, too, ducked as he approached the struggling man.

"There!" said the minister triumphantly. "Observe an answer to our prayers. Because of that service we held, the Lord has preserved our friend from the hungry sharks."

"Well, that may be," said the Doctor dubiously, "but personally I'm inclined to think it was professional ethics."

ETIQUETTE

A chorus girl introduced her sweetheart to another chorus girl and was angered when he transferred his affections to the new charmer. Her anger was not directed at him, but at her rival. But when she exploded in an angry vituperative letter, she did not forget the proprieties:

"Look here, you little cat, you know blamed well we had been going together for months. Wait till I lay my hands on you, you good-for-nothing bleached blonde. I'll scratch your eyes out, pull your hair, your teeth, and throw acid on you.

Yours truly, J. R.

P.S. Please excuse pencil."

EULOGY—Reluctant

Called upon for a few words of condolence at the death of one he cordially detested, Voltaire at first refused. He was finally persuaded and penned this brief but reluctant statement: "I have just been informed that Monsieur Blank is dead. He was a sturdy patriot, a gifted writer, a loyal friend, and an affectionate husband and father—provided he is really dead."

EUPHEMISM

The pastor was calling when the youthful son and heir approached his mother proudly and exhibited a dead rat. As she shrank in repugnance, he attempted to reassure her: "Oh, it's dead all right, mama. We beat it and beat it and beat it, and it's deader n' dead." His eyes fell on the minister and he felt that something more was due to that reverend presence so he continued in a tone of solemnity: "Yes, we beat it and beat it until—until God called it home!"

EVIL—Avoidance

A steamboat captain was seeking a pilot. "Do you know where all the snags are in this river?" he asked. "No, sir," was the reply, "I don't know where all the snags are, but I reckon I do know where they are not and that's where I do my sailing."

EVOLUTION

Three monkeys sat in a coconut tree, discussing things as they're said to be. Said one to the other: "Now, listen, you two, there's a certain rumor that can't be true—that man descends from our Noble Race. The very idea! It's a dire disgrace! No monkey ever deserted his wife, starved her baby and ruined her life. And you've never known a monk mother to leave her babies with others to bunk until they scarcely knew who was their mother. And another thing, you'll never see a monk build a fence 'round a coconut tree and let the coconuts go to waste. Why, if I'd build a fence around this tree, starvation would force you to steal from me! Here's another thing a monk won't do: go out at night and get on a stew; or use a gun, or club, or knife to take some other monkey's life. Yes, man descended, the ornery cuss—but brother, he didn't descend from us!"

EXAGGERATION

A man noted for his tall tales was relating a hunting experience he had in the Canadian north woods.

"The trees were huge and thick as the hairs on a dog's back. They were so thick I had to turn sideways to get through them. One day as I was walking through the woods I looked up and here was a huge buck coming right toward me. He had beautiful antlers that reached high above his head. He was a magnificent animal."

"Say," interrupted one of his listeners, "you just said the trees were so thick you had to turn sideways to get through; now how could a deer come through such a forest?"

"The deer," answered the hunter, "pulled in his horns, like the rest of us have to do once in a while."

✧   ✧

Two children on a train were arguing over who should have dibs on a box of candy reposing on the seat between them. Pushing the box behind him, the boy looked the little girl square in the eye. "I bet I can remember longer'n you can," he wagered. "I can remember when I was born."

"That's nothin'," she snapped. "I can remember before I was born. I can remember when God said, 'Stan' up Patsy, and let me put your eyes in.' Now you gimme that candy!"

✧   ✧

A much beloved minister, who preached good sermons, had a habit of exaggerating—always, however, on the side of good. But finally the elders decided that they would have to speak to him about it, which, of course, they disliked very much to do, but they finally got up the courage and spoke to him. When they got through, he said: "Oh, brethren, don't I know it? And it has caused me to shed barrels and barrels of tears."

✧   ✧

Leopold Godowsky, noted pianist and composer, was talking shop with a well-known violinist who was in the habit of exaggerating his successes. The violinist had just returned from a European tour, and was eager to tell the pianist about his triumphs.

"I was a sensation!" he boasted. "Everywhere I went, I had to play at least ten encores!"

"Then your tour was a success, eh?" asked Godowsky politely.

"A success! Guess how much I made, Leopold? Just guess!"

Godowsky calmly looked the other in the eye and answered: "Half."

✧   ✧

Two commercial travelers were swapping tall wireless stories in the presence of an old countryman whom they were trying to impress.

"You got a radio set?" asked one of the travelers.

"Yes, sor," said the countryman. "I got a very good one."

"Does it have good selectivity?" asked the traveler, with a knowing wink at his companion.

"Well, yes," said the old fellow, "it has. The other night I was listening to a quartet, and I didn't like the tenor, so I just tuned him out and listened to the other three."

❖ ❖

A Texas man went over into Arkansas with the idea of buying a farm. A real estate man showed him the tract. It was good soil but low land, and close to a creek. The keen eye of the Texan observed the marks of dark, rich land on the trees, about 5 ft. from the ground.

"Looks like this land is overflowed in high-water time," he commented.

"No, suh," assured the agent. "This heah land never is overflowed. Them marks is where the hogs come up from the bottoms and rub the mud off their backs."

The prospect pondered silently. Having completed his inspection, he gave his verdict: "I don't hardly reckon I'd be interested in the land," he said, "but—I shore would crave t' have about six carloads o' them hogs!"

❖ ❖

A motion picture mogul, as a gesture of courtesy, attended a preview of a film sponsored by a much smaller operator. Later, he was asked by press representatives to express an opinion, and found himself in rather a warm spot. To indicate an attitude of friendliness, with just the right note of condescension, required a bit of tact. Our mighty mogul was equal to the occasion.

"Ah," he beamed, "it was colossal, colossal—er, in a small way, of course."

❖ ❖

Exaggeration is the fountain of much of America's humor. . . . There was the dust-bowl joke about the man who felt the first drops of rain after the long drought, fainted, and had to be revived by having a couple of buckets of dust thrown in his face.

❖   ❖

"Johnnie," asked his mother, "what is all that noise on the back porch?"

"There's a thousand cats out there, fightin'," said Johnnie, after a survey.

"Johnnie, you shouldn't exaggerate so. Now, how many are there."

"There's five hundred, anyway."

"Are you sure?"

"Well, there's fifty."

"Johnnie, did you count them?"

"Well, there's our cat and Thompsons' and I won't come down another cat!"

EXAGGERATION—Deflated

Harry Hershfield tells of a fellow who opened a delicatessen in a block that boasted two salami salons. One promoted his line of bologna with this line of baloney: "Finest in the world!" The other delicatessen declared, "Best in the universe." Hershfield's hero put up a sign: "Nicest in the neighborhood!"

EXAMPLE

A traveler in Scotland stopped to ask a little bare-legged urchin the way to the nearest golf course.

"Weel," said he, "ye'll gang straight alang here till ye come to the first on yer richt, an' ye'll see a minister—I mean a sign post," he corrected hastily, "and ye'll git the road frae it."

Thanking him for the information, the traveler inquired why he called the finger-post a minister.

Shuffling his feet and gazing longingly at the copper the man held in his hand, he stammered, "Folks ca' it a minister," he replied, " 'kase it pints the richt road but disna gang itsel'."

❖   ❖

The waves had receded, and two crabs were strolling about the beach. Suddenly the mother cried out to her daughter: "It displeases me that you shift from side to side as you do. . . . You should go straight forward. There is no sense in doing otherwise. See that you heed what I say."

"Well, mother," replied the young crab, "do but walk straight yourself and show me how, then I will follow you."

❖ ❖

For many years Monterey, a picturesque California coast town was a pelican's paradise. As the fishermen cleaned their fish, they flung the offal to the pelicans standing expectantly by, and the birds grew fat, lazy and contented. Now, however, the offal is utilized, and there are no tidbits for the pelicans. When the change came, the pelicans made no effort to fish for themselves; they waited hopelessly around, grew gaunt and thin, and slowly starved to death. They had forgotten how to fish for themselves! The problem was solved by importing some strange pelicans from down the coast, birds accustomed to foraging for themselves. They were placed among their starving brothers, and the newcomers immediately began the joy of catching fish. Before very long, every hungry pelican in port followed suit, and the famine of Monterey was ended.

EXCITEMENT

A party motoring through Idaho came upon a lonely sheep-herder high up in the mountains; and asked him what he did to amuse himself.

"Oh, I hold up motorists and rob 'em," replied the sheep-herder.

"But aren't you likely to be arrested and sent to jail?"

"Nope, I do it this way. Ye see this hairpin bend in the road? Well, I hold up the people right here, and when they go on I duck over the hill, take off my mask, put on my badge an' meet 'em down at the bend. 'I jist caught that fella that robbed ye,' I sez. 'Here's yer valuable.' There's no danger in it and it's kinda exciting."

EXECUTIVE—Duties

As everybody knows, a boss has practically nothing to do—that is, nothing except: Decide what is to be done; tell somebody to do it; listen to reason why it should not be done; why it should be done by somebody else, or why it should be done in a different way, and prepare arguments in rebuttal that should be convincing and conclusive. The boss must follow up to see if the thing has been done, and if it hasn't been done, to inquire why not; then to listen to excuses from the person who should have done it. Another chore is to follow up a second time to see if the thing has been done, discover that it wasn't done right, and to conclude that it might as well be left as it is, reflecting that the person at fault has seven children and that no other boss would put up with him for a second. A boss must ponder how much simpler and better the thing could have been done if he had done it himself; to reflect sadly that if he had done it himself he could have finished the task in twenty minutes, but as it was he had to spend four days trying to find out why it had taken somebody else three weeks to do it wrong.

EXERCISE

A guest at one of those Florida health resorts where everyone is expected to exercise, stubbornly refused to comply. "I came here to eat and rest," he insisted. "I refuse to exercise."

As the guest was checking out, the proprietor pleaded: "Before you leave, just do one bit of exercise for me—to keep my record clear. Please just bend down, keep your knees stiff, and touch your valise." The man bent over and said, "Well, I'm touching my valise. What now?" "Open it," said the proprietor, "and give me back my towels."

EXHIBITIONISM

Little Willie, exhibiting his skill in riding a new bicycle, came down the street in front of his home: "Look, Mama!" he cried, folding his arms, "no hands!"

Again, he came into view, this time coasting, with his feet off the pedals: "Look, Mama! no feet!"

Half an hour passed and Little Willie again put in his appearance. This time, somewhat subdued, he gurgled: "Look, Mama! no teeth!"

EXPEDIENCY

Jim Corbett ... was telling the story of his life and said: "When I left home my father warned me: 'Remember, a rolling stone gathers no moss.'

"But when I returned after a successful career, he changed his tune to: 'Just as I told you, son, it's the wandering bee that gathers honey.'"

EXPENSE ACCOUNTS

There is a historic story in newspaper circles of a certain reporter who was dispatched to the northern wilds with a rescue party in quest of lost or misplaced arctic explorers. Returning to the office he found great difficulty in making his expense account balance. Finally, an associate suggested helpfully that one of the sledge dogs might have died, as a result of exposure. Sure enough! An uncommonly fine animal, too, the reporter recalled, as he entered an item of $250 for the dog. And since there still remained a sizable deficit, he added, on sudden inspiration: "Flowers for bereaved bitch, $50."

EXPERIENCE

The sheepskin conferred on a student by a college, hardly compensates for the human hide that will be knocked off him later in the school of experience.

❖ ❖

When Frederick the Great was discussing the plans of a military campaign, he expressed a poor opinion of a certain general who had been recommended to be placed in charge of a strategic division. One of the emperor's staff ventured to remonstrate, reminding him that the general in question had been through ten campaigns. Old Fritz retorted: "Yes, and that mule over there also has been through ten campaigns, but he knows no more of war than when he began."

❖ ❖

The seniority of a teacher had been overlooked in making a promotion. Naturally disgruntled, he demanded to know why his twenty years of experience had been overlooked.

"My friend," said the principal, "in reality you haven't had twenty years' of experience—you have had one year's experience twenty times."

EXPLANATION

A father took his little daughter on a shopping tour. In a crowded department store elevator, a stout woman gave the man an outraged look and smacked him squarely in the face. The victim compressed his lips and said nothing. As they emerged on the ground floor, his daughter said, "I hated that woman too, papa. She stepped on my foot so I pinched her."

❖ ❖

A geology professor took his eager scholars out to view some samples of glacial drift. He pointed out a number of huge boulders, explained that they'd been rolled down from Canada or some place by prehistoric glaciers.

"But," said a rather stupid student, "where are the glaciers now?"

The professor snorted, "The glaciers, my dear young lady, have gone back for another load of rocks!"

EXPLANATION—Futility of

Most of us who talk in public have had the experience of having some forecast go spectacularly sour. And these wrong guesses have a way of coming back to plague us. Well, it usually is best not to try to trot out too many alibis. Just take your medicine, and ease it down with a story—such as this one:

The Negro guide had assured the Nawthern gen'l'men that he knew the precise spot for perfect fishing. Nevertheless, two hours had passed without a nibble.

"Look here, Bob," a member of the party suggested, "are you sure this is the spot you bragged so much about?"

"Yas, sah! Dis de eye-dentical spot."

"Well, is the weather right for fishing today?"

"Yas, sah. Weather jes' perfeck, sah."

"How about the bait?"

"Done got de right bait, sho'."

"Is the tide okay?"

"Tide mighty fine fo' fishin', sah."

"Well, then, Bob, with all those inducements, what's the trouble? Why aren't we catching some fish?"

The old Negro scratched his head in deep perplexity. "Well, boss, hit jes' seem dat de fish ain' heah what de 'ducements calls fo'."

FAITH—AND WORKS

A colored church congregation had met to pray for rain to release a long dry spell. The preacher looked severely at his flock and said:

"Brothers and Sisters, yo' all knows why we is here. Now what I wants to know is—where is yo' umbrellas?"

✧ ✧

Most of us think we could move mountains—if someone would clear the hills out of the way.

FAITH—Faltering

The varsity football team was resting between halves in the field house, and the coach had finished his pep talk. Talk turned to other than athletics.

"My girl said she'd be faithful to the end," claimed one of the boys.

"Why, that sounds all right."

"Yeah, but I'm a quarterback."

FAITH—Limited

The southerly wind had dried the land, and the crops were suffering, so the farmers of the parish waited on the minister with a request to "put up a word or two for rain."

The minister, who had a reputation for the efficacy of his supplications on previous occasions, heard the deputation gravely, and after a silence, during which he carefully scanned the horizon, replied: "A wull, but A'll bide a wee till the wind's mair in the east."

FAME

Once at a dinner a lady said to Lord Northcliffe: "Thackeray awoke one morning and found himself famous."

Lord Northcliffe answered, "When that morning dawned, Thackeray had been writing eight hours a day for fifteen years. The man who wakes up and finds himself famous, Madam, hasn't been asleep."

FAMILY LIFE

A hunter down in Maine captured an elk, and being an enterprising chap, conceived the idea of putting it on exhibition, to make some money.

Amongst the prospects at the box office one afternoon, the exhibitor noted a man, his wife, and so many children that he grew dizzy trying to tally them. "Are they all yours?" he asked incredulously.

"Oh yes," beamed the citizen. "Sixteen of 'em. Do I get a special family rate?"

"Well, I'll tell you," pondered the owner of the exhibit, "I'm going to let the whole bunch of you in free. I figure it's worth as much for my elk to see your family as it is for your family to see my elk."

FAMILY PRIDE

A dispute arose between two hearty Scots, Campbell and MacLean, concerning the antiquity of their respective families. MacLean would not permit Campbell to claim a family tree as ancient as his own, contending that the history of his own forebears went back to the beginning of the world.

"What about the flood," asked Campbell.

"Pooh you and your flood," replied MacLean. "My clan was before the flood."

"I have not read in the Bible," said Campbell, "of the name of MacLean going into Noah's Ark."

"Noah's Ark," snorted MacLean, "whoever heard of a MacLean that had not a boat of his own?"

FASHION

"Now," said the saleslady in a hat shop, assuring a prospective customer, "here's a number that will never go out of style. It will just look ridiculous year after year."

FATALISM

A London Cockney was asked if he wasn't scared when a bad blitz was on.

"Well, no, guv'nor," he answered. "Yer see, I count me chances. Jerry has got t' take off all right, ain't he? Then 'e's got t' cross the Channel, and that ain't too easy fer 'im. Then 'e's got t' git by the coast. Then comes the Thames Estuary, and that ain't all he likes. Then comes London. He can't miss that. But then 'e's got to find Ammersmith, then Acacia Road, then No. 87, and then most likely I'll be at the pub."

FEAR

Participants in the Navy college training program at Miami University are taught to abandon ship in the municipal swimming pool.

During a recent practice session, a student perched on a diving board was reluctant to leap.

"Go ahead!" ordered the instructor. "Jump!"

The youth hesitated. The command was repeated.

"What would you do," asked the exasperated teacher, "if that diving board were a sinking ship?"

"I would wait," said the frankly scared pupil, "until it sank about ten feet more!"

✧   ✧

As one Navy craft sailed out into the English Channel on the eve of D-Day, the skipper called the crew together, and delivered a lecture on fear.

"Fear," he said, "is a very healthy thing."

A third-class yeoman near the front spoke up.

"Cap'n," he said, "you're lookin' at the healthiest sailor in the United States Navy."

FEAR—Effect of

There is the old story of the fellow who refused to pass a grave-yard at night because he was afraid of ghosts. When told that ghosts never hurt anybody, he replied, "Yes, I know that ghosts can't hurt you, but they will make you hurt yourself."

FIRST AID

A young matron taking first aid training, during the war period, had reached the Resuscitation Stage. One evening returning from a Red Cross meeting, she observed a man, on a darkened side street, sprawled face downward.

"Aha," thought the matron, "Providence has sent me hither to minister to this poor unfortunate." Parking her car nearby, she rushed over and began giving the treatment for resuscitation.

Presently the man stirred, looked up, and spoke with great difficulty:

"Lady," he said, "I don't know what you're up to, but I wish you'd quit tickling me. I'm holding a lantern for a guy workin' down in this manhole."

FLATTERY

"You know, Larson," said the minister, "flattery falls off me like water off a duck's back."

"That's okay," replied the deacon, "but the ducks like it and always come back for more."

❖ ❖

A Hollywood director was asked to write a letter of recommendation to aid a friend in securing a coveted position. He did so, then called his pal and read the letter back to him. "That's great, wonderful," enthused the friend.

"I thought you'd like it," said the director. "All the time I was writing it, I kept thinking of General MacArthur!"

FOOD

"Have you lived a good life?" asked St. Peter of a timid female knocking at the heavenly gate.

"I excelled in only one thing," said the woman dolefully. "I was a good cook."

"Come right in," invited St. Peter, throwing wide the gate. "Good cooks have saved more men from damnation than a dozen missionaries!"

✦ ✦

"We got peach and apple pie," said the waitress.

The patron ordered apple. Later he called the waitress in high dudgeon. "Say, what kind of pie did you bring me?"

"What does it taste like?" inquired the waitress cautiously.

"Tastes like glue," opined the patron.

"Then it must be apple. Our peach pie tastes like putty."

FOOLISH QUESTIONS

At a local first-aid class the question of fainting came up. The instructor explained to the class that the cause of fainting was primarily a fault of circulation and that it could be prevented by getting the head lower than the heart.

"For instance," he said, "if you feel faint and don't want to call attention to it, just lean down and tie your shoe-lace over again."

A woman in the front raised her hand and asked, "What sort of knot is used?"

FORTITUDE

When asked why Daniel was not devoured by the lions, Chas. H. Spurgeon once opined: "Most of him was backbone, and the rest grit."

FRIENDSHIP

Secretary of State Elihu Root and his fellow cabinet members were discussing a very wealthy man whose brusque manner had made him universally disliked.

"Well, one thing I will say about him," said one cabinet member. "He never bothers anyone to get positions for his friends."

"That certainly is in his favour," admitted Root, "unless——"

"Unless what?"

"Unless he has no friends."

❖　　❖

O'Toole was the questioner and he was of a curious nature. "Phwat's the matter that ye didn't spake to Mulligan just now? Have ye quarreled?"

"That we have not," answered O'Brien. "That's the insurance av our fri'ndship."

"Phwat do ye mane?"

"Sure, it's this way. Mulligan an' I are that devoted to wan another that we can't bear the idea of a quarrel; an' as we are both moighty quick-tempered we've resolved not to spake to wan another at all, for fear we break the fri'ndship."

❖　　❖

As Margaret Lee Runbeck puts it: Strangers are just friends that you don't know yet.

FUND RAISING (see also CHURCH—CONTRIBUTIONS)

A small boy, sobbing disconsolately, was asked the cause of his tears.

"My pa's a millionaire philanthropist," he replied, brokenly.

"Well, well! That's nothing to cry about!"

"It ain't, eh? Then you don't know my pa. He just promised to give me $5 for my birthday, provided I raise a similar amount."

❖　　❖

Civilization is a state of affairs where nothing can be done without first being financed.

❖　　❖

Old Uncle Joe was called upon to make a contribution to the church building fund.

"Lawsey," he confided to the solicitors, "I sho' would like t' help, but I jest ain't got it. It's all I can do to pay a little on my bills roun' heah."

"But, Uncle Joe, you owe the Lord something, too."

"Yeah," conceded the old man. "Yeah, dat's so. But de Lawd ain't pushin' me lak my othah creditors is."

❖ ❖

Benjamin Franklin who, among other things, was one of the best money-raisers of his generation, once set forth his principles for the guidance of a committee:

"First, call upon all those whom you know will give something; next apply to those you are uncertain whether they will give or not. Finally, visit those you are sure will give nothing, for in some of these you may be mistaken."

❖ ❖

At a meeting of the official board of a needy church the pastor was asking for funds to take care of some urgent repairs. The appeal was so strong that one member, known for his miserly contributions, rose and offered to start the fund with five dollars.

While he was yet on his feet, a piece of plastering fell, hitting him on the head. Surprised, and somewhat disconcerted, he mumbled, "I—I think I'd better make that *fifty* dollars!"

An irreverent voice in the back of the hall pleaded, "Hit him just once more, Lord!"

❖ ❖

Dwight L. Moody, the great evangelist, was calling with a certain minister, on a wealthy lady, to ask her help in a building operation. On the way over, Moody asked the minister what sum he had in mind. "Oh," said the pastor, "perhaps $250."

"Better let me handle the matter," suggested the evangelist.

"Madam," said Moody, after the usual introductions, "we have come to ask you for $2,000 toward the building of the new Mission."

The lady threw up her hands in horror. "Oh, Mr. Moody!" she exclaimed, "I couldn't possibly give more than $1,000!"

And the pair walked away with a check for that sum.

❖ ❖

Dwight L. Moody, the famous evangelist, had a wonderful faculty for getting money, whether it was a simple collection to meet some current expenses, or some large subscriptions with which to erect a new school building. Asked once as to the secret of his success in this particular line, the great preacher replied: "I urge people to give until they feel it, and then to keep on giving until they don't feel it."

❖ ❖

A colored preacher was delivering a "trial sermon" before a congregation that was about to call a new pastor. "Brethren," he said, the church that I'se the pastor of has to get up and run," and brethren all replied, "Amen—let 'er walk." The preacher talked on about building up the church to a place of influence in the community, gradually warming up to where he said: "Brethren, the church that I'se the pastor of has to get up and run," and the brethren responded, "Amen—let 'er run." Considerably encouraged, the preacher warmed up the congregation a few degrees further and let go with: "Brethren, the church that I'se pastor of has got to get up and fly," and again the brethren echoed in unison, "Amen—let 'er fly." The preacher, reaching his climax, wound up with, "Brethren, if this church is gonna fly it has to have money." The brethren all sat up like a bolt of lightning had struck and the rafters echoed as they shouted, "Let 'er walk!"

FUSSINESS

A fussy little woman had driven the grocer nearly frantic helping her figure out her ration points and find what she wanted during the busiest time of the day. At last he managed to satisfy her.

"Do you know, Mr. Peck," sighed the shopper in relief, "when I came into your store I had a dreadful headache. I've quite lost it now." "It isn't lost," growled the distracted grocer. "I have it!"

FUTILITY

Down in Kentucky, not so long ago, a local oracle was approached by a young farmer, who wanted to know how to rid himself of sassafras sprouts in his field.

"Well, son," said the wiseacre, "off and on I've given the subject of sassafrack sprouts considerable study durin' the past forty-five years. And here sometime ago I come to the opinion that the only way to git shet of sassafrack sprouts, when they start in to take a place, is to pack up and move off and jest natchelly leave 'em."

FUTURE

An elderly couple had been sitting in front of the evening fire a long time without speaking. At last the husband inquired, "What are you thinking about?"

To which the wife replied: "I was just thinking how long we had lived together and that it couldn't go on forever like this and that the time will soon come when one of us will have to go."

"Yes," assented the old man, "but it is no use to worry about that now, Mother."

"No," was the calm reply, "but I was just thinking that when it does happen, I would like to go to California to live."

FUTURE—Planning

Sometimes those of us planning for the future must feel a good deal like a near-sighted man in a dark room, wearing boxing-gloves, and attempting to measure the thickness of a jellyfish with a pair of rubber calipers.

GAMBLING

Papa was reading his sports page of the daily paper when Junior, who had been listening to the radio, asked, "Papa, what is the race problem?"

Without a moment's hesitation, the father answered, "Picking winners, my boy."

❖ ❖

Thomas Jefferson Brown and George Washington Johnson had just heard the rumor that their boss had lost heavily in the stock market.

"What's he mean when he says his stock done drop below margin?" asked Thomas Jefferson.

"Dat," answered George Washington, "is white man talk fo' 'seven come eleben—it reads a five!'"

❖ ❖

Two boys were in loud dispute, the elder evidently trying to convince the other of his prowess in a certain direction.

"I tell you," asserted the elder boy, "I did!"
"Will you swear that you did?" asked the younger.
"Yes."
"Take your oath?"
"Yes."
"Your Bible oath?"
"Yes."
"Will you bet a nickel you did?"
"Naw!"

GAY LIFE

Bob Burns, with his stories of the Van Buren relatives, tells of an old uncle of his who was such a gadabout that the aunt, who was a stay-at-home, couldn't keep up with his social activities. In one week, he said, the old fellow attended the lodge meeting on Monday night, the ice cream social on Tuesday, the session meeting of the church on Wednesday, the YMCA lecture on Thursday, and Friday night when she saw him go into the bedroom and wipe off his celluloid collar, she just stepped in and reproachfully inquired:
"Where you goin' tonight, play boy?"

GERMS

Little Elizabeth was a scientist's daughter, and when she was taken with the measles she heard a good deal about germs and microbes.
One evening, some time after her recovery, she heard her mother singing a lullaby to baby Jack.
"Oh, mama! You must not sing that. You sang it to me when I had the measles, and there may be microbes in it."

GIFTS—Giving

The old Scotsman was dying, reports a book published in London in 1880. He summoned the minister to his side. "Will I be placed among the elect," he whispered, "if I leave ten thousand for Free Kirk sustentation?"
The canny minister replied, "It's an experiment well worth trying."

GIVING—RECEIVING

A famous philanthropist was once asked: "How are you able to give so much, and still have so much?"

"Well," replied the generous man, "as I shovel out, He shovels in; and the Lord has a bigger shovel than I have."

GOD—AND MAN

Some of us, when things are going well, are inclined to take a little too much personal credit. We overlook the help we've had along the way. In that respect, we're a good deal like the old Negro that E. V. Durling tells about. This energetic old fellow had taken over a vacant lot packed with weeds, tin cans, rubbish, etc., and after months of hard work, made a garden spot of it. The preacher, looking over the fence, was much impressed.

"Rufus," he said appreciatively, "de Lawd and you has done a wondahful job here."

"Yas, sah," said Rufus meditatively. "Yas, sah. But you should a' seen dis heah place when de Lawd was takin' care ob hit Hisse'f."

❖   ❖

A clever moppet had figured out as long as no one saw him it didn't matter if he took things that weren't his own or played on forbidden ground. Whippings and scoldings were of no avail. The young offender would counter: "But nobody saw me!" One day his mother said: "God sees you. God sees everywhere you go and everything you do."

The kid's face flushed with indignation. "Is that all He's got to do?" he demanded with scorn. "Lay on His stomach all day and watch me?"

❖   ❖

In the juvenile section of a big bookstore, a small girl was found busying herself with a box of crayons. A clerk uneasily asked the child what she was about.

"I'm drawing a picture of God," was the surprising reply.

"But how do you know what God looks like?"

"That," said the little girl succinctly, "is why I am drawing Him. I want to find out."

❖ ❖

Talking to a group of small youngsters during a vacation Bible school, a pastor sought to emphasize God's loving and protecting care by drawing a familiar parallel.

"Now, I wonder," he said, "if any of you can tell what a shepherd does for his sheep besides feeding them?"

"I know," said practical Tommy. "He shears them."

❖ ❖

A minister who had given a liberal turn to his Sunday message was being taken to task by a prominent member. He replied, "Was the message in line with Christ's teaching on the matter?"

"Yes," said the frank layman, "I'm not questioning that, but this is one of the emphases of Christ that I don't approve of."

❖ ❖

Rich Mr. X was showing an acquaintance around his tremendous estate.

"Beautiful lawn," murmured the visitor.

"Ought to be," said X complacently. "Had the whole thing brought here as sod at $1 a square foot."

"And those trees!" exclaimed the other. "I've never seen more perfect specimens!"

"Had 'em transplanted," confided X. "Cost me $2,000 each."

"Ah," sighed the visitor meditatively, "what God could have done if He'd had all your money!"

❖ ❖

In the English and American colony of business exiles at Tientsin, China, the visit of the Episcopal bishop is an outstanding social event. Not long since, his eminence did a certain household the honor of dining in its company. The Chinese cook was duly impressed with the importance of the occasion and was stimulated to do his best. He responded nobly. The menu was all that the most exacting ecclesiastic could have desired, but the top notch of achievement came with the dessert, the pièce de résistance a magnificent frosted cake on the surface of which the chef had embossed these words:

"Hurrah for God!"

❖   ❖

Little Janet came running into the house one morning sobbing. Throwing herself into her mother's arms, she cried:

"God doesn't love me any more, mother!"

"Why, Janet dear," said the mother. "Why do you say that? God loves everyone."

"No, mother. He doesn't love me," wailed the little girl. "I know He doesn't. I tried Him with a daisy."

❖   ❖

An Englishman who had been visiting a Kentucky Colonel living in New York, decided to go to Virginia to spend the winter. After he had been away for a couple of weeks he wrote enthusiastically to his southern friend in New York:

"Oh, I say, old top, you never told me that the South was anything like I've found it, and so different from the North. Why, man, it's God's country!"

The Colonel, a voluntary exile from Kentucky, promptly wired back:

"Of course it is. You didn't suppose God was a Yankee, did you?"

❖   ❖

In the days when balloon ascensions were infrequent spectacles in the deep South, an intrepid bird-man, arrayed in silks and spangles descended in a cotton field, where a gang of Negroes were at work. The frightened hands departed hastily—all except one old uncle who, through valor, curiosity, or rheumatism, held his ground. With head thrown back and mouth agape, he watched the balloonist descend from the heavens, and when at last he came within shouting distance, the venerable darky raised his hat, and his voice: "Good mornin', Massa Jesus. How's yo' Pa?"

GOD—The Provider

God gives every bird its food—but he does not throw it into the nest.

GOOD DEED

Dr. Bronson Ray, a brain surgeon of considerable repute, was walking in the Park one afternoon when a little boy on a scooter ran into a tree and sustained a pretty severe scalp wound. Dr. Ray dispatched one of the bystanders to call an ambulance and was administering first aid when a lad only a couple of years older than the victim pushed his way through the crowd. "I'm a Boy Scout," he said to the Doctor. "You go along, sir, and I'll take over."

GOOD DEEDS—Misinterpreted

An old Negro man, injured in a traffic accident, was taken to the charity ward of the city hospital. A few days later he handed a grimy letter to an interne, asking him to mail it. Mildly curious, the young doctor noted the address, "The Lord, in Hevin," and decided to open the missive. It proved to be an earnest plea for the Lord to send $10 to meet a pressing need.

Touched by the simple faith of the old Negro, the interne tucked the letter in his pocket. Attending a lodge meeting that evening he showed it to some of the brothers. They resolved to preserve the old man's childish faith, and between them raised a total of $4.60. The interne added 40 cents and the following morning handed the money to the delighted Bash, explaining that it was in answer to his letter, sent via the Masonic Lodge.

Bash was profuse in his thanks, but a few days later the interne intercepted a second letter:

"I thanks you, Lord, for the moneys you sint me so quick. But nex time ples Sir sen it to Olive Branch church. The las monies you sen Lord the masuns done kep haf of it."

GOOD—EVIL

A colored divine was once asked to explain the doctrine of election. Said he, "Brethren, it is this way: The Lord he is always voting for a man, and the Devil he is always voting against him; then the man himself votes, and that breaks the tie!"

"GOOD OLD DAYS"

An Associated Press dispatch reports that in Tulsa a horse pulling a bakery wagon ran away. The driver pulled on the reins; a policeman gave chase—and still the horse galloped on. Then an old-timer yelled, "Whoa!" and the horse stopped at once.

While we are devising new techniques, maybe we should revive some of the old ones.

❖ ❖

An old-timer is one who remembers when he could buy a pound of steak for a dime, but forgets he had to work an hour to earn the dime.

GOOD RIDDANCE

Mr. Babcock was driving through the country, trying to buy a mule. He was directed to a colored man who had one for sale.

"Do you want to sell a mule?" asked Babcock.

"Yaas, suh," replied the owner. "May Ah ask whar yo' live, suh?"

"What has that got to do with it?" queried Babcock.

"Well," explained the negro, "Ah, ain't gwine ter transfer dat mule to nobody who lives less dan two hundred miles away from hyah. When Ah sells dat mule Ah wants to git rid not only ob de mule, but ob all conversation appertainin' to him."

GOSSIP

Ever notice how often a narrow mind and a wide mouth go together?

❖ ❖

So live that you wouldn't be ashamed to sell the family parrot to the town gossip.

❖ ❖

"I am more deadly than the screaming shell from the howitzer. I ruin without killing; I tear down homes, break hearts and wreck lives. I travel on the wings of the wind. No innocence is strong enough to intimidate me; no purity pure enough to daunt me. I have no regard for truth, no respect for justice, no mercy for the defenseless. . . . My victims are as numerous as the sands of the sea, and often as innocent. I never forget and seldom forgive. My name is—GOSSIP!"

GOVERNMENT

A group of children was playing recently, when a two-year-old set up a squall because he wanted the toys with which his older companions were engaged. So they started piling the toys up around him. A father of one of the lads came by and inquired into the unusual procedure.

"Oh," explained a seven-year-old, "we're playing that Billy is the government, and we're giving him everything we've got!"

GOVERNMENT PERSONNEL

They tell this story in Washington.

The chief of a certain bureau decided he had need for a weather prophet. Accordingly, he searched the highways and byways and employed one.

As he was leaving the office the first night, he asked the weather prophet what the weather would be.

"It will be a bright, clear night, with no rain at all," said the weather expert.

The chief, who had an engagement that evening, took the weather prophet at his word, put on a nice white suit, left his umbrella at home, and started out. As he walked along, glancing up at the dark clouds, he met a farmer leading a donkey.

"What's the weather going to be like, dad?" he inquired.

"It's going to rain," said the farmer.

A few minutes later, the skies opened up and it poured, drenching the chief to the skin. Disgusted, he went back in search of the farmer.

"I want to hire you as my weather prophet," he told the farmer.

"It ain't me," said the farmer, "it's my donkey. Every time that critter's ears hang down, it rains sure as shooting."

"Okay," said the chief, "then I'll hire the donkey." Which he did.

And there have been jackasses in Washington ever since.

GRACE

A young husband did not like hash. His wife acquired a French cookbook giving many recipes for using left-overs. The next evening she had one of the fancy mixtures in a covered dish on the table. The husband reached over and raised the cover, but the wife said, "Why don't you ask the blessing first, dear?"

The husband replied, "I don't believe there is anything here that hasn't already been blessed."

GRATITUDE

The minister was consoling an old lady who had had many troubles but who made a habit of looking on the bright side.

"I'm pleased to see, Mrs. Hoskins," he said, "that all your misfortunes have not soured you; that you are still grateful to the Almighty."

"Oh, yes, sir, I'm still grateful," she said. "My rheumatiz is awful bad, but I thank Heaven I still have a back to have it in!"

❖   ❖

A traveler for a big publishing house couldn't wait to get to St. Louis, where his oldest friend owned a prosperous bookstore. "Sam," he said to the owner the moment they were alone, "I want you to lend me $2,000.00." "The answer, Joe," said Sam, "is positively no." "But, Sam," protested the salesman, "in 1929, when Bond and Share broke from 189 to 50, who gave you ten thousand dollars to keep you from being wiped out?" "You did," admitted Sam. "And in 1931, when your daughter Shirley had that tropical disease, who took her down to Florida because you couldn't get away from business, who did, Sam?" "You, my friend, you did." "And in 1933, when we were fishing together, who dove into the rapids and saved you from drowning at the risk of his own life?" "You did, Joe. It was wonderful!" "Well, then, Sam, in Heaven's name, why won't you lend me $2,000.00 now when I need it?" "All the things you say are true," said Sam, nodding his head slowly, "But what have you done for me lately?"

GRATITUDE—INGRATITUDE

An ungrateful man is like a hog under a tree eating acorns, but never looking up to see where they come from.

GRATITUDE—Lack

A clergyman included in his annual parochial report the item "Nine persons lost at sea." When the congregation expressed shock and amazement, he said, "Well, eleven persons requested prayers for those going to sea, and only two asked me to give thanks for a safe return, so I assume that the other nine were lost at sea."

GUIDANCE

The sea was calm and the captain decided it would be a good time to satisfy the cabin boy's desire to take the helm. He pointed out the North Star to the boy and gave him explicit directions to steer toward it all the time.

For a while everything went well but finally the young pilot got into difficulty. "Captain," he called, "I've passed that star. Will you please come and pick out another?"

HABIT

"It's habit," says Bruce Marshall, "not hatred, that is the real enemy of the Church of God."

❖　❖

Someone has advanced the theory that the best way to break habit is to drop it.

HAPPINESS

The teacher of a primary class in Sunday school was mildly hipped on the happiness theme. It was her custom on Sabbath morning to inquire of each tiny tot what he or she had done in the course of the week to make some person happy.

When it came little Eunice's turn she deliberated for some time and finally said, "Well, I spent an afternoon at my aunt's house—and when I went home she was happy."

❖ ❖

Philosopher—And what do we want in this world to make us perfectly happy?

Battered Cynic—The things we ain't got.

HAPPINESS—MISERY

A psychologist says it is natural for people to be happy and self-satisfied after they have done a good piece of work. That accounts for much of the misery and gloom that we find in the world.

HARD-OF-HEARING

The radio salesman found the elderly farmer pitching hay in the barn. "How do you do, sir?" he began. "I want to introduce you to a brand new type of radio. It operates on batteries, and you can take it with you wherever you go, and—"

The farmer cupped his ear. "Eh?" he queried, "I can't hear you."

The salesman repeated.

"Sorry, son," drawled the farmer. "But I cain't hear a word you say."

The salesman gulped. "All I said was this:" he screamed. And another repetition.

The farmer shook his head and grunted, "No, siree, I don't need no radio. My wife plays the harmonica."

The salesman, hoarse from shouting, climbed back into his car; drove four miles to the nearest neighbor; knocked on the door of this farmhouse. A woman answered.

"Pardon me, lady," the salesman began. "But I have here a new type of radio and—"

The woman scowled. "Not interested, mister," she interrupted. "And, besides, I heard you the first time!"

HARDSHIP

"When I was a boy," Grandpa began, "I had to walk seven miles to school, with the snow sometimes up to my neck."

"I had a purty hard time of it, too," crowed Grandpa's son. "I had to drive a buggy and sleigh over four miles of rough dirt road to school. And did I get my ears froze!"

Then Chester, the ten-year-old grandson had his turn: "Believe me, I've had some hard times, too. Why one morning last winter, we had to ride the whole mile to school in the bus with the heater not even working!"

HARD TO GET

"I like the shy demure type," observed a sailor of our acquaintance, "you know—the kind you have to whistle at twice."

HATRED

A little boy was playing with his sister. A most unpleasant woman who lived near had been finding fault with them, and the boy said, "I just hate her." His little sister, greatly shocked, said, "Oh, no! The Bible says we must love everyone."

"Oh, well," he remarked, "old Mrs. Blank wasn't born when that was written."

❖ ❖

An Englishman, on a tour of the Western United States, came to a desert filling station. Above the door was a sign: "Joe Bevins, 200% American."

After the scowling and surly proprietor had filled the gas tank, the visitor ventured a question: "Would you mind, Mr. Bevins," he said, "telling me just what is a 200% American?"

"Well," said the filling-station man belligerently, "You heard o' 100% Americans, I reckon—they hate all other nationalities. Me— Well, I'm 200%—I hate everybody!"

HEAD MAN

Mr. Williams had hired Sambo to paint his shed at the stipulated price of $2.50. Reappearing on the scene some time later he found Sambo lying in the shade, enjoying himself, while another nego was busy wielding the brush.

"How is this, Sambo?" asked Mr. Williams. "I thought I hired you to do this job."

"Yes, suh, Mr. Williams, Ah knows you did, but Ah sublet de contrack fo' $3."

"But," remonstrated Mr. Williams, "I pay you only $2.50, so you are losing money on this job."

"Yes, suh; yes, suh, Ah knows Ah is," was the reply, "but it's wuth somethin' to be boss."

HEALTH—DISEASE

"Last night," said the club bore, "an old friend of mine cornered me and spent three hours telling me about his asthma."

"Well, why didn't you trump with the story about your diabetes?"

"Heck, I led with that!"

HEAVEN—HELL

When his lifelong enemy finally died, Barker weakened. "I'm glad the poor old feller died that way," he said. "Sorry he's gone; but if he had t' go, 'twas the best way he could h' done it."

Some interest was expressed by a friend as to the why and wherefore of this remark.

"Why'm I glad he's gone to his last accountin' drowned? Well, becuz I knowed him well enough to know that the place he's a-goin' to he'd better go thar wet than dry."

✧ ✧

There was a play given in New York a few years ago in which in the first act the soul awakened in the next world after death, and found himself in a vast expanse where he was exceedingly comfortable. He rested for awhile and then, becoming somewhat bored, he shouted out, "Is there anybody here?"

In a moment a white-robed attendant appeared and asked, "What do you want?"

"What can I have?" was the answer.

"You can have whatever you want," replied the attendant.

"Well, then bring me something to eat."

"What do you want to eat?" asked the attendant. "You can have anything you want."

And so they brought him just what he wanted, and he went on

eating and sleeping and having a glorious time. At last, he wanted something more and asked for games. They brought him all the games, all the books, everything he wished. He went on getting everything he wanted whenever he asked for for it, but at last he got more than a little bored and summoned the attendant and said:

"I want something to DO!"

That request the attendant could not comply with. "I am sorry, but that is the only thing we cannot give you here."

And the man said, "I am sick and tired of it; I'd rather go to hell!"

"And where," exclaimed the attendant "do you think you are?"

❖ ❖

One thing about hell—it's the only institution still mentioned without a prefixed "pro" or "anti."

❖ ❖

Spurgeon was asked if the man who learned to play a cornet on Sunday would go to Heaven. The great preacher's reply was characteristic. Said he, "I don't see why he should not, but," after a pause, "I doubt whether the man next door will."

❖ ❖

"Mother," said little Mabel, "do missionaries go to heaven?"

"Why, of course, dear," her mother replied.

"Do cannibals?"

"No; I'm afraid they don't."

"But, mother," the little girl insisted, "if a cannibal eats a missionary, he'll have to go, won't he?"

❖ ❖

Little Mary was heartbroken when her pet canary died, and to pacify her, her father gave her an empty cigar box and, with much ceremony, assisted in burying the box in the garden.

"Dad," whispered Mary, after the funeral was over, "do you think my little canary will go to Heaven?"

"I believe he will, dear," replied the father. "Why?"

"I was only thinking," murmured the youngster, "how cross St.

Peter will be when he opens the box and finds it isn't cigars after all."

❖ ❖

"Stand up," shouted the colored evangelist, "if you want to go to heaven!"

Everyone got up but one old man.

"Don't you want to go to heaven, Brother?" shouted the preacher.

"Sho," said the old man, "but Ah ain't goin' wid no excursion! Ah's crowded 'nuff down heah."

❖ ❖

A colored preacher was trying to impress on his flock the heat and fury of hell.

"You-all is seen melted lead running out a furnace, ain't you?"

"Amen," they answered in the affirmative.

"Wal, dey uses de stuff fer ice cream in de place I'm speaking of."

HELPFULNESS

A lady with a cold and hacking cough went to the movies. She reached in her medicine cabinet before she left for a box of cough-drops and dropped the package in her bag. As always happens when one goes forearmed, she didn't cough at all but the lady in front of her did. Tapping her on the shoulder she offered her a drop. The cougher took it gratefully and coughed no more. Late that night the solicitous one opened her medicine cabinet. There lay the box of cough-drops. In utter panic she rushed to her bag. In it was a box of Vigoro tablets, those pellets you drop in with the flowers and pray they'll grow. The thought of what she had done to the movie cougher was intolerable. Calling the druggist she asked frantically, "Will it hurt her?"

"No, ma'am, it won't," soothed the druggist, "but it may make her sick. You fed her about two spades full of manure."

❖ ❖

A salesman from New York disembarked from the ferry in Jersey City and walked up the street questioningly. Finally, he stopped two "bohunks" and asked one of the pair:

"Say, can you tell me where the macaroni factory is located?"

The one addressed gave an inquiring look at his friend, but seeing no hope, turned to the questioner, shaking his head.

"No, we don't know vere is de magoroni factory."

The salesman started on, but was overtaken by the "bohunks." The one to whom he had first addressed an inquiry spoke:

"Say, Mister, maybe you mean de noodle factory?"

"Yes," the salesman brightened, "that's what I mean—the noodle factory. Where is it?"

"Vell, dot's vat my friend and I began to think, but ve don't know vere de noodle factory iss also."

❖ ❖

The only time a hog helps the community is when he dies. Don't be a hog.

❖ ❖

The "suggestion box" as a technique for gaining and holding employee co-operation has become firmly established during the period of increased war production. Many important contributions have been made and these suggestions, collectively, have resulted in substantially increased industrial efficiency.

Certainly among the more practical suggestions should be included this one found recently in a midwestern factory collection: "Suggestion: Move the suggestion box. It's right where I always bump my head on it."

HENPECKED HUSBANDS

"What are you doing with those papers spread out there?" the wife asked sternly.

"I am making a wish," said the husband.

"A wish?"

"Yes, my dear. In your presence I shall not presume to call it a will."

HEREDITY

You can't do much about your ancestors, but you can influence your descendants enormously.

HEROISM

Some persons get credit for heroism when in reality they are just too lazy to get out of the way of impending disaster.

The school teacher was coaching her class of little boys on what to do in case of air raids.

"Now let us make believe," she stated, "that we hear the sirens warning us that planes are coming—whoooooooooo!"

As she imitated a siren all but one lad dived under his desk for protection.

"Sammy!" almost shrieked the teacher. "Why are you sitting there with your chin cupped in your hands so indifferently? Run for your life! Don't you know that this is war?"

Returned Sammy:

"And don't you know that there are heroes?"

HIDE AND SEEK

A salesman making a two-weeks stay in town, bought some limburger cheese to eat in his room. When he got ready to leave, he still had about half of the cheese left. He didn't want to pack it nor did he want to leave it lying in the room. He went over to the window sill, carefully removed a plant from its pot, buried the cheese and replaced the plant. A few days later, he received a telegram from the hotel: "We give up, where did you put it?"

HOME LIFE

Dr. S. Parkes Cadman used to tell about a girl who detested housework and saw no need for it. When the young man to whom she was engaged showed her a house he planned to buy, she commented: "A home: why do I need a home? I was born in a hospital, educated in a college, courted in an automobile, and expect to be married in a church. We can live out of the delicatessen and paper bags. I spend my mornings on the golf course, my afternoons at my clubs, and then my evenings at the movies. When I die I am going to be buried at the undertaker's. All I really need is a garage!"

HOMEY TOUCH

One hillbilly's wife is visiting another's and the hostess calls the visitor's attention to some gossamer hangings across the empty window space.

"New curtains, eh," sniffs the visitor. "Gittin' a mite hightoned, ain't ye?"

"Naw," says the hostess. "Just got us a new spider."

HONESTY—DISHONESTY

"Why do you call your dog 'Swindler'?"

"Oh, for the fun of it. When I call to him on the street, half the men almost jump out of their skins!"

HOPE

An examination was being held in little Emma's school and the question was asked:

"Upon what do hibernating animals subsist during the winter?"

Emma thought for several minutes and then wrote: "On the hope of a coming spring."

HOSPITALITY—Limited

In the days of the Forty-Niners, in California, a Scotsman who maintained the reputation of his brethren for thrift, made a moderately rich strike and came to town on a Saturday night to celebrate.

Under the mellowing influence of alcoholic beverages, he finally staggered to the bar and in a loud voice called: "When I drink, everybody drinks!"

With a grand gesture, he summoned all to join him—customers, waiters, singers. Everybody took a drink. Then Sandy incredibly ordered again. "When I take another drink," he said woozily, "ev'body takesh 'nother drink." So again all gathered round.

As he finished his second drink, Sandy cautiously took a dollar from his pocket, slapped it on the bar.

"When I pay," he said thickly, "ev'ybody paysh!"

❖   ❖

Mandy, garbed in deepest black and waving an ebony-hued palm-leaf fan, approached the railway ticket window: "Ah wants two round-trip tickets to Dothan," she said, "an' one ob 'em mahrked 'corpse.' "

"Don't you mean one round-trip ticket and a one-way ticket marked 'corpse'?" suggested the helpful ticket agent.

"Naw, sah," said Mandy with an air of finality. "Ah's takin' mah daid husban' down dere so' his folks kin see he's daid. Den Ah's bringin' him back heah t' bury him. An ain' goin' t' hab dat pack of trash comin' heah an' eatin' off'n me foh a week."

HOT NEWS

The enterprising editor of a small newspaper in a southwestern state cares little for national or international news, but is bedeviled by an intense desire to "scoop" the other papers in the region on local and sectional news.

One day he accomplished the minor triumph of being the first and only editor to report a certain disaster in a nearby town.

The following week he scored another beat with the announcement:

"We were the first to announce the news of the destruction of Jenkins' paint store last week. We are now the first to announce that the report was absolutely without foundation."

HUMAN NATURE

"What's wrong with the world?" It is said that this question was once addressed to Will Rogers and the Sage of Oklahoma replied, "Oh, I reckon, just folks!"

❖   ❖

An elevator man of our acquaintance, in a downtown office building, grew weary of repeated requests for the time. So he put up a shelf in the corner of his elevator, placed a small clock on it. Now people ask: "Is your clock right?"

HUMILITY

Harvard's Emerson Hall was in the process of construction. The design included an inscription over the door-way which the Department of Philosophy had decided should read, "Man is the measure of all things." But President Eliot quietly decided otherwise. When the professors returned from the summer vacation they found the building essentially complete, and cut into the stone were the words, "What is man that Thou art mindful of him?"

HYGIENE

War has spurred Mexico's national health program. The children are becoming conscious that health starts with nutrition. But sometimes there are perplexing and revealing questions, as in the case reported by Verna Carletan Millan. A school teacher who distributed tooth brushes to pupils was asked: "Must we brush our teeth even when we have nothing to eat?"

HYPNOTISM

A wife married to a hypnotist, brought her husband to court charging him with cruelty. "Your honor," she complained, "my husband is the meanest man in the world; he hypnotized me into thinking I was a canary and gave me birdseed for breakfast, dinner and supper."

The husband appeared very distraught; "I beg your pardon," he said, "but I don't think that was mean."

The magistrate's eyes popped. "No," he asserted. "I could have hypnotized her into thinking she was a sparrow and let her find her own food."

HYPOCHONDRIA

At two o'clock in the morning a physician had been summoned four miles in the country, to attend a chronic hypochondriac.

The patient admitted he suffered no particular pain, just had a feeling that something was wrong. Gravely, the doctor felt the man's pulse, listened to his heart. "Umph . . ." he said at length. "Have you made your will?"

The patient turned pale, answered tremblingly that he hadn't.

"Better send for your lawyer," counseled the physician. "And who's your pastor? Better send for him, too. Notify your father— and is there any one else?"

By this time the man, thoroughly terrified, was moaning piti-fully: "Oh, Doctor, oh, this is terrible. Do you really think I'm nearing the end?"

"Certainly not," said the physician in icy tones. "There isn't a thing in the world wrong with you. But I'd hate to be the only man you've made a fool of on a night like this."

HYPOCRISY

"He prays on his knees on Sunday—and on his neighbors the remainder of the week."—Definition of a hypocrite, given by a camp-meeting evangelist.

IGNORANCE

At a meeting a self-made man got up and talked at length about how thankful he was that he had never come into contact with the pernicious influence of any schools. He had no formal education and was proud of it.

"Do I understand," inquired the chairman at the conclusion of these remarks, "that you are thankful for your ignorance?"

"Well," said the speaker, "I suppose you could put it that way."

"Then," continued the chairman, "I just want to point out that you have a great deal to be thankful for."

IMAGINATION

Imagination was given to man to compensate him for what he is not; and a sense of humor was provided to console him for what he is.

IN A NUTSHELL

A baffled lady once turned to Edward Gibbon, the not-too-easy-to-read historian, and asked him to tell in a few words what actually caused the decline and fall of the Roman Empire.

He proved equal to the occasion with this reply:

"The bottom dropped out of it."

INCENTIVE

A small party set out on a bear hunt down in the southern part of the United States, and took along with them as a guide a Negro, native of the region. The Negro was stationed to watch a certain part of the trail and to give ample warning if a bear came near. But the Negro fell asleep, as Negroes often do, even in the ticklish position in which he had been left. Suddenly he was wakened by a huge, shaggy bear sniffing at him. With a war whoop of unbelievable volume, the Negro was well on his way homeward, the bear lumbering speedily behind.

As the pair approached the Negro's cabin, his wife heard the panting and grunting, as well as the sound of flying feet, and rushed to the door to see what was the matter. Realizing her spouse's predicament, she began to shout words of encouragement. "Run! Ephr'im, run!" she screeched from her place of vantage behind the door. Ephraim, exerting every ounce of reserve, reached his goal with a scant margin of safety.

Some minutes later, when he had partially recovered his breath, he panted to his wife from the floor where he had been lying exhausted, "Carolina, what foh you make sech a fool of youhse'f? How come you-all yells at me t' run? Does yo' s'pose Ah's gwine lie down in a race lak dat?"

INCONSISTENCY

A Chinese visitor says: "Funny people, you Americans. You take a glass, put in sugar to make it sweet and lemon to make it sour. You put in gin to warm you up and ice to keep you cool. You say, 'Here's to you!' and then you drink it yourself."

❖   ❖

Ross Hadley, the sportsman flier, wanted to take Mahatma Gandhi on his first flight, but the Indian leader demurred: "I'd have wings if I were meant to fly."

"Ah," said Hadley, "but you take an automobile ride every afternoon. Where are your wheels?"

INDIVIDUALISM

Guthrie Burton tells the story: It was at Miss Florance's dancing school that one of the young terpsichoreans, failing to note any connection between rhythm and the esoteric maneuvers required of her feet, brought out Miss Florance's controlled inquiry: "Little Miss Watson, don't you hear the piano?"

"Yes," said little Miss Watson, "I hear it—but it doesn't bother me any."

INFALLIBILITY

A new member of a certain government bureau made life miserable for his associates by pretending to absolute infallibility. One day, however, he startled his co-workers by admitting that once he had been wrong.

"You wrong?" exclaimed one of his listeners.

"Yes," replied the infallible man. "Once I thought I was wrong when I wasn't."

INFLATION

At Sadieville, Kentucky, a tourist once called to an old native of the village: "Hey, uncle! How far is it to Lexington?"

"I dunno, Mister; hit used to be 'bout 25 miles; but th' way things has gone up around here, may be near 40 by now."

INFORMATION

On a little service station away out on the edge of a western desert there hangs a shingle, bearing this strange legend: "Don't ask us for information. If we knew anything we wouldn't be here."

INGENUITY

A young doctor and a young dentist shared the services of a receptionist and both fell in love with her.

The dentist was called away on business, so he sent for the receptionist and said: "I am going to be away for 10 days. You will find a little present in your room."

She went in, and found 10 apples.

❖   ❖

A youngster returned from summer camp. His fond parents asked him dozens of questions, one of which was: "How on earth did they manage to wake 350 boys every morning?"

"Well," he said, "they blew a bugle—at first."

"At first?"

"Yeah. But after a while they couldn't find the mouthpiece of the bugle."

After the veteran had gone to sleep, the parents struggled to unpack his bags. Out of one bag rolled a small, curious object. On close inspection it turned out to be the mouthpiece of a bugle.

❖   ❖

A lady of our acquaintance commissioned a painter to decorate the bathroom of her apartment during a period when she was to be out of town. She gave the workman an ash tray enameled in the exact color desired.

For two days the painter struggled in vain to mix the required shade. But happily when the lady returned and gazed upon his handiwork, she was enraptured by the perfect match obtained. "And to this day," chuckles the painter, "she don't know that I repainted that fool ash tray with the same paint I put on the bathroom!"

❖   ❖

A man came into a bank and wanted to borrow $5. He was told that the bank did not lend such small sums.

"But," he went on, "lending money is your business, isn't it?" The banker admitted it was.

"Well, I've got good security," said the stranger, "and I want to borrow $5."

Finally the banker agreed to make the loan. When the note was drawn and the interest of 30 cents paid, the stranger drew from his pocket $10,000 worth of Government bonds and handed them over as security. Before the banker could recover from his astonishment the stranger said, "Now, this is something like it. Over at the other bank they wanted to charge me $10 just for a safety deposit box to keep these things in."

❖   ❖

Bobby had attended a birthday party. "I hope," his mother said a bit apprehensively, "you didn't ask for a second piece of cake."

"Oh, no," replied Bobby. "I only asked Mrs. Smith for the

recipe so you could make some like it. Then she gave me two more pieces."

✧   ✧

Once there was a Scotch giant who journeyed to Ireland, to mop up a certain Irish giant, of whom he'd heard much loud talk.

The Irish giant looked out the window, saw the Scotch mountain moving in his general direction; observed that he was about twice his size, and plenty tough.

With rare presence of mind, the Irishman climbed into his baby's carriage, and let his feet hang out.

The Scotch giant approached the house, saw the big pair of feet hanging out of the baby carriage and said to himself, "If the Irish giant has a baby that size, the old man must be tremendous. Maybe there was something to those stories I've been hearing." So he turned away, and went back to Scotland.

✧   ✧

Oliver Herford had a neat knack of disposing of pestiferous people. One afternoon Albert Bigelow Paine was at Herford's studio when some one knocked at the door in a peculiar manner. "Sh-h-h," admonished Herford, and he and Paine were silent until the caller left.

"He's a frightful bore," explained Oliver. "He comes here and talks all afternoon."

"But how did you get him to knock in that special way?"

"Oh," explained Herford. "I told him a lot of people came and bothered me, and that I was giving that knock to a few particular friends!"

✧   ✧

In a high school class the students were instructed to express themselves on the subject: "The Most Beautiful Thing in the World."

A lazy lad in the back of the room pondered briefly, wrote a single line, lapsed into slumber. Curious, the teacher read over his shoulder: "My girl—too beautiful for words."

✧   ✧

There is an Irish priest in the province of Quebec who deserves a little credit for ingenuity. He is a hail fellow well met with every one in the village, asks for contributions, and gets liberal ones, from Protestants and Catholics alike. One day a delegation of Baptists called on him—men who had frequently contributed to Father W.'s church—told him they were going to erect a new Baptist church, as the old one was too small, and asked him to subscribe to the fund.

"Well, boys," he said, after a slight hesitation, "you know my religion forbids my doing that, but I will give you fifty dollars to help tear the old church down."

❖ ❖

In Eatonville, there were some doubts as to Deever Spillkins' fitness for a position on the school board, owing to certain lapses in his early education; but his first speech in his official capacity silenced the tongues of all critics.

He listened to several recitations with a grave and interested air, and at the end of the last one he rose to address the school, "by request."

"Some things are in my province as member of the school board, and some are not," he said, with a genial smile.

"It's within my province to say that I never heard scholars answer up more promptly than you children of District Number Four. As to whether your answers are or are not correct, it is not my place to say. Your teacher knows, and in her hands I leave the matter."

❖ ❖

An American flight commander in England took the opportunity of a bad day to give his men a taste of what it might be like to find their way back to the airfield after a forced landing. He took them out in a bus through twisting lanes, twelve miles away from base and six miles toward it. The more cunning navigators tried to work out a course with a milometer and compass. Others tried to remember the turns in the devious route. One hundred cigarettes was the prize for the first man back to the airfield. After the flight commander had been back an hour, he went to the orderly room to see if any of his flight had arrived. Two sergeants had returned before him and left their report: "Natives apparently friendly and using remarkably civilized methods of transport."

INSOMNIA

For many years Moss Hart, the playwright, was plagued by insomnia and finally made up his mind to consult a psychoanalyst. Pianist Oscar Levant wondered whether the doctor's advice had proved constructive.

"No," admitted Hart, "but my attitude toward insomnia is much better."

INSPIRATION

In 1924, when Notre Dame went to Princeton, Knute Rockne had such a sore throat that he could not deliver his pre-game oration. In the adjoining room, the Irish could hear Roper exhorting Princeton to fight valiantly and well.

"There's the best pep talker in the world," Rockne told his men, nodding to the next room. "Listen to him and win with his fight talk." They did.

INSTALLMENT PLAN

A colored preacher wanted to be a D. D., just like many white preachers. He wrote to a certain institution of very dubious standing and asked them to confer on him this honorary degree. Finally some unscrupulous individual wrote that if the preacher would send $25, he'd see what could be done. The colored brother did not have the twenty-five dollars but was determined to get the degree. He wrote, "Enclosed please find the sum of $12.50 for which I kindly ask you to please send me one 'D.' As soon as I get the money I will send for the other 'D.' "

INSTALLMENT SELLING

The only reason a great many American families don't own an elephant is that they have never been offered one for a dollar down.

INSTRUCTION

A jaguar asked a cat to teach him how to jump. The cat obliged. After the first lesson, they took a walk together. Presently the cat, who was very hungry, saw a mouse passing by and pounced on it.

The jaguar, who was hungry too, took advantage of the situation, and decided to jump on the cat—only to have the greatest deception of his life. The master, with the rapidity of lightning, jumped backwards. The jaguar, missing him, fell squarely on the ground.

"That is not fair," complained the big animal. "You did not teach me that trick!"

The cat smiled quietly and said, "A good teacher, my friend, never teaches all his tricks."

INSULT

A dentist in a middle western town had had considerable difficulty in collecting a bill, which he had sent each month regularly for a period of a year to an individual for whom he had made an especially fine set of artificial teeth.

When he returned home after resorting to another method, his wife asked:

"Well, did a personal call do any good? Did he pay you?"

"Pay me!" repeated the dentist, in a rage. "Not only did he not pay me, but he actually had the nerve to gnash at me with my teeth!"

INTERPRETATION

The young matron had just gleaned a delightful bit of information and hurried over to drop a verbal bomb in the immediate vicinity of her female parent.

"Oh, by the way, mother," she presently remarked with exaggerated nonchalance, "Henry's going in for anthropology. You know, I always said he had big-time brains!"

"Humph! Anthropology!" sniffed the parent. "That flatfoot couldn't even pronounce the word! What gave you that crazy notion?"

"Well," continued the young matron complacently, "I found some green tickets in his pocket, marked 'Mudhorse 15 to 1.' When I asked him about them he told me they were relics of a lost race."

❖ ❖

The young matron listened attentively while her doctor prescribed a remedy for her nervous condition. "Madam," he said, "you require frequent baths, plenty of fresh air; also you should dress in warm clothes."

That evening she told her husband all about it: "The doctor said I'm in a highly distraught condition, dear, and that it is essential for me to go to Palm Beach, then to a dude ranch out west and to buy myself a new ermine wrap."

INVENTION

After the Armistice of World War I, a pigeon-hole in a desk at the English War Office was being cleared out. Among some dusty papers in the receptacle was a design for a tank, the inspiration of a Nottingham plumber. It had been submitted to the War chiefs in 1911.

Across the drawing was written the official comment in red: "The man's mad."

ISOLATIONISM

A small boy quarreled with his playmate from across the street. The neighbor went away in a huff. "All right," said the small boy, "let him go home. I don't need him. I can play by myself."

"Fine," said his father, "and now you can go out in the yard and play on your teeter-totter—by yourself."

JOINER

Two little boys were bragging about the relative accomplishments of their respective fathers. Billy appeared to have an edge when he insisted, "My father's an Eagle, an Elk, a Moose and a Lion."

"Yeah?" responded the incredulous companion. "How much does it cost to see him?"

JOY-OF-THE-JOB

A small-time vaudeville couple, playing a dismal little circuit, were standing weary and cold at the curb. They had finished their last turn and were on their way to a cheerless room in a cheap, shoddy theatrical hotel. In prospect was a miserable midnight meal, cooked over the flickering gas jet—a 4:00 A.M. call and a long day-coach journey to the next engagement.

As they waited there for a street-car, a costly limousine turned the corner. The little thespians caught a glimpse of richly-attired people—furs, jewels, opera hats.

"Looks pretty wonderful," sighed the actress.

"Yeah," asserted her partner. "Yeah; it looks wonderful. But, remember, they can't act!"

JUDGMENT

The late Simon Bolivar Buckner used to tell a story of an old resident in his Kentucky home who was celebrated for his wisdom.

"Uncle Zeke," a young man once asked, "how does it come you're so wise?"

"Because," said the old man, "I've got good judgment. Good judgment comes from experience, and experience—well, that comes from poor judgment!"

❖   ❖

Some visitors who were being shown over a pauper lunatic asylum inquired of their guide what method was employed to discover when the inmates were sufficiently recovered to leave.

"Well," replied he, "you see, it's this way. We have a big trough of water and we turn on the tap. We leave it running and tell 'em to bail out the water with pails until they've emptied the trough."

"How does that prove it?" asked one of the visitors.

"Well," said the guide, "them as ain't idiots turns off the tap."

❖   ❖

Fighting spirit is fine, but every executive must impress upon subordinates the importance of careful preparation and sound judgment. After all, when you fight blindly you're likely to get gory, rather than glory.

"This here's the fightin'est dog in the country," a farmer boasted. Just then another dog came along and after a short struggle subdued the farmer's dog completely.

"I thought you said your dog was a great fighter," a bystander remarked scornfully.

"Oh, he is," insisted the farmer, "he is. But he's a kinda poor jedge o' dogs."

JUDGMENT—Lack

Earl Gwin of Hot Springs, Virginia, once put his dog, Trailer, on the scent of a wild turkey that had disappeared in the brush. Unfortunately, the dog took up the back scent of the bird, which was an old bird. So Trailer just trailed and trailed. He must have trailed over half of Virginia, and, since he was on the back trail, never caught up with the bird. Instead, he was found barking at the nest in which that turkey had been hatched many years before.

JURY DUTY

A woman called up for jury duty refused to serve because she didn't believe in capital punishment.

Trying to persuade her, the judge explained: "This is merely a case where a wife is suing her husband because she gave him a thousand dollars to pay down on a fur coat and he lost the money in a poker game."

"I'll serve," she said, "I could be wrong about capital punishment."

JUSTICE

In a courtroom in the Arkansas hills, the judge drawled: "Who's the defendant here?"

A lean character in the jury box arose and said, "I'm him."

"What are you doing in that jury box?" asked the judge.

"They picked me," was the reply.

"You can't be both the defendant and a juror," pointed out the judge.

"No?" said the hillbilly. "I was thinkin' I was kinda lucky."

❖   ❖

In the early days of Phoenix, Arizona—about the turn of the century—an old-timer was elected justice of the peace. As was usual—he knew no law. When cases were brought before him, he had a fine-looking binder inside of which he had fastened a Sears-Roebuck catalog and he would get out his volume with a great flourish, thumb over the pages, put his finger upon a given point and pronounce judgment.

He did so one day when he had a man up for trial. Thumbing over the pages, he put his finger on a point, and said, "You are fined $4.98." The man got up to expostulate.

"Sit down!" hoarsely whispered his lawyer, pulling at his coattail. "You're just plain lucky he turned to Pants instead of Pianos."

❖ ❖

Out in Nevada a mining claim was pending before a certain oldtime western judge with a reputation for a rather rough-and-ready brand of justice. One morning his honor made the following remarkable statement:

"Gentlemen, this court has in hand a check from the plaintiff for $10,000 and a check from the defendant for $15,000. The court will return $5,000 to the defendant, and then we will try this case strictly on its merits."

JUSTICE—Foiled

A merchant was called upon to defend a suit brought against him by a dissatisfied customer. Just before the conclusion of the proceedings, the merchant had to go on a trip to another state. Accordingly, he instructed his attorney to telegraph him when a decision had been reached by the judge trying the suit. When the merchant arrived he received a message from his lawyer, saying: "Right has triumphed."

The merchant hastily wired his lawyer: "Appeal at once."

JUSTICE—Weighted

The Deacon's Board of a Colored Baptist Church called on a lawyer who had just taken office as Judge of the 4th Alabama Circuit.

They wished to employ him to represent their church in an equity suit filed in that court.

"Thank you very much for the honor, gentlemen," said the lawyer, "but having become the judge of this court, I can no longer accept employment in any case."

"Yes, sir," replied the chairman of the distinguished and solemn group, "we knows 'bout yo' 'lection; that's the reason we wants you on our side."

"JUST SUPPOSE—"

A certain little four-year-old girl can ask more questions than Dr. I. Q. Not only that but her questions are the chain type—that is, one question always leads to another. Her favorite method of carrying on the stream of questions is to say: "Suppose . . . suppose this, or suppose that."

One day, with many other things that at the moment seemed to be far more important, her father commanded: "Stop supposing."

She paused for a minute and a bright twinkle came into her eyes. "Daddy," she asked, "can I if?"

KEEPING UP

Cemeteries are so quiet because the boys under the headstones are not trying to keep up with the mausoleum crowd.

KNOW—HOW

"Sculpture is very easy, isn't it?" asked a sweet lady at an exhibition of statuary.

"Very, very easy," smiled the sculptor, "and very, very simple. You just take a block of marble and a chisel and knock off all the marble you don't want."

✧   ✧

A business man had occasion to consult a lawyer and went to his office for advice. Later, he ran into an acquaintance and told of his experience.

"But why spend money for a lawyer?" he was asked. "When you sat in his office, didn't you see all the law books there? Well, you see! What he told you, you could read for yourself in those books."

"Yes," said the business man, "yes, that's very true, but that lawyer knows what page it's on."

KNOWLEDGE

A preacher, in a sermon on "Wisdom," said to his small flock, "Brethren, it isn't the things we know that get us into trouble. It's the things we know for sure that aren't so!"

❖   ❖

At a political picnic, a newspaper reporter had listened for too long, as a proud father recounted the exploits of his 10-year-old son.

"That boy knows everything," the politician said. "And geography! He's terrific at geography! Why he can name every hemisphere!"

❖   ❖

While the late Dr. Charles W. Eliot (of "Five-Foot Shelf" fame) was head of Harvard University, someone asked why that noble institution had acquired a reputation as the nation's greatest storehouse of knowledge.

"I'm sure I do not know," responded the good Doctor, "unless it is because the Freshmen bring us so much of it, and the Seniors take so little away!"

❖   ❖

Woodrow Wilson, while president of Princeton University, once addressed a group of alumni. "You write in," he confided, "to ask why we do not make more of your boys. The answer is simple: it is because they are your boys."

KNOWLEDGE—Specialized

They are still laughing in Chicago judicial circles over the Italian street-peddler who applied for citizenship papers.

Asked by an examining judge how many states there are in the Union, the push-cart operator pondered deeply, and then, his countenance brightening, asked if he might put a query to the Court.

"Mr. Judge," he said, bowing respectfully. "You knowa your

business. I knowa my business. You ask me how many states is it in a Union. I ask you, How many bananas in a bunch?"

LABOR RELATIONS

A city boy, visiting his country cousin was walking through the pasture when he heard a peculiar buzzing sound. He looked around to find out what it was. "Come away from there!" the cousin shouted. "It's a rattlesnake! If you go near it, it will strike." "Gosh," said the city boy, "do they have unions, too?"

LANGUAGE

A Frenchman, struggling with the English language, turned to an American friend for counsel:
"What," he asked "is a polar bear?"
"Polar bear? Why he lives 'way up north."
"But what do he do?"
"Oh, he sits on a cake of ice and eats fish."
"Zat settle! I will not accept!"
"What in the world do you mean, you won't accept?"
"Ah," explained the other, "I was invite to be a polar bear at a funeral, and I will not accept."

❖   ❖

A young lad was leafing through a current magazine and after looking for some time at a certain advertisement he finally asked his mother: "What does 'budget' mean? Is it something like a camel?" She thought she had understood him correctly at first, but after the last query asked him to spell the word. "B-u-d-g-e-t" he said, carefully spelling it out, "It says here—'See Egypt on a budget.'"

❖   ❖

A favorite gag around Washington involves a new clerk in one of the bureaus. In the midst of the day's dictation he became a little hazy as to terminology and appealed to his secretary in some embarrassment. "Er—ah—do you 'retire' a loan?"

And she answered demurely, "No; I sleep with mama."

❖ ❖

"Some of our most amusing anecdotes, it has always seemed to me," says Dr. Adolph Keller, the Swiss theologian, "results from unintentional misinterpretations of the English language.

"Once, a good many years ago, I was dictating a sermon to a stenographer in an American city. I used the phrase, 'Salvation is a cosmic process.' When the young lady submitted the typed version it read, 'Salvation is a cosmetic process.'

"From one point of view, at least, the error resulted in an improvement of the sentence."

❖ ❖

In discussing the advantage of membership in a certain order, a friend of mine stressed to his wife the point that the group met in a spirit of friendly informality.

At this point the colored maid entered the room, and hearing the remark, she commented: "Da's what I likes about our lodge meetin', too, Mistah Blank. We meets in friendly immorality."

❖ ❖

"What do you use for fuel?" someone asked a South American engineer.

"Sometimes coal; more often wood; but always the catalogs of American manufacturers, printed in a language we do not understand."

❖ ❖

A Southerner once dictated a letter in which he rejected an insurance policy because the applicant had a heart murmur. Transcribed by a Northern girl who hadn't learned to decipher the lilting lingo of the land of Margaret Mitchell, the insurance was denied because policy seeker "had a hot mama."

❖ ❖

A little girl, daughter of an English mother and an American father, was asked how she felt about the differences in British and American pronunciation.

"Oh," she replied, "I'm half and hawlf."

LANGUAGE—French

An English soldier in a French village, seeing a wedding in process at a church, asked a Frenchman whose wedding it was. "Je ne sais pas, M'sieu," answered the Frenchman.

A few hours later the same soldier saw a coffin going into the same church, and, curiosity getting the better of him, he again asked the identity of the individual.

"Je ne sais pas," was the response.

"Blimy!" ejaculated the Tommy, "he didn't last long!"

LAUGHTER

A ham actress was belittling the late Marie Dressler's comedy. "What dignity is there in making people laugh?" she squeaked. "I make them cry." Miss Dressler retorted: "Any onion can do that. Show me a vegetable that can make people laugh."

LAW—Enforcement

For the first time in the history of the state, Negroes were permitted to vote in the 1946 Texas elections. Two colored men duly presented their poll tax receipts at a voting place in Lamesa and requested to be shown how to mark the ballots. "We just want to vote for Sheriff Buck Bennett and County Attorney Bob Huff," one of them explained.

The clerk in charge asked why they did not care to vote for the candidates for other offices. The big Negro spokesman scratched his head. "Well," he said respectfully, "we don't know nothin' about them. But this Mister Buck, he caught us with a load of bootleg whisky, and Mister Bob he persecuted us and made us pay a fine. We know they's very efficient gentlemen and ought to keep their jobs."

LAW—LAWYERS

The famous Choate, than whom there was never a shrewder cross-examiner, was questioning a witness in an assault case in which his client was the accused. He maneuvered the fellow into admitting that he hadn't actually seen the offense committed.

"So," purred the famous attorney, "you say you didn't actually see the defendant bite off this man's ear?"

"Naw," growled the witness, "I didn't see him bite it off. I just seen him spit it out on the ground!"

❖ ❖

A young lawyer attended the funeral of a millionaire. A friend arrived at the service and took a seat beside him. He whispered, "How far has the service gone?"

The lawyer nodded toward the clergyman in the pulpit and whispered back: "Just opened the defense."

❖ ❖

A manufacturer received a whopping bill from his lawyer. He stood for everything until he came to this item: "For crossing the street to talk to you and discovering it wasn't you: $500."

LAZINESS

There's a Missouri story about a hound sitting in a country store and howling as hounds howl. In comes a stranger who says to the storekeeper, "What's the matter with the dog?" "He's sittin' on a cocklebur." "Why doesn't he get off?" "He'd rather holler."

❖ ❖

"Sometimes," confided Mrs. Longwed, to her intimate friend, "I think my husband is the gentlest, most patient, best-natured soul that ever lived. And sometimes I think it's just laziness."

❖ ❖

Bobby Coltrin, major league baseball scout, tells this one:

"If I am ever asked to name the laziest man I have encountered in my travels, I'll have no hesitancy at all in handing the palm to a pitcher I encountered in Arkansas, while I was umpiring a ball game.

"This pitcher took his stance facing the plate and never altered direction in the slightest degree. During the course of the game he addressed me on the hill, speaking out of the corner of his mouth: 'Anybody on base?' I answered: 'One.' When he followed this with the query, 'Which base?' I was pretty sure I had met my champion. 'Second base,' I answered. And his third question cinched the title: 'How big a lead has he got?' "

LEADERSHIP

A leader is anyone who has two characteristics: first, he is going somewhere; second, he is able to persuade other people to go with him.

✧ ✧

A little boy was trying to lead a large dog. "Where are you taking that great dog?" asked a man in passing.

"I-I'm waiting to see where he w-wants to go, then I'll t-take him there."

LEAST RESISTANCE

A church custodian, with a record of long and harmonious service, was once asked how he managed to get along with the various women's groups who held frequent meetings in the building.

"Oh," he replied philosophically, "I just git in neutral and let 'em push me about."

LEISURE

Millions long for immortality who do not know what to do with themselves on a rainy Sunday afternoon.

✧ ✧

A farm wife was being interviewed by a social worker, intent on filling out one of those surveys studded with interminable—and intimate—questions.

The interviewer was bent on learning how her subject spent the day. Patiently the farm wife detailed her duties, from the rising hour of 5:30—through the cooking, baby-tending, cleaning, washing, ironing, mending, farm accounts, gardening, and so on and on.

"Yes, yes," said the interviewer, a trifle impatiently, "but your free time. What do you do with your free time?"

The woman pondered the question a moment, and replied: "I go to the toilet."

LIFE

BIOGRAPHY: Apron strings, heart strings, purse strings, harp strings.

❖ ❖

When you have to keep your back to the wall and your ear to the ground . . . your shoulder to the wheel and your nose to the grindstone . . . your head level and both feet on the ground—you're not a contortionist; you're just like the rest of us.

LIFE—LIVING

A prayer many of us need is that of the old Scot who feared that he might become like so many he saw around him—dead from the chin up—and hence this daily petition: "O Lord, keep me alive while I am still living!"

LITERATURE

At a dinner-party one evening the venerated Columbia professor, Raymond Weaver, was queried by a bright young thing, in her most buffed and polished finishing-school voice, "Mr. Weaver, have you read So-and-so's book?" (naming a modish best-seller of the moment). Mr. Weaver confessed he had not. "Oh, you'd better hurry up—it's been out over three months."

Mr. Weaver, an impressive gentleman with a voice like a Greek herald, inquired, "My dear young lady, have you read Dante's Divine Comedy?" "No." "Then you'd better hurry up—it's been out over six hundred years."

❖ ❖

A writer of popular stories was one day being shown through a book shop in New York. A small table was devoted to the new books, and all the rest of the space was taken up with gorgeous editions of Stevenson, Dickens, Scott, Thackeray, Fielding, etc.— fine leather-bound volumes at very modest prices.

The writer indicated with a sweep of his arm this collection of books and observed:

"Literature would pay better if there were not so many dead men in the business."

LOGIC

As the Santa Maria was tossing about in a storm, a worried seaman approached Christopher Columbus.

"Captain Columbus," he blubbered, "if the world is really flat, like everybody says—"

"Stop fretting," interrupted Columbus impatiently, "I'm telling you the world isn't flat."

"But what makes you so sure?" persisted the seaman.

"If the world was flat," returned Columbus, "where would I have gotten the money to make this trip?"

❖   ❖

When bread-slicing machines were introduced, a bakery in a small town decided to make a survey and find out what the housewives thought of this new convenience.

A dapper young man was hired for the job and sallied forth with notebook and pencil. He found one woman who was very enthusiastic about the new machine.

"And why, madam," he asked curiously, "do you favor the machine-slicing so strongly?"

"Well," she replied, "mainly because we ain't got no knife."

❖   ❖

The Federal judge, after explaining at some length the history of Old Glory to a group of aliens seeking citizenship papers, asked one of the applicants: "And now, tell me, what flies over the city hall?"

The alien blinked a moment and then triumphantly replied, "Peejins!"

❖   ❖

McTavish had taken up riding, and he was going into it with all the thoroughness of his race. He had completed his outfit except for one thing, and this he set out to purchase. He strode into the harness store with the self-assurance of a veteran and asked for one spur.

"One spur!" exclaimed the clerk. "But we never sell a single spur. They come in pairs, and if you want them for horseback riding you will have to have two."

"Coon, lad, I dinna need but one spur. If I can get the right side of the hoorse a-goin', the left side weel coom right along."

❖ ❖

A roadside sign in Normandy reads, "Pasture your horse here. Short-tailed horses, 20c a day."

A local peasant, asked to explain the distinction, answered: "A short-tailed horse is bothered all the time by flies. To shake them off he has to use his head, and while doing that he can't eat. A long-tailed horse can handle the situation with his tail without raising his mouth from the grass. The men of Normandy would never pay as much for grazing a short-tailed horse as a long-tailed one."

❖ ❖

The teacher was giving her kindergarten class a lesson in cubes, and she asked for examples. Each child in turn named something shaped like a cube—a box, a block, a cake of ice—and finally one little boy shouted, "I know—a half pound of butter."

"Yes, that's good," said the teacher. "Now let's have one more."

The class was silent, apparently having exhausted its originality, until another little boy raised his hand. "The other half pound of butter," he said.

LOST AND FOUND

"Now, Sandy McDorr," the teacher said. "Tell me where the elephant is found."

The boy hesitated for a moment, then his face lighted up. "The elephant, teacher," he said, "is such a large animal it is scarcely ever lost."

LOVE

If a woman can stand a man: who eats celery audibly; who would rather spend an evening at home listening to the radio than go to a dance; who always forgets to return his partner's lead; who quarrels with waiters; who always gets theater tickets in the next to the last row, well over to the side; who has never learned the new dances, and talks about the old days when they used to waltz and two-step and polka; who forgets her birthday, but remembers her age; who disapproves of her new gown because it is cut too low, and then spends the evening talking to Mrs. Smith in one six inches lower; who believes in economy—feminine variety only; who believes a toothpick should be used in public; who wears a toupee; well, if a woman can stand a man through all that—that is love!

❖   ❖

A distinguished actor, showing guests about his country place, had come to his particular pride: a flock of sheep. Halting at the gate, the proud proprietor uplifted his voice, whereupon the group came flocking to him, thrusting their noses through the pasture bars, nuzzled their owner's hand, and greedily gobbled up the tidbits which he had brought in his pocket.

"Ah," said the actor, his eyes alight, "see how they love me!"

"Yes," interposed a guest, "but you feed them."

"My friend," said the actor, "at my age we call that love."

❖   ❖

A friend of ours, in charge of decorations for an elaborate wedding reception, decided to reproduce the nuptial scene in miniature. Recounting his plans in the family circle, he explained that he had obtained a small reproduction of a church with appropriate dolls to represent the parson, the bridal couple and attendants. "All I need now," he concluded, "is a little auto with a placard, 'Just Married!'"

His 5-year-old-son, who had made no comment up to that point disappeared into his play room and presently returned with a favorite toy, a very rakish sport model auto. "Daddy," he said solemnly, proffering his contribution, "I think this expresses love."

❖   ❖

A lovelorn sailor decided to celebrate pay day by sending a wireless to his girl in Duluth. After chewing on his pencil for several minutes, he finally turned in a cable that read: "I love you, I love you, I love you. John."

The clerk in the cable office read it over and said, "You're allowed to add a tenth word for the same price."

The sailor pondered for several minutes and then added his tenth word. It was "Regards."

LOVE—AND LIFE

"Engaged couples," says Mary Borden, in *The Technique of Marriage,* "are like a couple of explorers starting off with a bagful of sweetmeats as provisions."

MAN

There are three classes of men in the United States—the intellectual, the handsome, and the majority.

MAN—AND HIS WORLD

One Sunday afternoon, in order to have a little rest, Daddy tore a picture of the map of the world from a newspaper, sheared it into a number of odd-shaped pieces, and sent Joan into the living room to "put the world together again."

He hoped for an hour of quiet but in five minutes Joan was back, announcing that the map of the world was all laid out on the floor.

"How did you ever do it in so short a time?" asked the incredulous parent.

"Oh, that was simple," explained Joan. "There was a picture of a man on the other side of the map. I just put the man together correctly—and then the world was all okay."

MANNERS

"Have you any abnormal children in your class?" a harassed-looking teacher was asked.

"Yes," she replied, "two of them have good manners."

❖   ❖

A diffident young magazine editor from New York went to Hollywood. Invited to a motion picture party, he determined to throw off his shyness and behave with abandon, as he had heard the Hollywooders did at parties. He did his best in that direction, giving most of his attention to a young actress.

At the peak of his reckless abandon, the editor was somewhat disconcerted to find the actress weeping. "Oh-h-h," she boo-hooed, "I've been here almost a year now, and you're the first fellow who's acted to me like a gentleman."

MARRIAGE (see also MARRIED LIFE, DIVORCE)

The local reporter was interviewing the grandfather of a Hollywood star.

"Does Bill ever come back to the old farm since he's such a big shot in the movies?" he asked.

"Every summer," said the old man proudly. "Every one of the five summers he's been away.

"And did he bring his wife with him?"

"Every time," replied Grandpa. "And they was five as purty gals as you ever laid eyes on."

❖   ❖

An old bachelor was asked which he thought were the happier, people who were married or those who were not.

"Well, I don't know," he replied. "Sometimes I think there is as many as is that ain't, as ain't that is."

❖   ❖

When our Psychological Warfare department started working with the French, they had a terrible time explaining to one Frenchman just exactly what this psychological warfare was. Finally he got it. "Ah," he said, "I see what you mean. It is just like marriage."

❖   ❖

Max, the marriage broker, took a client to look over a certain female prospect. From a distance in the room the anxious youth made an inventory of the lady. He then whispered to the marriage broker: "She's too fat, her nose is terrible, she's knock-kneed, her hair is bleached, and she's missing two teeth." "You can talk louder," said the marriage broker. "She's deaf also."

❖ ❖

The bride tottered up the aisle on the arm of her father, who was wheeled in his armchair by three of his great-grandchildren. She was arrayed in white and carried a big bouquet of white rosebuds; her hair, though gray, was bobbed, and she smiled and nodded to acquaintances.

The groom was able to walk, aided by two handsome mahogany crutches. His head was bald, and his false teeth chattered a little nervously.

And so they were married—the couple who waited until they could afford to get married.

❖ ❖

"Pa," said Mrs. Hidgson, with evident anxiety in her voice, "I'm gettin' real worried about Elmer. Seems like he just don't want to marry."

"Shucks, Ma," Mr. Hidgson spat philosophically, "don't you worry a mite about Elmer not wantin' t' marry. He will when the wrong girl comes along."

❖ ❖

Getting a husband is like buying an old house. You don't see it the way it is, but the way you think it's going to be when you get it remodeled.

MARRIED LIFE (see also MARRIAGE, DIVORCE)

I always try out my jokes on my wife. You know, if your wife laughs at a joke, you can be sure that it's either a darned good joke, or you've got a darned good wife. In my own case—well, I think I've got a good wife!

❖ ❖

A certain happily married college professor, delivering a graduation address, gave this sage counsel:

"Gentlemen, many of you will marry. Let me entreat you to be kind to your wives. Be patient with them. When you are going out together, do not worry if your wife is not ready at the appointed time. Have a good book nearby. Read it while you wait. And, gentlemen, I assure you that you will be astonished at the amount of information you will acquire."

❖ ❖

Chauncey M. Depew had an old friend at Peekskill who, after courting the same woman for twenty years, married her.

"Josephus," said Chauncey, "why did you not marry that splendid woman long before now; why did you wait all these years?"

"Chauncey," explained the other, "I waited until she talked herself out. You see, I wanted a quiet married life."

❖ ❖

"By whom?" asked a husband when told that his wife was outspoken.

❖ ❖

Mrs. Peck: Now, Henry, what are you thinking about? I can tell when you are entertaining some thought you want to conceal from me. Out with it!

Henry: Very well, my dear; I was just wondering what the Mormons could possibly see in polygamy.

❖ ❖

"Now that we're married," said the groom, with a certain air of superiority, "perhaps I'll be permitted to point out a few of your defects."

"It won't be necessary," was the reply of his loving bride. "I know them too well. They kept me from getting a better man than you."

❖ ❖

"Boohoo," boohooed the bride, "to think my cake would turn out this way when I put my heart into it!"

"Never mind, honey," comforted the groom, "next time try baking one when you're light-hearted."

❖ ❖

Down in the Blue Ridge mountains of Tennessee, a "good woman" is expected to do all the housework and chores, raise a dozen children, a few hogs, a couple of cows, and not be too proud to help a bit with the crops if need be. The mountaineer, on an average, wears out about three wives.

A "city-feller," planning a summer home in the mountains, consulted a local contractor. All went well until the wife of the city resident insisted that the walls of the living room be panelled in native chestnut. Finally, the contractor took the city man aside. "I know yer wife's a holdin' out fer that thar ches'nut," he said, "but if 'twas me I shore wouldn't have hit. Y'know, there's one p'int you maybe hain't considered: yore nex' wife maybe wouldn't like it!"

❖   ❖

The archbishop had preached a fine sermon on married life and its beauties. Two old Irishwomen coming out of church were heard commenting on the address.

" 'Tis a fine sermon his Riverance would be after giving us," said one to the other.

"It is, indade," was the quick reply, "and I wish I knew as little about the matter as he does."

❖   ❖

They had just come from watching the Falls at Niagara and were returning to their hotel when the bride sighed and remarked:

"Just think of it, Henry dear! Fifty years from yesterday will be our golden anniversary!"

❖   ❖

"Susannah," asked the preacher, when it came her turn to answer the usual questions in such a case, "do you take this man to be your wedded husband, for better—for worse . . . ?"

"Jes' as he is, pahson," she interrupted, "jes' as he is. Ef he gets any bettah Ah'll know de good Lawd's gwine to take 'im, and ef he gets any wusser, w'y, Ah'll tend to 'im mahself."

❖   ❖

There was a certain chap who was fond of playing poker. At one of the regular sessions, which lasted until the early morning hours, the caretaker politely told the players they would have to get out.

As they left the building, this chap suggested that the gang come on up to his house and continue the game.

"What! At this hour? What will your wife say?"

"Oh," said the chap "that's all right. She's a good sport—and besides, I'm the Czar in my household."

So they went along. And, sure enough, the Mrs. greeted the group with tolerance if not cordiality. The chap told her of the assurances he had given his friends, even adding the comment about being the Czar in his household.

The lady of the house showed the boys a room, told them there was plenty of cards, chips, food in the icebox, liquor on a shelf. Then she concluded:

"You can amuse yourselves to your heart's content—the Czar is going to bed!"

❖   ❖

Patrick, having consumed his repast, turned attention to the bit of newsprint in which it had been wrapped. "Michael," he said presently, turning to a companion, "it speaks here o' the 'witching hour.' An' what time would that be, pray?"

"Shure, Pat," said the other workman, "that's the hour of two in the mornin' when yer wife meets ye wid, 'Witch story is it this time?'"

❖   ❖

A man who claims he's boss in his home will lie about other things, too.

❖   ❖

After a few years of marriage, it is said a man can look right at a woman without seeing her—and a woman can see right through a man without looking at him.

❖   ❖

A rather loud-mouthed employee in a large mid-western office was given to boasting that he always had the last word in his household. One of his associates who chanced to call at the home was impressed by evidence to the contrary.

"Well," said the somewhat chastened husband, "I still have the last word. Don't you always hear me say, 'All right'?"

❖ ❖

The honeymoon has ended when a wife stops making a fuss over her husband, and begins to make a fuss with him.

❖ ❖

There comes a time in every man's life when his wife remarks complacently, "I can read you like a book, John."
And we've just heard the appropriate reply:
"Why don't you, then? You skip what you don't like in a book, but in me you linger over it."

❖ ❖

A couple who had been having rough sailing asked their minister to call. During the course of the evening he remarked: "Just look at that cat and dog lying there so peacefully before the fire. They are not fighting even if they do not see eye to eye on everything."
"Yeah," spoke the husband, "but you just try tying them together and see what happens!"

❖ ❖

At the beginning of their married life an English couple made the following arrangement: Whenever he had a bad day at the office, he would put his hat well over on the left side of his head on returning home. If she had a bad day at home, she would put her apron on backwards.
Each undertook to respect the other's danger signal. They are still happily married after 48 years.

❖ ❖

At a wedding breakfast little Eric was given a seat near his adoring aunt.
"Well," said the old lady, "what kind of a wedding will you have, Eric?"
"I'm never going to get married."
"But why won't you ever get married?"
Eric was silent for a few minutes as he gazed across the table at

his admiring parents. Then he answered very positively: "Because, Auntie, I've lived with married people too long already."

❖ ❖

An old Negro, speaking of his wife, said:

"She ain't got so many faults, but she sho' do make the mos' o' dem she got."

❖ ❖

When the colored preacher's knock on the door of the modest little shanty brought a woman attired in heavy mourning, the good man solicitously inquired, "Is yo' husband daid, sister?"

"Oh, no, suh, he ain't daid," was the reply.

"Then, why is you in mournin', sister?" the preacher asked.

"Well, suh," explained the woman, "it's like dis: Mah present husband has been naggin' and botherin' me so much that I'se went back into mournin' fo' mah fust husband."

❖ ❖

"I wear the pants at our house."

"Yeah, but I notice that right after supper you wear an apron over them."

❖ ❖

Before a feller gets married he kin git his girl in most any sort of a shindig with an invitation er a ticket but after th' ceremony it takes a completely new outfit an' $4 worth of beauty work.

❖ ❖

Not too long ago we heard a preacher rise at a banquet and say, "Tonight marks the fortieth anniversary of my marriage; in all that time, my wife and I have never had a spat." He was followed by a hard-bitten old Bishop who said soberly, "Now, my friends, there are two things to keep in mind about the brother's statement. One is that it may not be true. The other is that if it is true, how ghastly!"

MATHEMATICS

Recently a Canadian editor was in a gun plant where extremely fine tooling operations were being carried on.

"What are your tolerances on this job?" he asked a man at a lathe.

"One five thousandth of an inch," replied the workman.

The figure conveyed little to the editor. He asked, "How fine is that?"

The workman, too, seemed puzzled. He called to his neighbor on the next machine: "Bill, how many five thousandths are there in an inch?"

Bill scratched his head. "Gee, I don't know. But there must be millions of them."

MEDIOCRITY

A lawyer was cross-examining a negro witness in a Georgia court, badgering the poor darky with a barrage of questions. He was getting along fine until he asked the witness to state again his occupation.

"Ah's a carpenter, suh," the witness replied.

"What kind of a carpenter?"

"Jest a jack-leg carpenter, suh."

"And, pray tell the court, what kind of a carpenter is a jack-leg carpenter?"

"Well, suh, he ain't 'zackly a fust-class carpenter."

"Explain more fully what you mean by that."

"Ah means, suh, dat a jack-leg carpenter is diffunt f'm a fust-class carpenter, jes' like you is diff'unt f'm a fust-class lawyer."

MILLENNIUM

Do you recall the ancient jest about the soapbox orator who shouted, "Comes the revolution, the rich man will eat your moldy bread, while you eat his strawberries and cream."

"Strawberries," a hearer protested, "always give me hives."

"Comes the revolution," the orator thundered, "strawberries won't give you the hives!"

MIRACLES

Adm. Nimitz and Gen. MacArthur went fishing together. In a sudden squall, the boat capsized, and the eminent fighting men were floundering helplessly in the water.

The Admiral was first to reach the boat. With the aid of an oar, he finally got the General aboard. "Now, Mac," he cautioned, "don't mention this to anyone. I'd be disgraced if the men of the Navy learned I can't swim."

"Don't worry," MacArthur replied. "Your secret is safe. I'd hate to have my men find out I can't walk on water."

"MISERY LOVES COMPANY"

A mountaineer woman of eastern Tennessee was asked how she and her husband were making out.

"Well, the corn and 'taters didn't make it a-tall," she replied. "The beetles have got all the string beans and the cabbage never did head up. Fact is, we h'aint got a bit. But, thank God, neither has no one else in our neighborhood."

MISINTERPRETATION

Two travelers in Ireland, returning home late one night, lost their way.

Said one, "We must be in a cemetery. Here's a gravestone."

"Whose is it?" asked the other.

The more sober of the two, having struck a match said, "I don't know, but he seems to have lived to a ripe old age—175."

"See if you can read the name," insisted his companion.

Another match being lit—"I don't know him, some fellow called 'Miles from Dublin.' "

MISPLACED METAPHORS

A Bishop relates the following experience: After the service one Sunday morning he was approached by an old lady who expressed great appreciation over his discourse. "Why, Bishop," she said, "you can never know what your service meant to me. It was just like water to a drowning man."

"MISSED THE MARK"

Will Rogers used to tell a story about a friend of his, who was crazy about hunting, in spite of being a miserable shot. One day he met the friend, coming home from a day's shooting and obviously in the dumps.

"Didn't you get anything?" asked Will.

"Not a durned thing," said the man. "I was so ashamed to face my wife again that I went to one of the local butchers who obligingly tied a live rabbit to a tree for me to take a shot at."

Seeing that he had no rabbit with him Rogers exclaimed.

"What! Mean to tell me you even missed that?"

"Oh I made a swell shot," said the fellow gloomily, "hit the rope clean in the middle, and I haven't seen the rabbit since!"

MISSIONARIES

A young lady, seeing a group of admirers gathered around a woman who had given a faithful and successful service in a foreign field, said she would like to be a returned missionary if it were not for being an outgoing missionary.

MISSIONS

A little girl in a Sunday School class was listening to the story of missionaries in far-away lands, trying to convert cannibals to Christian ways of life. When the teacher asked, "What do you think is the first thing the missionaries should teach the cannibals?" The little girl answered promptly, "They should teach them to be vegetarians!"

❖ ❖

The new minister was enthusiastic about foreign missions and one of his first tasks was to call upon parishioners whom he knew to have money and enlist their support. "I'm sorry," replied one wealthy farmer, "but it's no use asking me. I don't approve of foreign missions."

"But surely," the minister persisted, "you know that we are commanded to feed the hungry."

"That may be," came the grim reply, "but can't we feed 'em on something cheaper than missionaries?"

MISUNDERSTANDING

In his lonely cabin sat the game warden when the phone on the wall jangled. A sweet voice inquired if he were the game warden. He assured her that he was.

"Oh, I'm so glad to have the right person at last. Would you mind suggesting some nice games for a children's birthday party?"

✧ ✧

Jimmy Durante, reporting on his Alaskan trip, told Garry Moore he saw a sign outside an igloo which read, "Eskimo Spitz Dogs—five dollars each."

"Well, what's so unusual about that?" said Garry.

"Unusual!" exclaimed Jimmy. "I got fifty dollars that says the Eskimos can't do it."

MIXED METAPHORS

"When I look," thundered the orator, "down the untrodden paths of the past, I see in the future the dim outlines of the footprints of an unseen hand."

✧ ✧

Westbrook Pegler, in an unguarded moment (he has so many of 'em) once referred to Townsend Old Age Pensioners as "itchy old loafers." Naturally, this was very hot stuff for presiding officers at Townsend meetings.

"Itchy old loafers!" thundered one foaming forensic. "Why that's an insult to every man who has attained the ripe and honorable age of three score. Loafers, indeed! I say to you, my friends, that beneath many a pair of patched pants there beats a heart as brave. . . ."

MODERN MAID

A small boy returned home from school and told his father he was now second in his class. The top place was held by a girl.

"But surely, John," said his father, "you're not going to be beaten by a mere girl."

"Well, you see, father," explained John, "girls are not nearly so mere as they used to be."

✧ ✧

After listening to the usual damaging comparison between girls of today and the girls of years ago, pert Miss Teenage remarked: "Well, if they were so darned innocent, how did they know when to blush?"

✧ ✧

"You must have gotten in quite late, dear," remarked the modern mother. "Where were you?"

"Oh," replied the equally modern daughter, "I had dinner with —oh, well, you don't know him—and we went to several places I don't suppose you've been to, and we finished up at a cute little night club. I forget the name of it, but it's in the cellar of an old house on the North Side. It's all okay, isn't it, Mother?"

"Why, of course, dear. It's only that I just like to know."

MODERN TOUCH

Having finished a lesson on the Feast of the Passover, a church school teacher asked, "Now, why was it that Mary and Joseph took Jesus with them to Jerusalem?"

Mary, aged four, smiled understandingly. "I guess," she ventured, "they didn't have a sitter."

✧ ✧

Grandma could never quite reconcile herself to the ways and wiles of a younger generation. "And where are you going now, my dear?" she asked an 18-year-old granddaughter.

"Oh," was the bright response, "Billy and I are off to the lake on an all-day picnic."

"Humph," humphed Grandma, "in my day no nice girl would think of traipsing off with a man unless she was engaged to him!"

"Oh, that's all right, Grandma," confided Millie, "Billy is one of my fiances."

✧ ✧

Two old sailors were sitting, rather uncomfortably, in what evidently had been their favorite barroom. Since their last visit the

old place had been completely done over in a new art style and
was now filled with gay young people. Both tars fell to reminisc-
inging on the good old days. Said one:

"I suppose it's all right, George, the new-fashioned trappings;
but I miss the old spitoon."

"Yes, Jack," answered the other, "you always did."

MONEY

During a lull in A. E. F. activities a colored boy from Chatta-
nooga got in a poker game with a few English chaps. Picking up
his cards he found four aces. Someone had just bet one pound and
the colored boy said, "I don't know how yo' boys count yo' money,
but I'll just raise yo' one ton."

❖ ❖

Money doesn't bring happiness. The guy with ten million dollars isn't a bit happier than the guy with nine million.

❖ ❖

This may help you to appreciate how much a billion is: Suppose a business started in the year 1, A.D. with $1,000,000,000 cap-
ital. Supposing further that the concern was so unsuccessful as to
lose $1,000 a day. It would still be in business today, after having
lost $1,000 daily for 1941 years, and could continue almost 800
years longer, or until the year 2739 A.D., until its original capital
of one billion dollars was exhausted.

❖ ❖

It might be well to bear in mind, Olin Miller reminds us, that
while "billion" and "million" are similar in sound, their ratio is
the same as that of a ten-dollar bill and a penny.

MONOLOGUE

Herbert Bayard Swope had been in town attending a racing
commission meeting. He sat next to the late Mrs. Pat Campbell
at dinner. Swope started one of his brilliant if long discourses and
occasionally Mrs. Campbell made a slight sound. After the third
time she had done so he stopped abruptly.

"What is that sound you are making?" he asked.

Explained Mrs. Campbell, "It's a word trying to get in edge-wise."

MONOTONY

A Greek refugee arrived in the United States speaking not a single syllable of English. He stayed with some compatriots in New York City, and being a curious guy he decided to look around the city. So he asked his friends to teach him how to order something—anything—in a restaurant. They decided the most practical thing was "apple pie and coffee." So laboriously, syllable by syllable, they taught him the phrase. The Greek tried it the first day and was delighted with the food and his skill in getting it—but after two weeks he was so sick of apple pie and coffee, it was coming out of his ears. At last he began to plead with his friends to help him vary the menu. This time they carefully instructed him on "chicken sandwich."

The following day he went on his usual sightseeing tour. Come lunch time, all hungry and excited, he walked into a busy cafeteria.

"Chicken—Sand-witch."

"Huh, buddy?"

"Chicken Shand—vitch!"

"How will you have it?"

"Chikun Shandvitch!"

"Yeah, I know, but how—whole wheat, rye, lettuce, trim the edges, mayonnaise, white meat?"

Sadly the Greek shook his head, drew a deep sigh, and said:

"Appeal pie and cawfee."

❖   ❖

Bishop Doane, of Albany, keenly interested in the abolition of the divorce evil, once paused for a moment in an earnest discussion of divorce to narrate this pet anecdote.

"The motive of these people," he said, "is like the motive of a Scot who was found weeping one day by his comfortable hearth.

" 'Eh Saunders, mon,' said a neighbor peeping in at the open door, attracted by the sounds of woe, 'what's ailin' ye?'

" 'Oh, dear; oh, dear,' sobbed Saunders, 'Donald Mackintosh's wife is dead.'

" 'Aweel,' said the neighbor, 'what o' that? She's nae relation o' yours.'

" 'I ken she's no',' wailed Saunders. 'I ken she's no'. But it just seems as if everybody's gettin' a change but me.' "

MORALE

"The best morale," said the Colonel, "exists when you never hear the word 'morale.' Count on this: when you hear a lot of talk about it, it's lousy."

✧   ✧

"Morale," said the colored sergeant, "is what makes your laigs do what your haid knows ain't possible."

MOTHERHOOD

A mother is a woman who runs a temperature of 103 every time her child's temperature hits 100.

"MOUTHS-OF-BABES"

Precocious, four-year-old Janie insisted upon joining her mother's bridge party for a few minutes' visit. She perched herself on the arm of a chair and proceeded to examine each lady present. The bidding and playing went ahead as usual, but young Janie was unperturbed at being ignored. At last, when her careful and candid diagnosis was concluded, she scrambled down from the chair, halted at the door and announced in her childish voice, "There are four ladies here who look exactly like monkeys!"

MULES

At a Texas Army camp, a long-eared, sad-eyed mule named Brad had done his work well and faithfully. Just before the outfit shipped for overseas, a long list of promotions for the enlisted personnel was placed on the bulletin board.

Beneath it, the men tacked on a resolution:

"Whereas the mule, Brad, has performed acts beyond the call of duty, and whereas he has gained the respect and admiration of this company, be it resolved that, henceforward, he shall be addressed by the more dignified name of Bradford, and that he is hereby promoted to the rank of horse."

MYSTERY

Some of the common mysteries in many a mystery novel are who killed the deceased, where the suspects were at the time of the murder, and why the book was ever published.

NATIONALITY

A columnist interviewing William Saroyan, the playwright, was trying to find out about a "short" on which Saroyan was working.
Columnist: "What nationality is the little old guy?"
Saroyan: "The human nationality. That's all there is, the human nationality."

NEIGHBORS

In the very center of the vast George Vanderbilt estate near Asheville an old Negro owned a tiny plot of land which no money could buy. Within sight of the palatial Vanderbilt mansion he sat on his small veranda, contentedly surveying his own domain. Every possible inducement was offered the man to sell his land and move, but to every tender he invariably made the same reply:

"Now look here, sah," he would explain, as he leaned back in his old rocker, "all my life I'se been bothered with bad neighbors. Dey comes home 'toxicated and smashes my fence and steals my bacon. Now Colonel George here treats me square. He leaves my bacon alone. Now I'se got a good neighbor, I'se going to stick to him."

❖ ❖

According to a Mexican legend, San Ysidro was plowing his garden when an angel appeared: "The Lord wants to see you, Ysidro. Come with me." But Ysidro was busy. He refused the command.

Again the angel appeared: "Unless you come at once, the Lord will send hot winds and drought to wither your corn." Ysidro was unperturbed. He had fought the wind before; drought could be relieved by river water.

Twice more the angel appeared, but Ysidro would not leave his work. The fourth time, the angel said simply: "If you do not come with me, the Lord will send you a bad neighbor."

Ysidro paused in the middle of the row and turned to the messenger. "I'll go with you now," he said quietly. "I can stand anything but that."

NEW WORLD

If we wish to make a new world we have the materials ready; the first one was made out of chaos.

NO CHOICE

A doctor said to a woman who complained that she did not like the night air: "Madam, during certain hours of the 24, night air is the only air there is."

OBJECT LESSON

Cuthbert had been listening for half an hour to a lecture from his father on the evils of late morning rising.

"You will never amount to anything," said his father, "unless you turn over a new leaf. Remember, it's the early bird that catches the worm!"

"Ha, ha!" laughed Cuthbert. "How about the worm? What did he get for turning out so early?"

"My son," replied the father, "that worm hadn't been to bed all night; he was on his way home!"

OBSTACLES—Imaginary

A Scotsman who had worked for many years on railroads in his native land, came to the United States and settled in a remote section of the middle west. Soon after his arrival there was a project for a railway through the district.

"Hoot, mon," said the Scot to a neighbor who brought the exciting tidings, "ye canna build a railway across this country."

"And why not, Ferguson?"

"Why not? You ask me, 'Why not?' Dinna ya see the country's flat as a floor? Ye hae nae place at all t' run your toonels through."

OCCUPATION

A little lad paused at the window for a last look at the starry heavens before he said his good-night prayers. "Mummy, will I go to heaven some time?" "Yes, dear, if you love Jesus." "And will you be there?" he asked again. "I hope so, and Daddy'll be there, too." The little fellow shook his head emphatically. "My Daddy won't be there; he couldn't leave the store."

OLD STORIES

Times change, but many of our good old "laugh-tested" stories remain pretty much the same.

The small boy's mother—or was it his teacher?—said to him after the battle, "When the other boy threw stones at you, why didn't you come and tell me instead of throwing them back at him?"

To which the boy answered, "What good would it do to tell you? You couldn't hit the side of a garage."

Now, when we first heard the story, the boy used the word "barn" instead of "garage."

Of course stories must be kept up to date. The boy of the coming generation probably will have to use the word "hangar."

ON-THE-JOB

A girl entered the manager's office to apply for a job, and when asked if she had any particular talents, stated that she had won several prizes in crossword puzzles and slogan contests.

"That sounds good," the manager told her, "but we want somebody who will be smart during office hours."

"Oh," she explained brightly, "this was during office hours."

OPINION

"Lord, give me this day my daily opinion, and forgive me the one I had yesterday."

OPPORTUNISM

The optimist takes the cold water that others throw on his proposition, and with the heat of his enthusiasm turns it into steam to get over the hill.

OPPORTUNITY

The man who says he did not have enough opportunities is like the man working on a mathematical problem who complains, "I can't work this because I have no figures to work with."

Opportunity is unlimited. The supply is there to be used.

✧　✧

An ambitious young man asked the great merchant for the secret of success.

"There is no easy secret," replied the merchant. "You must jump at your opportunity."

"But how can I tell when my opportunity comes?"

"You can't," snapped the merchant. "You have to keep jumping."

✧　✧

After Carl Sandburg's six volumes of Lincoln were published someone once commented in his presence that the book was "so very American."

"Yes," Sandburg agreed. "It's a book about a man whose mother could not sign her name, written by a man whose father could not sign his. Perhaps that could happen only in America."

OPPORTUNITY—Lost

When Florence Finch Kelly, pioneer newspaperwoman, visited Yosemite Valley in the late eighties, she had an opportunity to talk with one of the pioneers who had discovered it. She asked him about his reactions when he and his party came upon the valley, with its mountains, trees and waterfalls which have since attracted so many hundreds of thousands of visitors. The man looked about reflectively for a moment, then answered:

"Well, I'll tell ye. If I ha' knowed it was going to be so famous I'd ha' looked at it."

✧   ✧

Last month, a friend invited me to his office to see a chair that he said had cost $5,000.

"You must be kidding," I said. "That chair is not worth $5,000."

"Maybe it isn't worth that money," he agreed, "but that's what it cost me last year, just sitting in it, when I should have been up and after business!"

OPPORTUNITIES—Realized

Here is an excellent story for a sales executive to tell, emphasizing the importance of "cleaning up" a territory thoroughly. It's also a good one for the chairman of a fund-raising committee.

A kid from the Kentucky mountains entered the army as a raw recruit. On his first trip to the rifle range he hung up a new record for consecutive hits. The commanding officer was astonished. He wanted to know "how come?"

"Aw, shucks," said the mountaineer. "That wasn't nothin' special. You see, every mornin' since I kin recollect Pa's been handin' me the old muzzle-loader, with a charge o' powder an' one bullet. 'Here, boy,' he says, 'go hit breakfast.' So you see, I ain't used to missin' much."

OPTIMISM

One morning, Thad Sherod's store in Keosauqua, Iowa, burned to the ground. And Thad had neglected to renew his fire insurance.

Later in the morning, a neighboring tradesman met Thad, whistling, on the street and, wishing to express sympathy, as midwesterners do, without blowing his top off about it, slapped Thad on the shoulder and said, "Hi, fellow—how's things going?"

"Fine," said Thad, "fine. I had breakfast, and it ain't time for dinner yet."

"ORDERS IS ORDERS"

The young and keen police officer was being shown his new night beat by the sergeant. "D'ye see that red light in the distance? Well, that is the limit of your beat. Now along with you."

The young policeman set out, and was not seen again for a week. When he did show up at headquarters, the sergeant demanded furiously where he had been.

"You remember that red light?" asked the cop.

"Yes."

"Well, that was a bus bound for Chicago."

OSTENTATION

A sabled Mabel dismissed waiters, captains and headwaiters who came to take her order in Romanoff's. Nothing would do but to have the proprietaaah himself wait upon her.

"I would like some caviaaaaah," she said, when Mike put in an appearance. "Have you got imported caviaaaaah?"...

"Yes, Moddom," Romanoff replied.

"Well, that's what I would like—but it must be imported," reiterated the gal. "Now are you really sure it's genuine imported caviaaaaah?"

Mike, starting to burn, said: "Look, Moddom, you are talking to His Royal Highness, Prince Mike Romanoff! I assure you we have genuine imported caviar!"

"I hope you're right," drooled the dame. "You see, I want to be certain—because I wouldn't know the difference!"

PATIENCE

Polish statesmen and pianist Ignace Paderewski very humanly enjoyed adulation but when it was overdone, his reactions were decidedly unfavorable. Following a concert, a prattling woman approached the artist and gushed her saccharine comments.

"You must have had a world of patience to learn to play as you do," she cooed.

"It's not that at all," confessed Paderewski. "I have no more patience than anybody else. It's just that I use mine."

❖ ❖

A doctor was once asked by a patient who had met with a serious accident, "Doctor, how long shall I have to lie here?"

The physician answered cheerfully: "Only a day at a time."

PEACE

Gracie Allen may be a dumb dame on the radio, but she said a mouthful when she observed: "Peace is different from butter and lamb chops. The more people want it, the more there is to go around."

❖ ❖

The late Ramsay MacDonald, former prime minister of England, was discussing the possibility of lasting peace with another government official. The latter was unimpressed with the prime minister's viewpoint.

"The desire for peace," he said cynically, "does not necessarily insure peace."

"Quite true," admitted MacDonald. "Neither does the desire for food satisfy hunger. But at least it gets you started toward a restaurant."

PENANCE

Pat and Mike, having been to confession, had to do penance by walking several times up and down a steep hill with their shoes filled with peas. After they had done so several times, Pat said to Mike:

"How is it ye can walk so aisy an' niver a bit complain of yer feet being sore?"

"Begorra," answered Mike, "an' didn't ye boil yer peas before puttin' them in yer shoes?"

PERFECTION

There's a story going the rounds of a man who met an acquaintance on the street, and observed that he was apparently deep in the dumps:

"What'sa matter, pal?"

"Oh, nothing; nothing at all—except that, after a lifelong search, I have finally found The Perfect Girl."

"Well, what's so bad about that?"

"Oh, it's just that—well, she's looking for the *perfect man!*"

PERSISTENCE

Two mice fell into a deep bowl of cream. One couldn't see the use of swimming. He gave up—and drowned. The other was discouraged, too, but didn't know how to quit. He just kept on swimming. Finally, when things looked the blackest, a miracle happened. The churned cream hardened, turned to butter—and the mouse was able to jump out alive.

❖   ❖

One raw cold morning in January, a snail started to climb the trunk of a cherry tree.

As he inched painfully upward, a wise-guy beetle stuck his head out a nearby crack and called, "Hey, buddy, you're wasting your strength. There ain't any cherries up there."

But the snail scarcely paused as he replied: "There will be when I get there."

❖   ❖

Big shots are only small shots who keep on shooting.

❖   ❖

The traveling man arrived in Memphis one morning, early but not very bright. He had spent the night in a day coach and was in anything but a jovial mood. Illogically, perhaps, he was "taking it out" on the bellboy who showed him to a room.

Having performed his customary services, the bellboy paused expectantly. No tip was forthcoming. Politely and pointedly, he called attention to the fact that there were plenty of towels, fresh soap. He offered to get an extra blanket for the bed.

The traveling man said nothing, and began to remove his shirt.

"Is there anything else, sah?" the boy asked.

"Nothing," replied the guest, "except that you can get out. I'm tired and want to be let alone."

"Yes, sah. Maybe you might want t' write some letters later on. Better let me bring you a fresh pen?"

"No."

"S'posen I sends up a dinin' room hand t' take yo' odah for a morsel o' breakfast?"

"No breakfast. Now, get out."

"Yes, sah."

With one hand on the door knob, the boy persisted. "Any clo's t' be pressed, sah?"

There were none. The boy retired, but he was not yet beaten. A moment later he again opened the door, poked his head in and presented his last forlorn hope.

"Sah, iffen yo' should tek a notion t' cut yo' hair, I could bring up a nice new pair of scissors."

❖ ❖

Rex Beach, the novelist, asked the secret of his success, answered with the story of a Swede in Alaska—the owner of several rich mines. Once he was asked how he managed to become so success-ful.

"Ay never tolt anybody before," he replied, "but Ay tell you. Ay yust kept diggin' holes."

❖ ❖

As someone, writing in *The Upper Room* observed: "A saint is a sinner who keeps on trying."

❖ ❖

An elderly Negro had a hen that contributed an egg now and then for her keep. One day she became broody and started to set. The old man tried every device he could think of to discourage the maternal instinct and finally appealed to an experienced poul-tryman, "Dat ol' hen," he said, "she sot an' sot. I done ever'thin' I knows, but hit ain' do no good." The poultryman suggested putting some thorns in the nest.

"I done dat, too," said Mose, "I puts thorns an' briars under her—an' doggone if she don't stood up an' sot!"

PERSPECTIVE

One of Strickland Gillilan's sure-fire stories concerns the fellow who was lying in a drunken slumber on a hotel lobby floor one early morning. A wag slipped out to an all-night delicatessen and came back with a portion of limburger cheese which he smeared on the drunk's thin mustache. Finally, the stew staggered to his feet and shuffled toward the door. Walking about, in the fresh air awhile, he came back and sat down dejectedly to mutter:

"Ain't it awful?" Finally someone queried "What's awful?" He wailed: "Why the whole world smells."

❖ ❖

A good many of us in these busy, bustling times are rather in the position of a visitor to the nation's capital who, on a sightseeing tour, was whisked into an elevator and taken to the top of Washington Monument. She looked about, bubbling ecstatically. "Oh, this is marvelous! Why I can see all of the points of interest. There's the Capitol, the White House . . . and the Lincoln Memorial, but—but, where's the Washington Monument!"

❖ ❖

Did you hear about the couple driving across the Mojave desert? In the distance they saw a tiny black speck which, when they approached it, turned out to be a man wearing only his swimming trunks.

The man hailed them and said, "How far is the ocean?"

Somewhat surprised, the couple explained that the ocean was a few hundred miles away, on the other side of California.

"Good Lord," said the man, staring at the sandy waste, "what a beach!"

❖ ❖

An old man, away up in the Ozarks was giving his summary of the war situation. "If the Japs ever git t' this side o' the water," he concluded, "this here town will be the fust one that will be bombed!"

"Hardly," objected a bystander. "This town is a long way from the coast."

"Sure, it'll be bombed," persisted the prophet. "It's the county seat, ain't it?"

❖ ❖

Orville and Wilbur Wright had tried repeatedly to fly a heavier-than-air craft. Finally one December day, off the sand dunes of Kitty Hawk, North Carolina they did what man had never done before. They actually flew! Elated, they wired their sister Katherine, "We have actually flown 120 feet. Will be home for Christmas."

Hastily she ran down the street, shoved the telegram—the news scoop of the century—at the city editor of the local paper. He read it carefully and smiled, "Well, well! How nice the boys will be home for Christmas!"

PESSIMISM

A farmer was among those watching from the shore of the Hudson, as Robert Fulton's Clermont got up steam for its first up-river run.

"They'll never start her," the farmer predicted gloomily.

Then, as the boat moved off and gathered speed, he gave out another dire prophecy:

"They'll never stop her!"

PESSIMISM—Unfounded

The composer, Brahms, was occasionally given to fits of depression. One night he stood on a bridge with a friend and exclaimed dejectedly, "Everything fine in music has been done. There is nothing more for men to do."

"Look down there," said his companion. "There comes the last wave."

"Ridiculous," said Brahms. "There is no last wave."

"And so it is in music," agreed his friend.

PHENOMENON

A young Boston woman, extremely athletic, rode very well, and, seated astride her horse, she resembled a handsome boy. Riding one day in her masculine habit, she had the misfortune to be thrown. An old sea captain hastened to her aid. Raising her gently, he touched her corset, and shouted in wild alarm to a bystander: "Get a doctor, quick! Here's a young chap's ribs runnin' north and south instead of east and west."

PHILANTHROPY

The kids were holding forth at length on their future careers. "And what are you going to be?" someone asked Freddy.

"Oh," replied that observing youngster, "I'm going to be a philanthropist. Those fellows always seem to have such a lot of money!"

PHILOSOPHY

A modern philosopher is a person who redoubles his efforts after he loses sight of his objective.

✧   ✧

Philosophy is the discovery that you might be worse off than you are.

✧   ✧

Philosophers are people who talk about something they don't understand, and make you think it's your fault.

✧   ✧

In a baseball game between two negro teams, the slugger of one team who was also a church deacon, was at bat. The pitcher slung one right down the middle, waist high. The deacon let it go. The umpire yelled, "Ball!" The next pitch came high and inside, right at the deacon's head. As he ducked the umpire yelled, "Strike!" The deacon started angrily for a second. Then he muttered softly, "De Lawd giveth, an' de Lawd taketh away."

PLAGIARISM

Ralph Waldo Emerson once lent a copy of Plato's Essays to a neighbor in Concord. In a few days the neighbor returned the book.

"Did you enjoy reading the book?" Mr. Emerson inquired.

"Yes," said the neighbor, "I liked it very much. That fellow Plato has got a lot of my ideas."

PLATITUDES

Walter Bullock, a movie script writer, was having a conference with his producer. They were discussing a scene that called for a husband to make a corny compliment about his wife. The producer objected to the line.

"That's terrible!" he said. "That's old-fashioned."

"But that's the kind of character he is," Bullock tried to explain. "He's the type of fellow who talks in platitudes."

"Okay, okay," said the producer, "but at least let's get some fresh platitudes."

POLITICS

A professor of Arabic at Cambridge was something of a mystery. His politics were unknown even to his intimates. Some friends, determined to solve the mystery, asked how he voted: "Oh, I vote Liberal," he said. Asked why, he explained: "I like for Mr. Gladstone to be in office, because then he has no time to write about Holy Scripture."

❖   ❖

An 8-year-old girl, accompanied by a 6-year-old companion, ordered 15 cents worth of cheese in a market on South Fourteenth street. The butcher jokingly asked if she wouldn't rather have some braunschweiger or bologna.

The girl explained that her family being Catholic did not eat meat on Friday, to which her companion added brightly:

"We're Republicans at our house and we eat meat any time we can get it."

❖   ❖

Bill Johnson, candidate for Attorney General, never lost an opportunity to make votes. At each town he would tear around getting acquainted and distributing campaign cards.

On one occasion, he walked into a back yard where a girl was milking a cow. He introduced himself; explained that he was campaigning for the office of Attorney General.

Just then the mother stuck her head out the back door and called, "Mary, who is that feller you're talking to?" Mary explained that the visitor was a politician named Bill Johnson.

"You come right in the house," commanded the mother, with great concern in her voice. And as an afterthought, she added: "and if that feller is a politician, bring the cow along!"

❖ ❖

In March, 1894, John Kendrick Bangs, American humorist and writer, ran for mayor of Yonkers. It was a Republican year but his name appeared on the Democratic ticket. The close of election day found Bangs loser to his opponent by 207 votes.

"To what do you attribute your defeat?" asked the New York World.

Bangs barked out briefly, "Not enough votes!"

❖ ❖

Two Arkansas farmers had been feuding for more than 20 years. One morning one of them hitched up his mule and drove to the property fence. Pretty soon the other one came along in his buckboard.

"Mawnin' Jeff," said the first farmer.

"What in tarnation you speakin' to me for after 20 years?" asked the second one suspiciously.

"I'm just here to tell you that I'm aimin' to run for Congress and I don't want you nor none of yours a-votin' for me."

"Now looky here," said Jeff, "me and my kin's been a-votin' the straight Democratic ticket since grandpappy came to these hills, and if you don't want us a-votin' for you you can get off the ticket."

❖ ❖

It was, I think, Bertrand Russell who remarked that, should the temperature of a room unhappily become the subject of political controversy, two political parties would hold two views—one would stand for boiling-point, the other for freezing.

❖ ❖

There is an old true story of a Republican political leader in Vermont who always showed up at Democratic rallies. He seemed to take grim pleasure in attending these gatherings, somewhat to the discomfort of assembled Democrats. His presence made their parties seem less homey.

At last, one day, a Democratic leader asked the old fellow why he came to their meetings. "Is it in your mind that you might get converted, or somethin'?"

"Oh, no," said the Republican, "Nothin' like that. I'll tell ye, I jes' come aroun' t' yer meetin's so's t' keep my disgust fresh."

❖ ❖

Politics is the art of looking for trouble, finding it everywhere, diagnosing it wrongly, and applying unsuitable remedies.

❖ ❖

A mysterious stranger had appeared away back in the mountain canyon in the Ozarks, and was occupying a lonely hut, keeping to himself, and telling "nobody nuthin'." Naturally he became the object of intense curiosity and suspicion. On Saturday night when the old "he coons" of the mountains gathered round the stove in the local grocery store, the mysterious stranger was the glib subject of conversation.

"I'll tell yer what I think," said one. "I think he's a hoss thief, an' we better watch our stock."

Said a second: "I believe he maybe kilt somebody back whar he come from, an' he's hidin' out."

A third had another opinion: "I'm afeared he's a revenooer an' maybe he's a spyin' on us."

But the fourth speaker had still another idea:

"I bin watchin' him and checkin' up on him," he said, "and I'll tell you what I think. I think he's a Republican."

"Oh, no," they all cried at once. "He can't be that bad!"

"I ain't so sure 'bout that," declared the fourth, with much confidence. "The gol durned scoundrel can read."

❖ ❖

"I am very much impressed," remarked the personage from abroad, "by the extreme generosity displayed mutually by the gentlemen who designate themselves as Democrats and Republicans."

"I don't quite see where you get that generosity idea," said the somewhat rugged native.

"I am surprised that you should fail to note how industriously each party points out to the other exactly where it is making its most serious mistakes."

❖ ❖

Fondly the parents looked into the cradle of their delightful child.

"I think he is going to be a politician," said the father.

"Oh, how can you say that?"

"Well, he says more things that sound well, and mean absolutely nothing than any other human I ever saw."

❖ ❖

"I suppose, Uncle Jim, you remember a good deal about the politics of the early days?"

"Well, I never tuk much int'rest in pollytics, but I kin recollect when Wm. Jennings Bryan was 'lected President."

"Bryan! Why, Bryan, was never elected."

"He wun't? Well, now, that gets me. I heerd a leadin' speaker talk the night 'fore 'lection, an' he said if Wm. Jennings Bryan wun't 'lected the country would fall to ruin an' everybody would have to shut up shop. Course I didn't take the papers; but, noticin' thet things went on 'bout the same as before, I calculated Wm. Jennings won. So he wun't 'lected? Well, B'jinks! Thet gits me!"

❖ ❖

"What became of Tom Smith?"

"Well," said Uncle Josh, "Tom tried farming for a while and failed at that. Then he attended law school, and after three years trying to make a living at law in the county seat he failed at that."

"That's too bad," interrupted the man from the city. "Tom was a good fellow! Everybody liked him. I'm sorry to hear that he's such a failure."

"Failure, heck!" exclaimed Uncle Josh. "He's our congressman!"

❖ ❖

A candidate rushing to address a meeting at an election was accosted by a friend.

"What do you think about the political situation now?" the friend asked.

"Don't bother me!" replied the candidate. "I've got to talk. This is no time to think."

✧ ✧

Politics is the art by which politicians obtain campaign contributions from the rich and votes from the poor on the pretext of protecting each from the other.

✧ ✧

Politics is a game with two sides—and a fence.

✧ ✧

An old farmer kept interrupting the Republican orator to announce that he was a Democrat.

"And why are you a Democrat, may I ask?" the orator finally exploded.

"My father was a Democrat and his father before him."

"Well," said the orator, finding his opening, "suppose your father was a fool, and your grandfather was a fool. What, according to your argument, would you be?"

"Oh, then," said the farmer, "I'd be a Republican."

PORTENT

It was at Mt. Wilson observatory.

A distinguished scientist was scanning the heavens through the huge telescope. Intent upon the sight, he remarked to his colleagues without turning his head, "It's going to rain."

"What makes you think so?" queried a brother scientist.

Still peering at the heavens, the astronomer replied:

"Because my corns hurt!"

PRACTICE vs. THEORY

There was a famous insurance case in San Francisco in which one of the important questions was what exactly was the cause of the death of the insured. Many eminent medical specialists went on the stand and testified they had examined the decedent and that he was suffering from a shrunken liver.

Presently, a young interne came on the stand. He testified that, instead of a shrunken liver, the dead man had an abnormally large liver.

"Do I understand you to sit there and swear that this man had an enlarged liver, when all these eminent specialists have said the opposite?" thundered the cross-examining lawyer.

"I do," the interne replied calmly.

"How does it come that you set yourself up against these great physicians?" shouted the lawyer. "You, a mere whippersnapper of a young doctor, only a few months out of medical school. It is preposterous. How do you know he had an enlarged liver?"

"I performed the autopsy," the young doctor explained.

PRAISE

Ding, the famous cartoonist, expressed once a feeling that most creative artists have. The wife of one of his good friends came into his office, and looking about her, remarked: "You must get a great deal of praise from all sides."

"Not a whit more than I need," he answered.

PRAISE—Meager

A close-fisted, hard-bitten citizen died. After the funeral, as neighbors loitered at the cemetery, one broke the awkward silence: "Well, I can say one good thing about John: he wasn't always as mean as he was sometimes."

PRAISE—Restrained

"When I think of what you've meant to me for all these years," the taciturn Vermonter said to his spouse, "sometimes it's more than I can stand not to tell you."

PRAYER

"It's no use telling me the angels write down in their books if I'm naughty," said a small boy. "I might as well tell you they think up in Heaven that I'm dead."

"But why should they think that?" his mother protested.

"Because I haven't said my prayers for two weeks."

❖　❖

Three-year-old Nancy had spent the evening in rapt attention to the new radio. Finally it was time for bed and prayers. Kneeling before her bed she repeated her "Now I lay me," then stopped at the close, paused for a moment, changed her voice slightly and said: "Tomorrow night at this time there will be another prayer."

❖　❖

A farmer whose barns were full of corn was accustomed to pray that the needy be supplied; but when any one in needy circumstances asked for a little of his corn, he said he had none to spare. One day after hearing his father pray for the poor and needy, his little son said to him, "Father, I wish I had your corn."

"What would you do with it?" asked the father. The child replied, "I would answer your prayer."

❖　❖

Coach of little Western Kentucky State Teachers College is Ed Diddle, in his playing days a blocking back for Bo McMillin and Centre College's famed Praying Colonels. Diddle liked the idea of praying before a game and brought it with him to Western.

Diddle had a new captain one season and was trying to explain to him how to pray "just right." Instructing him before the opening game of the season, he said: "Say a nice, modest, humble prayer, but don't ask for a victory. Just ask that you be able to give a good performance."

A bit shaky over the strange assignment, the captain huddled his players and began the prayer, with Coach Diddle standing off a few paces.

All was quiet for a couple of minutes, then suddenly the subs on the benches and the people in the stands were startled by a yelp.

"Damn it!" roared Diddle, crashing the huddle and interrupting the ceremony, "I told you not to ask for victory!"

❖　❖

"Do your folks have family prayer before breakfast?" asked Georgie.

"No," replied young Albert, "we have prayers before we go to bed. We ain't afraid in the daytime!"

✧   ✧

"Mommie," said 6-year-old Judy, "while you were away last night I looked for somebody to say my prayers to, but Nursie had gone and Auntie was talking on the phone, so I just said 'em to God."

✧   ✧

A GI en route to Europe during the period of the submarine menace, when the alert signal was sounded, prayed in this manner: "O Lord, thou art our refuge and fortress, our ever present help in time of trouble. Save us from being torpedoed." Then suddenly there was a terrific explosion, and the GI cried out in despair, "O Lord, we've been hit. Why hast thou forsaken us?" And then, realizing that his ship still plowed ahead on even keel, he looked about and joyously exclaimed, "Thank God, it was the other ship!"

✧   ✧

A little boy who had been taught to pray found himself sliding down a roof, apparently to a serious fall.

"O, Lord," he prayed hurriedly, "save me! Save me!"

Just then a nail caught his pants, and he added a postscript: "Never mind, Lord; a nail has done it for you."

✧   ✧

Little Judy had disobeyed and was sent tearfully to bed to ponder her sins. The tears did not last long. In less than ten minutes she was talking away at great rate. Her mother, in the next room, caught this much of the conversation:

"Now you see, God, what a lot of trouble You got me into. When I went to bed last night I said my prayers and asked You to 'make me a good girl, amen,' and You didn't do it. So it's all Your fault, God, and not mine at all, and it's up to You to fix things up with my mother."

❖ ❖

Do you know what is wrong with the world today? There's too much theologian and not enough kneeologian!

❖ ❖

When life knocks you to your knees—well, that's the proper position in which to pray, isn't it?

❖ ❖

One of our ministerial friends was telling about making a pastoral call on a parishioner who had been confined to his bed for several weeks. As he was about to leave the minister asked if he should offer prayer.

"Oh, I guess you needn't mind," the patient replied. "I don't think I'm that sick."

❖ ❖

The woman was strong-minded, and she was religious, and she was also afflicted with a very feminine fear of thunderstorms. She was delivering an address at a religious convention when a tempest suddenly broke forth with a din of thunder and flare of lightning. Above the noise of the elements, her voice was heard in shrill supplication: "Oh, Lord, take us under Thy protecting wings, for Thou knowest that feathers are splendid non-conductors."

❖ ❖

Rastus came to his colored pastor and asked him to pray for his floating kidney. "That's a somewhat strange request, Rastus," the pastor said.

"Ah know it is," said Rastus, "but mah kidney is givin' me trouble, and anyway, last week yo' prayed fo' de loose livers!"

❖ ❖

Little Ben, growing out of early childhood, was being taught to address his parents as "Father" and "Mother."

One night, saying his prayers, he followed the usual practice,

"Lord bless Daddy and Mommy." Then suddenly he paused and in a most solemn and respectful manner offered a revision: "Excuse me, Lord, I should have said Father and Mother." He meditated briefly, then concluded, "But, Lord, they are the same old parties."

✧ ✧

Lincoln himself liked to tell the story about two Quakeresses who had a spirited discussion concerning himself and Jefferson Davis.

"I think Mr. Jefferson will win this war," said the first one.

"Why does thee think so?"

"Because Jefferson is a praying man."

"And so is Abraham a praying man."

"That's true," answered the first, "but the Lord will think Abraham is joking."

✧ ✧

There were once two men who were the only survivors of a shipwreck. For two days they floated in an open lifeboat with nothing to eat or drink.

When their plight became desperate, one of them decided to pray. He dropped to his knees and began, "I've been leading the wrong kind of life for a long, long time. But if I am allowed to get out of this I promise for the rest of my days on earth—"

"Hold on a minute," said the other man. "Don't commit yourself. I think I see land!"

✧ ✧

Here is an old Negro prayer, well worth preserving:

"O, Lawd, give Thy servant dis mawnin' de eye of de eagle and de wisdom of de owl; connect his soul with de gospel-telefom in de central skies; 'luminate his brow with de sun of Heaven; saturate his heart with love for de people; turpentine his magination; grease his lips with 'possum; loosen him with de sledge hammer of Thy power; l'ectrify his brain with de lightnin' of Thy word; put 'petual motion in his arms; fill him plum full of de dynamite of glory; 'noint him all over with de kerosene oil of salvation and sot him on fire!"

❖ ❖

A little girl was on her knees one night, and auntie, staying at the house, was present.

"It is a pleasure," said auntie, "to hear you saying your prayers so well. You speak so earnestly and seriously, and mean what you say, and care about it."

"But auntie," the little one answered, "you should hear me gargle!"

❖ ❖

" 'O Lord, dis yer little congregation ob mine am prone to gossip! O Lord, dis yer little congregation ob mine am prone to bear false witness! O Lord, dis yer little congregation ob mine am prone to steal! O Lord, dis yer little congregation ob mine am prone to do things what am unmentionable in de house ob de Lord! O good Lord! deliver dem from de prone!' "

❖ ❖

Remember the story of the British tar who was asked by a foreign sailor why the British Navy always won?

"That's easy to answer," replied the bluejacket. "We always pray before we start fighting."

"But so do we," retorted the foreigner.

"Yes," came the rejoinder, "but we pray in English."

❖ ❖

In a rural community of Kentucky a family was in desperate circumstances as a result of continued illness.

The church board and the preacher met to plan for their relief. A deacon, called on by the preacher to pray, waxed eloquent.

"Oh, Lord," he prayed, "help us to act as Thy messengers here on earth to these poor people. Help us not only to pray for them but to supply their need of food, Oh Lord. Put it in our hearts to carry them a barrel of flour, a barrel of pork, a barrel of sugar, a barrel of pepper—oh hell, that's too much pepper!"

❖ ❖

In a northern public school foot-race, a small colored boy breasted the tape about two inches ahead of his swiftest and closest rival. One of the observers had noticed that the lad's lips were busy throughout the last two or three laps of the contest. Taking the little fellow aside afterward, he said:

"Boy, I noticed you were talking while you ran."

"Ah was prayin',' Mister."

"What were you saying in your prayer?"

"Ah, was sayin', 'Lawd, You lif' 'em up, Ah'll put 'em down; You lif' 'em up, Ah'll put 'em down; You lif' 'em up, Ah'll put 'em down'—alla time Ah says dat, and youall sees whut happen!"

❖ ❖

The evening lesson was from the Book of Job, and the minister had just read, "Yea, the light of the wicked shall be put out," when a fuse blew and the congregation was left in total darkness.

This minister was of stern stuff, though, and with scarcely a pause he met the situation.

"Brethren," he said, "in view of the sudden and startling fulfillment of this prophecy, we will spend a few minutes in silent prayer for the electric-light company."

❖ ❖

Two little girls were in danger of being late for school.

"Let's stop and pray for God to get us there in time," said one.

"No," said the other, "let's run with all our might, and pray while we're running."

PRAYER—AND ACTION

The celebrated William Ewart Gladstone used to tell friends about a neighbor's little girl who really believed in prayer.

Her brother had made a trap that caught little sparrows and she prayed that it might fail. Suddenly for three days her face was radiant when she prayed and her absolute faith in the futility of the trap so noticeable that her mother asked: "Julia, how can you be so positive?"

She smiled, "Because, dear Mama, I went out three days ago and kicked the trap to pieces!"

PRAYER—Answered

Frederick Douglas said that when he was a slave he prayed seven years for liberty, but received no answer. Then it occurred to him he must answer his own prayer. And, when, with his eyes fixed on the North Star, he prayed with his legs, his prayer was answered.

❖ ❖

A little Kansas town underwent an extended drought a few years ago. The mayor heard that the local parson was very effective in praying for miracles, and so, with the community assembled in the town square, the minister raised his arms and prayed for rain.

It began to sprinkle, then to pour, and it didn't stop. It rained, and the fields grew green with crops and it still didn't stop. The streams flooded, the crops washed away, houses floated down the streets. The mayor called on the parson again.

Again in the town square the minister raised his arms and prayed. "Six months ago, Lord," he said, "I prayed for rain and it came—but, after all, this is ridiculous!"

❖ ❖

In Scotland there lived an old woman who believed implicitly in the efficacy of prayer. One night two young rogues heard her praying for bread. As a joke, they brought two loaves from the village baker, climbed to the roof of the cottage and dropped them down the chimney.

Later, they called at the old woman's home to hear her tell of what she considered a miraculous answer to her prayer. The scamps then laughed at the old woman, and related how they themselves had dropped the loaves down the chimney.

The old woman's faith was not shaken. "I still say God sent it," she declared, "though the devil's imps may have brought it."

PREACHERS—PREACHING

The little daughter of a colonel living on an army post was taken to church for the first time. The minister was one of the old-fashioned type who believed in illustrating his sermons with vigor. She stared in awe at the old minister, shut up in a box pulpit, thumbing the Bible, and waving his arms wildly. Finally, unable to stand it any longer, she whispered to her father in a frightened voice: "What'll we do if he gets out?"

❖ ❖

Out under the old brush arbor meeting place, Aunt Becky, 250-pound Negro mammy, was punctuating the preacher's sermon with "Amen! Amen! . . . Praise de Lawd! . . . Hit's God's own truth, Brother!" etc., while the parson lit into every sort of sin from bloody murder to shooting craps. But when he moved on against snuff-dipping, all applause suddenly ceased as Aunt Becky turned to her next neighbor and exclaimed:

"Dar now, dar now! He's done stopped preachin' and gone to meddlin'!"

❖ ❖

Business men expect to get what they pay for except when they hire a preacher. Then they expect $5,000 value for $800.

❖ ❖

A young Carolinian was studying at a backwoods theological school to become a minister. One day, just before graduation, his professor asked him to demonstrate his ability to outline a sermon from any text that might be selected from the Bible. The boy stood up and was given this text:

"The wild ass sniffeth up the wind with his nostrils."

The boy shifted uneasily from one foot to the other, obviously at a loss how to begin. Finally he blurted out exactly what was in his mind: "It would take him a damn long time to get fat on it."

❖ ❖

Dr. S. Parkes Cadman had been telling his small granddaughter a bedtime story. At the end of the tale she demanded, "Grandfather, was that a true story, or were you just preaching?"

❖ ❖

A traveling man inquired of the hotel porter how the big convention of clergymen was getting on.

"Well, sah," said the porter, "dey is diff'rent from mos' men at a convention. Dey comes in wid a copy ob de Ten Commandments in one han' an' a ten-dollah bill in de othah, an' us portahs don't believe dey is broke either one ob dem yit!"

❖ ❖

A visiting minister denounced horse racing in a town famous for the sport. Later, someone pointed out to him in the congregation, one of the principal patrons of the track, a wealthy citizen who was also a generous contributor to the church.

"I am afraid," said the minister, when he met the gentleman, "that I touched on one of your weaknesses in my sermon today."

"Oh, that's all right," said the sportsman genially. "It's a mighty poor sermon that don't hit me somewhere."

❖ ❖

The new preacher had covered almost the entire list of human wants in his prayer. A deacon asked the Negro janitor if he didn't think that the minister had offered up a good prayer.

"I most suttinly does, boss," said the janitor. "Why that man asked de Lawd fo' things de othah preacher didn't eben know He had!"

❖ ❖

A Yankee soldier was being shown over an old church wherein hundreds of people were buried.

"A great many people sleep within these walls," said the guide, indicating the inscription-covered floor with a sweep of his hand.

"So?" said the tourist. "Same way over in our country. Why don't you get a more interesting preacher?"

❖ ❖

"I am entertaining two locust preachers in my home."

"You mean *local,* of course, my dear."

"No; I said locust and I *meant* locust."

"But locusts—why, locusts are things that come in swarms, and eat everything up, and . . ."

"Don't I know it!" snapped the complainer. "And I'm entertaining two of 'em in my home this week."

❖ ❖

Dr. Edgar DeWitt Jones give this recipe for a good preacher:

"He should get religion like a Methodist; experience like a Baptist; be sure of it like a Disciple; stick to it like a Lutheran; pray for it like a Presbyterian; conciliate it like a Congregationalist; glorify it like a Jew; be proud of it like an Episcopalian; practice it like a Christian Scientist; propagate it like a Roman Catholic; work for it like a Salvation Army Lassie; enjoy it like a colored man."

✧ ✧

In outlining the characteristics of a modern clergyman, Dr. Edgar DeWitt Jones said, "The minister of today needs the courage of a lion, the skin of a hippopotamus, the endurance of a camel, the sagacity of an elephant, the patience of a donkey and as many lives as a cat."

✧ ✧

The late Bud Robinson, evangelist, was once asked by a lady in one of his congregations if he had not preached that same sermon before in another city.

"Yes, sister," he admitted readily.

"You see, I got new sermons until I learned it was easier to get new congregations!"

✧ ✧

Little Willie, who had heretofore shown no strong religious convictions, suddenly expressed the intention of becoming a preacher. His delighted mother pressed the lad to determine the source of his recent spiritual enrichment.

"Well," said Willie, with an air of resignation, "I s'pose I've got to go to church all my life anyway, and it's a good deal harder to sit still than to stand up and holler."

✧ ✧

A steward came to the presiding elder and asked for a preacher. "How big a man do you want?" asked the elder. "I do not care so much about his size," said the steward, "but we want him to be big enough to reach heaven when he is on his knees."

❖ ❖

Wesley was once asked how he got the crowds. He replied, "I set myself on fire, and the people come to see me burn."

❖ ❖

The tramp stopped at the home of a minister and asked for a handout. Upon presenting the plate of food, the pastor exhorted him to become a Christian.

"I am a praying man," said the aimless wanderer. "Don't you see the knees of my trousers are worn out from praying so much?"

"Yes," said the clergyman, "and I notice the seat of your trousers is worn out from backsliding!"

❖ ❖

As John Wesley and a friend were passing through Billingsgate Market, two women were quarreling furiously, using that forceful language which has given to English speech the word "Billingsgate." Wesley paused and listened.

"Pray sir, let us go," suggested his horrified companion.

"Stay, Sammy," replied Wesley, "stay and learn how to preach."

❖ ❖

Three small boys were bragging about the prowess of their respective dads.

"My dad," said one "writes a few short lines on a piece of paper, calls it a poem—and gets $10 for it."

"My dad," said another, "makes some dots on a piece of paper, calls it a song—and they pay him $25 for it."

"That's nothing," said the third. "My father writes a sermon on a sheet of paper, gets up in the pulpit and reads it—and it takes four men to bring in the money!"

❖ ❖

An irate old gentleman strode into the railroad station and, without preamble, proceeded to tell off the ticket agent, including in his denunciation everybody from the president on down. He ended by lambasting the trains for their failure to run on time. The agent finally cut in with: "Do you do much traveling on this road?" "Don't do any," replied the man; "but on Sundays, our preacher always finishes his sermon right after the noon train whistles—and the danged thing's been late the last three Sundays!"

❖   ❖

In these manpower-shortage days, it is coming to a point where even the wearer of the cloth is assured no special considerations. It is reported that one, lately come to a community, inquired of his laundryman, "Because I am a minister, do I get anything off?"

The laundryman's reply was prompt and to the point: "Yes, sir; all your buttons."

❖   ❖

And there's the kid who, on his examination paper, wrote that a prime minister is a preacher at his best.

❖   ❖

A young deacon had to read one of his own sermons to his bishop. The bishop heard it in stony silence. Then, trembling, the curate said, "Will that do?"

And the bishop retorted sharply, "Do what?"

❖   ❖

Two brothers—one a famous baseball pitcher, the other a preacher—met after a long separation. Some time was spent in exchange of reminiscences. Then the preacher said: "How is it, Bill? I've spent four years in college, three years at the seminary, and you've never done anything but play ball, and now you're getting a salary of $10,000 a year while I get $900. I can't understand it."

Bill thought a minute, then he said: "I'll tell you how it is, Jim: it's all in the delivery."

❖   ❖

> I never see my pastor's eyes,
>   He hides their light divine;
> For when he prays, he shuts his eyes;
>   And when he preaches, mine!

A preacher once said he had been preaching twenty years and no one had ever gone away angry or come around to challenge his message. An older minister answered, "Of course not. No one ever challenges an echo."

❖ ❖

A pastor, says James Street, needs the tact of a diplomat, the strength of Sampson, the patience of Job, the wisdom of Solomon— and a cast-iron stomach.

❖ ❖

A preacher was visiting at the home of a parishioner.

"I see you have a new maid," observed the clergyman. "How do you like her?"

"Oh," said the lady of the house, "she's all right, but," (pointing to a small child playing on the floor) "I don't want to say anything now because she repeats everything she hears us say."

Promptly, the little daughter looked up very innocently and remarked: "Dr. Brown, you preached too long last Sunday!"

❖ ❖

If a writer of fiction lambasts us, we think he's a genius.

But let some preacher say, "God says you are a sinner," and some in his audience will mutter, "Listen to the old mossback. I wish I had not dropped that nickel in the collection."

❖ ❖

"I was preaching in the Yale Chapel," says Prof. Wm. Lyon Phelps; "A little girl sat with her father and mother. After I had finished, she said, 'Mama, during Professor Phelps' sermon I didn't itch once.'"

❖ ❖

The minister's little daughter, watching him prepare his sermon, asked: "Daddy, does God tell you what to write?"

"Certainly, my dear."

"Then why do you scratch out so much of it?"

❖ ❖

The philosophy of a veteran Southern evangelist: "I make 'em feel the flames; I make 'em hear the harps!"

A minister was asked if he was making many new friends in his new charge.

"Well," he replied, smiling, "I must say I noticed quite a few nodding acquaintances in my congregation this morning."

✧ ✧

Just down below here they have had a great installation service. A minister is taking a new parish and they have been getting him suitably parked.

"What do they do when they install a minister, Papa? Do they put him in a stall and feed him?"

"Oh no, son, they hitch him to a church and expect him to pull it."

✧ ✧

A village clergyman said, "Well, George, how is it that you have not been to church lately?"

"Ain't got no Sunday trousers," replied George.

"I have an extra pair I'll send you," replied the clergyman.

The trousers were sent, and George was at church the three following Sundays.

A month later, the preacher met the parishioner and reminded him again that he was missed at church.

George answered, "Look here, parson, I like for a man to speak plain. You're thinking about them trousers. I come to church three Sundays, and if you don't think I've earned them, tell me how many more Sundays it'll take, and I'll either come to church or send them back."

PRECISION

The harassed attache of the American Consul at Lisbon swears this happened: A small, shy little man leaned confidentially across his desk and said, "Please, Mister, could you tell me if there is any possibility that I could get entrance to your wonderful country?"

The attache, pressed by thousands of such requests and haggard with sleepless nights, roughly replied, "Impossible now. Come back in another ten years!"

The little refugee moved toward the door, stopped, turned, and asked, with a wan smile, "Morning or afternoon?"

PRECISION—Lack

"I am never well—I can't say why," said the patient. "I get a sort of pain, I don't know exactly where, and it leaves me in a kind of—oh, I don't know."

"This," said the doctor, "is a prescription for I don't know what. Take it I don't know how many times a day for I can't think how long, and you will feel better, I don't know when."

PREJUDICE

"Yes," said the dear old lady, "I think the United Nations conference was a good idea, but it's a pity they have so many foreigners in it."

❖ ❖

Prejudice is a great time-saver. It enables one to form opinions without bothering to get the facts.

PREPAREDNESS

President Truman used to tell this one in the day when he was a Senator from Missouri:

In a Pennsylvania Dutch family, the old gentleman had been very ill, and on a restricted diet. Finally one day the doctor told the family that the old man was going to die and they might as well let him have anything he wanted to eat.

So Mama, without, of course repeating the doctor's dire forecast, went in to take Papa's order for supper. When finally the old man realized he could have anything he wanted, he asked for corned beef, fried potatoes and half a gallon of coffee. "And," he concluded, "you might be giving me a slice of that well-cured ham in the smokehouse."

"Ah, Papa," said the obedient frau, "the corned beef, the fried potatoes and the coffee I am fixing yet, but the ham—ach, that we should save for the funeral."

❖ ❖

Father, exasperated by little Billy's constant querying, observed: "I wonder what would have happened to me if I'd kept asking my father questions when I was your age."

"Well," said Billy, unperturbed, "perhaps you'd have been able to answer some of mine!"

PRETENSE

A certain small-town lawyer whose pretensions of importance were somewhat greater than his actual merit went about the village with head held high and an expression of superiority on his countenance. "Charlie," he remarked to the courthouse caretaker one morning, "why do you persist in shambling about with your head hung down and that everlasting dreamy look on your face? You should stand up straight and proud like I do!"

"Mr. Tucker," rejoined Charlie, "have you ever noticed in passing a wheat field that some of the plants stand up straight while the others bend low?"

"Of course I have," the lawyer rejoined impatiently.

"Well," observed Charlie, "the wheat that stands too straight hasn't any grain on it."

PRIDE—In Work

Robert Henri, the well-known artist, was attending a private showing of new pictures in a New York gallery. He was standing before a fine Sargent, when his attention was attracted by a big brawny individual, who looked like anything but an artist, engaged in admiring the same canvas and murmuring: "They have given me a good place at last."

Henri was immediately interested. "You are in this sort of work?" he inquired.

"Been in it for twenty years," replied the brawny one, "and this is the first time I ever got on the line."

"Ah, indeed?" exclaimed Henri. "And where is your picture?"

The stranger pointed to the Sargent. "Right there," he replied.

"That?" said Henri. "Why, Sargent painted that!"

"Painted it!" sniffed the brawny man. "Yes, I think Sargent was the name of the man that painted the picture, but it was me who made the frame."

PROBLEM

A farmer, visiting his son's college and wandering into the chemistry class, saw some students experimenting.

"What are you trying to do?" he asked.

"We're endeavoring," replied one of the students, "to discover or invent a universal solvent."

"What's that?"

"A liquid that will dissolve anything."

"That's a great idea," agreed the farmer. "When you find it, what are you going to keep it in?"

PROFANITY

The first and second grade boys were using pretty naughty language on the playground. Finally, the superintendent called them together and said he would not tolerate the use of swear words or dirty words. "Now," he concluded, "do you all know what I mean?" One little fellow replied: "Yes, you don't want us to talk like our daddies do at home."

❖   ❖

A certain parson in the Australian bush country took exception to the contention that bullocks cannot be successfully driven without blasphemy.

Challenged to prove his case, the parson cracked his whip, cleared his throat, and in roaring tones addressed the animals: "You rapturous archangels! You sublimated cherubims! You sanctified innocents! Get ye up and hence!"

The bullocks slowly gathered themselves together and moved off!

❖   ❖

A witness, an old darky, was undergoing a cross-examination. "Did the defendant use improper language when he was beating his horses?" asked the lawyer.

"Well, he talk mighty loud, suh."

"Did he indulge in profanity?" The witness seemed puzzled, and the lawyer put the question in another form: "Uncle Amos, what I want to know is, did he use words that would be proper for your minister to use in a sermon?"

"Oh, yes, suh," the old man replied with a grin, "but they'd have to be 'ranged diff'rent."

✧ ✧

The preacher was out on the golf course, and thought that a small moral lesson might not be amiss.

"I notice that the players who get the lowest scores are those who do not swear."

The gloomy golfer dug another slice of turf. "What do they have to swear about?"

✧ ✧

An Irishman had been having a long struggle with a balky horse on a steep hill, and he had given vent to exasperated language quite unfit for publication. On reaching the top he addressed the refractory animal reproachfully:

"Shure, 'tis the likes of ye that keeps me out of the Howly Name Society."

PROFIT

The tailor was packing up the coat which Brown had just purchased.

"You know, sir," he said, "I am letting you have this garment at a sacrifice."

"Indeed," said Brown, who considered he had paid quite a fair price.

"Less than it cost me to make," said the tailor, busy with the parcel.

Brown couldn't stand this. "Look here," he said. "You're always telling me that. How on earth do you make a living?"

The tailor smiled meekly. "I make a small profit on the paper and string."

PROFIT & LOSS

Three salesmen were eating dinner in a Washington hotel. The bill was $30 and all reached for the check. The first fellow said his firm was in the 50 per cent income tax bracket, and that the bill actually would cost him only $15. The second man said, "Let me pay it. We're in the 80 per cent bracket and it will cost me only

$6." The third one said, "I'll pay the check. My firm is working on a cost plus basis and we'll make $3 on the meal."

❖ ❖

A young college graduate was entering the retail business, conducted for 40 years by his father.

"Dad," he asked, "when are we going to take inventory and learn how much we have made?"

"Son," said the father, "measure that bolt of calico on the top shelf and figure what it's worth. That's what I started with. All the rest of this place is profit."

❖ ❖

The accountant of a store dashed into the office of the head of the firm. "After 5 long years," he chortled, "we are no longer in the red."

"Glory be," cried his boss. "Make up 5 copies of the annual report at once so that I can show them to the bank."

"But I have no black ink," said the accountant. "We haven't needed any in so long."

"Run out and buy a bottle," said the boss.

"I should say not," was the reply. "Then we'd be back in the red."

PROGRESS

Progress of a Great Man:
1. Quits shining his own shoes.
2. Quits writing his own letters.
3. Quits writing his own speeches.

❖ ❖

Life is like a ladder, every step we take is either up or down.

❖ ❖

Progress always involves risks. You can't steal second base and keep one foot on first.

❖ ❖

Little Jill approached her teacher as the other children were leaving for home.

"Miss Blivins," she inquired diffidently, "what did I learn in school today? My daddy always wants to know."

✧ ✧

Our attitude towards life largely determines our altitude.

✧ ✧

Little Oswald was taking violin lessons and kept trying to push ahead of the training exercises into the advanced pieces. Finally the teacher exclaimed in exasperation, "No, no—you want velvet draperies before you have plaster on the wall!"

PROGRESS—Lack

Mandy positively refused to ride on the merry-go-round at the county fair. To her protesting friends, she declared: "No indeed! Ah don't travel on dat thing. De other day I seen Rastus Green get on an' ride an' ride, till I was dizzy watching him. When he gets off, I sez to him, 'Rastus, yo' spent yo' money, but whar yo' been?'"

✧ ✧

Too often, we only make motions when we think we're making progress. In such situations the speaker, gently chiding a group, may find this tale a timely one.

Two negroes met in New Orleans. One was a big fellow who had traveled as far as Canada; the other a little chap known as Sam.

"Nice place up in Canada?" inquired the latter.

"Finest in the world."

"Any room fer me up in Canada?"

"Yessah, dey like us folks up dere."

"How do Ah get dere?"

"Why, you jes' gets into a row-boat right hyah on the Mississippi Riber, and you rows and rows, and den you're in Canada."

Early the next morning Sam got into a boat and rowed and rowed. But the Mississippi current is swift, and Sam was puny. He rowed from 6 A.M. to 6 P.M., attending strictly to business and keeping his eyes glued on the bottom of the boat. By the end of that time he had lost about six feet. His big friend happened to stroll down to the river bank, saw him rowing frantically, and called out:

"That you, Sam?"

The latter looked up, startled.

"Goodness sakes!" he exclaimed, "who knows me way up hyah in Canada?"

PROMISE—Fulfillment

"Honey," said the young man, "if you will marry me I'll put in electricity, get some modern kitchen things, paint the house inside and out, and also buy a milking machine."

"Henry," sighed the wise young lady, "suppose you do all those things—and ask me again."

PROPINQUITY

It seems that a girl and a boy were madly in love. So great was their love, in fact, that when fate separated them and sent the boy to a distant city, he telegraphed messages of his devotion and affection each morning. Every day for three years, the same Western Union messenger boy knocked on the girl's door bearing the message of undying love. At the end of three years they were married—the girl and the Western Union boy.

PROVINCIALISM

At the mouth of the Clyde are small islands called the Cumbraes. An old story has it that the minister there used to pray every Sabbath, "O Lord, grant Thy grace to the Greater and the Lesser Cumbraes; and O Lord, in Thy great mercy, remember also the neighboring islands of Great Britain and Ireland."

❖ ❖

Two elderly Boston ladies were visiting in California one summer when the temperature reached 98 degrees. "I declare!" exclaimed one, "I have never seen such heat. It isn't ever like this in Boston."

"Of course not, my dear," her sister pointed out. "After all, we are 3,000 miles from the ocean!"

❖ ❖

"Well" said a city man to a rural resident, during an historic war week, "lots of things have happened since the last time I saw you, Walter."

"Yep," Walter said. "Sure have. Been some snow, and the lake's most froze over solid."

PSYCHOLOGY

A soldier asked a dining car waiter which breakfast combination was best. "It doesn't make much difference," said the man. "Nothin's any good." He ordered a Number 3, Spanish omelet and things, and when he'd finished, called the waiter back. "Say," he said, "That was fine. What was your idea?"

"I always tells 'em nothin's any good," the waiter said. "Then they're pleasantly surprised," and leaning over, he almost whispered, "Ya see, I'm a psychologist."

PUBLIC RELATIONS

Public relations work is generally considered to be a relatively new development. Actually Clifford B. Reeves points out, the principles involved are as old as the ages. The 9th Verse, 14th Chapter of First Corinthians reads: "Except ye utter by the tongue words easy to be understood, how shall it be known what is spoken? For ye shall speak into the air."

✧   ✧

A young man, seeking a job as press agent, was having little luck with a Hollywood movie tycoon. The latter kept insisting that he needed no press agent.

"Have you heard of Napoleon?" asked the applicant.

"Sure; everybody's heard of Napoleon. What's that got to do with giving you a job?"

"Well," persisted the young man. "Have you heard of Wellington?"

"Wellington?" mused the tycoon. "Was he maybe an actor?"

"Wellington," said the job-seeker impressively, "was another one of those men who didn't need a press agent. He defeated Napoleon at Waterloo. But who knows that? All you hear is the story of Napoleon—the fellow with a good press agent."

The young man was placed on the pay roll.

"PUTTING ON AIRS"

Asked if a year of college had made any difference in his eldest son, a deep-South farmer reflected: "Well, he's still a good hand with the plow, but I notice his language has changed some. It used to be, 'Whoa, Becky! Haw! and Git up!' Now, when he comes to the end of a row, he says, 'Halt, Rebecca! Pivot and proceed!'"

❖ ❖

A Chicago capitalist planned a rather elaborate fishing lodge in the North Woods of Wisconsin. He employed a local contractor to put up the structure. Plans were duly dispatched, and in a few days the capitalist received word from his much perturbed local supervisor. "These plans is all wrong," the contractor wrote. "I can't do nothing until you get up here to straighten things out. Why, if I was to build that house the way it's laid out here you'd have two bathrooms!"

❖ ❖

Professor Willis A. Sutton, former superintendent of Atlanta public schools, tells of an old colored mammy who had been lured by a wealthy northern family to serve in their New England home. A few months later he encountered this mammy on the streets of Atlanta.

"Why, Rachel," he said in some surprise, "are you back home again?"

"Yessah!" the mammy declared with much emphasis. "Yessah! Mistah Sutton, Ah done come back to res' up and git me a mess o' eatments."

"What's the matter, Rachel, didn't that fashionable northern family give you enough to eat?"

"No, sah! Dey sho' didn'. An' work! Mah goodness! Mistah Willis, Ah nevah seen so much shufflin' o' de dishes fo' de fewness ob de vittles!"

PUZZLE

Pat and Mike were watching the construction of a building.

"Mike," said Pat, "is it ye kin tell me what kapes them bricks together?"

"Shure, now," replied Mike, "An' 'tis the mohrtar."

"Not at all, not at all," insisted Pat, "that's what kapes 'em apart!"

QUARRELS

Tired of being betrothed, Bennie decided to cancel the engagement in a diplomatic manner.

"Sadie," he said one day, "ve vas nefer meant to be mates. By us is too difference de temperaments. Ve vill only be bickering weet fighting."

"Vy, Bennie," said she, "you got wrung de idea. Ve luffink itch odder like two turdle doves."

"Rilly, Sadie, mine dollink, ve'll nefer agree, und vill be by us ull de time freection."

"No, Bennie, It'll be like Rumeo wit Jooliat. I'll making a poifect wife end it'll nefer be a quarrell."

"Sadie, I'm tellink you by us vill be nottink but arguments wit quarrelling!" insisted Bennie.

"But, Bennie, I say . . ."

"See," yelled Bennie. "Vot did I tell you! Ve're fighting ulraddy."

QUO VADIS?

Too many of us, confused and confounded by the contemporary scene, are a good deal like the old Negro uncle who, very late in life, undertook to gain an elementary education. When someone asked how he was progressing, he made reply:

"Well, Ah reckons Ah is doin' right peart. Yas, sah! Ah's comin' 'long. Now, when Ah comes t' a road sign Ah kin read how fer, but not wheah to."

❖   ❖

Having extended her visit longer than she meant to, the old English lady was going home in London after dark—and the blackout was on.

Presently, in spite of all her care, she bumped into a dimly-seen man and they both crashed on the pavement. At once the man was all apologies.

"So sorry," he murmured. "Careless of me. Let me help you up. So sorry."

"Never mind all that," returned the old lady curtly. "Will you please tell me which way I was facing before I was knocked down?"

RACE PREJUDICE

Many colored folks in Los Angeles hold war jobs that pay them generously. They believe in spending their money on the same generous scale.

Recently, a colored woman was in one of our large department stores looking for a hat. She found a lavishly-decorated number which at first seemed to strike her fancy. After viewing herself in the mirror, however, she cast it aside in disgust. "No," she told the sales girl, "I can't wear that one. It makes me look Jewish!"

REACTION

A lunch-counter patron ordered four poached eggs and chips, a dozen oysters, and a grilled steak.

After wading through these he finished off with four dough-nuts and two cups of coffee.

When the waiter had finished serving, he commented: "You must enjoy your meals."

"No," said the patron. "No; it isn't that—but I'm nuts about bi-carbonate of soda."

REALISM

The celebrated Greek artist, Zeuxis, painted a picture of a boy carrying a basket of grapes, and so lifelike were the grapes that the birds flew down and pecked them. Friends of the painter exclaimed over this wonderful manifestation of his genius, but Zeuxis was bitterly disappointed in his work.

"The boy must be very poorly painted," he confessed, sadly, "else his presence would have frightened the birds away from the grapes."

REASSURANCE

A timid old lady approached the captain of a steamboat on the Missouri river. "Captain," she said anxiously, "they say a great many men have been drowned in this river. Is that true?"

The captain smiled reassuringly. "My dear madam," he said, "you must not believe everything you hear. I assure you I have never yet met a man who had been drowned in the Missouri river."

REFORM

The average man doesn't oppose reform. What irks him is being reformed by somebody no better than he is.

❖   ❖

What this country needs is dirtier fingernails and cleaner minds.

❖   ❖

The reformer heard of a case which interested him more than the ordinary, so he sought out the reformed one and asked: "You stopped smoking because she asked you to?"

"Yep."

"And you stopped drinking because she asked you to?"

"Yep."

"And you stopped swearing because she asked you to?"

"Yep."

"And you gave up your poker parties and went into refined serious society for the same reason?"

"Yep, yep."

"And yet you never married her!"

"Well, you see, after I'd reformed like that I found I could do better."

❖   ❖

If God had made no reformers, men would still be living in caves; if He had made only reformers, no men would still be living.

REFORM—Dangers of

The speaker usually wants to reform somebody or something. But he needs a story to warn listeners against too sudden or violent change.

The wife and mother had been a constant nagger, a chronic complainer. The family had become accustomed to her whining voice and sour face. Then one day she attended a lecture. The subject was "The Face With a Smile Always Wins!"

The woman reformed. She reformed suddenly and overwhelmingly. The next morning she got up early, got a good breakfast for the family, and as they filed into the dining room, greeted them with a beaming smile. This was too much for the husband. He took a lingering look at his spouse, and collapsed into a chair:

"Oui! Oui!" he groaned. "Along with everything else, she's gone and developed lockjaw!"

REGRET

An English drill sergeant, whose extreme severity had not exactly endeared him to his men, was putting a squad of rookies through the funeral exercise.

Opening ranks, so as to admit the passage of the cortege between them, the sergeant walked down the lane thus formed, saying as he did: "Now I am the honored dead. See that you do the proper thing. Attention!"

At the end of the lane he turned around, scrutinized the squad with a practiced eye, and then remarked, "Your 'ands is right your 'eads is right, but you 'aven't got that look of regret you ought to 'ave."

RELIGION

There are 200 brands of religion. But that isn't too many when you remember that there are about 78,962,354 brands of cussedness.

✧   ✧

Phillips Brooks was once greeted by a lady who had brought a new religion back from the Orient. She vowed this would trans-

form the race. "How did you get it through the Customs?" asked
Brooks. "The Customs? What have they to do with religion?"
"Ah," replied he, "then it has no duty connected with it?"

❖   ❖

A minister's wife was pleased with the way her three-year-old
son had learned some of the simpler phases of religion that she had
taught him, but was entirely unprepared for the question he asked
one day when he was in a reflective mood.

"There are two kinds of goats, aren't there?" he asked. "Billy
goats and holy goats."

❖   ❖

If all churches were closed, and all Sunday schools forbidden,
and all Bibles destroyed, some people would be glad, some would
be sad, and still others would be mad—if they ever discovered it.

❖   ❖

A colored cook came in still shouting from a religious meeting.
Her mistress tried to tell her that religion didn't need so much
noise, and cited the example of Solomon's temple which had been
raised without the sound of hammers.

"Yes'm," agreed the cook, "but we ain' ready t' build yit. Us is
jest a-blastin' now."

❖   ❖

In a certain town are two brothers, who are engaged in the
retail coal business. A celebrated evangelist visited the town, converted the elder brother of the firm. For weeks after his conversion
the brother who lately "got religion" endeavored to persuade the
other to join the church. One day, when the elder brother was
making another effort, he asked: "Why can't you be a good man
and join the church like I did?"

"It's all right for you to be a member of the church," the un-
holier brother replied, "but if I join who's going to weigh the
coal?"

❖   ❖

An old darky got up one night during a revival meeting and
said:

"Bruddern an' sistern, yo' know Ah knows dat Ah ain't been what Ah oughter been. I'se robbed henroosts an' stole hawgs an' tole lies, an' got drunk, an' slashed folks wi' mah razo', an' shot craps, an' cussed an' swore; but Ah thank de Lawd der's one thin' I ain't nebber done: Ah ain't nebber lost mah religion."

❖ ❖

A housewife, interviewing a new maid, asked her if she had any religious views. The girl hesitated, then replied, "No, but I have some good pictures of the Great Lakes and Niagara."

❖ ❖

"I would like," said the lady, "a nice book for an invalid."
"Yes, madam," said the clerk. "Something religious?"
"Er-no," replied the lady; "the doctor told him this morning he was going to get well."

❖ ❖

Some folks' religion is like cider—sweet enough until it begins to work.

❖ ❖

"What did the Puritans come to this country for?" asked a teacher of a class in American history.
"To worship in their own way," said Willie, "and make other people do the same."

RELIGION—Conversion

A priest had a tamed parrot who had learned to speak Latin. One day the parrot disappeared. Sometime later the priest was sent on a Jesuit mission to the interior of South America.
One day, when the priest was deep in the forest, he heard mysterious voices in Latin. He listened attentively. To his amazement he discovered it was the celebration of a solemn mass.
"Dominus vobiscum . . ." said one voice.
"Et cum spiritu tuo . . ." answered another voice.
The priest looked in to a nearby tree, saw his escaped parrot,

proudly perched among hundreds of other parrots he had converted to Catholicism.

✧   ✧

That early American settler, Captain John Smith, was continually pestered by a Society in London which had contributed their means to convert the American savages. Their frequent solicitations for conversions sent Smith into deep perplexity until at last he hit upon an idea.

A party was sent into the swamp to capture an Indian. The unlucky brave was shipped across the seas to the English Society with this message from Smith:

"Here's an American Indian. See if you can convert him!"

RELIGION—Practical

Dr. J. M. Buckley was conducting an "experience meeting" at a Negro church, when an impressive-looking, modishly attired colored woman arose and in glowing terms bore witness to the many blessings she had gained through religion.

"That's wonderful, sister," said the white minister. "But what about the practical side? Does your religion make you strive to prepare good meals for your husband? Does it inspire you to make your home more comfortable and cheerful for him in every way?"

Just then Dr. Buckley felt a tug at his coat-tails, and turning, met the anxious gaze of the Negro pastor, who with great urgency whispered, "Press dem questions, doctor, press dem questions. Dat am my wife!"

RELIGION—Revival

You may have heard many people say, "Oh, well, I don't like revivals. They don't last." Well, neither does a bath.

RELIGIOUS INSTRUCTION

A visitor to Coleridge argued strongly against the religious instruction of the young and declared his own determination not to "prejudice" his children in favor of any form of religion, but to allow them at maturity to choose for themselves. The answer of Coleridge was pertinent and sound.

"Why not let the clods choose for themselves between cockle-berries and strawberries?"

REPARTEE

A woman who had been having trouble with public laundries shrinking her unmentionables found a large railroad spike and tied a tag to it with the inscription, "Try and shrink this."

When her laundry was returned, she opened it and found a small carpet tack with a tag tied to it saying, "We did."

REPENTANCE

Repentance was once defined by a small girl: "It's to be sorry enough to quit."

✧ ✧

A Christian is a man who feels
Repentance on a Sunday
For what he did on Saturday
And is going to do on Monday.

REPUTATION

Make ten consecutive correct guesses and you've established a reputation as an expert—which will last until you make one little mistake.

RESEARCH

Dr. George Washington Carver, the world-famed scientist in Tuskegee Institute, who came up out of slavery, has discovered 150 products that can be gotten out of the common sweet potato, and 300 products from the humble peanut. E. Stanley Jones asked Carver how he came to make all of those discoveries. The devout scientist replied, "One day I asked God what could be made out of a peanut. God said to me, 'You have brains; find out for yourself.'"

RESOURCEFULNESS

One is ready to forgive the boasting implied in the story of the answers given by a Christian, a Mohammendan and a Jew to the question:

"What would you do if a tidal wave drove the mighty ocean waters deep over your land?"

"We would die with the sign of the cross and beg the Lord to open for us the pearly gates of heaven," said the Christian.

"We would pray to Allah and be consoled in our Kismet, fate. As it is destined to be, so it is. Allah be praised," said the Moslem.

"We," said the Jew, "would learn to live under water."

❖   ❖

Although the Charleston earthquake called forth liberal charity, the public was just as ready to respond to the wants of the sufferers from the Johnstown flood which so rapidly followed the other disaster.

The old darky, appealing to a lady for aid, told her that by the Johnstown flood he had lost everything he had in the world, including his wife and six children.

"Why," said the lady, "I have seen you before, and I have helped you. Were you not the colored man who told me you had lost your wife and six children by the Charleston earthquake?"

"Yes, ma'am," replied the darky, "dat was me. Most unfort'nit man dat eber was. Can't keep a fam'ly nohow."

RESTRAINT

Constance Hope, the publicity gal, tells a story of Bruno Walter, famed European conductor. He once walked into rehearsal, bowed a courtly good morning to the musicians, then raised his hand for silence. "Now, gentlemen," he said, "the opening of this symphony must be piano—softly, but very, very softly. It opens like a whisper. Now!"

He raised his baton. Tensely, the men placed their instruments in position, but before even a single note was played, Walter lowered his baton.

"No, no, gentlemen," he said solemnly. "Already too loud."

RETRIBUTION

One of Winston Churchill's most persistent critics once said to the Prime Minister, "I am a firm believer in fighting the enemy with his own weapons."

Churchill took a deep puff on his cigar and said: "Tell me, how long does it take you to sting a bee?"

RETROGRESSION

A short story entitled "Three Generations": Grandfather had a farm. Father had a garden. Son had a can opener.

REVENGE

Some people do odd things to get even.

REVIVAL

"Yes," said the old man. "I have had some terrible disappointments but none stands out over the years like the one that came to me when I was a boy."

"And what was it?"

"When I was a boy I crawled under a tent to see a circus and discovered it was a revival meeting."

REWARD

As a reward for bravely undergoing an operation, a little girl had been promised the finest kitten to be had. Coming out from the influence of the anesthetic, the child muttered: "It's a bum way to get a cat!"

ROMANCE

One reason romance lasted longer in the old days was that a bride looked much the same after washing her face.

RULE-OF-THUMB

The sergeant asked recruits why walnut was used for the butt of a rifle.

"Because it has more resistance," volunteered one.

"Wrong."

"Because it is more elastic."

"Wrong."

"Because it looks nicer than other woods," a third suggested timidly.

"Don't be so dumb," snapped the sergeant. "It's simply because it is laid down in the regulations."

RUMOR

When a man talks of uncertainties and rumors he has heard, ask him if he has ever awakened in the dead of night to hear a neighbor's dog barking. Soon his own dog starts to bark, and several others join in the chorus. A lot of dogs barking, yet only one knows what he is barking about—and the chances are he's aroused by a false alarm!

SABBATH—Observance

Five-year-old William had been taught that Sunday is not a day for play. One Sunday morning his mother found him sailing his toy boat in the bathtub.

"William," she said, "don't you know it is wicked to sail boats on Sunday?"

"Don't get excited, Mother," he replied calmly. "This isn't a pleasure trip. This is a missionary boat going to Africa."

✧   ✧

A Scottish minister of the old style was asked if he thought it wrong to take a walk in the country on Sunday afternoon.

"Weel," he responded cautiously, "I ken 'tis nae harm takin' a bit o' a walk on the Sawbath, sae long, mind, as ye dinna enjoy yourself."

✧   ✧

Speaking in London, Canon Ottley told the following story as illustrating some folks' idea of keeping the Sabbath. A Scotchman one Sunday went into his backyard to mend a barrow. The loud banging which accompanied the driving in of the nails brought his wife to the door. "Donald, Donald," she cried, "what are ye about on the Sabbath?"

"I tell ye, I must mend the barrow. I want to use it," answered her husband.

"Ye must not," was her reply. "What'll the neighbors say? Or if ye do, ye must use screws."

❖ ❖

Joe Morgan, a darky living in an Alabama town, was confiding to a friend the fact that work was scarce just then.

"But I got a job last Sunday that brought me six dollars," said Joe.

"What!" exclaimed the friend, "you don't mean to tell me that you broke the Sabbath?"

Joe was very apologetic. "Well, suh, it was lak dis: it was one or de odder ob us dat had t' be broke."

❖ ❖

Joseph was a solemn-eyed, spiritual looking child.

"Nurse," he said one day, leaving his blocks and laying his hand gently on her knee, "nurse, is this God's day?"

"No, dear," said the nurse, "this is not Sunday, it is Thursday."

"I'm so sorry," he said sadly, and went back to his blocks.

The next day and the next, in his serious manner, he asked the same question, and the nurse tearfully said to the cook: "That child is too good for this world."

On Sunday the question was repeated and the nurse with a sob in her voice said: "Yes, Lambie, this is God's day."

"Then where is the funny paper?" he demanded.

❖ ❖

It was one of those bright Sunday afternoons when the minister called at the home of one of his members who was not in pews that morning. The little boy came to the door when he knocked.

"Is your daddy at home?"

"No, he went out to the Golf Club today."

"Golf on Sunday?"

"No, he isn't playing golf. He just went out for a couple of highballs and some stud poker."

❖ ❖

The new vicar was making pastoral calls in his parish, and stopped to converse with a small boy at the garden gate. "And where does your father go on Sundays, my little man?"

"Well, on fine Sundays he goes golfing, and on wet Sundays he turns us all out to church so he can have a bit of peace in the house."

❖ ❖

On Thanksgiving day, 1713, the governor of Connecticut and the king's commissioners were just preparing to dine when it was announced that the bear prepared for the occasion had been "shot on ye Lord's Day." At that dismal news none would touch a morsel of the roast bear, until it was decided that the Indian who shot the animal should be whipped and made to restore the price paid for the meat. Then, having inflicted a "just and righteous sentence on ye sinful heathen," the company fell upon the roast bear with clear conscience and left nothing but the bones.

❖ ❖

A farmer wrote to a newspaper that he had plowed his land on a Sunday, sown his seed on a Sunday, reaped his harvest on a Sunday, and done his threshing on a Sunday. When October came he said he found he had better results than any of his neighbors who had not worked on Sunday. He asked the newspaper how this could be explained. The editor's note below the farmer's letter consisted of a single line: "God does not make up His accounts in October."

❖ ❖

Little Marian, four years old, was busy ironing her dolly's new gown on the Sunday after Christmas. Her nurse remonstrated, "Don't you know it's a sin, any work to begin on the Sabbath?"

Marian looked up and calmly answered, "Now, don't you suppose the Good Lord knows this little iron ain't hot?"

❖ ❖

Although they were partners in many financial deals, Jay Gould and Jim Fisk were never on especially friendly terms.

On one occasion a clergyman, talking with Fisk, was insisting that Mr. Gould had his good points. "At any rate," he defended, "You must admit that he keeps the Sabbath."

"No doubt," said Fisk icily, "Mr. Gould keeps everything he lays his hands on."

❖ ❖

A Kentucky mountain woman was asked if she had noticed any difference in her Abner since he joined the church.

"Oh, yes," she said, "before, when he went to do any carpentering on Sundays, he'd carry his hammer and saw on his shoulder—but now he carries them under his coat."

❖ ❖

Marjorie Kinnan Rawlings tells about Grampa Hicks who lived in a palmetto-log shack at the edge of Cross Creek. . . . He existed by the illegal trapping of fish in Orange lake and by renting other men's rowboats, without permission, to fishermen from Jacksonville. If a customer's outboard motor lacked gas, he shuffled mysteriously to the other side of the bridge across the Creek, where lay beached other boats and motors, and returned with fuel. If catfish were scarce on his own lines, he ran the other fellow's.

Man's law is one thing, God's another.

One Sunday morning we asked Grandpa to go fishing with us. He knew where the bream were biting and we had had no luck for weeks. He spat.

"I don't fish on Sundays," he said haughtily. "I wa'n't raised up that away."

❖ ❖

A small boy had a little wagon that was a new possession and the delight of his heart, but when he brought it out to the front walk one morning he was told that he must play with it at the back of the house, "This is Sunday," added the father by way of explanation. The boy obeyed, but he questioned wonderingly as he trudged away. "Isn't it Sunday in the back yard too?"

SAFETY—SAFE DRIVING

Nowadays drivers seldom sound their horns; Gabriel does it for them.

❖   ❖

More people have been killed in car accidents during the fifty years since the automobile was invented than have been killed through all the wars in American history.

❖   ❖

Recipe for a Wake—Take one stewed prune, one pickled peach, and one date. Saturate the peach and the prune with brandy or gin; if unable to procure these, beer will do. Place on the seat of a high-powered car and leave on the road for thirty minutes. Then garnish with broken glass, gravel, and serve cold on a stretcher. Very attractive in light-colored box, decorated with flowers.

❖   ❖

An Englishman, visiting in this country, borrowed an automobile from an American friend and was setting out with considerable trepidation to tour the countryside. Scrupulously observing all of the roadside admonitions, he presently came to one reading, "Drive Carefully! This Means YOU!"

"Righto!" said our British cousin, slowing down to a conservative twenty miles per hour. "But I say," he mused to himself, snailing through the village, "how do you suppose they knew I was over here?"

❖   ❖

He was dug out of his wrecked car and hurried to a doctor's office.

"I can't do much for you," confessed the doctor. "You see, I'm a veterinary surgeon."

"That's all right, doc," replied the patient weakly. "I guess they brought me to the right place. I was an ass to think I could do fifty on those tires."

SAGACITY

"There are two things necessary for success, my boy," cautioned a fond father. "They are honesty and sagacity."

"What is honesty, father?"

"No matter what happens, or how adversely it affects you, always keep your word, once you have given it."

"And sagacity?"

"Never give it."

SALESMANSHIP

Once, many years ago, when Firestone, Edison and Ford were touring the west, Firestone and Ford got into an argument as to which was the better salesman. They determined to test their abilities at the next village, with Edison as arbitrator.

Ford closeted himself with the leading citizen, a wealthy Indian. He struggled for an hour to sell the chief a car, but returned empty-handed.

It was now Firestone's turn. But what earthly use could a man have for the Firestone product, if he wouldn't even consider the purchase of an automobile? Undaunted, however, Harvey Firestone went to meet his man. In a few minutes he returned, smiling. He had sold the tire, all right. It was to be used by the chief's son *as a hoop!*

SALESMEN—SALESMANSHIP

Merchants should remember
When
Dealing with a Supersalesman
That, as in shooting at a
Target
They must allow for the wind.

❖   ❖

A tribute to our era of super-salesmanship forms the basis of this story—a favorite of L. H. Hubbard, president of Texas State College for Women, in Dallas.

The alert salesmen for a milking machine had exhausted his

goodly store of adjectives in a vain effort to "warm up" his obdurate prospect. The old farmer refused to be moved. "Hit ain't a mite o' use in your talkin' thataway," he counseled, "I ain't got only one cow t' milk nohow."

Undaunted by this cold blast, the salesman continued, "But this machine will save time in milking even one cow," he insisted. "Look! It's just about milking time now. Come on down to the stable and let me show you."

So together they departed. The salesman set up his machine and began the demonstration, continuing meanwhile his ready flow of persuasive talk. In spite of himself, the old man began to take a keen interest in the proceeding. His eyes "bugged out" as he beheld the wondrous efficiency of the milker.

"Well, Mister," he conceded at long last, "that shore is some device o' yourn. I'd like mighty well t' have it, but—" and his face clouded with evident disappointment—"but I ain't got no money, and no way o' gettin' holt o' any." He paused and looked longingly at the shining machine. "I'll tell you, though, what I'm willin' t' do—I'll let you take the cow as a first payment!"

❖   ❖

A salesman was demonstrating a meat slicer to an old German market man. Everything seemed to be going smoothly. The market man emitted encouraging clucks of pleasure as each new feature was explained.

Finally the salesman, out of breath, paused to wipe a perspiring brow. "Pretty slick, eh?"

"Shure. Best I ever seen."

"Then, why don't you buy it?"

"Vell, why don't you *ask* me?"

More than one salesman has made the fatal error of neglecting to *ask* for an order—and ask repeatedly.

❖   ❖

A wholesale hardware salesman had been calling on a dealer for more than a year, without a chance to decorate his order book. The dealer was friendly—almost too friendly. He was constantly promising to "give your house some of my business." Finally the salesman pinned him down to a definite promise: "Next time you come in," he said, "I'll surely have an order for you."

The salesman walked away. Half an hour later he returned. "Well, Fred," he greeted the surprised tradesman, "you told me you'd have an order for me next time I came in. This is the 'next time.' Let's go!"

It worked!

❖   ❖

And it came to pass that there dwelt in a Certain Land a Player of Poker who delighted to sit in a Game. Yet he would make no bets. Each hand he laid down in disgust, because the Flush of Royal Hue was not dealt unto him.

And behold his stack dwindled and became as naught, for he had fed his substance unto the Kitty.

And there were in the same land Salesmen who erred like unto the Player of Poker. For, lo, they antied their days away. And the order-writing arm was not exercised. Thus they spake one unto another saying, "Come, let us go forth unto the Dutchman's and shoot a couple of games. For no one hath a desire to buy, so why should we waste time calling upon them?"

And it came to pass that there were others who didn't know that Sales couldn't be made. So they called upon the Prospects. And, behold, orders were booked in goodly number, and their sales flourished and blossomed even as the Bay Tree, while the Wailers and Waiters fell upon evil days and cursed "Conditions."

❖   ❖

"Digging up prospects" is a perpetual problem in almost any sales organization. And where is the sales executive who can't use another good "prospect" story?

On his way to confession, Mike encountered a kindred spirit, confided that he had participated in intimate relations with a lady of the neighborhood, but that he purposed not to reveal the name of his partner to the priest. "Shure, and he'll get it from ye," prophesied the associate. "Ye can't keep nothin' from the Father."

True to forecast, the priest was most insistent. But the sinner gave no ground. "I'm not tellin' ye, Father. Let 'er be comin' in t' do her own confessin'."

The priest was not easily dissuaded. "But you must tell me, Mike. You must tell me everything. Was it Mrs. Mahoney?"

"Faith and 'twas not."

The priest looked quizzically up. "Was—was it—Miss McCarthy?"

"It was not. And 'tis no good your askin' me, Father, for I'll tell ye no name. You're wasting your breath."

And thus the interview terminated. But Mike's friend was waiting for him, eager for an admission that the priest had again triumphed. "An' did ye tell him the name, Mike?"

"Shure an' I did not," Mike beamed proudly, "but—I got two blamed good prospects!"

❖ ❖

A salesman in a rural territory in Illinois had made a remarkable record in merchandising a low-priced car. The factory became interested in knowing the whys and wherefores. A zone manager was sent out to interview the man and study his methods.

"Well," said the salesman, deeply flattered at the special attention accorded him, "I ain't rightly got no secret, I reckon. Mostly I look around for a likely prospect, and then I jest *constipate* on him."

❖ ❖

Customers are often more receptive than we think. Their defensive attitude is merely a mask to hide their natural desire for what we have to sell. (Proceed with this story to illustrate the point.)

"What yo' so skeered of, woman?" Mose asked the comely young mulatto.

"I'se skeered yo' gwine kiss me."

"How I gwine kiss yo' when I's got a bucket on mah haid, a wash pot in one han' an' a turkey gobbler in de udder?"

"Oh, well, yo' fool, I wuz thinkin' yo' could set de bucket o' watah on de groun', put de turkey down an' turn de wash pot over him, den set me on de wash pot, frow yo' ahms 'roun me—an' des he'p yo'se'f."

❖ ❖

"The trouble with most salesmen," a veteran of the road declares, "is that they don't expect enough." This uncertainty and lack of confidence reminds us of the man who put a sign on his property:

"FOR RENT—$50 a month—or at the very least, $40."

❖   ❖

Some salesmen electrify their prospects; others merely gas them.

❖   ❖

She wanted to buy a stove.

She listened meekly to the sales patter. She heard about non-corroding bolts and patented insulation material and the gauge of steel used, and tricky controls, and over-size combustion chambers, and all the other things that are so startlingly new in an old lady's world that you'd think they would impress her mightily. Finally the salesman paused, and she still waited with patient expectancy.

"Well, madam, I've told you everything about the stove," the salesman declared. "Is there anything else you'd like to know?"

"Yes," she answered. "Will it keep an old lady warm?"

❖   ❖

"I had a marvelous day," said the First Salesman. "Made lots of friends for the Company."

"Me, too, Bill," said the Second Salesman understandingly. "I didn't sell anything either."

❖   ❖

"Well, what are you selling?" growled the gruff prospect, looking up from his desk.

"N—nothing, sir," stammered the timid tyro, "and is my boss raising a row!"

❖   ❖

Alfred Schindler tells this one:

I once hired an Iowa farm boy to sell stock feed. He was an earnest young fellow, very persistent and consistent in making his calls, but the tangible returns were negligible. Finally, one day, I said, "Son, I'm afraid you are in the wrong spot. You just can't sell."

The lad looked at me in earnest perplexity. "Mr. Al," he said, "I'm selling—I'm selling all the time. The trouble is that folks just ain't buyin'!"

❖ ❖

A good salesman should have—
The curiosity of a cat.
The tenacity of a bulldog.
The determination of a taxicab driver.
The diplomacy of a wayward husband.
The patience of a self-sacrificing wife.
The enthusiasm of a co-ed.
The friendliness of a child.
The good humor of an idiot.
The simplicity of a jackass.
The assurance of a college boy.
The tireless energy of a collector of past-due bills.

SANCTIMONIOUS

Catherine, the maid of all work, was telling Henry McLemore, the syndicated columnist, about a friend, a colored woman who was prominent in her little town.

"She is a sanctified saint in our church," Catherine said, "and a mighty fine woman. Good and true. Sweet and pure. But Mr. Henry, you know, she has one hindrance. Even her dearest friends ain't fond of her."

SARCASM

Knute Rockne, the celebrated Notre Dame football coach was once deeply disappointed at the showing made by his team in the first half of a crucial game.

At the intermission, the chagrined teammates huddled miserably together, anticipating a terrific tongue-lashing from their mentor. But Rockne failed to put in an appearance. Finally, at the last possible moment he strolled up, remarked casually, "All right, girls, it's time for the second half." That did it! Notre Dame won by three touchdowns.

SATAN

Sam had fallen again, and his pastor was upbraiding him for it. "How come, Sam," he queried, "you-all don' say, 'Git behin' me, Satan'?"

"Ah does say dat, pastor. I says dem very words. Den Satan he say, 'All right, Sam, I'll git behin'. Since we bofe goin' de same way, hit mek no diff'ence wid me who take de lead.'"

❖ ❖

An old Scottish woman who had never been known to say an ill word about anybody was one day taken to task by her husband.

"Janet," he said impatiently, "I do believe ye'd say a guid word fer the de'il himself."

"Ah, weel," was the reply. "He may nae be sae guid as he micht be, but he's a very industrious body."

❖ ❖

One of the members of a colored church in Alabama was talking to the pastor about the temptations Satan places in one's path, when the old preacher grunted and replied: "Folks make me tired representin' Satan as runnin' aftah dem to tempt dem. De truf is, my friends, dere is so many pullin' at de debbil's coat-tails dat he ain't got much time to chase anybody."

❖ ❖

A little girl in an Indian mission made this engaging supplication: "And, O God, I pray for the devil. He must have some good points, but everybody here seems to be against him."

❖ ❖

The politician had just concluded an eloquent plea for the support of his audience. A man in the back of the rom jumped up and angrily cried, "I'd rather vote for the devil!"

"Quite so," agreed the unruffled candidate. "But in case your friend declines to run, may I not then count on your support?"

SECRECY

Secretary of State William H. Seward, attending a Washington gathering, had commented freely upon various subjects. But when

the discussion turned to troop movements that had recently occurred, he immediately became silent.

Several of the group voiced speculation, and then one of the
young women present turned to the statesman.

"Mr. Seward," she beamed, "what do you think? Where are
the troops going?"

The secretary smiled.

"Madam," he replied, "if I did not know, I would tell you."

SECRETS

At a dinner party the guests were discussing whether women or
men were the most trustworthy in business. "No woman can keep
a secret," said one man scornfully.

"I don't know," retorted the forbidding-looking woman sitting
opposite him. "I've kept my age a secret ever since I was 24."

"You'll let it out someday, though," replied the man.

"I doubt it," was the answer; "when a woman has kept a secret
for 20 years, she can keep it forever."

SELF-ANALYSIS

"I got off a street car this morning," said a doctor, "and being
in no hurry, I began moralizing on the actions and probable character of three men who had alighted just ahead of me. The first
one was even then halfway down the block. . . . There, thought I,
goes a hustler—a man who's bound to succeed in life. The second
man was walking rather slowly and impressed me as one who
would do fairly well, perhaps. But the last fellow was just dawdling
along in the most shiftless sort of way. I very quickly set him down
as a loafer. Just then a thought came to me. All three were ahead
of ME!"

SELF-APPRAISAL

You grow up the day you have your first real laugh—at yourself.

SELF-APPRECIATION

"Elmer, do you love me?". . ."I'll say.". . ."Do you think I'm beautiful?". . ."You bet.". . ."Are my eyes the loveliest you have gazed

into?"..."Shucks, yes."..."Is my mouth like a rosebud?"..."Sure it is."..."Is my figure divine?"..."Uh-huh."..."Oh, Elmer, you say the nicest things! Tell me some more!"

SELF-DEFENSE

Asked if he thought it wrong to learn the art of self-defense, a minister replied:

"Certainly not; I learned it in youth, and have found it of great value."

"Did you learn the old English system, or Sullivan's system?"

"Neither; I learned Solomon's system. You will find it in Proverbs:

" 'A soft answer turneth away wrath.' It is the best system of self-defense I know."

SELF-IMPORTANCE

Joe, disconsolately looking out the window, noticed a very large log floating down the river. He said, "Now that's typically Washington."

Moe looked and said he couldn't see anything unusual except the log was pretty big.

Joe said, "Yes, I know, but if you'll look closely, you'll notice that there are 100,000 ants on that log and each one thinks he's steering it."

SELF-INTEREST

"What is the first step in cleaning a rifle?" asked the instructor of a rookie.

"Look at the serial number and make sure it's your own gun."

❖ ❖

The telephone rang in the fire station office. The Chief took up the receiver.

"Is that the fire station?" asked a timid voice.

"Yes," answered the Chief eagerly.

"Well," continued the voice, "I have just had a rock garden built, and I've put in some new plants . . ."

"Where's the fire?" asked the Chief.

"Some of these new plants are very expensive, and . . ." the voice continued.

"Look here," said the Chief at last, "you want the flower shop."

"No, I don't," said the voice. "I was coming to that in a minute. My neighbor's house is on fire, and I don't want you firemen to tread all over my garden when you come in."

❖   ❖

A customer, waiting for a small job to be done on his car, watched a mechanic change the oil in another car without spilling a drop, check the radiator, clean the windshield, wipe away all the greasy finger marks, place an clean cloth over the upholstery, wash his hands thoroughly and drive the car slowly out to the street curb. "Now, there's a real mechanic," the customer observed to the foreman. "Oh," explained the foreman, "that's his own car."

❖   ❖

When radios were something of a novelty, an Arizona trader imported one from Chicago and was demonstrating it when the chief of a neighboring Indian village wandered in. "This is Chicago speaking," said the manager. Then, turning the dial: "Now, we hear New York." And again: "That voice comes to us from Los Angeles."

"Ugh," commented the Chief. "What they say in my hogan?"

When he learned that the little box couldn't tell him that, he lost interest and wandered away.

❖   ❖

A couple of majors on a mission that took them to a good many army posts in this country found that most of the men assigned to chauffeuring them drove with a true soldier's disregard of life and limb. When, at a midwestern camp, they were assigned a colored corporal who drove them at a conservative 30 miles an hour, they felt impelled to compliment him. The soldier acknowledged the commendation with a modest rejoinder. "Well, suhs," he said, "Ah, looks at it dis way—Ah's in diss-here jeep too."

❖   ❖

Little Lydia had been given a ring as a birthday present, but, much to her disappointment, no one of the guests at dinner noticed it. Finally, unable to withstand their obtuseness or indifference, she exclaimed:

"Oh, dear, I'm so warm in my new ring!"

✧ ✧

The teacher was making the point that history repeats itself, and that many things which happen today are the counterpart of similar things that happened years ago.

"Now, will anyone tell me of anything new of importance that has happened during the last twenty-five years?"

"Me," answered one of the pupils.

SELF-MADE MAN

"Yes, I am a self-made man," boasted the magnate.

The quiet gentleman in the clerical collar looked at him reflectively. "Sir," he replied, "you relieve the Lord of a great responsibility."

SELF-RELIANCE

An old southern darky was soliloquizing, "When ah asks de Lawd to send me a chicken, ah hardly evah gets a chicken. But when ah asks de Lawd to send me after a chicken, ah always gets me a chicken."

✧ ✧

In saying good-by to his son, who was leaving his home to make his way in another city, a Chicago businessman gave him the following advice:

"Remember, son, that you must place a certain amount of dependence upon yourself. The man who goes about seeking advice is liable to find himself in the position of the man who gets so interested in reading the timetable that he misses his train."

SERVICE

A young woman hurried into a new delicatessen in her neighborhood to pick up some things on her way home from the office. The man behind the counter strove to please her in every way, going to considerable trouble to make careful selection of each item. When she thanked him for his painstaking service, he said cheerfully, "Oh, that's all right, miss. There's our motto." He waved to a printed card on the wall: OUR BEST IS NONE TOO GOOD.

❖ ❖

The new station agent flagged No. 10, a train that was known not to stop at his station. The train ran past the station and had to back up. The conductor stepped to the platform and asked.

"What did you flag us for? There's no one to get on."

"No," said the new agent, "but I thought someone might want to get off."

❖ ❖

A rather fussy young woman had spent nearly two hours inspecting the stock of linoleums in a certain shop. Roll after roll was brought out by the perspiring salesman, but still she seemed dissatisfied. The salesman judged from the woman's dress that she was a person of wealth, and, therefore, likely to give a fine order. When finally he had shown her the last roll he paused in despair.

"I am extremely sorry, madam," said he apologetically, "but if you could wait I could get some more pieces from the factory. Can you call again?"

Whereupon the young women gathered her belongings together and rose from the chair.

"Yes, do," she said, with a gracious smile, "but ask them to send something with very small designs, suitable for putting in the bottom of a canary's cage."

❖ ❖

A bellboy burst into a Texas hotel room and was reproved by the guest for lack of manners.

"But didn't you ring?"

"Yes, of course I rang."

"Three times?"

"Perhaps; I was in a hurry for ice water. But that doesn't excuse you for bursting in here without knocking."

"Mister," said the boy, "you ought to read the bell card. It's one ring for the porter, two for me, and three for a gun. And when s guest rings for a gun, orders are to get it to him before the other fellow can beg his pardon."

❖   ❖

The small, mild little Jewish man, seated in a remote corner of the busy restaurant had ordered steak—and was having a difficult time trying to carve it.

A waiter paused at the table. "Tough?" he asked solicitously.

The exhausted patron turned to the waiter, with defeat in his eyes: "When I am ordering beef," he said patiently, "and you serve horse, I am not saying a vord. I don't like it to mek a fuss. But the next time I am esking, if you will please be so kindly, to tek the harness off before you are serving."

❖   ❖

If you would be satisfied with your lot in life, build a service station on it.

❖   ❖

One of those fussy guys ran into a brand new waitress the other morning. "Two eggs," he ordered, "and, mind now, don't fry them a second after the white is cooked. Don't turn them over. Not too much fat. Just a pinch of salt on each. No pepper. . . . Well, what are you waiting for?"

"The hen's name is Betty," the waitress said demurely, "Is that all right, sir?"

❖   ❖

A lady called up the clerk in a general store and said: "Send me a bucket of lard, tell my husband to come home, send a spool of No. 60 cotton thread and vote the straight Democratic ticket for me."

❖   ❖

Mrs. MacGillicuddy walked into the butcher shop and said, "I'd like to have you cut me, please, six and seven-eighths pounds of flank."

It was an unusual request, but the butcher thought maybe his customer had a special recipe. Once, twice, three times, he was a bit short of the mark. Finally, he got a piece of meat that was exactly the right weight.

"Well, Mrs. MacGillicuddy," he said, sighing with relief, "will you take it with you or shall I send it up?"

"Who wants it?" answered the customer. "I'm dieting and that's how much I lost. I want to see how it looks in one lump!"

SERVICE—Limited

A Naval ensign got off a troop train at LaGrange, Georgia, to mail a letter. Unable to locate a post-box he asked a sleepy-eyed native to post the letter for him.

"Whar's hit a-goin?" drawled the cracker.

"New York City," answered the ensign.

"Wal," said the other meditatively, "reckon you'd better mail hit summers else. Ain't no train heah runnin' t' New Yawrk. They all goes t' Atlanta!"

SEX

The gentleman was late. For twenty minutes the beautiful show girl had been standing on that corner, growing more and more angry with each passing moment. At last he came, apology in his face and the speed of Mercury in his feet.

Without waiting for his excuses, she proceeded with a thorough tongue lashing.

"But, dear," he finally interposed, "let's talk this thing over dispassionately."

She eyed him icily. "If you're going to bring sex into it," she said, "I'm going home right now."

SEXES

Tommy had a charming and personable manner, which he exercised with telling effect upon little Mary, who sat next to him in school. Unfortunately, he was an indifferent student.

Observing the attraction between the two youngsters, the teacher devised a subtle appeal to Tommy's ambition.

"Tommy," she warned, "you must study harder or you won't be promoted.

"How would you like to have to stay in this class and have little Mary go ahead of you?"

"Well," said Tommy philosophically, "I guess there'll be other little Marys."

❖ ❖

Two maiden ladies were discussing a favorite topic—men.
"Which," asked one, "would you desire most in a husband—brains, wealth, or appearance?"
The second hesitated not a moment. "Appearance," she replied decisively, "and the sooner, the better."

❖ ❖

Miss Jones remarked that she had never met a man really good enough to marry.
"You'll be left waiting," cautioned her friend. "Other women are snapping the men up pretty fast."
"Oh," replied Miss Jones, "there's plenty fish in the sea yet."
"That's true. But aren't you afraid of your bait getting stale?"

❖ ❖

Carl Van Doren tells the story:
"Why 'n't you ask one o' the gals hereabouts t' go with y' to the carnival?" one of our hired men asked, in the days of my early youth.
I replied that I was awkward and unschooled in the art of persuading females. "I wouldn't know," I confessed, "how to ask 'em."
It was then that this sage philosopher gave me counsel I have sought ever to remember:
"Heck, bub," he said, "there ain't no wrong way!"

❖ ❖

How to tell the sexes apart now that both are wearing pants: The one listening is the man.

❖ ❖

"Mandy," Uncle Ephraim said to his wife the other day, "I has noticed one big difference twixt men and women."
"Whut's dat?" asked Mandy.
"Jes' dis," answered Uncle Ephraim, "a man'll gib $2 fer a $1 artickle dat he wants, an' a woman'll gib $1 fer a $2 artickle dat she doan want."

Stories about men and women are the speaker's stock in trade. In a mixed audience, you can hardly get along without a sprinkling of each. They are sure-fire. When you talk about men, how the women will howl! And vice versa.

A little girl wrote this essay on men:

"Men are what women marry. They drink and smoke and swear, but don't go to church. Perhaps if they wore bonnets they would. They are more logical than women, also more zoological. Both men and women sprang from monkeys, but the women sprang farther than the men."

SIMPLE SOLUTION

An eastern visitor to the wide open spaces of the West was captivated by that diminutive beast of burden, the burro. He bought one; ordered it shipped to his country estate. The animal was billed, "one Burro, crated."

A freight clerk, checking way-bills en route, finally balanced his records with the notation: "Short: one bureau. Over: one jackass."

SIN

Sonny, walking through a cemetery with his father, was reading the inscriptions.

"Gee, Pop," he asked as they reached the gate, "where are all the wicked people buried?"

❖   ❖

A prominent churchman had occasion to visit New York, where he remained for a few days. In writing of his experience to his wife in the West he had this to say: "New York is a great city, but I do wish I had come before I was converted."

❖   ❖

The other fellow's sins, like the other fellow's car lights, always appear more glaring than our own.

❖   ❖

Sin is an old-fashioned word used to describe what is now termed "experience."

"Bredern!" exclaimed the preacher as he came across a portion of his flock engaged in pursuing the goddess of chance. "Don' yo' all know it's wrong to shoot craps?"

"Yassah, pahson," admitted one parishioner sadly, "an' believe me, Ah's payin' foh mah sins."

SNOBBERY

Nikolaus Ruediger, the famous anatomist who taught at the University of Munich toward the end of the last century, had been a barber until a small inheritance which came to him in middle life made it possible for him to begin his academic career.

Several of his aristocratic students, however, regarded his early life as a barber with disdain. One day in the dissecting room Professor Ruediger noticed one of those students working carelessly with a dull scalpel. "Why don't you sharpen your blade?" he asked the young Count.

"I don't know how to sharpen blades," was the reply. "You see I've never been a barber."

The Professor regarded him quizzically. "I'm sure you haven't," he commented, "if you ever had been one, you would have remained one."

SOCIALISM (see also COMMUNISM)

The late Baron de Rothschild is said once to have employed an excellent valet who, for a time became persuaded to the tenets of socialism, and met regularly with a group who advocated this social reform.

Some time later the Baron, noting that Alphonse no longer attended these meetings, asked the valet if he had lost interest. "Sir," he was told, "some of my former colleagues have calculated that if all the wealth of France were divided equally, each individual would be the possessor of 2,000 francs."

"Well," said the Baron, "what of that?"

"Sir," said the enlightened Alphonse, "I now have 5,000 francs."

❖   ❖

The socialistic father had his young son on the carpet for skipping school. In his hand, the father held a note from Junior's teacher, suggesting that ample punishment be dealt to the truant.

"Junior, just what do you mean by staying away from school? If you have a good reason, you'd better tell me. Come, come, what was your reason?"

"Class hatred, Father. Class hatred."

SOLUTION

A woman sent her little boy to the store for two pounds of plums. Presently she telephoned the grocer to complain that she had weighed the plums and found only a pound and a half.

"I am sure my scales are correct," insisted the merchant. "Have you weighed your son?"

❖   ❖

Ralph, the diminutive office boy for one of the great Eastern financial institutions, approached an executive of the bank one morning with the assurance that he now knew what was wrong with the country. Invited to give his opinion, the lad observed:

"Why, we're trying to run America," he asserted, "and right now we haven't even *one* vice-president!"

❖   ❖

The city slicker, fascinated by the sight of an old man sacking eggs in a grocery store, asked, "Do you know how many eggs in a dozen?"

The worker allowed as how he didn't.

"Then how do you know how many you're putting in the sack?"

Replied the old man: "I can count up to nine, and then I just add three more eggs."

SPEECH—SPEAKING

Charles H. Spurgeon, the noted preacher, was emphasizing to his "sermon class" the importance of making the facial expression harmonize with the speech.

"When you speak of Heaven," he said, "let your face light up, let it be irradiated with a heavenly gleam, let your eyes shine with reflected glory. But when you speak of Hell –well, then your ordinary face will do."

✦ ✦

Words are like sunbeams—the more they are condensed the deeper they burn.

✦ ✦

In the days of Balaam it was considered a miracle when an ass spoke. Things have changed.

✦ ✦

"As we grow older," says Robert Quillen, "our bodies get shorter and our anecdotes longer."

✦ ✦

In Japan speeches at public dinners are made before dinner. Who said that we know everything?

✦ ✦

A certain man had an aptitude for after-dinner speaking. His wife was asked which of his speeches she preferred. Without hesitation she replied:

"The best after-dinner speech I ever heard him make was this: 'Dear, I'll help you with the dishes.'"

✦ ✦

We should pause once in a while and ask ourselves where we are going in all this hurry, and whether, after all, speed is as important as we customarily believe it to be. Maybe we're just victims of the "hurry" habit.

"I'm in a great hurry to get to New York," said the man with the valise. "How soon can you get me there?"

"The train will start in a few minutes," answered the ticket agent, "that will get you there in twenty hours. Tomorrow evening, though, we shall put on a train that will make the distance in eighteen hours."

"All right," rejoined the man, "I'll wait till tomorrow evening."

❖ ❖

A stable boy who had been loud and lusty in praise of the fleet feet of a potential Kentucky Derby entry, was approached by the hireling of a rival stable. "Black boy," said the challenger, "Ah axes you, who is de sire ob dat won'erful colt you speaks so highly ob? Ah craves me to know, who is his pappy?"

The braggart was only momentarily taken aback.

"Well, t' tell you de truth," he rejoined, "dis heah colt is so fas' —an' he done run away from home so quick—he nevah learned his pappy's name."

STABILITY—Lack

An old Oriental fable relates that a woman, observing a man following her (yes, it is a very ancient custom!) paused and asked him why.

"Because," said the man, "I have fallen in love with you."

"Ah," said the woman, "but my sister, who is coming after me, is much prettier than I."

So the man, meditating for a moment, retraced his steps in search of the sister. However, the next woman he met was very ugly. Angrily he hastened after the first, who had pleased him, and asked, "Why should you tell me a lie?"

"Because," said the woman, "it was my wish to test you. Had you been in love with me you would not have gone back looking for another woman."

STANDARDS—Advancing

As a patroness of struggling and discouraged artists, Mrs. Gilling was not markedly successful, although she had plenty of money and a warm heart, and was interested in art and artists.

"I've brought some of this year's sketches to show you," said one poor young man whom she had asked to call upon her, "but I do not feel satisfied with them. They are not as good in some ways as the work I did a year ago."

"Nonsense!" said Mrs. Gilling, with loud cheerfulness, patting

him on the shoulder. "You paint just as well as you did last year—
as well as you ever have. Your taste's improving, that's all."

STAY-AT-HOME

The colored private, a passenger on the ship going across the
ocean, became very seasick and was being kidded by one of his
buddies. "You all is jest a landlubber."

"That's right," replied the private. "Dey ain't no arguments
dere. Ah's a landlubber and ah's jest findin' out how much ah
lubs it."

STRATEGY

John Hay, the famous American diplomat and statesman, before being admitted to the Illinois bar, was called before a committee of prominent lawyers for examination. A member of the
committee, in an attempt to confuse the young lawyer, cited a very
difficult and involved case in great detail and then turning a forbidding eye upon the fledgling, said:

"And now, Mr. Hay, let us suppose that a client came to you
with such a case. What would you tell him?"

Young Hay had become lost in the maze of data and was thoroughly bewildered. Inwardly he swore that he would kill the first
man who came to him with such a problem. But after a moment of
nervous reflection, he looked up and said:

"I would ask him for $50 and tell him to call again in the morn-
ing."

The committee murmured its approval.

"Mr. Hay," said his questioner with a twinkle in his eye, "you
are admitted."

❖ ❖

An elderly plutocrat went to a rejuvenating expert and asked:
"Can you make me twenty-five again?"

"Yes," was the reply, "but it will cost you $500."

"Can you make me eighteen?"

"Yes, but it will cost you $2,500."

"I'll have the operation for eighteen."

Six months later the expert called for his money.

"Nothing doing," said the patient, "I'm under age, and if you say I'm not I'll sue you for fraud."

❖ ❖

A freckle-faced young hawker was trying to get himself and his basket through a jam-packed throng of fans in a passageway at Yankee Stadium. "Gangway, gents!" he kept shouting, but nobody paid the slightest attention. Finally he yelled, "Gangway—watch out for the mustard!" Everybody clutched his jacket protectively and shrank back to let the youngster past.

The boy wasn't selling hot dogs at all—just peanuts.

❖ ❖

In the book *Kabloona*, Father Henry, shepherd of the Eskimos at Pelly Bay, tells how he employs strategy in handling his charges.

"You gain naught in urging an Eskimo to hurry," said the wise Father. "When I must send a sled on a quick trip, I call an Eskimo: 'I want you to go to Repulse Bay. It will take a good bit of time. You are young; probably you do not know the way very well; your dogs are not worth much. Still, nobody else is available, so go along.'"

Thus pricked in his vulnerable pride, the young Eskimo outdoes himself; may make a 17-day journey within two weeks.

❖ ❖

The customer, with a puzzled expression, contemplated a display of half a dozen dressed chickens.

"You see," she confided to the butcher, "I keep boarders. I wish you would pick out the three toughest hens in this lot."

The butcher gladly complied.

"Now," said the customer, "that's fine. I'll take the other three!"

❖ ❖

Jones, a good family man, had been inveigled into a poker game, and experienced growing apprehension as the hands of the clock moved relentlessly on toward morning. Finally, at 3 A.M. he had a sudden inspiration. He called his home and when, finally, the little woman answered the phone, he shouted in frenzied haste, "Don't pay the ransom; I'm back!"

❖　❖

A shrewd and thrifty farmer got into a boundary dispute with his neighbor. The battle waxed from warm to hot and the farmer sought legal aid.

After stipulating that there was to be no fee unless there were grounds for legal action, he gave the lawyer a detailed and elaborate account of the trouble.

"Fine!" the lawyer said. "The case is air-tight. The other fellow hasn't got a leg to stand on. My advice is ten dollars, and for a forty dollar retainer I'll start a suit at once."

"No," said the farmer. "No, I guess you better not. I gave you the other fellow's side."

STUPIDITY

A farmer engaged a young man from town and discovered that he was not very bright.

The new man was constantly putting the end boards of the cart on wrong. He would put the front board on behind and the back board in the front. Finally, the farmer painted a large "B" on each board and called the man's attention.

"Now, blockhead," he said, "you can't make any more mistakes. That 'B' is for 'before' and this 'B' is for 'behind.' "

❖　❖

When a man acquires a wooden leg, it is not inherited or transmissible, but when he acquires a wooden head it is.

SUBTERFUGE

Too often, in our supplications, we are inclined to try to "fool God." And we are not always so frank about it as was the little girl who concluded her prayer:

"And, dear Lord, please send the beautiful snow to keep the little flowers warm through the winter."

Climbing into bed, she confided: "That's the time I fooled Him. I want the snow so I can go sliding with my new sled!"

SUCCESS

Nothing recedes like success.

SUCCESS—Formula

"How can I get promoted?" a young boy employed in an Oregon lumber yard asked an efficiency expert.

"Wear a red shirt and work hard," was the answer. "The red shirt will catch the eye of the boss; the hard work will win you a better job."

SUCCESS—Popular

One of Abraham Chasins' most successful compositions was a piano piece called "Rush Hour in Hong Kong."

Discussing the piece with his friend Moritz Rosenthal, the composer said, proudly, "It was published only seven months ago, and it has just gone into its 17th edition!"

"Mm-m," was the reflective response. "I was never crazy about that piece, Abe, but that bad I didn't think it was!"

SUPERMAN—Deflated

Bernard DeVoto, the author, was taking his 12-year-old son to the broadcast of Cavalcade of America. The lad wasn't much interested until he recognized the voice of the announcer, Clayton Collier, as that of Superman.

After the broadcast, DeVoto and his young son sought out the announcer, who readily admitted his dual role.

"Umph," said the 12-year-old, speculatively eying Collier, "I'll bet you couldn't even push over the RCA building!"

SUPERSTITION

Baseball players are notoriously superstitious, and most agree that an empty barrel is a sign of success.

Before a crucial series with the Cubs, the Giants fell into a slump. Manager McGraw entered the locker-room smiling broadly. "Our troubles are over, boys," he called cheerily. "I just saw a truckload of empty barrels."

That afternoon the team made hits at will off the Cubs' pitchers. The following day, the second baseman announced that he had seen some barrels. Again the Giants pounded the Cubs. It was the same story in the final two games.

After the last game, a big fellow wearing a trucker's apron came in.

"Where's McGraw?" he demanded. "I've been driving my truck past here with empty barrels for four days, and I want the pay he promised me!"

❖ ❖

A black cat following you is bad luck, depending upon whether you're a man or a mouse.

❖ ❖

Lowell Thomas tells of three Jews who were traveling from Hollywood to New York—film executives, I suppose. They came through, all the way, in the same Pullman with the same Pullman porter. Morning, noon, and night they had the colored porter on the run, opening bags, closing bags, and running endless errands. Not once during the entire four-day journey did they give him so much as a dime. Just before pulling into New York, the porter brushed them off in style—still no tip. The vestibule of the Pullman was piled high with their bags. He unloaded them onto the platform at Grand Central. Still no tip.

The three Jewish gentlemen picked up their bags as though about to start off. Then, with a sudden recollection, one of the group paused, thrust his hand into his pocket, and came up with a five dollar bill, which he presented to the despairing servitor. The second, taking the cue, produced a ten spot, and the third, not to be outdone, came forth with a crisp twenty-dollar note.

Accepting these gratuities with profuse thanks, the Pullman potentate mopped his perspiring brow and turned to an associate. "Sam," he said, a relieved note creeping into his voice, "Sam, Ah bets you de Jews didn' crucify Christ. Dey jes' worried him to death!"

TACT

"I don't think that man upstairs likes to hear Johnnie play his drum, but he's certainly tactful about it."

"Why?"

"This afternoon he gave Georgie a knife and asked him if he knew what was inside the drum."

❖　❖

A captain, owner of a fine milk cow, lived alongside a corporal whose proudest possession was a thriving strawberry patch. Staking his cow near the strawberry patch to graze, the captain often helped himself to a handful of the choicest berries. The corporal knew it would be impossible to accost his captain. He racked his brain for a tactful but effective solution. Then it came. He nailed a sign on the fence-post:

"Notice: Anyone caught stealing strawberries from this patch will get his cow shot!"

TALK

Orville Wright was reproached for not taking up the challenge of the Smithsonian Institute that it was Langley, not the Wrights, who was the first to fly.

"The trouble with you, Orville," said a friend, "is that you are too taciturn—you don't assert yourself enough. You should press-agentize more."

"My dear friend," Orville Wright answered, "the best talker and the worst flier among the birds is the parrot."

❖　❖

Of the sounds the human ear cannot hear, it is a sad fact that none are made by the human tongue.

❖　❖

Bill Jones stopped in at a pet store and was entranced by a remarkable bird that was not only beautiful to look at but also spoke fluently in eight languages. He paid a good round sum for the bird and asked to have it delivered to his house.

Reaching home at dinner time that evening, he asked, "Has the bird come?"

"Yes, dear," his wife replied. "It's in the oven now."

"What!" he exclaimed. "In the oven? Why, that bird could speak eight languages!"

"So?" said the unperturbed frau. "Then why didn't he say something?"

❖   ❖

"I believe," said Ephraim Tutt, the fabulous character created by Arthur Train, "the curse of the world to be that it is governed by talkers. I do not care for government for, of or by the larynx."

❖   ❖

When you talk you only say something you know—when you listen you learn what someone else knows.

❖   ❖

A drunk, attending an auction, began bidding on a parrot. Each bid brought an answering offer, just a trifle higher. Finally, the bird was knocked down to the inebriated one for $17.40.

Taking Polly under his arm, the successful bidder stumbled out of the auction house and down the street. At the corner, he paused and exclaimed to himself: "G-g-good grief! Here I've gone and paid $17.40 for a parrot, and I don't even know whether the blamed bird can talk!"

"Talk?" squawked Polly. "Say, who do you suppose was doing that bidding against you?"

TANK TOWN

The motorist was on unfamiliar ground, and directly before him was a fork in the road with no signpost to tell him which way to go.

"Which way to Stumpville?" he asked of a dejected looking man who roosted on a fence near at hand.

The native languidly waved his hand toward the left.

"Thanks," said the motorist. "How far is it?"

" 'Tain't so very far," was the drawling reply. "When you get there, you'll wish it was a durn sight farther."

TASTE

Two old-time legislators, Senator Blackburn and Senator Beck, from below the Mason-Dixon line, were reputed to be excellent judges of liquor. A certain Washington whiskey dealer was preparing to fill the order of a fastidious customer from a barrel of fine old bourbon he had just received, when it occurred to him to have the two experts pass upon the quality of the product.

Blackburn tasted the bourbon, smacked his lips and said he believed there was a little iron in it. Beck then sampled it and said, "Very good, but I think I detect the taste of leather."

In the bottom of the barrel was found a carpet tack with a leather cap.

TAXES

Michael Faraday, father of our electrical age, was giving a demonstration before the British Royal Scientific Society of London. A rising young politician of the day, Wm. Gladstone, was present. He evinced polite interest at first and then became bored, saying, "It's all very interesting, Mr. Faraday, but what in God's earth good is it?"

"Some day," answered Faraday, "you politicians will be able to tax it!"

❖   ❖

This conundrum, attributed to Mark Twain, was contributed by a long-suffering taxpayer to the columns of the New York Herald-Tribune:

"What is the difference between a taxidermist and a tax collector?"

"The taxidermist takes your hide only."

❖   ❖

Walking up the street, a Federal officer heard frightful screams coming from a house. He ran to investigate; found a small boy had swallowed a quarter. His mother, not knowing what to do, was frantic.

The man caught the little fellow by the heels and holding him up, gave him a few shakes. The coin dropped to the floor.

"Well," exclaimed the grateful mother, "you certainly know what to do! Are you a doctor?"

"No, madam," replied the official, "I'm a collector of internal revenue."

❖   ❖

When an old South African native was told he had to be taxed because the government, like a father, protected him from enemies, cared for him when he was sick, fed him when he was hungry, gave him an education and, for these reasons, needed money, the old native said:

"Yes, I understand. It is like this: I have a dog, and the dog is hungry. He comes to me and begs food.

"I say to him, 'My dear faithful dog, I see you are very hungry. I am sorry for you. I shall give you meat.'

"I then take a knife, cut off the dog's tail, give it to him and say: 'Here, my faithful dog, be nourished by this nice piece of meat.'"

❖   ❖

People who squawk about their income taxes may be divided into two classes. They are: men and women.

❖   ❖

At a certain State institution for the mentally muddled, they were testing inmates here awhile back, and put the query:

"Which would you rather have—$10 or $10,000?"

"I'll take the $10," replied a "guest" promptly. "I couldn't pay the tax on $10,000."

They let him out; he was cured!

❖   ❖

The months during which we feel free from income tax worries are those that have an X in the spelling.

❖   ❖

Once, in Milwaukee, says Geo. Raft, the movie star, I was approached by a panhandler. I reached into my pocket for some small change, and finding none, in a sudden burst of generosity, I pulled out a dollar bill and handed it to the man.

To my complete amazement he carefully counted out 90c in

change and handed it over to me. "Those dollar contributions," he explained blandly, "bring my tax up too high."

❖ ❖

Legislators casting about for new sources of tax revenue during the war seem to have overlooked a promising proposal once offered to England and the world by Jonathan Swift.

"I propose," said the satirical Swift, "that a tax be levied on female beauty."

"But could we make the women pay enough to make it worthwhile?" a listener inquired.

"Ah, yes," replied the wily Dean. "Let every woman be permitted to assess her own charms—then she'll be generous enough."

TEACHING (see also EDUCATION)

For months the sculptor had been working over a bust, chipping off a bit of marble here and a bit of marble there, but never getting it quite right. Finally, one afternoon, while the sculptor's back was turned, the statue said reproachfully: "Why don't you stop this foolishness and let me alone? You have neither the talent nor the knowledge to be a sculptor."

Convinced that the statue was right, the sculptor put away his tools forever. He is now writing a treatise on "How to Be a Sculptor."

❖ ❖

Teacher had called on Johnny's mother, and told her that Johnny wasn't co-operating to the fullest extent in helping his education along. After the teacher left, his mother asked Johnny for an explanation. "Well, it's like this," he said, "she just doesn't teach anything I want to learn."

TEMPER TEMPERED

There was a man who had a grouch and a pretty daughter. The daughter attracted young men. The grouch drove them away.

One afternoon a young man called. Waiting for the daughter on the front porch, he tried to start a conversation.

"Looks like rain, Mr. Brown."

" 'Tain't goin' to rain," said the father.

There was silence for some time, then the father asked, "What's your name, young man?"

"My name's Jones, Richard Jones. I'm the son of Newton Jones."

"Well, well," said the father, "so you're the son of my old friend, Newt Jones? Mm-m-m, well, it may rain."

TEMPTATION

An old Negro preacher once cautioned his flock, "When you're lookin' at your neighbor's melon patch, bredderin, you cain't keep your mouf from waterin', but you kin run."

❖ ❖

Small Bobby was trying to save all the pennies he could to buy war stamps. But it was a difficult job. One night he was saying his prayers when his mother heard him plead earnestly:

"Lord, please help me save my money—and don't let the ice cream man come down this street!"

TEMPTATION—Yielding

"Ruth," moaned the long-suffering husband, "you promised you wouldn't buy a new dress. What made you do it?"

"Dear," replied the modern Eve, "the devil tempted me."

"Why didn't you say, 'Get thee behind me, Satan?'"

"I did," the little woman replied, "and then he whispered over my shoulder, 'My dear, it fits you just beautifully in the back!'"

TESTS

The star of a North Carolina team had to take a history test to be eligible for Saturday's game. The professor asked one simple question: "What is the capital of North Carolina?"

"Pikeville," was the reply.

"Well," said the professor, "if you had answered correctly, you would have had 100. Since Pikeville is only 15 miles from Raleigh, I'll give you 85 and pass you."

THE CHAMP

Ingrid Bergman recently asked a book clerk for an instruction manual on boxing. "We have a book," said the salesman, "by

Jas. J. Corbett who was world's heavyweight champion. He knocked out Jas. L. Sullivan, and never lost a fight in his life except when he was knocked out by Bob Fitzsimmons. Would you like to see the book?"

Miss Bergman hesitated and replied, "Have you a book by Bob Fitzsimmons?"

THEORY vs. PRACTICE

A theorist is a feller that don't work, but who has a lot of ideas that he thinks will.

❖ ❖

A professor was teaching a class of nurses. He had been explaining the use of the tourniquet in stopping the flow of blood.

"The pressure should be applied between the cut and the heart," he stated, illustrating the fact with great simplicity.

Then in order to see if the flow of words had penetrated the brain, he popped on them a trick question:

"What would you do in case a man had a brain hemorrhage?" Back came the answer from a literal-minded student:

"I'd put a tourniquet on his neck!"

❖ ❖

He was the four-year-old offspring of the beloved minister of a well-known and popular church—a minister renowned for his eloquent appeal to the practical as well as the spiritual side of life.

One day the young son and heir was having trouble with his gocart when a neighbor passing by was appealed to for help. The neighbor felt incompetent to advise and asked:

"Why don't you go to your father and find out what's the matter? He'll know."

"No use," said the little chap in disgust. "He won't know. He don't know anything except about God!"

THOROUGHNESS

When United Air Lines helped launch the 5th War Loan by scattering leaflets in the Loop from a Mainliner, it recalled to Tonky Martin an incident of his barnstorming days.

Martin and his partner contracted with a small town theatre

owner to toss handbills from their plane. The showman insisted on accompanying them. They were flying high above the town's Main street, Martin piloting, the partner pushing the leaflets out of a window when the theatre owner shouted excitedly: "Throw some out the other side!"

"But why?" asked the birdman.

"Why," the showman explained, "Naturally, I want the handbills on both sides of the street!"

THOUGHT

Most folks have presence of mind. The trouble is absence of thought.

❖   ❖

Minds are like parachutes—they only function when open.

❖   ❖

The world's best safety device is located an inch or two above the eyebrows.

❖   ❖

Men have from time to time proposed the axiom, "No work, no bread!" But no man has ever dared to threaten the calamity of "No thought, no talk!"

❖   ❖

The minister, visiting newcomers in the community, admired a bright-plumed bird that sat silently brooding in its cage.

"What a beautiful parrot! Does it talk?"

"Well, no," admitted the lady of the house, "it doesn't talk much, but," she added defensively, "it thinks a great deal."

❖   ❖

"How can I tell what I think," queried the debutante, "until I hear what I say?"

TIME

Tired and hungry after walking uncounted and unrewarded miles on a hunting trip in Louisiana last year, my companion and

I came to an old trapper's cabin. The owner was dozing in the shade that was slowly creeping across the porch floor. I called to ask what time it was.

He stirred, cocked one eye to the floor, and drawled, "Oh, about fo' planks till dinnertime."

❖   ❖

An engineer engaged on railroad construction in Central America explained to one of the natives living alongside the right-of-way the advantages the new road would bring to him. Wanting to illustrate his point, he asked the native, "How long does it take to carry your produce to market by muleback?"

"Three days, senor."

"Then," said the engineer, "you can understand the benefit that road will be to you. You will be able to take your produce to market and return home on the same day."

"Very good, senor," the native agreed courteously. "But, senor, what shall we do with the other two days?"

❖   ❖

Farmer Jones had a reputation for driving his hired men. And the reputation was fully deserved. About four o'clock one Monday morning he was seen, armed with a huge bell, which he rang vigorously as he called out to his hirelings at the top of his voice:

"Today's Monday, the next day's Tuesday, after that comes Wednesday. Half the week's gone, an' you slugabeds ain't up yet!"

❖   ❖

The lady pigeon sat in her nest impatiently waiting for her husband to come home. He was over two hours over-due, and the worm they were to have for dinner was getting cold. Finally he flew up to the tree to face the ire of his wife. "Where," she pouted, "have you been so late?"

"Well, I'll tell you, dear," answered the tardy one. "I was up in the Bronx this afternoon when I started home—and it was such a beautiful day—I thought I'd walk!"

❖   ❖

It was a hot August afternoon at one of our southern Army camps. A tough, seasoned sergeant had been drilling raw, awkward recruits until the men were ready to drop.

A captain, passing, paused for a moment to eye the spectacle with evident displeasure. An especially clumsy recruit had the ill luck, at that precise moment, to drop his rifle. The captain called the culprit out of line. "How long," he asked witheringly, "have you been in the Army?"

The recruit looked up, all the weariness and woe of the world writ upon his countenance as he stammered, "A-a-all day, sir."

TRADITION

This is a story about Russia in the days of the Czars. In the park of St. Petersburg's Winter Palace there was a beautiful lawn, on that lawn a bench, and next to that bench, two guards. Every three hours the guards were changed. No one knew why.

One day an ambitious young lieutenant was put in charge of the Palace Guard. He started wondering, and asking questions. In the end, he found a cobwebby little old man, the Palace historian.

"Yes," the old man said, "I remember. During the reign of Peter the Great, 200 years ago, the bench got a fresh coat of paint. The Czar was afraid that the ladies in waiting might get paint on their dresses. So he ordered one guard to watch the bench. The order was never rescinded. Then in 1908, all the guards of the Palace were doubled for fear of a revolution. So the bench has had two guards ever since."

TRAVEL

She insisted on taking innumerable frocks with her and they arrived at the station loaded with luggage.

"I wish," said the husband thoughtfully, "that we'd brought the piano."

"You needn't try to be sarcastic," came the frigid reply. "It's not a bit funny."

"I'm not trying to be funny," he explained, sadly. "I left the tickets on it."

❖   ❖

"A thing that still amazes me," says Erna Barschak, "is the desire people have to do as much as possible in as short a time as possible. I once talked with an American tourist in Switzerland who was admiring the grandeur of the Alps. 'How I wish I could stay here longer,' the tourist sighed.

" 'Why not?' I asked. 'You will find nothing more beautiful in Europe in the summertime.'

" 'Yes,' assented the lady, 'but you see we decided to make fourteen European countries on this trip. We've covered only twelve so far.' "

❖   ❖

A lady got on the Madison avenue bus in New York; took the only empty seat—next to a harmless-looking little drunk—and opened a map—a detailed map of Manchuria. The drunk studied the map for a time, too, and finally addressed the lady: "Are you sure," he asked, "you're on the right bus?"

❖   ❖

A wealthy Beacon Hill spinster announced she had never spent a night in a sleeping car. Someone expressed astonishment. "Why should I travel?" asked the Beacon Hiller with some asperity. "I've always been here!"

❖   ❖

A Viennese Jew entered the office of a travel bureau and said to one of the clerks, "I want a steamship ticket."

"Where to?" asked the clerk.

"Where to? Yes, where to?" repeated the Jew meditatively. "I wish I could answer this question. Let me look at your globe, if you don't mind."

Thereupon the Jew turned the globe around several times, studying carefully countries and continents. After a few minutes, he raised his eyes to the clerk and said, "Is this all?"

TRAVEL—Cost

As John Mason Brown, the popular lecturer, once put it: "In a hotel you are your own guest. You think you own the place when you are in it and know you do when you leave it."

TROUBLE

The pastor called on Aunt Mandy, and suggested that she ignore some of her troubles and spend more time counting her blessings.

"Not sure about dat, parson. I ain't seein' how de Lawd would keep sendin' me tribulations lest He spect me to tribulate."

TROUBLE—Blessings of

Thomas Sugrue has very well said that if man had not been troubled millions of years ago he would still be living in caves. If he is not troubled, he will soon be back in the caves.

TROUBLE—Borrowed

About an hour after the children had been sent to bed, dad heard Billy, the youngest, screaming at the top of his lungs.

Dad rushed upstairs and into the nursery.

"What's the matter, Billy?"

"Johnny scared me-e-e!"

"How?"

"He said a big bear was goin' to get me."

"That's nonsense. There are no bears within a hundred miles of this house. Go back to sleep like a good boy."

Dad returned to the living room, re-lit his pipe and settled down with his book. Almost immediately there was renewed yelling from the nursery.

This time dad took the stairs two at a time. It sounded serious.

"What's wrong now, Billy?"

"Ow-w-w-w! Johnny says that a hungry bear can run a hundred miles in five minutes."

TRUST

Aunt Lizzie had been converted during a winter month and the colored parson wanted to baptize her in the river, but through fear for her health the convert objected.

"Doan't ye trust in de Lawd?" asked the parson.

"Ah sure does, brudder," she asserted. "Ah trusts pintedly in de Lawd, but Ah ain't gwine to fool wid him."

TRUTH

It is possible for one to tell you all the facts and still not all the truth.

TRUTH—UNTRUTH

If tombstones told the truth, everybody would wish to be buried at sea.

✧　✧

A liar has been defined as one who has no partition between his imagination and his facts.

✧　✧

Four-fifths of the perjury in the world is expended on tombstones, women and competitors.

TRYING

Tommy's first school report, which was promising, read, "Trying." The second report raised the parents' hopes by simply stating, "Still trying." The next report, however, dashed all hopes to the ground. It read, "Still very trying."

TURNABOUT

Last summer a rancher living some miles out in the hills saw a car from the capital city drive up beside his place. The family scrambled out of the car and climbed over the rancher's fence for a picnic under his trees. In the evening, after the visitors had gone, the rancher spent a weary hour cleaning up the rubbish left on the ground. Tin cans, empty bottles and cartons, lunch paper, sandwich wrappers, etc., etc.

The next day a car drove up and stopped in front of a fine house in the city. The rancher got out and lugged a box up on the velvety lawn, where he dumped out its contents—an assorted lot of rubbish. The owner of the house dashed madly out, roundly abused the rancher, and ordered him to remove the stuff.

"Brother," replied the rancher calmly, "it's all yours—I'm just returning it. You forgot it at my place yesterday. Luckily I got your license number, or I might never have been able to locate you."

UNSELFISHNESS

Speaking of unselfishness, what form could go deeper than that expressed in the maiden's prayer: "O Lord, I ask nothing for myself, but will you please send dear mother a son-in-law!"

USEFULNESS

An elderly man, strolling about the London menagerie one Sunday afternoon reached the area where a camel was lolling about. He was puzzled. The camel just didn't make sense. He approached an attendant and asked for an explanation of the beast's hump.

"It's pretty useful, sir," he was told. "The old camel wouldn't be much good without it."

"Why not?"

"Well, now, you don't suppose people'd pay sixpence t' see 'em if 'e 'adn't got an 'ump?"

VALOR—Limited

There is a story of a 4th-rate prize fighter who after a few rounds was thoroughly beaten and ready to give up. His eager manager, standing at the ringside, urged him on: "Get back in there!" he ordered. "You got him goin'. You're winnin'!" Encouraged by this assurance the bruiser went back in. At the end of the 7th he emerged, blood-drenched and wobbly. He approached his manager and asked huskily, "I ain't winning now, am I, Jake?" Again assured, he went back for another round, only to have his opponent catapult him half way out of the ring. With a groggy glance out of one half-closed eye, he mumbled, "Am I still winnin'?" "Sure," said the manager. "Then," declared the pug, crawling out of the ring, "I quit winner!"

VALUES

Once upon a time (said Wm. Dean Howells, veteran author and editor) there was a horse trade between a farmer and a broker. After a long-drawn-out discussion of the horse's good points, the broker asked:

"What is the rock-bottom price you will take for the horse?"

"One thousand dollars," said the farmer.

"I'll give you $100," agreed the broker.

"Okay," said the farmer, "I'll take it. I won't let a little matter of $900 stand between me and a horse trade."

✧   ✧

The late Archbishop of Canterbury, Dr. Wm. Temple, used to drive home his points in workaday metaphors. Once he conjured up an ironmongery (hardware store) in which a prankster switched price tags. Lawnmowers were two for 5c, nails $25 each, a gallon of paint, a penny. All the values were wrong. "That," he concluded "is what has happened to our civilization, and we shall not come to order and peace until our price tags tally with God's."

VANITY

A matron of great beauty was calling one day on a friend, accompanied by her ten-year-old daughter, who promised to be as handsome as her mother.

They were shown into a room where the friend had been receiving a milliner and many hats were scattered about. During the conversation the ten-year-old amused herself by trying these on. She was particularly pleased by the effect of the last one. Turning to her mother, she said:

"Mother, I look just like you now, don't I?"

"Hush!" cautioned the mother, with uplifted finger. "Don't be vain, dear."

VARIETY

For three days the wind had been blowing hard in Zion National Park, Utah, location for a special movie sequence.

When it was rolling up the most dust and knocking down several big light reflectors, the producer turned to one of the natives who had stopped to see how motion pictures were made.

"Up here does it always blow this way?" he asked.

"Nope. Not always. Some days," the native said, pointing a lank finger eastward, "she blows that way."

VIEWPOINT

Every day a British Army officer would take his little boy to the park to admire the statue of "Chinese Gordon" astride his favorite camel. Finally, when the family was moving, the child asked to go tell Gordon good-bye. He stood with tears in his eyes saying a last fond farewell, while the father beamed with pride recognizing in his son a great admiration for his own hero. On the way to the station the small boy turned back to wave once more; then, with his face upturned to his father, he asked, "Daddy, what's the name of that man riding Gordon?"

❖　❖

Speaking to one of his friends at the club, a man said, "What's the matter with you Jim? You look as though you had lost your last friend." "You would, too, if you had been through what I've been through." "What happened?" "I got home last night and found that my wife had taken my car and run away with another man." "My God, man! Not your new car!"

❖　❖

To the Pessimist, O symbolizes zero. To the Optimist it is the beginning of Opportunity.

❖　❖

A traveler from the well-wooded East passing through a barren part of North Dakota got into conversation with a rancher. "Nice view from here," he said ingratiatingly, pointing to three trees in the distance which broke the monotony of flat prairie. They were the only trees in sight.

The rancher slowly swept the unobstructed horizon with a satisfied glance. Then he noticed the trees, and spat. "Yes," he pronounced. "Pretty nice, except where them darned trees cut off the view."

❖　❖

A copy of MacKinlay Kantor's *Long Remember* found its way into the hands of a sergeant on Guadalcanal. In the thick of battle, when Japs were throwing everything they had, he continued to read, huddled in his foxhole.

"Must be quite a story," an officer remarked.

"Yes, sir," sighed the sergeant, "they sure had a tough time of it back in those Civil War days."

❖   ❖

An old salt who has spent two terms in the Navy, and who is never quite happy anywhere except on the bounding main, has viewed the encroachment of the airplane with something less than wholehearted enthusiasm.

"Well, I s'pose it's all right," he agreed grudgingly, when he viewed a recent aerial demonstration with his mates. "I got to admit the airplane has its place, but what I say is what's the good o' havin' an ocean if you aim to fly over it?"

❖   ❖

The immediate past is always in disrepute. Grandmother's gowns are quaint. Great-grandmother's are simply too adorable. But Mother's dresses are just old-fashioned.

VISION—Lack

It is told that a group of citizens in Lancaster, Ohio, a little over a century ago, petitioned the school board for the use of the schoolhouse for a discussion of the new invention, the steam locomotive. The school board gave careful consideration to the petition and then gave its decision: "If God in His infinite wisdom had intended mankind to be hurtled through space at the outrageous speed of 15 miles an hour He would have said so in His Holy Scripture. Petition denied."

"WAIT-YOUR-TURN"

Back in the good old pre-bomb days, a village fire chief, busy with his only engine at a big blaze in the local factory, was called to the telephone to hear of a distressing coincidental conflagration two miles across the country.

His instant response:

"You'll just have to keep your fire going until we get finished over here."

WAR—AND PEACE

This younger generation of ours is plenty smart. Take the boy who had asked his father how wars started.

"Well," said Dad, "suppose America quarreled with England and—"

"But," interrupted the mother, "America must never quarrel with England."

"I know," said the father, "but I am only taking a hypothetical instance."

"You are misleading the child," protested the mother.

"No, I am not," shouted the father.

"Never mind, Dad," put in the boy, "I think I know how wars start."

WAR—Memories

A negro soldier, who had been wounded overseas, lay in the sick bay of a hospital ship entering New York harbor. A medical officer stopped by on a last-minute checkup to ask the soldier whether he had any personal belongings which he wished carried ashore. The colored boy shook his head.

"You don't mean to say that a soldier who saw as much action as you did has no souvenirs," exclaimed the officer.

"Captain," said the soldier, "I don't have no souvenirs—cause all I wants of this here war is jest a faint recollection!"

WARNING

The Quaker had heard a strange noise in the night, and waking, found a burglar ransacking the kitchen. He took his fowling piece and called from the landing of the kitchen stairs, in plain sight of the intruder: "Friend, I would do thee no harm for the world and all that is in it—but thee standest where I am about to shoot." The burglar fled.

WATER

A party of eastern autoists was passing through the western section of Kansas when one of the party, in need of water, stopped

a farmer along the road, who was hauling several barrels of water
on his wagon.

After negotiating with the farmer for the much needed water the
driver inquired, "Well, my friend, tell me how far do you have to
haul this water?"

"Oh, only 'bout ten miles," the farmer dryly answered.

"Land sake!" exclaimed the stranger. "Why don't you dig a
well?"

"What's the use?" drawled the farmer. "It's about as far one
way as 'tis the other."

"WHO'S CRAZY?"

A new patient at a sanitarium for the mildly deranged complained to the attending physician:

"What's the idea of sticking me in a room with that crazy guy?"

"Well, I'll tell you," said the Doctor placatingly, "It's the only
room we have available just now. Is your roommate really trouble-
some?"

"Why the guy's nuts! He keeps looking around and saying, 'No
lions, no tigers, no elephants'—and all the time the room's full of
'em!"

WILL POWER

A farmer, wrestling with a stubborn mule, was asked, "Man,
where's your will power?"

"Will power?" he puffed, wrestling with the balky critter. "You
just come here and get the feel of this animal's won't power!"

❖   ❖

Dr. Adam Clarke, the great commentator, was a slow worker,
and he could only produce his wealth of literary treasure by long
and patient toil. He therefore made it his custom to rise early
every morning. A young preacher anxious to emulate the distinguished doctor, asked him one day how he managed it. "Do
you pray about it?" he inquired. "No," said the doctor, who was
a great man of prayer, "I get up."

WISDOM

When you notice how much smarter you are today than you were ten years ago, don't stop there. Follow the same line of thinking until you partly realize how much dumber you are today than you will be ten years hence. That ought to hold you for awhile.

WOMEN

A woman is old when she stops patting herself on the back and starts patting herself under the chin.

❖ ❖

Two men who hadn't seen each other for fifteen years met and began reminiscing.

"Is your wife as pretty as she used to be?" asked one.

"Oh, yes," replied the other, "but it takes her quite a bit longer."

❖ ❖

Give a woman an inch and she gets the idea she is a ruler.

❖ ❖

Womankind is divided into two classes—the careless ones who lose their gloves, and the careful ones who lose only one glove.

WORK

There's the farmer who was asked what time he went to work in the morning.

"Son," he replied to the interrogator, "I don't go to work in the morning. I'm surrounded with it when I get up!"

❖ ❖

Any time you want to wipe out hard luck, just use hard work for an eraser.

WORKMANSHIP—Faulty

The foreman employed by a big contractor rushed into the office of the boss, wide-eyed and palpitating. "Boss," said he in an agitated voice, "one of them new houses of ours fell down in the night!"

"What's that?" exclaimed the boss, jumping right up and beginning to take notice. "What was the matter? How did it happen?"

"It was the fault of the workmen, boss," answered the foreman. "They made the mistake of taking down the scaffolding before they put on the wallpaper."

WORK—Shift

The city slicker visited the hills to see how the mountaineers lived. He came to a farm where a man reclined on the front porch, smoking a cob pipe while a woman worked in the garden.

"Isn't that hard work for your wife?" asked the city dweller.

"Yep," he said, "but we work in shifts, hereabouts."

"Oh, I see. When she gets tired, you take over."

"Nope," said the native. "When she gits tired out in the garden she shifts to the house chores."

WORK—Virtue of

A man who keeps his shoulder to the wheel, is rarely seen giving others trouble. He's like a mule in the respect that when he's pulling, he can't kick, and when he's kicking, he can't pull.

WORRY

A Chicago physician specializing in research on ulcers told recently that his laboratories had been obliged to abandon the use of dogs in their experiments. The fool critters just wouldn't worry—and worry is the thing that makes ulcers and keeps them active. You can inflict an ulcer upon a dog by artificial methods and he will sit down placidly and cure himself by refusing to be bothered about anything. It's just possible that there might be a lesson here for humans!

❖   ❖

If you must worry, always do your worrying in advance; otherwise you will miss most of the chances.

WORRY—Freedom from

A Chinese pauper couple regularly slept under a bridge spanning the Yangtse River. One night as they were about to retire, the wealthiest man in town—a banker—trudged across the bridge muttering to himself about his losses that day at the market place. Hearing him the pauper wife remarked: "Lucky are those of us without financial worries!"

And the husband, taking his cue rose to his feet, thumped his chest proudly and said: "Yes, and to whom do you owe your fortunate position?"

WORRY—Futility of

An old mammy in the Carolinas was asked the secret of her youth and well-being. Her answer: "When I works I works hard. When I rests I rests easy. When I worries I just go-o-es to sleep."

WRONG NUMBER

The phone rang recently in the press room at the White House. A reporter, who picked up the receiver, heard a Negro voice say, "Hello—this Doctah Brown?"

"No," answered the reporter, "this is the White House."

"O—oh!" There was an awed silence. And then: "Pahdon me, wrong numbah, Mistah President!"

YOUTH—Superficiality

A boy went to work in an engineer's shop and after three weeks announced his intention of quitting. Asked his reason, he replied:

"Well, the hours and wages are all right, but I just don't like the work, and I am sorry now that I learned the business."

*A Few Characteristic Examples of that Unique American
Institution Known as the*

SILLY BILLY

*The Silly-Billy is as American as apple pie or Yankee pot roast—
and considerably less satisfying. Indeed, the hallmark of a true
Silly-Billy is that it leaves the auditor in a frenzy of frustration.*

*The Silly-Billy is silly. It is fantastic, implausible, incomprehensible, and more often than not, completely pointless. Just
about the time a Silly-Billy begins to look as though it might possibly make sense, it ends on a note of abrupt futility.*

*The best counsel we can give is this: Don't ever try to understand a Silly-Billy. For that way lies madness. If you must take
them at all, take them as they are. And in homeopathic doses.*

*No one knows what started this Silly-Billy business. Or when.
It has been going on for a lot longer than even the longest-winded
public speaker you can recall. Often the Silly-Billy, handed down
through generations, possesses an enduring folk charm. But authentic new ones are bobbing up all the time.*

*Authorship of the Silly-Billy is rarely known. They just seem
to grow. With understandable restraint, the creator seeks no
credit. The present compiler admits that some few of the widely-copied specimens in this collection are of his brain brood. But on
advice of counsel he refuses specific identification.*

*The Silly-Billy is best related on those occasions when, as Antonio put it, "we purpose merriment." The company should be
small and select. (The Silly-Billy sounds pretty awful in an auditorium!) To tell a Silly-Billy really well you should probably be a
fit subject for psychiatric examination. And if those who listen
are similarly impaired, so much the better!*

At the height of the drive to obtain castoff apparel for destitute
Europeans, a small and emotionally distraught Jewish tradesman
made his way to one of the great warehouses where multiplied bales
of clothing awaited shipment.

His wife, explained the frantic man, had, in his absence, given
to the drive a certain suit, in the lining of which he had imprudently hidden his total savings of $218.00.

The director emitted a horse-size sigh, and called for a description of the apparel.

The color, it developed, was approximately that of red winter cabbage, and by way of further description, the unhappy tradesman added that there was a stripe, "as vide maybe lak a tepe line."

In a spirit of hopeless helpfulness, the director set his men to work. Bale upon bale they opened, sorted, cast aside. Finally, after a couple of hours, one searcher pulled out a suit that seemed to fit the description. Triumphantly, the director held it up for inspection. Slowly and deliberately the little Jew walked about the suit, examining the texture, poking a tentative finger into the lining. Then sadly he shook his head.

"The color," he said, "is being lak mine. The stripe is also hokay. But the suit mine wife is geeving avay is heving no pants!"

❖ ❖

The hour was late, the night bitter cold. A numb and weary Jewish traveling man stumbled into the lobby of a small residential hotel in a mid-western city, made his way to the desk and asked for accommodations. The clerk shook his head regretfully. There was no room in the inn.

But the traveler was desperate. "Surely," he insisted, "you must be heving something . . . a pool table, maybe, vere I can lie down for a few hours. I am not heving it the straingth to vace dat storm again. And I am gedding up to mek a tra-a-in by nod later as vive o'clock anyvay."

"Well," said the clerk helpfully, "there's one thing I can do. We have a permanent guest here—fellow by the name of Judkins—who has two beds in his room. Once in awhile he lets us rent that other bed in an emergency."

"That is being hokay," said the traveling man, "an' you should call me ad vive o'clock—mek no mistake—ef you will please be so kindly."

So, in the forlorn darkness of five A.M., the Jewish traveler answered the phone, stumbled sleepily into his apparel, and made his way down to the desk.

"Ah, good morning Mr. Judkins," said the clerk. "You're a bit early this morning, eh?"

"Judkins?" mused the wayfarer to himself. "The clerk is being nod yet avake. So long he t'inks I am maybe a rag'lar guest, I em leaving do key an' nod mendioning a night's ludgings vat I am owing."

At the door, the little Jew whistled for a cab. "Right here, Mr. Judkins," said an alert cabbie, coming up on the double-quick. "To the railway station, sir?"

"Vell, anyvay," said the puzzled pilgrim, settling himself comfortably, "you are heving t' say dis fal_ow Judkins is a men vat gedts service!"

Arriving at the station, a red cap promptly claimed the baggage, again calling the name of Judkins, while our bewildered traveler made his way toward a ticket window. Suddenly, halfway there, he caught a quick reflection of himself in a slot-machine mirror. Startled, he paused for a long, lingering inspection, then suddenly emitted a shriek of wild dismay:

"Dis is being tarrible," he cried. "I *am* dat fallow, Judkins! The hutel is vaking a wrong man!"

❖ ❖

It was Springtime. Springtime in the South. The flowers were putting forth their gayest blossoms. The bees were buzzing. And in yonder fragrant honeysuckle vine a little lady humming bird hummed happily. For Love had come into her life. A he humming bird—big, and strong, and handsome—had made it clear that their life henceforth was to be as one. Even now, the little lady humming bird was planning her nest.

Ah, what happiness they shared together in those ecstatic days of early Spring! What joy it was to fashion their snug little nest, straw by straw. They chose the site with care—a big magnolia tree, near the edge of a clearing. Then, proudly, the little lady humming bird deposited a single egg—a beautiful, beautiful egg. How faithfully through the weeks she sat upon that solitary egg, while the he humming bird brought refreshing drops of nectar to the nest.

At long last, the miracle unfolded. There came a plaintive pecking on that solitary egg—that beautiful, beautiful egg. And out scrambled the wettest, ugliest, scrawniest baby bird that ever you beheld. Yes, and the *hungriest,* too.

But the parents were proud, as parents ever are. Away they foraged, farther and farther from the little nest. For it takes a heap of nectar to satisfy a baby hummer. And one afternoon they found themselves miles, and miles, and miles from home. Suddenly the he humming bird cocked an eye, looked up and observed, "Ah, the hour is late. We must be heading for the nest."

"But it isn't late at all," insisted the lady humming bird, "and we haven't half enough nectar for little Nectarine. See, it is that cloud—that big, black cloud—that gives the look of night."

And, sure enough, it *was* the cloud that had blotted out the sun. Even as they looked, it came closer and closer to them, gathering up everything in its path. And they knew then that this was no ordinary cloud but a great destructive cyclone. Then, suddenly, the cloud swerved, headed eastward with renewed force. The humming birds looked at each other and grew suddenly pale. For it was following the path from whence they had come, the trail that led straight to their nest, and to the tiny hummer. Without a word, they turned and began to fly, as they had never flown before. But the cyclone was far ahead, and they could not outpace it.

On and on they flew. Tongues were hanging out of their long, graceful beaks. Drops of perspiration were blinding their bright little eyes. But there was no time to pause. All that mattered now was to reach the nest, and the little hummer!

Finally they saw it, there in the distance—the big magnolia tree. It still stood! And—wonder of wonders!—the nest was there, too, as staunch and sturdy as ever. But what of the baby hummer— had he been harmed? In a sudden frenzied flight, the little lady humming bird, far outdistancing her mate, headed straight for the magnolia tree, and the trim little nest. Tremblingly, she balanced herself on a branch—looked down. There nestled the baby hummer, snug and secure. He lifted his head, opened his baby beak— and what do you suppose he said:

"MAMA!"

❖   ❖

A wee little mousie was scampering about in the basement of a tavern, gleaning an occasional delectable drop of whiskey that oozed from the spigots of barrels stored there.

And then—quite unexpectedly, you may be sure—this wee little mousie made a Great Discovery. He came upon a barrel whose head had been partially broken, exposing a vast sea of this wonderful beverage. The mousie soon found that by standing on the broken edge of the barrel head, and taking a long, long stretch, he could just reach the liquid contents, and thus get himself a sizable swig. This he proceeded to do. Then, bracing carefully, he took a second swig. And, after that, a—

Well, no, that isn't precisely accurate. He really didn't get that third swig. For, somehow, he reached a little *too* far, lost his balance, and tumbled head-first into the barrel of whiskey. There he swam around for a long, long time, growing more and more giddy as he swallowed vast quantities of the once-cherished liquid refreshment. And all the time, you may be sure, he was squeaking at the top of his voice for help.

But, of course, there was no one to hear. No one, that is, until at long last a young Tom Cat came by on a stealthy search for— well, whatever do you suppose?

The cat heard the mouse's wail, now growing very faint, indeed. Springing nimbly to the top of the barrel, he looked in and saw the miserable mouse swimming around very, very slowly.

"Well, well, little mousie," he said, "and whatever *are* you doing there?"

"I—I fell in," said the wee little mousie, "and now I can't get out again. Oh, Mr. Cat, if only you'll help me out, you can do anything with me you want—anything at all! But I d-don't want to drown!"

So the cat stuck in a paw, and pulled out a very moist mousie. "Aha!" he said, licking his whiskers, "you're just about the size I had in mind. I think I'll just eat you here and now!"

"Oh, Mr. Cat, I wouldn't do *that!*" exclaimed the horrified mousie. "I'm all soaked with whiskey, and you know what alcohol does to your sinus! Besides," squeaked the mousie hopefully, "I have a heavy date tonight. Please, ple-e-ase let me keep that date, then you can come around tomorrow morning—you know where I live. I'll be all dried out, and I'll make you a won-n-derful breakfast!"

"We-e-ll," said the Tom Cat, thinking it over, "I guess maybe you're right. Till tomorrow morning, then, run along and have fun. I'll be seeing you at six!"

"Okay," squeaked the wee little mousie, "and be sure you're prompt." Then he scampered away.

Right on the stroke of six, the cat was standing in front of the mouse's hole. But the little mousie was nowhere in sight. So the cat lifted his paw and rapped sharply on the door. There was no answer. So he rapped again. And then again. Finally a sleepy, squeaky voice from away inside asked, "Who's at my door at this unearthly hour?"

"It is I," said the cat. For he was a pedigreed Persian cat and very precise in his use of grammar.

"And who are you?" squeaked the voice.

"I am Mr. Cat," said the cat, who was now quite annoyed, "Mr. Thomas Cat. I have come for my breakfast."

"Well," said the wee little mousie, "I'm sorry, but I'm not in the restaurant business, and besides I have an awful hangover. Why don't you go talk to the cook?"

"But you don't understand," said the cat. "I saved your life yesterday when you were swimming around in that barrel of whiskey. Don't you remember?"

"Oh, yes," said the mousie, "yes, indeed, Mr. Cat, and I am very grateful to you."

"Then come on out," said the cat sternly, "and let me eat you up. That's what you promised, you know."

"I—what?" squeaked the mouse.

"You promised to let me eat you for breakfast," said Tom Cat, now terribly annoyed, "and I can tell you I'm getting pretty tired of waiting. Get a move on you now!"

"Well, all I can say," replied the wee little mousie, hiccuping as politely as possible, "all I can say is that if I told you *that*, I must have been drunk!"

❖   ❖

An impoverished cobbler had an incredibly ugly and stupid daughter. He had long abandoned hope of getting her off his hands, when one day the local matchmaker dropped this bombshell: "I have a match for your daughter."..."It can't be," the cobbler exclaimed. "Who is the man?"..."Count Petrovsky," calmly announced the matchmaker.

The father was stunned. Count Petrovsky, the richest, most aristocratic, the most handsome—no, he couldn't permit it. "My daughter would only be unhappy," he said. "She wouldn't know how to act in his company. The Count is out of her class."

But the matchmaker was not to be easily dissuaded. "Let us go," he suggested," and lay the case before the Mayor. He has had experience in such matters. Surely, he will counsel wisely."

But the Mayor, too, was perplexed. "In all my experience," he confessed, "I have not had another case such as this. Here are involved not only the question of social caste, but spiritual factors, as well. Your daughter, Sir, is a pious and devoted ascetic. Count Petrovsky, though a member of the Church, is scarcely celebrated for his reverence. Let us go, therefore, and present this matter to the Priest. By his decision we shall be guided."

And it was even so. The little band went forth to seek the man of God. The Priest listened carefully, then furrowed his brow in deep perplexity. "Truly," he said at long last, "I know not what to say. Let me pray and meditate upon the matter. Come again tomorrow and you shall have my decision."

Promptly at the appointed hour they met at the Priest's domain—the cobbler, the Mayor, and of course the matchmaker. The Priest greeted them with a fond paternal smile. "I have thought well into the night," he said, "and my decision is ready. Though logic points to many pitfalls, none the less, I have resolved that true love must not be thwarted. It is my conclusion that the wealthy and illustrious Count and the humble cobbler's daughter may marry. When they come before me I shall be happy to give them my blessing."

At this point the cobbler looked up to see that the matchmaker had already snatched his hat and was making a hasty departure. The cobbler dashed after him, grabbed him by the sleeve, and asked: "Tell me, where are you going in this unseemly haste?"

"Don't stop me," said the matchmaker breathlessly. "Now, all I have to do is sell the idea to Count Petrovsky!"

❖   ❖

Aristides McSwiggle ambled slowly down Cedar Street, his mind occupied with a Great Problem. The time was 4:37. If he should call now upon his beloved Desdemona could he wangle an invitation to supper? And could he be reasonably assured of a generous portion of that incomparable strawberry shortcake? Or, suppose again that he should delay his call for another half-hour. That would leave fewer awkward moments to be filled with conversation. And they could hardly avoid asking him to eat . . . but, well, would that be a little too obvious?

Engaged in this momentous mental struggle, Aristides scarcely noticed the long, black foreign limousine that turned in from the main highway and sped on down Cedar Street. The car had gone perhaps half a block before he saw Her there, sitting alone in the luxurious splendor of that back seat. She was slim, radiant, altogether lovely, with hair the color of shocked corn.

Aristides was a little shocked, too. For at that moment the Vision smiled, threw him a kiss and, stretching a daintily-gloved arm out of the car window, she dropped a note—and was gone.

Our hero did not hasten his pace. He was not a man to be deeply moved by romantic interludes. But when, in due course, he came up to the note, lying there in the street, idle curiosity moved him to reach down and pick it up. Ah, fateful gesture that was to change the course of a promising young life!

The note was in an envelope, fastened securely with an embossed seal. Even through the heavy covering Aristides could detect the entrancing odor of what he rightly took to be costly foreign perfume. Taking a knife from his pocket, he ripped the envelope, removed the sheet of embossed stationery. It was covered with writing, in a bold, intriguing feminine hand. But that was about as far as young McSwiggle could go. He saw the words clearly enough, but could make no meaning of them. Some of the symbols seemed a little like Greek. And then, again, they had the look of Latin.

For a few moments Aristides stood with furrowed brow, pondering the weird script. Then he put the note in his pocket. Well, at any rate, he reflected, his Great Problem was now solved. He would go on to Desdemona's. Now, they would practically have to ask him to supper. . . . Then he remembered. Desdemona was rather good at languages. He would show her the note, get her to tell him the meaning.

It was much later in the evening when a very full and deeply contented Aristides again bethought himself of the note. He told Desdemona of the adventure, reached into his pocket and brought out the missive. She took it from him in eager expectancy, opened the sheet and began to read. She read it once, and then again—slowly, deliberately, as the blood drained slowly from her rosy cheeks.

When at last she had completed the reading, a wan, ethereal Desdemona refolded the sheet with exaggerated care, placed it in the envelope, quietly stripped from her finger a half-carat diamond solitaire, placed it atop the envelope and with a stifled, heart-breaking sob ran from the room.

Aristides left. After all, he had had his double-portion of strawberry shortcake and there seemed no particular point in lingering longer. But the next morning, after a deep and dreamless sleep, he was reminded of his romantic episode when he saw the envelope lying where he had carelessly tossed it atop the dresser. Now he was beginning to be just a little curious. Again he tried to decipher the strange words. What was in the blamed note, anyway? It wasn't like Desdemona to act so flighty.

But a second attempt brought him no nearer a satisfactory solution. So once more he returned the note to his pocket. . . . At Centerdale high, where he was now a senior, there was a language prof who would know what it was all about.

It was midafternoon before the note came again into McSwiggle's thoughts. He went to hunt the professor and found him busily engaged in grading papers. A bit stumblingly he told his story and passed over the scented script. The old prof smiled amiably. Ah, these youngsters and their petty affairs! For a time the learned man read in silence. Aristides watched fascinated, as a look of terror and incredulity spread over the once-kindly countenance.

"McSwiggle," the professor thundered, and there was no mistaking the portent of that voice, "I am astounded. I can scarcely credit the evidence of my own eyes. I can only say, sir, that your fiancee's actions were altogether fitting and proper. She took the only course open to her . . ."

"But, professor, I—er—ah, uh—" Aristides was floundering miserably.

"Go!" barked the professor sternly. "Go, at once—from this room—from this school. If you delay for a moment I shall be forced, much as I shrink from doing so, to lay this matter before our Principal, and I shudder to think of the consequences. Here—take this—this miserable thing with you." He thrust the note into the young man's shaking hands. "Begone! And remember, you must never, under any circumstances, darken our portals again. Go, now, and try, as humbly as you may, to atone in some measure for this incredible and inexcusable incident!"

With no clear notion of where he was going or what he was to do, poor Aristides McSwiggle turned toward that section of Cedar

Street, where the fateful note had come so romantically and so disastrously into his possession. Presently he recalled that there was, not far away, a little shop presided over by an old Jewish watchmaker, a kindly man well versed in languages of the Old World. Aristides had spent many pleasant hours with the old man. Surely here was one who would unravel the growing mystery.

The watchmaker clucked commiseratingly. "Such a nondsense!" he said, "You should geeve me the note, Aristide-e-s. I vill do for you vat I can." Confidently our troubled adventurer handed over the now badly-rumpled envelope—and waited in tense silence.

He waited for what seemed a very long time while the watchmaker adjusted his glasses, read and re-read the fateful words. Before his uncomprehending eyes, Aristides saw his mentor age a decade in a space of seconds. In the eyes of the old, old man was the sadness of centuries, as he carefully folded the sheet, placed it in the envelope, and silently returned it to the doomed lad.

Questions rushed at flood pace to the lips of young McSwiggle. Vainly he pleaded, begged, cajoled. The watchmaker could only look blankly into space.

"There is nuddings I can say, Aristide-e-s," he mumbled abjectly. "There is nuddings I can do. Id is best you go now, and you plize, I am vishing you nod to come back."

It was weeks later that a motorist on the Eastern seaboard picked up a hitch-hiker who seemed to carry on his dejected shoulders the woes of all the world. As they rode along together through a peaceful valley, the motorist's kindly questioning finally brought from reluctant lips a strange, fantastic story. A story so incredible that it seemed sheer madness to harken seriously to a single syllable.

But the motorist was a deeply understanding man. And some quality of earnestness in the lad's trembling voice appealed to him. "How fortunate," he said at length, "that I came upon you in this way. For I have an old aunt who lives scarcely ten miles from here. Her mind is a store-house of strange lore. She will know the answer to your fateful adventure. And because she can refuse me nothing, I know that she will tell us the truth, and relieve your troubled mind. Come, we shall go together and see her."

And so they went, the motorist and the strange young hitch-hiker, now aged and broken by the strain of an uncomprehended sin. In the end, it was the motorist who did most of the talking. The hitch-hiker could manage little more than an affirmative nod.

"I must know!" he babbled, again and again. "I—*must*—know!"

"Very well," said the little old lady, when she had heard them through, "I will help you, if I can."

"You will tell me the truth—no matter how terrible it may be? You—you promise to do that?"

"Yes," said the motorist's aunt. "Yes—I promise. Come, give me the script."

With a gesture of indescribable relief, Aristides McSwiggle reached into an inner pocket—

—and found that he had lost the blamed note!

❖ ❖

A Scotsman, who was in every cents a Scotsman—if you know what we mean—was busily engaged in measuring feed for his horse. A wayfarer paused to observe the process.

To a quart of oats, the Scotsman carefully added a quart of sawdust; then, another measure of oats, another measure of sawdust.

"What in the world are you doing?" the observer asked. "What's the idea of mixing sawdust with oats?"

"Aye, mon," said the Scot, looking up, "an' hae ye no seen? 'Tis a strategy tha' saves many a muckle. I mix the sa'dust wi' the oats measure for measure—my hoorse being blind in one eye!"

❖ ❖

The Mighty Lion was on a rip-roaring rampage. Through the forest he slashed and thundered, challenging any and every animal to come and do battle with him. But there were no takers. The frightened animals ran in fear of their lives. Even the elephant prudently tucked in his trunk and set out for regions remote.

Finally the Lion came to the lair of the Little Mouse. There he gave forth a roar that shook the earth. "Come out!" he challenged, "Come out and do battle with the King of Beasts!" From far inside the lair came a faint squeak:

"Who, me?" said the Little Mouse, "why I—I've been sick!"

❖ ❖

The screwball entered a drug store. "Do you handle pills that contain Vitamins A, B, C, D and G?" he inquired.

"Yes, sir," replied the druggist.

"And," persisted the nut, "are they guaranteed to give you pep and energy? Are they supposed to make a man of you, and supply you with verve and bounce and extra dash?"

"Oh, yes," assented the druggist.

The screwball sighed. "Gosh," he murmured wistfully, "how I wish I needed them!"

❖   ❖

A department store elevator operator blinked and wondered who had spiked his glass of beer at lunch, but a second look confirmed the impossible. Walking up to his elevator was a horse, led by a man.

Recovering, the operator barked, "You can't bring that horse in here—get out before I call a cop."

"Oh, please," begged the man. "I've just got to take him up in the elevator."

"Oh, you've got to take him up in the elevator—would it be asking too much to know why?"

"Because," replied the man, "he always gets sick if I take him on the escalator."

❖   ❖

A motorist on a lonely road passed a car stuck in a ditch. On second thought, he stopped, went back to help. He found the driver using some string to harness a pair of squirrels to the front bumper.

"You aren't trying to pull that big car out with those squirrels, are you?" asked the aghast spectator.

"Why not?" the motorist responded irritably. "I've got a whip."

❖   ❖

A young man was slightly under the influence of liquor, and was mounting the curb when he tripped and fell. A policeman was standing over him as he struggled to his feet.

"Did you see me fall?"

"Yes, I was standing right here. I saw you."

"Did you see me get up?"

"Yes, I saw you get up."

"Then what is my name?"

"How should I know your name? I never saw you before."

"Then how did you know that it was me that fell?"

❖ ❖

Working his way upstream without any luck, a fisherman came across an old negro stretched on the bank in such a position that he could keep an eye on three cane poles.

"Been fishing around here long, uncle?" he asked the darky.

The negro gave the question due thought and finally nodded. "Ah guess I'se been fishin' heah always."

"I am a newcomer myself and"—he looked at his own expensive rod and reel in disgust—"I could use some good advice."

"De bes' way is to get yourself sum cane poles like I'se got. Don' git dem too long or dey hangs up in de limbs overhead when you jerk."

"Cane poles about as long as yours, eh? And your lines?"

"Dey is jus' ole cotton lines. Git w'ite ones an' let de mud color dem like de watah. Dey's got to be strong, or dey bust w'en de hook grab a root an' you try to pull."

"Strong cotton lines, eh? What size hooks?"

"Ah uster use de big size, but de big size is bad. Git de little size hooks, so dey don' tangle up in de underbrush."

"Little hooks, eh? And sinkers?"

"Bout six tenpenny nails on ev'ry line does de trick. De current's pretty swif' an' de line got to go to de bottom—dat's de bes'."

"And bait?"

"It ain't reportant, suh. Evah since Ah kin remember dey's been a dye works up f'om heah 'bout fo' mile dat kill out all de fish."

❖ ❖

Colonel Smith of Kentucky was the guest of Congressman Hard-Boiled Simmons in Washington, and was returning to his hotel in Washington late one night, when he lost his way. While browsing about aimlessly, he encountered a policeman.

" 'Scuse me, my frien'," said the Colonel, "but can you tell me which izzee opposite side o' ze street?"

"Why," explained the policeman, "it's over there—the other side."

"Zat's what I thought," confessed the Colonel, "but while I was walkin' over there a few minutes 'go, I asked a man an' he told me zis wazzee opp'site side!"

❖ ❖

An Englishman and an American soldier were motoring along an English road. At intervals the Englishman, who was driving, would stop and dust the roadside with white powder which he carried in a large can in the car.

Finally the GI could restrain his curiosity no further, and asked what it was all about. "Oh, this," said the Englishman casually, "is lion powder."

"Lion powder!" exploded the GI, "But you haven't any lions in England!"

"No," said the Englishman, lowering his voice to a confidential whisper, "and a good thing it is too, because this powder's no damned good."

❖ ❖

A dimwit bought one of those mail order houses that come in sections, and put it up himself.

"Howyuh doin'?" a friend asked shortly thereafter.

"Aw," mourned the moron. "I got troubles. Come on out and I'll show you."

"Well, for gosh sakes, Bill," exclaimed the friend, when he looked the place over, "you've put it together upside down."

"Darned if I ain't," replied the moron. "You know— bet that's why I keep falling off the porch."

❖ ❖

A psychiatrist, consultant on the staff of a large asylum, visited an inmate in solitary confinement and found the loon wearing nothing at all—except a top hat.

"How come no clothes?" asked the psychiatrist.

"Well, I'm warm enough; and then, too, nobody ever comes to see me here in solitary, so why bother to dress?"

"That seems reasonable," the psychiatrist conceded, "it's even sane! Only, why are you wearing the hat?"

"Oh," said the nut, "you never can tell. Somebody might come!"

❖ ❖

Two nitwits found a flashlight. After fiddling with it for several

minutes, one found the switch. First, he directed the ray of light at
the floor, then turned it toward the ceiling. His companion stared
thoughtfully, then challenged: "Betcha you can't climb up that
beam."

"Nothin' doin'," replied the other after deep meditation.
"About the time I was halfway up, you'd turn it off."

❖   ❖

An inmate in a mental institution was troubled by a cat in his
tummy. The feline, he told asylum attendants, tore around inside
and clawed him something fierce. One day the poor fellow got a
real pain—from a bad appendix. An operation was necessary, and
the surgeon figured that maybe this was his chance to cure the patient of his delusion. He sent out for a cat—a black one—and
when the patient came out of the ether the doctor held up the
animal and said, "You're all right now. Look what we got!"

The patient took one look, grabbed his tummy and howled:
"You got the wrong cat! The one that's been bothering me was a
gray one!"

❖   ❖

"Son, you air like Hazy Austin," grandfather said. "Hazy got
drunk from a jug while driving his hosses and buckboard out of
Telluride one night. He fell asleep in the wagon. When he woke
in the morning, his hosses had been cut loose and wandered off.
He looked around, then said: "If I'm Hazy Austin, I've lost two
hosses. If I'm not Hazy Austin, I've found a wagon.""

❖   ❖

A gentleman of our acquaintance went into a restaurant and
gave his order, asking for brown bread with his meal. The waitress
brought white. The third day this experience was repeated, and
thereafter for a solid week. It became a sort of game with our
friend. But finally he bethought himself of a sure-fire strategy.

"This restaurant," reasoned the patient and somewhat frus-
trated patron, "appears to go by opposites." So, having given his
order on the eighth day, he added, "And bring me some white
bread."

"But," said the waitress, "aren't you the gentleman who always has brown?"

✧   ✧

A guard from the lunatic asylum rushed up to a farmer on the road and said: "I'm looking for an escaped lunatic. Did he pass this way?"

The farmer puffed thoughtfully on his corncob pipe and asked: "What did he look like?"

"He's short," said the guard, "and he is very thin and weighs about 350 pounds."

The farmer looked at him in amazement.

"How can a man be short and thin and still weigh 350 pounds?"

"Don't act so surprised," replied the guard angrily, "I told you he was crazy."

✧   ✧

Mama Skunk was worried because she could never keep track of her two children. They were named In and Out, and whenever In was in, Out was out, and if Out was in, In was out. One day she called Out to her and told him to go out and bring In in. So Out went out and in no time at all he brought In in.

"Wonderful!" said Mama Skunk. "How, in all this great forest, could you find In in so short a time?"

"It was easy," said Out. "In stinct."

✧   ✧

Sir Lancelot was lost one dark night in a deep woods. He wandered about helplessly and after some hours encountered a handsome St. Bernard dog. The dog attached himself to Sir Lancelot, and they went on together for some time. Then the knight, exhausted, sat on the back of the magnificent animal. It dutifully took him straightway to a tavern. Sir Lancelot knocked at the door. "Could you give me bed and board?" he inquired of the proprietor. The tavern keeper peered out into the darkness. "Who am I to turn out a knight on a dog like this?" he answered.

An Exposition of that Universal Phenomenon—the Concoction of

TALL TALES

In a great museum of the Old World there is a remnant of pre-historic art, picturing a primitive man, spear in hand, exulting over the prostrate form of an enormously exaggerated beast.

There, mutely eloquent, stands the oldest Tall Tale of which we have record. The newest is being told somewhere in the world for the first febrile time as we draw this present breath.

The telling of prodigious stories is something more than an art. It is an impelling necessity. No people is so backward as to lack a folk lore; none so advanced as to dare dismiss the teller of tales.

The Tall Tale is man's psychiatric weapon against his fates; his mark of rebellion to the gods who set their curbs upon physical forces and leave imagination unfettered. So long as mind out-reaches muscle and vision journeys beyond the bounded body, just so long shall we nurture the Saga of the Super.

Yet in the end are the gods triumphant. For the wildest flights of man serve but to chart our distance from Olmpian heights.

Lion-hunters have strange adventures. This is the tale one tells:

"Unarmed as I was, I met a magnificent lion face to face. He lashed his sides with his tail, gave a loud roar, and jumped. But he missed me—his leap was too high—and he slunk off into the jungle.

"Next morning we started out to track the monster down. We found him within an hour. He had cleared a space under some trees and was practicing low jumps."

❖   ❖

"First I pour hair tonic in the stream," related Mr. Cross, "a technique developed in the land of Unadella, where fish grew beards after a native accidentally spilled hair tonic in their habitat.

"The only remaining step is to put up a barber pole and the

Police Gazette on the bank and shout, 'Next!' The fish jump out
of the water to get a shave."

✧ ✧

On a hunting trip in North Dakota in the year of the big bliz-
zard, my horse fell and broke his leg. I had to shoot him. I knew
I would freeze if I didn't do something quick. I cut the horse's
stomach open, removed the entrails, crawled inside and fell
asleep.

Next morning, I found the horse's stomach was frozen shut; I
couldn't pry my way out. I heard a pack of wolves howling and
knew they had scented the horse.

The wolves pounced on the carcass, growling and tearing away
the flesh. A thought struck me. I reached out and grabbed two
wolves by the tails. They let out frightened screams and started to
run, pulling me and the horse over slippery ground.

By pulling first one wolf's tail a little harder, than the other, I
could guide them. I headed the wolves for home. When pa saw
them coming toward the house, he shot them both.

✧ ✧

Bill Howie began to get fidgety as the yarns spun by his cronies
about the long shots they'd made grew in size. Finally he decided
it was time to cut in.

"Now, boys," Howie said, "those triflin' 300 and 400 yard shots
don't amount to nothin'. Take one time I was goin' along a mountain trail when these here telescope eyes of mine spots a buck. I
banged away, a mite hasty, and my first shot only clipped off a
branch over the critter's head. Quick-like, I rammed a new charge
down the bar'l, then some wadding, and a couple of ounces of salt.
I shoved a bullet in on top of that. When I let go with that second
shot the buck dropped in his tracks."

Bill's cronies thought that over a minute, then one of them
asked, "What in tarnation was the idea of puttin' salt in your
gun?"

"Shucks," Bill drawled, "that deer was so fur off I had to do
somethin' to keep the meat from spoilin' till I could git thar!"

✧ ✧

I was lying in bed one night when a huge mosquito bit me on

the arm. I pulled my blanket over me. But the same mosquito returned and bit me again, right through the blanket.

"That's going too far," I said, and covered myself with two blankets. The mosquito bit through both of them. He also bit through a third. When I put a fourth blanket on, that stopped him. But not completely.

I heard a commotion, put on the light and looked up. There was that damned mosquito on a rafter. He was working away furiously with a pipe wrench—changing bills.

❖   ❖

Some friends of mine were motoring in New Jersey and ran out of gas late in the evening. They put up at a primitive small-town hotel for the night. There were no electric lights; only candles. The bedroom proved to be so infested with Jersey mosquitoes that sleep was impossible. One of the boys suggested a way to get rid of the pests. As they were squatted all over the ceiling, it would be a simple matter to light the candles and burn them up. So they lit candles, stood on a table and proceeded to put the plan into action. It worked fairly well until one outsize specimen, feeling the heat, turned around and blew out the candle!

❖   ❖

Tigers had been ravaging a village, and the terror-stricken natives sent for the nearest white man to assist them.

This man was a crack shot, and had never been known to miss. His method was to tie a goat to the foot of a tree at dusk, climb the tree, and, when the tiger came for the goat, fire at the flash of their eyes. In the morning they would be found dead, shot straight between the eyes.

He followed his usual procedure the first night, but although he fired several shots, when the day dawned the goat was gone and there were no dead tigers.

This happened on two succeeding nights. Perturbed, he took a huge torch with him on the fourth night, and instead of firing at the flashing eyes, switched on his torch and saw, to his amazement, six tigers advancing in pairs, each with one eye closed.

❖   ❖

Aboard our ship we had an old tomcat whose leg was broken in an accident during a storm at sea.

The pharmacist's mate amputated the injured member, whit-

tled out a wooden leg for Tom. The poor animal was very unhappy. We could hear him clumping about top-side all night and
most of the day. It seemed that his career was over and that he
would have to live on our charity for the rest of his life.

But we were wrong.

One night we heard a terrific racket on deck. We rushed up with
flashlights to investigate.

There was Tom, holding a rat down with his good front leg—
and beating him to death with the wooden one!

❖   ❖

On a holiday excursion, the avid fisherman was finally forced to
give up and go home. Instead of baiting fish, he, himself, was bait
for the mosquitoes.

On his discouraged return, he reported: "During the first night
out I overheard two of the mosquitoes talking. They had just
killed a steer. The first mosquito said: 'Shall we eat it here or take
it home?' And the other replied: 'We better eat it here. If we take
it home the big fellows will take it away from us.'"

❖   ❖

Zeke Baskin's favorite story for the city slicker who visited his
Arkansas farm concerned the deadly cleverness of his old razor-
back hog, Horace.

Horace, he said, simply couldn't be kept within the bounds of
the hog enclosure. First Horace found a way to break through the
fence. When the fence was reinforced, Horace rooted a hole under
it. Then Zeke countered by sinking the foundations of the fence
so deep into the earth that the hog couldn't get under it.

"Guess you had him then?" the visitor would remark.

"No," Zeke would reply, with a doleful shake of his head, "that
didn't hold him either. That hog had just one more trick than I
did, and when he pulled it I plumb gave up in disgust. Horace
rolled his tail around in the mud until he had accumulated a large
mud ball. He let this ball dry in the sun until it was hard and
heavy. Then like one of them athletes making a hammer throw,
Horace swung that ball on the end of his tail around and around.
Stranger, he swung it so fast that finally the ball flew out into
space, over the fence, and carried Horace along with it."

❖   ❖

This is the season of weather stories. Which brings to mind the mighty winds which range the great open spaces of Eastern Oklahoma. Out there the wind blows so hard that the boys often use it to ride to town on. They stand out in the road and hold up their big hats like sails, and the next thing they know the breeze has set them down in front of the courthouse. Sometimes it turns wells inside out and spills water over seventeen counties.

One day a visitor noticed a log-chain hanging from a limb near a lonely cabin. He asked the settler what purpose it served.

"Well, stranger," the man replied, "when I wake up in the morning I peek through a crack in the cabin and take a look at that there chain. If it's a-hangin' down, everything is all right. But if the chain is a-stickin' straight out from that there limb, I figger it's too windy for me to work."

❖   ❖

A group of returned Australian service men were telling snake stories when "Shooftie," just back from the East Indies, spoke up:

"Those are only glow worms you blokes are talking about. You oughta been on Morotai.

"I jumped out of bed in the dark one morning, started pulling on my socks. One seemed pretty hard and rough but I rammed my foot in as far as I could, then struck a match. I found I had my foot half way down a crimson python's gullet.

"Well, I took him off and kept him in a box until I found another the same size and wore the pair as houseboots. Just the other day I sold them to a bloke without any points."

❖   ❖

They were discussing dogs, particularly the matter of canine intelligence, and the tales were becoming pretty tall, when one of the most veracious-looking of the group led off with this one:

"Smith had a most intelligent retriever. One night Smith's house caught fire. All was instant confusion. Old Smith and his wife flew for the children and bundled out with them in quick order. But alas, one of them had been left behind. Up jumped the dog, rushed into the house, and soon reappeared dragging the missing child. Every one was saved. Nevertheless, Rover turned and dashed through the flames back into the house. What did the dog do that for? No one could imagine. But presently, the sagacious animal reappeared—scorched and burned—and carrying—what do you think?

"Give it up!" chorused the eager listeners.

"Believe it or not, gentlemen, that dog had a damp towel in his mouth, and when they unfolded it, out dropped the fire insurance policy."

❖   ❖

"Yes," said the yarn-spinning old mariner, in the corner of the railway carriage, "for three days and nights we worked at the pumps, and still the water gained on us. At last we gave up the hopeless struggle. There we was—sinkin', sinkin', expecting to perish every 'arf a minute. It was horful time, believe me. Sudden-like we feels the wessel a-rising up through the water. She riz till her keel was a'most out o' water, and we rides into port right on top o' the waves. We was saved! 'Ow it happened was, we had a cargo of yeast on board, and when the water reached it, it rose and rose, till it fairly lifted up the ship!"

❖   ❖

Famous among the old storytellers of the West was Lyin' Jack, and his favorite tale was of an elk he once killed that had a spread of antlers 15 feet wide. He always kept these, as he said, in the loft of his cabin. One time after a long absence Lyin' Jack showed up in Benton. The boys were all glad to see him and, after a round or two of drinks, asked for a story. "No, boys," said Jack, "I'm through. For years I've been telling these lies—told 'em so often I got to believing 'em myself. That story of mine about the elk with the 15 foot horns is what cured me. I told about that elk so often that I knowed the place I killed it. One night I lit a candle and crawled up in the loft to view the horns—an' I'm damned if they weren't there!"

❖   ❖

Millionaire Jones was recalling the struggles of his youth.

"I was living in California, and my parents in New York," he said, "and I had just managed to save enough money to buy my-self a bicycle when my father wrote that my mother was ill.

"I jumped on my bicycle and rode across the continent, only to be told that California air was all that would save my mother.

"So I dragged the bike in beside the bed, let the California air out of the tires, and she lived to the good old age of 95."

❖ ❖

A purveyor of Tall Tales relates that, fishing in Canada, he came upon a most peculiar sight. In a little bed of rock where a rather deep little pool of water lay, was an enormous fish. Looking about in the crystal water he could see no minnows such as larger fish consume and he and his guide began to wonder how the fish survived. They took turns watching. Finally one day the mystery was solved.

A trickle of water flowed in and out of the pool and very tiny minnows came over in its current. They were so small the big fish could scarcely see them. However, since nature had provided him with peculiar eyes he was able to save himself from starvation. One eye was red and the other green. When he was hungry he would swim over and turn his red eye toward the incoming water. The minnows, seeing the stop light, would halt and wait for a go signal. When enough had collected for a large mouthful, the big fish would turn his green eye to the water. Then, as the minnows started to come over, he would open his mouth and gather in his dinner!

❖ ❖

Here is a corn-shucking story from the Middle West:

"They was havin' a contest and Maur drew a file that was all down from a hail storm. Well, sir, he just bent himself down and started shuckin'. You should have seen the corn fly agin' that bangboard! He was doin' right good until, in a hurry, he reached down and took hold of his own foot and threw himself into that wagon. And, would you believe it, he straightened up just in time to get hit on the head by four ears of corn that was still in the air!"

❖ ❖

A man was elaborating on the smartness of his dog. It seems he was out hunting quail and the dog suddenly ran into the brush. The hunter waited and in a moment a quail flew out. He shot it. Soon a second quail appeared and he shot that. A third and a fourth followed at intervals.

Curious as to why the birds were thus spaced, the man entered the brush and walked over toward the dog. He found that his clever animal had run a covey down a hole and was standing there with his foot over the opening, letting the birds out one at a time, so that the hunter could shoot them at his leisure.

❖ ❖

This outlandish yarn is credited to "Bo" McMillan, the football coach, at a dinner given in his honor by the alumni of Indiana University:

McMillan had just come from a coaching position out in Kansas, and he was speaking of the speed of the players he had coached out there. He told of one boy who had appeared at a Kansas school as a candidate for the football team, and had been so fast that he made all the others on the team look as stationary as the goal posts. The coach asked him how he had developed such phenomenal speed. The boy said he had done it chasing jack rabbits and catching them for his father's dinner.

"But," said the coach, "I have other boys who can catch jack rabbits, and you're a lot faster than they are."

"Well," the boy said, "pap was mighty particular. He'd give me a beatin' unless I fetched home a fat rabbit. You see, I didn't just have to catch 'em, I had to run along side of 'em and feel 'em to see if they was fat enough to suit pap."

❖ ❖

Easily qualifying him for a charter member of the Tall Story Club is the favorite anecdote of former mayor Louis Marcus of Salt Lake City, Utah.

"While fishing one day, I ran short of bait and was temporarily at a loss as to what to do. Upon looking down near my feet, I noticed a small snake which held a frog in its mouth. I removed the frog and cut it up for bait, feeling very fortunate that my eyes had lighted on the snake at that moment.

"I did, however, feel a bit guilty at relieving the poor reptile of his meal, and in order to give him a slight recompense for my supply of bait, I poured a few drops of whisky into its mouth. Fortunately for my conscience, the snake seemed to leave in a contented mood, and I turned and went on fishing.

"Some time had passed when I felt something hitting against the leg of my boot. Looking down, I saw the identical snake, laden with three more frogs!"

❖ ❖

"Are you a good runner?" asked the farmer of a student applying for a job on his ranch.

The student said he was.

"Well," said the farmer, "you can round up the sheep."

After several hours the student returned perspiring and out of breath.

"I got the sheep all right," he reported, "but I had a fierce time getting the lambs."

"The lambs?" said the farmer. "I haven't any lambs."

"Oh, yes you do," replied the student, "they're in the corral." Thereupon the farmer went to investigate. In the corral with the exhausted sheep he found half a dozen panting jackrabbits.

❖ ❖

"Why," said the Californian, "we grow cabbage so big that an army of soldiers can camp under one."

"That's nothing," said the New Englander. "We make copper kettles in New England so big that a thousand men can be riveting one and yet be so far apart they can't hear each other's hammers."

"Go on," said the Californian, "what would anyone use a kettle of that size for?"

"Why, to boil your California cabbage in," replied the New Englander.

❖ ❖

Whoppers are always good because they inspire more of their kind, and the woods is full of whopper tellers. One old fellow was trying to tell the tallest tall story in a group of tall story experts. He won on this:

"It was when I was a little boy visiting my grandpap in the mountains. We was sitting there on the steps, and grandpap was puffing away on the corn-cob pipe and telling me of the things he's seen in his time. I crawled down into the yard to get a stick to whittle on when out of the brush came a big grizzly bear. He grabbed me and knocked me down. I thought my time had come, when grandpap just takes a big puff of smoke and blows a ring so big it could have busted his cheek if he hadn't been an expert. It settled down on that bear's nose and jammed his jaws so tight together that he couldn't take a bite of me. While he was trying to claw it off, grandpap just blew one after another and bound that bear up so tight he died of strangulation."

❖ ❖

After having spent a fruitless afternoon in the city searching for a room, the cow-puncher from a Wyoming ranch sat disconsolately on a park bench. Beside him was a respectable looking fellow, so he struck up a conversation which began with the weather and ended with the following:

"Stranger," said the cow-puncher, "I'm durned if I could find a landlord who would rent me a bunk for the night."

"So?" said the stranger. "And why not?"

"Well, they say my legs is so bowlegged that I'd rub the danged paper off the wall."

❖ ❖

The young farmers were gathered around the village store discussing the size of various vegetables they had raised this excellent season, and old Uncle Abner listened to their chattering with an amused glance. Finally he said modestly that he had raised a huge squash.

"A squash?"

"And how big was it?" asked another.

"Well," said Old Uncle Abner with a sly wink in the general direction of no one in particular, "we never measured it, but we had to use the seeds for snowshoes."

❖ ❖

"Last summer," said the tall story teller, "I was off the coast on a fishing trip, and while we were out on deck early in the evening, smoking and chatting, a great cloud of mosquitoes, all of them monstrous birds, came out from shore and settled on the boat. And do you know, in fifteen minutes they had stripped it of every inch of canvas, and left the masts bare as beanpoles!"

The listeners were inclined to scoff at this relation, but one of the party interposed, "Well, don't be astonished. I can vouch for that. It was only a week after that I was on a trip along the coast, and one night the same swarm of mosquitoes came out after us."

The first speaker didn't seem to appreciate this unexpected support, for he said, "Humph! They did, eh? Well, how did you know they were the same mosquitoes?"

"How did I know?" repeated the other with a chuckle. "How did I know? Why, confound it, they all had on canvas overalls."

❖ ❖